Librarian's Guide
to Online Searching

Librarian's Guide
to Online Searching

Second Edition

SUZANNE S. BELL

A Member of the Greenwood Publishing Group

Westport, Connecticut • London

Library of Congress Cataloging-in-Publication Data

Bell, Suzanne S.
   Librarian's guide to online searching / Suzanne S. Bell.—2nd ed.
      p.   cm.
   Includes bibliographical references and indexes.
   ISBN 978–1–59158–763–7 (alk. paper)
   1. Database searching.   2. Electronic information resource searching.
I. Title.
   ZA4460.B45   2009
   025.5′24—dc22   2008035924

British Library Cataloguing in Publication Data is available.

Library of Congress Catalog Card Number: 2008035924
ISBN: 978–1–59158–763–7

First published in 2009

Libraries Unlimited, 88 Post Road West, Westport, CT 06881
A Member of the Greenwood Publishing Group, Inc.
www.lu.com

Printed in the United States of America

♾™

The paper used in this book complies with the
Permanent Paper Standard issued by the National
Information Standards Organization (Z39.48–1984).

10 9 8 7 6 5 4 3 2

To my grandfather, Augustus Hunt Shearer, librarian and teacher, and my father, Vern Coventry Bell, inventor and engineer. You may not have understood this book, but you would have appreciated it. Thank you both for the gifts that made it possible.

Contents

Preface xiii

Acknowledgments xvii

1—DATABASE STRUCTURE FOR EVERYONE: RECORDS, FIELDS, AND INDEXES 1

Historical Background 1
   Indexing and Abstracting Services   1
   From Printed Volumes to Databases   3

Database Building Blocks 4
   Fields and Records   4
   Quick Recap   5

Beyond Fields and Records: Field Indexes 6
   Quick Recap   11
   Examples of Indexes   11

Exercises and Points to Consider 16

Suggested Reading 17

Notes 17

2—WORKING WITH DATABASES THE SEARCHER'S TOOLKIT: PART 1 19

Searcher's Toolkit: Part 1 19
   Basic Tool No. 1: Boolean Logic   19
   Quick Recap   24
   Basic Tool No. 2: Controlled Vocabulary   24
   Basic Tool No. 3: Field Searching   26
   Terms in the Searching Lexicon   27
   Quick Recap   28

Applying the Tools 29
   MasterFILE Select: Notes and Search Examples   29

Exercises and Points to Consider 35

Notes 37

3—THE SEARCHER'S TOOLKIT: PART 2 39

Searcher's Toolkit: Part 2 39
  Basic Tool No. 4: Proximity Searching   39
  Basic Tool No. 5: Truncation   43
  Quick Recap   46
  Basic Tool No. 6: Limits to Constrain Your Search   46
  Basic Tool No. 7: "Pearl Growing": A Useful Search Strategy   46
  Quick Recap   48

Your Mental Toolkit 48

Summary and Advice 48

Exercises and Points to Consider 49

Suggested Reading 50

Notes 50

4—SOCIAL SCIENCE DATABASES 51

Introduction to Subject Databases 51

Library Literature & Information Science 52
  Background and Coverage   52
  Notes and Search Examples   52
  Working with Results: Mark and Output   60
  Quick Recap   61

ERIC via FirstSearch 61
  Background and Coverage   61
  Notes and Search Examples   62
  Working with Results: Mark, Functions, and Output   70
  Quick Recap   71

PsycINFO from Ovid 71
  Background and Coverage   71
  Notes and Search Examples   73
  Working with Results: The "Results Manager"   81
  Additional Feature: The PsycINFO Thesaurus   81
  Quick Recap   81

Exercises and Points to Consider 83

Notes 85

5—DATABASES FOR SCIENCE AND MEDICINE 87

MEDLINE and PubMed 88
  MEDLINE   88
  PubMed: More than MEDLINE   93
  Introduction to the PubMed Interface   94
  Output in MEDLINE and PubMed   100
  Getting to the Full Text   101
  Quick Recap   101

The Web of Science and the Citation Indexes 102

History of the Citation Indexes 102
Web of Science Content 103
An Index Focused on Citations 103
Additional Differences in Available Fields 104
Searching the *Web of Science*: Main Search Interface 105
Cited Reference Searching 108
E-mail, Print, Save, or Export Results 115
Advanced Features: Advanced Search and Analyze 117
Quick Recap 118

Exercises and Points to Consider 119

Notes 121

6—BIBLIOGRAPHIC DATABASES 123

WorldCat: The "OPAC of OPACs" 124
Background and Coverage 124
A Tool for Many Parts of the Library 125
Notes and Search Examples 126
Quick Recap 135

WorldCat.org 136
Background: The Path to WorldCat.org 136
Notes and Search Examples 138
Quick Recap 142

Revisiting Your Local OPAC 143

Exercises and Points to Consider 143

Notes 144

7—HUMANITIES DATABASES 147

America: History and Life 148
Background and Coverage 148
Notes and Search Examples 148
Related Records, Folder, and Output Options 154
Quick Recap 157

MLA International Bibliography 158
Background and Coverage 158
The Marked List and Output 166
Additional Feature: Directory of Periodicals 169
Quick Recap 169

Exercises and Points to Consider 171

Notes 172

8—NUMERICAL DATABASES 173

Finding Numbers 173
Concepts about Numbers 174
Quick Recap 177
A Comment about Searching for Numbers 177

LexisNexis *Statistical* 177
Background and Coverage 177
Notes and Search Examples 179

Working with Results: "Tag" and Output   188
Going from LexisNexis *Statistical* to Web Sites   189

American Factfinder 190
Background and Coverage   190
Notes and Search Examples   190

Bureau of Labor Statistics 195
Pay & Benefits at the Bureau of Labor Statistics   196
Occupation Information at the Bureau of Labor Statistics   199

Quick Recap 200

Numbers and the Reference Interview 201

Exercises and Points to Consider 201

Suggested Readings 202

Notes 202

9—FOCUS ON PEOPLE 205

Part 1: Information-seeking Behavior 206
Some Theoretical Background on Information Seeking   206
Applied Research on Information-seeking Behavior   208
Quick Recap   213

Part 2: The Reference Interview 213
What Is the Real Question?   214
Question Negotiation in the Reference Interview   216
Beyond the Face-to-Face Reference Interview   220
Why Is the Reference Interview So Important?   222
Quick Recap   222

Exercises and Points to Consider 223

Suggested Readings 223

Notes 223

10—CHOOSING THE RIGHT RESOURCE FOR THE QUESTION 225

Start with the Reference Interview 226

Questions for Databases 226
Why and When to Try a Database   226
Quick Recap   229
Choosing a Database   230

Questions for the Web 232
Personal Uses of the Web   232
Professional Uses of the Web   232
Quick Recap   234

Exercises and Points to Consider 234

Suggested Reading 234

Notes 234

11—EVALUATING DATABASES 237

Basic Facts and Figures 238
Initial Factual Information to Gather   238

Testing and Benchmarking 242
  Testing   242
  Benchmarking   247

Making a Request for Purchase 249
  Elements to Include in the Request   249

Exercises and Points to Consider 251

Suggested Readings 251

Notes 252

12—TEACHING OTHER PEOPLE ABOUT DATABASES 253

Teaching Principles 254
  Principle 1: Teach to Your Audience   255
  Principle 2: Avoid Lecturing   255
  Principle 3: *Wait* for Answers   256
  Principle 4: Less Is More   257
  Principle 5: Transparency in Teaching   257
  Principle 6: You Have the Right to Be Wrong   258
  Principle 7: Teaching with Technology   258
  Principle 8: Practice   259

Database Teaching Opportunities 260
  Teaching at the Reference Desk   261
  Teaching an Information Literacy Session   261
  A Staff Presentation   266
  The Full Semester Class   267

Exercises and Points to Consider 268

Suggested Readings 268

Notes 269

References 271
Index 283

Preface

Welcome to the wonderful world of database searching! Roy Tennant's (2003) now famous quote that "only librarians like to search, everyone else likes to find" has perhaps been too frequently repeated—but it's hard not to, because it's *true*. There are certain kinds of minds that enjoy solving puzzles and ferreting out information, and the owners of those minds often find a good talent "fit" in library careers. Librarians do like to search, although generally we aren't born knowing it: it's a realization that emerges later, with experience or in a class. If you are a researcher or a student, in the position of having to search for the information you need, you may also find that there can be some interest and pleasure in the process as well as the product.

If it is true that most people only want to "find," and are perfectly happy with the Google model of one simple search box and long lists of results, one might ask, "Why should I care about learning more sophisticated search techniques? Why should we still teach a course on database searching?" (or "Why should I buy a book on database searching?") "Will there ever be an opportunity to use this information again?"

In offering you this book, I wholeheartedly believe those questions can be answered in the affirmative. Yes, learning about more sophisticated search techniques continues to be helpful, and it will increase your effectiveness in helping others to do research, or your own productivity as a researcher. No matter how simple the initial interface becomes, it still helps to know something about database structure, that is, what is going on "under the hood." This is especially helpful for understanding what is *possible* with any given database: what degree of precision in searching you can expect, and thus what you can expect in terms of results. There will continue to be "Advanced" versions of the interface that will allow experts to do more efficient, targeted, and useful searches. Yes, people will do and are doing more searching on their own: if you are not a librarian and are looking at this book, it will introduce you to resources you might not have been aware of, and help you to be more effective. For librarians and library students, searching is a part of our profession, an area in which we need to be ready to offer our users more skills than they have on their own. Indeed, as users do more searching on their own, the questions that they approach librarians with become more difficult. They have taken care of the easy questions; librarians need to be ready for the hard ones. This is still an important part of our skill set.

Most of the techniques and strategies provided in this book are not particularly complex or hard to master, but they need to be stated and learned, because they are not generally how people think. You need to *learn* to parse questions into good search strategies. You need to really internalize how Boolean logic works to understand that when a search returns only a few results, the tactic to take is to use fewer, broader search terms, not add more, and more specific, terms. One of the most essential techniques sounds like the simplest: to use your eyes and truly analyze what is on the screen. This is something that very few people really do, however, so it is also something to learn.

One of the overriding goals in this book is to remain thoroughly grounded in the real world. The examples and exercises involving commercial databases work with ones commonly available at academic and major public libraries. When free Web sites are discussed, they have been carefully chosen for their expected longevity. The emphasis is not on providing every detail of every database presented, but rather how to look at any interface ("use your eyes"), to use a set of basic concepts to understand what you are seeing ("engage your brain"), and then to use effectively whatever search capabilities are provided. Once you have a basic idea of how databases are put together, and have grasped a collection of concepts and techniques (the "Searcher's Toolkit"), you should be able to plunge into any database that comes along and figure out how it works. In fact, the other main goal for this book is to help you learn to be flexible and adaptable. What more important skill can there be in our rapidly changing world?

This book will expose you to a whole range of databases: multidisciplinary, social science, medicine, science, bibliographic, humanities, and statistical/numeric. You will learn that even when you don't know anything about a subject, using some good, general principles, you should be able to use an unfamiliar database and do a reasonable search. A discussion of information-seeking behaviors and how to do an effective reference interview helps with this. Most important, you shouldn't be *afraid* of any subject area and declare it off-limits. As all of these choices begin to build up, however, the natural question is: how do you know which database to use? Or should you use the Web? We address these issues as well. Note that although the Web does enter into the discussion from time to time, this book does not attempt to teach you to search the Web better. There are already many excellent books on the market to fulfill that purpose. The focus here is on commercial, subscription databases. If you thought searching started and ended with Google, surprise! There's a whole other world waiting for you, through the library.

Not only will you learn to search databases, but you'll also learn something about passing your knowledge along: tips and guidance for showing others how to get what they need out of a database. In addition, we'll go over points to consider in evaluating a database, for purposes of writing a review, or, for librarians, as part of collection development. With budgets everywhere as tight as they are, librarians are more frequently finding themselves in the position of having to evaluate and choose among current resources.

If you are a library school instructor, you'll find that the chapters after the first three are almost completely freestanding. You can pick and choose, using them in whatever order best suits your needs or teaching style. Exercises and material that can be used as discussion-starters are included with each chapter, and "Recommended Readings" are provided for selected chapters.

We live in the age of the Web, with its incredible capability for change: vendors now change the appearance of their interfaces regularly, and it's crucial to be flexible. This book is intended to help you learn to adapt and change, as well as to give you the tools to understand and use what you're looking at, regardless of what the interfaces happen to look like in the future. I hope that the book achieves that goal for you, and in addition, that you'll soon join me in thinking that searching is just great fun.

Additional Thoughts for the 2nd Edition

Even as the first edition of this book was going to press, interfaces were changing, and it was frustrating to know that from the moment it first appeared it would be out of date. Two years later, it is definitely time for a new edition: some interfaces have changed a little, while others have changed a *lot*, and the online world being what it is, these interfaces may well have changed some more by the time this edition goes to print. But producing a new edition still seems worth it, for several reasons. Observing and analyzing the changes provides much fodder for discussion, and is educational in itself. (For example: "Why did the vendor make that change? Is it new, or are they imitating another interface? Compare it to what's printed in the book; which do you prefer? Which do you think will be easier for users to figure out?") Indeed, in working on the first edition, I expected the commercial vendor's interfaces to be more stable, and the free Web sites, such as the government sites in Chapter 8, to be more volatile. Time has shown the opposite situation to hold true more often. Several of the commercial databases did, in fact, change almost beyond recognition after the first edition came out, whereas the government Web sites are reassuringly similar. As repeated several times in the text: we just have to stay flexible and adaptable.

Creating this update from the first to the second edition has also highlighted for me an interesting trend across many of the interfaces. It seems that vendors have moved into an era of faceted results: there is a strong emphasis on providing options and opportunities to refine a search from the results page. To me, this shows recognition that "search" doesn't need to be—and probably won't be—perfect the first time, and that it's useful to give users options for "fixing" a search without having to go back to the search interface. Does this reduced emphasis on initial search skills mean librarians are out of a job? No, I don't think so, because no matter how easy the vendors try to make it for users, they still can't make people read or see what's on the screen, or grasp as quickly and easily what it all means. As trained professionals, we can do all that, and we also have a huge role to play simply in making users aware that the database is there and can help them.

Last, a word about the technology known as *metasearch* or *federated search*. This idea has been around for several years, and can be summarized as a way to search multiple databases through one very simple interface. Some academic libraries see it as an answer to getting students to use their subscription databases by providing a familiar, one-box, "Internet-like" search interface (Lampert and Dabbour, 2007). Because the federated search completely eliminates the vendors' individual interfaces and all their features, it is not a topic for this book. (An excellent discussion of this can be found in the Lampert and Dabbour article.) Will federated search put this book (and one of the most interesting parts of our jobs) out of business? All I can say is that I certainly hope not; I hope we can all keep skillfully searching for years to come. Let's get started—because searching really can be just as rewarding as finding.

Acknowledgments

Acknowledgments for the 1st Edition

There are many people who helped make this book possible. In particular, I wish to thank Alan Lupack, who has provided extensive advice, feedback, and mentoring—from project proposal to chapter reviews and comments. Susan Gibbons and Vicki Burns also provided very valuable commentary on the proposal, and have willingly read chapters and provided thoughtful feedback. Nora Dimmock, Stephanie Frontz, Beth Banzer, Helen Anderson, and others have also been eager readers and excellent commentators. I much appreciate Kostya Gurevich's good humor in the face of sudden phone calls requesting explanations of how OCLC works, and Melissa Mead's enthusiasm and assistance with images from Poole's Index. I also want to thank Ron Dow for being very supportive of the project and making my leave of absence possible, as well as my colleagues in the Management Library, who had to cover for me all summer. Sincere thanks go to the great students in the 2005 summer session of LIS 566RE: Digital Information Retrieval, who put up with the book in its "draft" version, and were wonderful at finding typos and letting me know what worked and what didn't. The book is also deeply indebted to the anonymous peer reviewers, who provided extremely helpful advice and suggestions. I don't know who you are, but please know I'm profoundly grateful. Any remaining problems are all my own.

My vision of the book as text supported by (lots of) screen shots would not have been possible without the vendors of these wonderful resources being willing to grant permission to use their material. I am deeply grateful to all the people who made this part of the project possible: Craig Hunt at ABC-CLIO; Duncan Campbell at Chadwyck-Healey; Ed Roche and Scott Bernier at EBSCO; Sherry Sullivan and Deborah Loeding at H.W. Wilson; Gwen Bole and Ryan Runella at LexisNexis; Joyce Rambo and Barbara Lynch at OCLC; Tracy Smith and Kim Landry at Ovid; Ed Yarnell at ProQuest; and Rodney Yancey and Brian McDonough at Thomson Scientific.

In addition, there would have been no book at all without the work of Vivek Sood and the incredible team at Techbooks (now Aptara). They pushed production through in record time, dealt with all those screen shots, and provided excellent copyediting. It was amazing and wonderful to do business so quickly and efficiently with a group so far away, and I am intensely grateful for Mr. Sood's attention to the project, his reliable and prompt communications, and his "can do" attitude.

Finally, a very, very special thanks to my husband, a walking Chicago Manual of Style, who gave me a gorgeous new computer to write on, has read every word (sometimes several times), provided excellent editing and advice, never lost his enthusiasm, and kept us fed throughout the project. I couldn't have done it without you, my dear.

Acknowledgments for the 2nd Edition

My list of thanks this time around is shorter, but no less sincere. First of all, to the alert readers who emailed me with thoughts and corrections, thank goodness for you! You caught things that everyone else missed, and I appreciate the feedback so much. Many thanks also go to Ron Maas, Sue Stewart, and wonderful Emma Bailey of Libraries Unlimited/Greenwood Publishing, for being responsive, helpful, and a pleasure to work with, as well as to Peggy Rote of Aptara, who was incredibly helpful and kind, and worked on this project even when she was supposed to be on vacation. My gratitude to my boss, Vicki Burns, and all my colleagues in the Reference Department of the University of Rochester's Rush Rhees Library, is unbounded, for letting me have the time off to write again. Thanks for covering for me, everyone. My great thanks, again, to all the vendors of these products that I so enjoy writing about, for giving permission to reproduce their screen shots here. Thanks especially to the people who got my permission requests "through the system," or who helped in other ways: Duncan Campbell at Chadwyck Healey; Kim Stam, Ed Roche, and Jim Kropelin at EBSCO, Cathy Dillon at LexisNexis, Barbara Lynch at OCLC, Kim Landry and Connie Hughes at Ovid, Grace Maselli at Thomson Reuters, and Deborah Loeding at H. W. Wilson.

Finally, where would we be without our tools and home support? Thanks, little MacBook with the hot pink skin, for allowing me to work anywhere and making the writing seem fun, and to your giant brother upstairs, for taking magnificent screen shots. My most heartfelt thanks, however, go to my husband, who has again put up my being totally distracted for weeks on end, who has again patiently read and provided invaluable editing, and altogether been a cheerful, supportive, and sustaining presence. You are the best, my dear.

1
Database Structure for Everyone: Records, Fields, and Indexes

In many library school programs, the database searching course is an upper-level, elective course. This means that some of you have had a chance to take a database course and are already familiar with the concepts in this chapter. My goal is to focus on helping you learn and develop strategies to search and interact more effectively with databases rather than getting into the real technology of how databases are built. This chapter provides a very brief and simple introduction to how databases are conceptually put together. In my experience, this is as much as you need to know to apply appropriate search techniques and use the database effectively. There's no point in piling on technical detail if it doesn't further your ultimate goal, which in this case is: searching.

It's always interesting to start with a little history, however. Electronic access to information by means of the Web is so pervasive that we take it for granted. You have undoubtedly already used databases somewhere in your academic life. But where did these "databases" come from? Why are they important? What *is* a database, anyway?

Historical Background

Indexing and Abstracting Services

In the Beginning...

There was hard copy. Writers wrote, and their works were published in (physical) magazines, journals, newspapers, or conference proceedings.

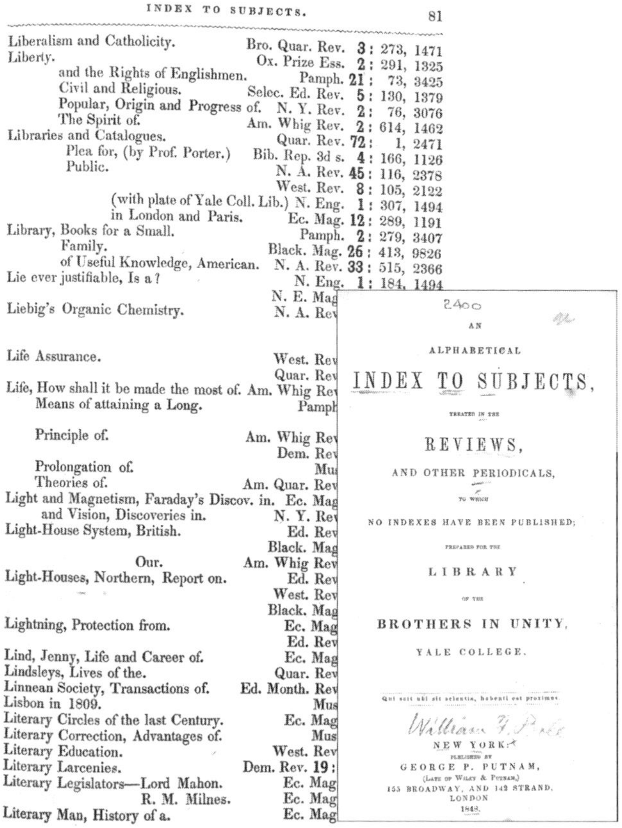
INDEX TO SUBJECTS. 81

Liberalism and Catholicity.	Bro. Quar. Rev.	3 : 273, 1471
Liberty.	Ox. Prize Ess.	2 : 291, 1325
and the Rights of Englishmen.	Pamph.	21 : 73, 3425
Civil and Religious.	Selec. Ed. Rev.	5 : 130, 1379
Popular, Origin and Progress of.	N. Y. Rev.	2 : 76, 3076
The Spirit of.	Am. Whig Rev.	2 : 614, 1462
Libraries and Catalogues.	Quar. Rev.	72 : 1, 2471
Plea for, (by Prof. Porter.)	Bib. Rep. 3d s.	4 : 166, 1126
Public.	N. A. Rev.	45 : 116, 2378
	West. Rev.	8 : 105, 2122
(with plate of Yale Coll. Lib.)	N. Eng.	1 : 307, 1494
in London and Paris.	Ec. Mag.	12 : 289, 1191
Library, Books for a Small.	Pamph.	2 : 279, 3407
Family.	Black. Mag.	26 : 413, 9826
of Useful Knowledge, American.	N. A. Rev.	33 : 515, 2366
Lie ever justifiable, Is a?	N. Eng.	1 : 184, 1494
	N. E. Mag	
Liebig's Organic Chemistry.	N. A. Rev	
Life Assurance.	West. Rev	
	Quar. Rev	
Life, How shall it be made the most of.	Am. Whig Rev	
Means of attaining a Long.	Pamph	
Principle of.	Am. Whig Rev	
	Dem. Rev	
Prolongation of.	Mus	
Theories of.	Am. Quar. Rev	
Light and Magnetism, Faraday's Discov. in.	Ec. Mag	
and Vision, Discoveries in.	N. Y. Rev	
Light-House System, British.	Ed. Rev	
	Black. Mag	
Our.	Am. Whig Rev	
Light-Houses, Northern, Report on.	Ed. Rev	
	West. Rev	
	Black. Mag	
Lightning, Protection from.	Ec. Mag	
	Ed. Rev	
Lind, Jenny, Life and Career of.	Ec. Mag	
Lindsleys, Lives of the.	Quar. Rev	
Linnean Society, Transactions of.	Ed. Month. Rev	
Lisbon in 1809.	Mus	
Literary Circles of the last Century.	Ec. Mag	
Literary Correction, Advantages of.	Mus	
Literary Education.	West. Rev	
Literary Larcenies.	Dem. Rev.	19 :
Literary Legislators—Lord Mahon.	Ec. Mag	
R. M. Milnes.	Ec. Mag	
Literary Man, History of a.	Ec. Mag	

2400

AN

ALPHABETICAL

INDEX TO SUBJECTS,

TREATED IN THE

REVIEWS,

AND OTHER PERIODICALS,

TO WHICH

NO INDEXES HAVE BEEN PUBLISHED;

PREPARED FOR THE

LIBRARY

OF THE

BROTHERS IN UNITY,

YALE COLLEGE.

NEW YORK:

PUBLISHED BY

GEORGE P. PUTNAM,

(LATE OF WILEY & PUTNAM,)

155 BROADWAY, AND 142 STRAND, LONDON.

1848.

Fig. 1.1. Index listing and title page (*inset*) from Poole's *Index to Periodical Literature*. (Courtesy of the Department of Rare Books and Special Collections, University of Rochester Libraries, Rochester, NY.)

Months or years afterward, other writers, researchers, and other alert readers wanted to know what was written on a topic. Wouldn't it be useful if there were a way to find everything that had been published on a topic, without having to page through every likely journal, newspaper, and so forth? It certainly would, as various publishing interests demonstrated: as early as 1848, the *Poole's Index to Periodical Literature* provided "An alphabetical index to subjects, treated in the reviews, and other periodicals, to which no indexes have been published; prepared for the library of the Brothers in Unity, Yale college" (Figure 1.1).

Not to be caught napping, the *New York Times* started publishing their *Index* in 1851, and in 1896, taking a page from Poole's, the *Cumulative Index to a Selected List of Periodicals* appeared, which soon (1904) became the canonical *Readers' Guide to Periodical Literature*. Thus in the mid-nineteenth century, the hard copy Index is born: an alphabetical list of words, representing subjects, and under each word a list of articles deemed to be about that subject. The index is typeset, printed, bound, and sold, and all of this effort is done, slowly and laboriously, by humans.

Given the amount of work involved, and the costs of paper, printing, etc., how many subjects do you think an article would have been listed under? Every time the article entry is repeated under another subject, it costs the publisher just a little more. Suppose there was an article about a polar expedition, which described the role the sled dogs played, the help provided by the native Inuit, the incompetence on the part of the provisions master, and the fund-raising efforts carried on by the leader's wife back home in England. The publisher really can't afford to list this article in more than one or two places. Under which subject(s) will people interested in this topic be most likely to look? The indexer's career was a continuous series of such difficult choices.

An index, recording that an article exists and where it would be found, was a good start, but one could go a step further. The addition of a couple of sentences (e.g., to give the user an idea of what the article is about) increases the usefulness of the finding tool enormously—although the added information, of course, costs more. But if they thought that their customers would pay the higher price, some index publishers added abstracts. Thus, *Abstracting and Indexing services* or "A & I," terminology that you can see in the library literature.

The abstracts were all laboriously written by humans. They needed to be skilled, literate humans, and skilled humans are very expensive (even when they're underpaid, they are expensive in commercial terms). Humans are also slow, compared with technology. Paper and publishing are expensive too. Given all this, how many times do you think an entry for an article would be duplicated (appear under multiple subjects) in this situation? The answers are obvious; the point is that the electronic situation we have today is all grounded in a physical reality. Once it was nothing but people and paper.

From Printed Volumes to Databases

Enter the Computer

The very first machines that can really be called *digital computers* were built in the period from 1939 to 1944, culminating in the construction of the ENIAC in 1946 (*Encyclopædia Britannica*, 2008). These machines were all part of a long progression of invention to speed up the task of mathematical calculations. After that, inventions and improvements came thick and fast: the 1950s and 1960s were an incredibly innovative time in computing, although probably not in a way that the ordinary person would have noticed. The first machine to be able to store a database, RCA's Bizmac, was developed in 1952 (*Lexikon's History of Computing*, 2002). The first instance of an online transaction processing system, using telephone lines to connect remote users to central mainframe computers, was the airline reservation system known as SABRE, set up by IBM for American Airlines in 1964 (Computer History Museum, 2004). Meanwhile, at Lockheed Missile and Space Company, a man named Roger Summit was engaged in projects involving search and retrieval, and management of massive data files. His group's first interactive search-and-retrieval service was demonstrated to the company in 1965; by 1972, it had developed into a new, commercially viable product: Dialog—the "first publicly available online research service" (Dialog, 2005).

Thus, in the 1960s and 1970s, when articles were still being produced on typewriters, indexes and abstracts were still produced in hard copy, and very disparate industries were developing information technologies for their own specialized purposes, Summit can be credited with having incredible vision. He asked the right questions:

1. What do people want? Information.

2. Who produces information, and in what form? The government and commercial publishers, in the form of papers, articles, newspapers, etc.

3. What if you could put information *about* all that published material into a machine-readable file: a database—something you could search?

Summit also had the vision to see how the technological elements could be used. The database needed to be made only once, at his firm's headquarters, and trained agents (librarians) could then access it over telephone lines with just some simple, basic equipment. The firm could track usage exactly and charge accordingly. Think of the advantages!

The advantages of an electronic version of an indexing/abstracting system are really revolutionary. In a system no longer bound by the confines of paper, space, and quite so many expensive skilled personnel:

*   Articles could be associated with a greater number of terms describing their content, not just one or two (some skilled labor still required).

*   Although material has to be rekeyed (i.e., typed into the database) this doesn't require subject specialists, simply typists (cheap labor).

*   Turnaround time is faster: most of your labor force isn't thinking and composing, just typing continuously: the process of adding to the information in the database goes on all the time, making the online product much more current.

*   If you choose to provide your index "online only," thus avoiding the time delays and costs of physical publishing, why, you might be able to redirect the funds to expanding your business, offering other indexes (databases) in new subject areas.

As time goes on, this process of "from article to index" gets even faster. When articles are created electronically (e.g., word processing), no rekeying is needed to get the information into your database, just software to convert and rearrange the material to fit your database fields. So rather than typists, you must pay programmers to write the software, and you still need those humans to analyze the content and assign the subject terms.

In the end, the electronic database is not necessarily cheaper to create; it very likely costs more! The costs have simply shifted. But customers buy it because...*it is so much more powerful and efficient.* It is irresistible. Given a choice between a printed index and an electronic version, most people under the age of 50 won't give the printed volume a second glance. The online database is here to stay.

Database Building Blocks

Fields and Records

In essence, databases are made up of fields and records. Fields are like one cell in an Excel spreadsheet: a bit of computer memory dedicated to holding one particular thing, one value (e.g., age) or type of information (e.g., letters, numbers, or an image). A set of fields makes up a record. An analogy would be a row in Excel: one row equals one record. If you prefer a good mental image, think of it as a whole line of shoeboxes with the lids off, and one thing in each box. Every time you add another record to your database, that becomes another line of shoeboxes, into which you put the appropriate bit of information into the box assigned to it (e.g., box 1 is always the number of the row, box 2 is always a last name, box 3 is always the first name, etc. Each record—each row of shoeboxes—will have the same number of boxes, but you might not have a piece of information for every box; that is, some fields might be blank. Altogether, all the rows (the records) make up the database.

Think about driver's licenses. They all have an ID number, the owner's name, address, date of birth, eye color, a bad photo, etc. I don't know if this is true in all states, but certainly in New York State all of that information resides in a database somewhere. It's easy to imagine the Department of Motor Vehicle's database having fields with names such as: Name, Addr, DOB, Eyes, BadPic, etc. Each record represents a person. The fields in each record represent every bit of information that appears on your license, and probably some that aren't actually printed on the license as well. When you send in the paperwork and the check to renew your license, they look your record up in the database, make any changes that you might have indicated in your paperwork (e.g., change the values in your fields), and hit print. Presto, you've gone from being a database entry to being a small card with an unflattering photo.

Decisions, Decisions: Designing the Database

The crucial task in developing a database is deciding what fields the records in your database are going to have, and how big they are going to be, that is, how many characters or numbers they will be able to hold. This "size" represents the computer memory allocated every time a new record is added. (Although memory is cheap now, in a huge project, how much memory will be allocated is still something to consider.) In the best of all possible worlds, a whole design team, including software engineers, subject experts, people from marketing and sales, and potential users, would wrestle with this problem. Nothing might ever get done in such a large and varied group, however, and so probably a more limited team of software engineers and content experts is the norm. The problem is that the design team had better make good choices initially, because it's very difficult, if not impossible, to make significant (if any) changes to the record structure later.[1] This is good and bad. It means there's a certain inherent stability, or at least pressure on these database products not to change too much, but when you wish that they *would* fix something, it can take a long time (if ever) for change to happen. You can take a certain amount of comfort, however, in the knowledge that however much the interface to the database—the way it looks—changes, behind the scenes the same types of information (fields), are probably still there.

Quick Recap

One full set of fields makes up a record. Every record in the database has the same set of fields (even if, in some records, some fields are blank). All of the rows (records) together make up the database.

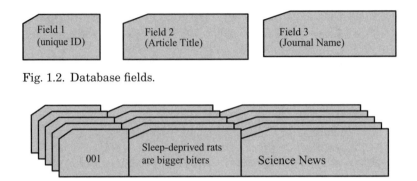

Fig. 1.2. Database fields.

Fig. 1.3. Database records.

Food for Thought

For an article database, you'd probably have a field for the article title, the name of the journal it appeared in...and what else? Think about the other information you would want to capture. Again, the process is something like this:

Define your fields (Figure 1.2):

...that make up records (Figure 1.3)...

...and form the basis of your database.

Beyond Fields and Records: Field Indexes

Fields and records are the basis, the "data" of a database. What makes a database fast, powerful, and efficient are the *indexes* of the fields. It would be very slow if every time you queried the database, it started at field1, record1, and searched sequentially through each field of each record—you might as well go back to hard copy at that rate.

An index, in the sense that we're discussing now, is a list of all the values from a particular field (or multiple fields), with some kind of identifier indicating from which record each value came. This is much like the index at the end of a book that indicates on which pages a word appears. It becomes part of the database but has a separate existence from the records. An index list can be alphabetized and in various ways optimized for searching. When arranged as a list of locations for a given word, this list is referred to as an *inverted file*. If we continue our very concrete mental image: Picture your rows of shoeboxes lying flat, covering your living room floor. Now imagine copying box 2 from each row, noting on the side of it which row it came from, and stacking those boxes vertically, off to one side. You can arrange that stack anyway you like. Maybe, to return to the driver's license example, that's the field for Last Name. You'd probably want to organize the stack (the index) alphabetically, so that if you wanted to find the record for Smith, John, you could zip to the Ss in the stack, pull out his box, see that it was marked "record no. 3," and run over to the third row of shoeboxes. Thus the order of the rows in your database, that is, what order you enter your records, doesn't matter at all. You simply build an index and search *that* when you want to find something in your database. Or you can build several indexes: you can make an index of any field you want. However, as always, there are costs and reasons why you might not index every field.[2]

A Very Simple Example

Say we have three articles:

Milky Way's Last Major Merger.

Science News. v. 162 no. 24 p. 376

It's a Dog's Life.

The Economist. December 21, 2002. p. 61

Manhattan Mayhem.

Smithsonian. v. 33 no. 9 p. 44

Let's enhance these just a little by adding a one-line description to each record (so we have a few more words to search on):

Record 1:

Milky Way's Last Major Merger.

Science News. v. 162 no. 24 p. 376.

New clues about galaxy formation indicate early collision affected Milky Way's shape.

Record 2:

It's a Dog's Life.

The Economist. December 21, 2002. p. 61.

From hard labour to a beauty contest, a history of the work and whims of dog breeding.

Record 3:

Manhattan Mayhem.

Smithsonian. v. 33 no. 9 p. 44

Martin Scorsese's realistic portrayal of pre–Civil War strife—*Gangs of New York*—re-creates the brutal street warfare waged between immigrant groups.

My database will have just four fields (Figure 1.4):

1. Record number (four number places, e.g., my database will never grow to more than 9,999 articles)

2. Article title

3. Journal name

4. Abstract

Fig. 1.4. A very simple database record.

Now we need to index the fields.

The initial list of words from the Article Title field looks like:

Milky

Way's

Last

Major

Merger

It's

a

Dog's

Life

Manhattan

Mayhem

More Database Decisions

There are various things about this list that one might question. What will our indexing program do with those possessives and contractions? Do we want to clog it up with little words like *a*? There are many decisions for database designers to make:

- How will the indexing program handle apostrophes and other punctuation? We take it for granted now that the system will simply preserve it, and users can search for contractions or possessives, but you may still encounter systems that insert a space instead of the apostrophe (dog s), or ignore it and treat the letters as a string (ending up with "dogs" for "dog's").

- What will the indexing program do with the "little words"? That is, words such as *a, an, by, for, from, of, the, to, with*, and so forth, which are usually referred to as *stop words*. These are words that are so common that the database designers usually decide they don't want to expend time and space to index them. Indexing programs are programmed with a list of such words and will "stop" indexing when they hit a word on the list. A more descriptive term would be *skip words*, because that's what really happens: the indexing program skips any stop list words and continues to the next word. Almost all databases employ a stop word list, and it can vary greatly from one vendor to the next.

- Should the system be designed to preserve information about capitalization, or to ignore the case of the words? We are so used to systems that do not distinguish upper and lowercase (so you don't have to worry how you type in your query), but there are times when you would really like the system to know the difference between, say, AIDS (the disease), and aids (the common noun or verb).

Because this is a modern system, we'll decide to preserve the apostrophes, and put *a* on our stop word list, so it won't be included in the index. We can then sort the list alphabetically:

Dog's

It's

Last

Life

Major

Manhattan

Mayhem

Merger

Milky

Way's

Can you see the problem here? We have neglected to include an identifier to show which record a word came from. Let's start over.

Better Field Indexing

Let's make sure that our index list includes the record number and which field the word came from:

0001	Milky	TI
0001	Way's	TI
0001	Last	TI
0001	Major	TI
0001	Merger	TI
0002	It's	TI
0002	Dog's	TI
0002	Life	TI
0003	Manhattan	TI
0003	Mayhem	TI

One more thing: we can include a number representing the *order* of the word within the field (why might this be useful?) We now have something like this:

0001	Milky	TI	01
0001	Way's	TI	02
0001	Last	TI	03

Now we'll sort again.

0002	Dog's	TI	03
0002	It's	TI	01
0001	Last	TI	03
0002	Life	TI	04
0001	Major	TI	04
0003	Manhattan	TI	01
0003	Mayhem	TI	02
0001	Merger	TI	05
0001	Milky	TI	01
0001	Way's	TI	02

Note how even though we deleted the stop word *a* in the title "It's a dog's life," the numerical position of "dog's" reflects that there was an intervening word there: its position is recorded as 3, not 2.

Because people might want to search on the name of the publication, it would be good to index that as well. Our index of the Journal Name field looks something like this:

0002	*Economist*	JN	02
0001	*News*	JN	02
0001	*Science*	JN	01
0001	*Science News*	JN	01, 02
0003	*Smithsonian*	JN	01

Note the multiple indexing of *Science News*. The technical term for this is *double posting*.

To make things even faster and more efficient, after indexing each field, combine the indexes so that you have only one list to search:

0002	Dog's	TI	03
0002	Economist	JN	02
0002	It's	TI	01
0001	Last	TI	03
0002	Life	TI	04
0001	Major	TI	04
0003	Manhattan	TI	01
0003	Mayhem	TI	02
0001	Merger	TI	05
0001	Milky	TI	01
0001	News	JN	02
0001	Science	JN	01
0001	Science News	JN	01, 02
0003	Smithsonian	JN	01
0001	Way's	TI	02

We undoubtedly want to index the content of the one-sentence "abstracts," as well. Here is a list of the words in raw form:

new	beauty	Pre-Civil
clues	contest	War
about	a	strife
galaxy	history	*Gangs*
formation	of	*Of*
indicate	the	*New*
early	work	*York*
collision	and	Re-creates
affected	whims	The
Milky	of	brutal
Way's	dog	street
Shape	breeding	warfare
From	Martin	waged
hard	Scorsese's	between
labour	realistic	immigrant
to	portrayal	groups
a	of	

Decisions and cleanup are needed on this list of words:

- Stop words—what will they be?
- Hyphenated words—how will they be recorded?
- Proper names—"double post" to include the phrase too?
- Alternative spellings—do we do anything about them or not? (What might you do?)

Luckily, software does almost all of this work for us. You probably will never see any indexes in their raw state. What we've been going over here is in real life very "under the hood," often proprietary material for the database vendors. You don't need to know exactly how any particular database works; you simply need to grasp some of the basic principles that govern how databases in general are put together and how they are indexed. This determines how you search them, and what you can expect to get out of them.

Quick Recap

Much thought goes into the initial database design (i.e., what fields to include, what they are called, how much space to allocate for each one), because the design cannot be easily changed later. The information contained in a database's fields can be extracted and used to build an index of terms in the database. Indexes make rapid searching of huge databases possible. Many decisions go into the design of indexes as well, for example, which fields will be indexed, how contractions and possessives will be handled, which words will be treated as stop words, and if and how identification of phrases will be supported.

Examples of Indexes

In the examples that follow, see if you can relate what we've just gone over with the "user's view" of the indexing scheme in these common databases. We'll start with the Subjects index in EBSCO's *MasterFILE Select*, a multidisciplinary database.

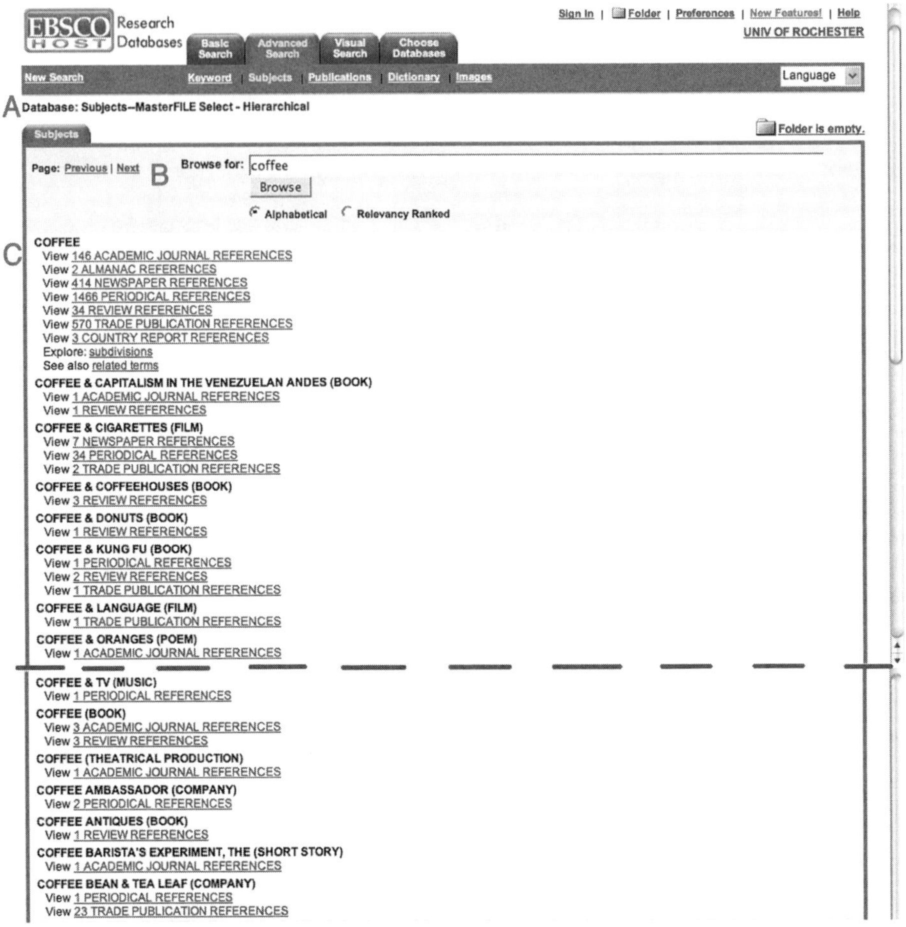

Fig. 1.5. The Subject Index in EBSCO's *MasterFILE Select*, showing two sections of the "coffee" entries. © 2008 EBSCO Industries, Inc. All rights reserved.

The EBSCO *MasterFILE Select* Subject Index

Even in a fairly simple display, there is a lot to look at and look for. In this view of the subject index in EBSCO's *MasterFILE Select* (Figure 1.5), *A* is the area identifying where we are: which database, and which part of the database. You are undoubtedly used to recognizing this without thinking about it, but what is the signal that we are in the *Subjects* function of the database?

The *B* section lets us jump around to any point in the index, that is, to the entries on and around whatever word we put in. Note that the results can be returned in alphabetical or in relevancy ranked order: we're seeing the inverted file at work—there are two ways to stack the shoeboxes.

In *C* the actual subject list is provided. The entries in bold and all-caps are values from the field designated as *subject* in this database. Note how the entries are a mixture of items: the thing itself (coffee), films, books, poetry, music, company names, and more. The View statements for each

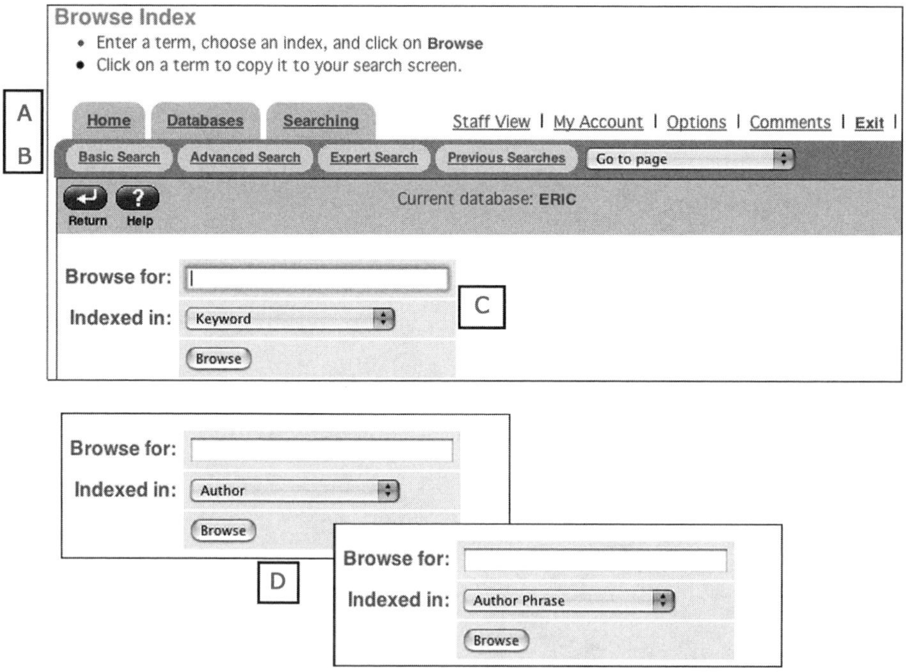

Browse Index
- Enter a term, choose an index, and click on **Browse**
- Click on a term to copy it to your search screen.

A

| Home | Databases | Searching | | Staff View I My Account I Options I Comments I Exit I |

B

| Basic Search | Advanced Search | Expert Search | Previous Searches | Go to page |

Return   Help   Current database: **ERIC**

Browse for: [   ]
Indexed in: [Keyword   ]   **C**
             [Browse]

Browse for: [   ]
Indexed in: [Author   ]
             [Browse]

D

Browse for: [   ]
Indexed in: [Author Phrase   ]
             [Browse]

Fig. 1.6. The initial Browse Index screen for the ERIC database as provided by FirstSearch®; examples of single-word and phrase indexes that FirstSearch® offers for many fields. Screen shots used with permission of OCLC; FirstSearch® and WorldCat® are registered trademarks of OCLC Online Computer Library Center, Inc.

entry tell you exactly how many times the term was assigned, and to which type of article (i.e., newspaper, periodical, or review). You can begin to tell what is being captured about each article in this database: subject terms assigned to it and the type of publication it appeared in.

FirstSearch Indexes for the ERIC Database

Moving on to another example, the FirstSearch databases provide examples of the use of *separate* indexes for many fields. In the Browse Index interface, as in EBSCO's Subject list above, you have the opportunity to roam around in the indexes, discovering what is there (and thus, what is possible), before committing to a search. There are even multiple indexes for the same fields, because they provide both single-word and phrase indexes for many fields, such as author name (Figure 1.6). The icon for accessing the Browse Index screen is part of the FirstSearch Advanced Search interface, discussed in greater detail in Chapter 4. For now, simply observe how it works.

In this case, the A area provides three major navigation tabs: you can go Home, change Databases, or go to the Searching interface from this Browse Index interface. The B area lets you jump directly to one of three kinds of search. Notice how the "where am I?" information also appears nearby, that is, the name of the current database. In the C area, the index field being

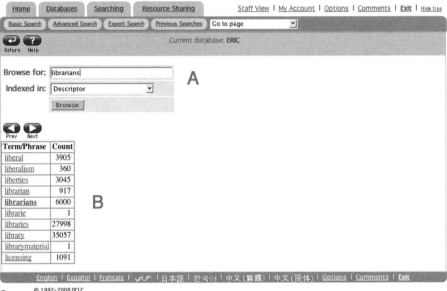

Fig. 1.7. Results from the single-word Descriptors index. Screen shots used with permission of OCLC; FirstSearch® and WorldCat® are registered trademarks of OCLC Online Computer Library Center, Inc.

searched is set to Keyword. In the screens marked *D*, the drop-down menu has been changed to Author, and Author Phrase.

Using the Descriptors Indexes

In Figure 1.7, we have looked up the word *librarians* in the Descriptors index (A) of a database called ERIC, which is a database that specializes and focuses on education literature. (*Descriptors* is the name FirstSearch has assigned to the field that EBSCO calls *Subject terms*: words assigned by indexers that capture the essence of an article's content.)

In the *B* area of Figure 1.7, we see the results of this search of the index. Note how the term searched on appears in the *middle* of the list, and is in bold. Why do you think the database designers have chosen to display the results this way? Note the two terms that only have a count of one. You can tell that the indexing process, the harvesting of terms from the field Descriptor, is done by a machine: it simply picks up whatever is there, typos and all. The Count field indicates how many articles in the database have been assigned to each Descriptor. The numbers tell you something about the overall content of the database, and how useful it might prove for whatever question you're working on. In this case, ERIC might not be the best place to look for information about liberalism (360 articles, once you add any other terms, will quickly disappear into nothing), but what do you think of ERIC as a place to look for information about libraries and librarians?

In Figure 1.8, we see the results of a search in the Descriptors Phrase index. You get a sense of the depth and history of this education database from the entry for *opaque projectors*, and how much the online concept

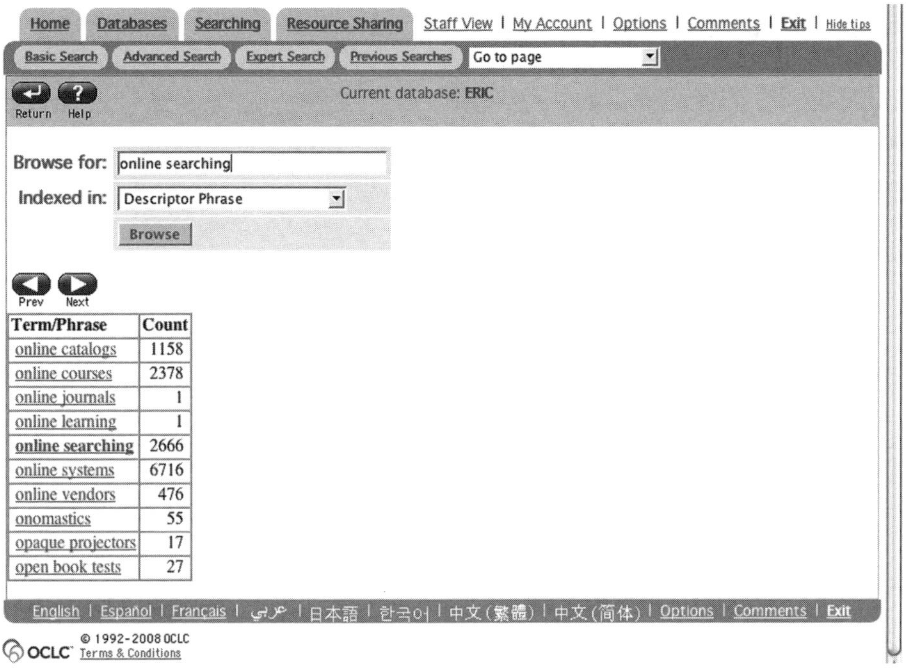

Fig. 1.8. Results from the multiple word Descriptors Phrase index. Screen shots used with permission of OCLC; FirstSearch® and WorldCat® are registered trademarks of OCLC Online Computer Library Center, Inc.

has taken over, by noticing the counts for *online searching* and *online systems*.

Record Structure Reflected in Fields Displayed

As a reminder, indexes are built from the fields included in a database record. The fields can be called the *record structure*, and you can get a sense of how simple, or elaborate, a database's record structure is by studying the fields displayed when viewing a record from the database.

The ERIC database on FirstSearch has quite an elaborate record structure; these database designers were making sure they didn't leave anything out, and that the most complete set of bibliographic information they could assemble would be available to users, as can be seen in a display of a full ERIC record (Figure 1.9).

The ERIC interface designers are trying to convey a large amount of information here, but they achieve their goal with clarity. Take some time to study the screen snap, noticing how they've used different fonts and alignments to convey meaning. If you can, go online and observe the colors used. The field names are lined up on the left, followed by colons. The contents of the fields appear to the right. Under the gray bar marked Subject(s), the terms are labeled Descriptors—a simplification over the past, when there were three types of subjects! Some of the fields probably seem quite mysterious, but think about the purpose of the others, and why the database designers decided to include them. ERIC has been around since the early 1960s, and if invented today, the database designers might have made different choices.

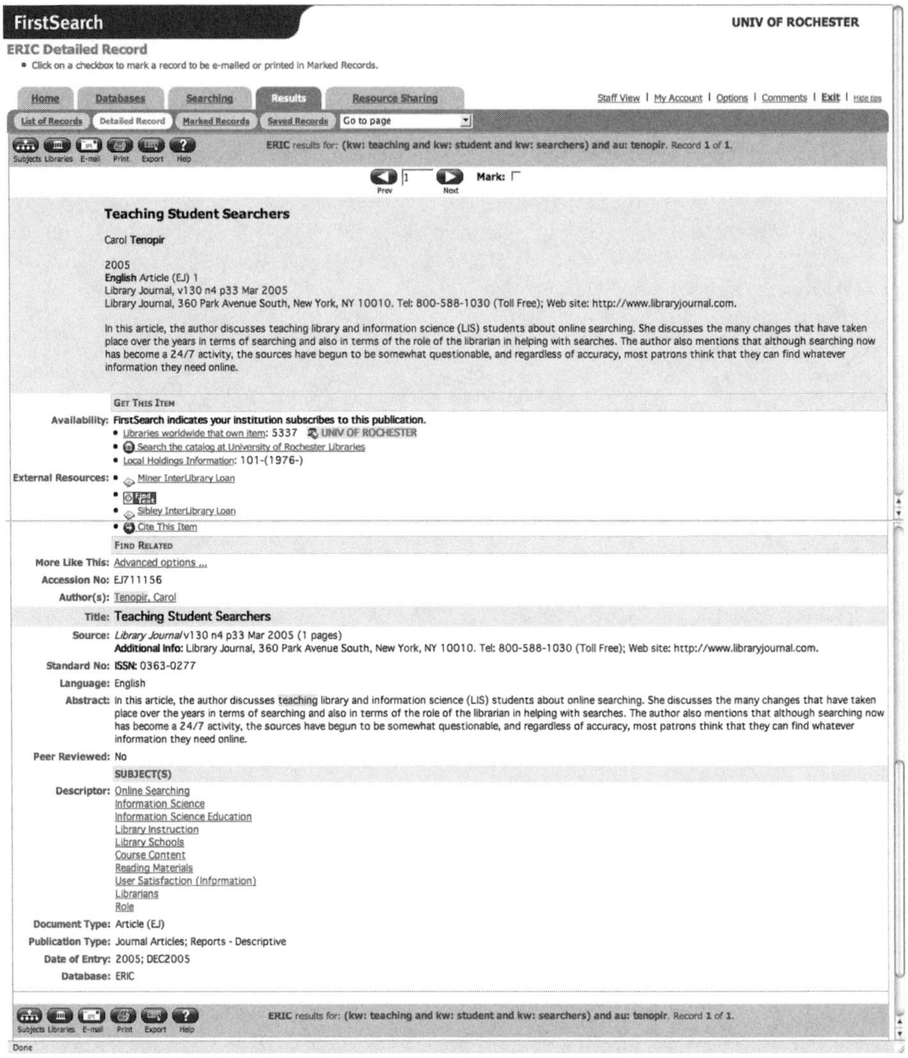

Fig. 1.9. A full record display from the ERIC database. Screen shots used with permission of OCLC; FirstSearch® and WorldCat® are registered trademarks of OCLC Online Computer Library Center, Inc.

Exercises and Points to Consider

1. What would *your* ideal database record for a journal article look like? Choose any article that interests you, and design a database record for it. What fields will you use? How big will each field be? What will you call them? Sketch out what the overall database would be like (and why this article would be included), and justify your choices.

2. Why do you think FirstSearch has separate one-word and phrase indexes for the same fields?

3. What is a useful piece of information that is provided when you browse the indexes (in both *MasterFILE* and the FirstSearch databases)? How might this affect your search strategy?

4. Go into the *MasterFILE Select* Subject index, and try looking up *self acceptance*. Page forward a few screens; have you found it yet? Start over at *self*, and page forward until you do find it, noticing as you go how the entries are sorted. (*Hint*: the hyphenated terms file after all the *self* (space) *word* entries.) Finally, look up *self acceptance* again, but this time sort the results by Relevance. Don't be afraid to break away from the straight alphabetical presentation of results if that approach doesn't appear to be working for you.

5. Can you do a field search with Google?

6. People generally think of Google as indexing all the words of all the Web pages that it visits.[3] In some sense, it offers one huge index labeled "all the text." Why do you think the commercial database vendors go to so much trouble to provide an elaborate record structure with indexed fields?

7. In the early days of online searching in libraries, only librarians performed searches, after a detailed and careful interview with the patron requesting the search. The librarian would plan the search carefully, and then "dial up" to connect to the database, using a password and employing a very terse, arcane set of commands to perform the search. Access fees were charged by the minute, with additional charges for records viewed. Try to picture this scenario, and then compare it with the situation today. How do you think the totally open, end-user access has affected databases and their interfaces? Can you think of anything about the current situation that is not an improvement?

Suggested Reading

Tenopir, Carol. 2005. Teaching Student Searchers. *Library Journal* 130 (March): 33.

Notes

1. If you're wondering why it would be so hard to change the record structure, remember to think of these databases as huge things: true, adding a new field to a database of just five records would be trivial. But a database of 500,000 records? How are you possibly going to retrospectively fill in the new field for all the existing records?

2. For one thing, the process of initially building the index can take hours. Although this does not mean that it can't be done, remember that every index has to be updated, frequently, to reflect any changes in your database. It just adds to the complexity of the whole operation.

3. Does Google have stop words, words that it ignores? And does it really index every page all the way to the end? Does this matter?

2
Working with Databases
The Searcher's Toolkit:
Part 1

In my experience, there are a finite number of concepts, techniques, and strategies for searching databases that make all the difference between aimlessly groping around, and efficiently and effectively retrieving useful material. If you spend your whole day searching, then you'll probably discover or develop many more, but for most researchers or reference librarians, the topics in this chapter and the next are most likely all you will ever need. I've dubbed this set of concepts the *Searcher's Toolkit*. All of them have applications in searching commercial databases, and some can be used with Web search engines (and once you've grasped these concepts, you'll start to see what's missing in the Web search products, and understand better why searching the Web is, well, the way it is: sometimes perfect, sometimes very frustrating).

Searcher's Toolkit: Part 1

Let us plunge right in with the most fundamental concept of all.

Basic Tool No. 1: Boolean Logic

In fact, this concept is so fundamental that you've probably run into it before, possibly several times through grade school, high school, and college. But do you *really* know what Boolean logic is and how it works, and how it will affect your searches? Bear with a discussion of it one more time—you may be surprised!

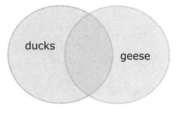

AND

Fig. 2.1. Boolean AND:
Ducks AND Geese.

In the database context, Boolean logic (after a fellow named George Boole [1815–1864])[1] refers to the *logical* (rather than arithmetical) operations on sets. That is, rather than manipulating numbers using symbols for plus, minus, multiply, or divide, Boolean logic controls what happens to sets of things when acted on by *logical operators*. The Boolean operators used in database searching are:

AND

OR

AND NOT (frequently expressed simply as *NOT*; more on this below.)

Venn Diagrams

Arithmetical expressions (2+2) result in some value (i.e., 4). Boolean expressions result in either a subset or superset of the original sets; rather than producing a specific value, logical operators have an *effect* on the sets, producing a different output set. The effects of Boolean expressions are traditionally illustrated with drawings called *Venn diagrams*. Venn diagrams are always done with circles and shadings as in Figure 2.1, which keeps them nicely abstract. Feel free to start thinking of the terminology "sets," and these circle illustrations, as "sets of database records" to make the concept more concrete. With just one operator in effect, Venn diagrams are quite simple to draw and to understand what the operator's effect is.

Boolean AND

In Figure 2.1, the circle on the left represents the set of all the database records that include the word *ducks*, a few of which also include the word *geese*. The circle on the right represents all records that include the word *geese*, a few of which also include the word *ducks*. A search for *ducks AND geese* retrieves only those records that mention *both* terms, represented by the smaller, overlapping section. It is easy to get confused here, because our regular use of the word *and* is additive, it produces more ("two scoops, and sprinkles, and some whipped cream"), but a Boolean AND is very different: an AND operator will always, in practice, return a set that is *smaller* than either of the original sets. Theoretically, the largest set it could return would still be only of equal size to the smaller of the original sets. For example, at one point in time, the ProQuest Research database contained

21,191 records that contained *Bush, George W* in a field called Person, and 15,216 records containing *Iraq* in a field called Location. A search on

Bush, George W in the Person field,

AND

Iraq in the Location field

produced 1,132 records.

Notice how even when the initial sets are quite large, the combined, "ANDed" set is considerably smaller. When one of the initial sets is much smaller than the other, the resulting set is affected even more. In the same database, at the same point in time, there were only 465 records for *Dean, Howard B* as a Person. Combining that with Bush, George W produced a set of only forty-six records.

AND says that *all* criteria must be met for an indicated action to happen (usually retrieval of a record). What the Boolean operators are really doing is evaluating true or false. The computer's thought process goes something like this:

If (ducks) is true (e.g., present in the record)

AND (at the same time, in the same record)

If (geese) is true

Retrieve the record.

So, to reiterate: the number of records meeting multiple conditions is, in practice, always smaller than the set of records meeting just one condition, and usually significantly smaller. The more conditions (criteria, terms) that you set, the smaller the number of records retrieved will be: there will be fewer documents about ducks AND geese AND loons than there are about just ducks AND geese. If one of the initial sets is very small, ANDing it with some other term is likely to reduce the results to zero.

Boolean OR

In Figure 2.2, the circle on the left represents all the database records that include the word *banana*, and the circle on the right represents all the database records that include the word *orange*. In this case, we don't care what other words they contain, or how much they overlap. Thinking of this as a search, the OR retrieves *all* the bananas records, plus *all* the oranges records (including records mentioning both), for a total of a LOT of records! Again, our common parlance can make this confusing: usually we use the word *or* to mean "either one or the other"—"I'll have the banana *or* the orange." We wouldn't expect to be handed both fruits in response to that statement. But in Boolean logic, OR means "either the one, or the other, or both." Either of the criteria can be met for the computer to retrieve the record:

If (banana) is true (e.g., present in a record)

OR

If (orange) is true (present in a record)

Retrieve the record.

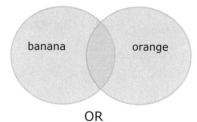

OR

Fig. 2.2. Boolean OR:
Banana OR Orange.

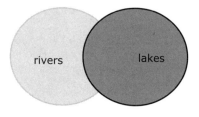

NOT

Fig. 2.3. Boolean NOT:
Rivers NOT Lakes.

Think of it this way: in practice, Boolean OR is (practically) always more.

Boolean NOT

Finally, Figure 2.3 represents the Boolean exclusion operator, which you'll see expressed as AND NOT and simply NOT with almost equal frequency. For our purposes, they are interchangeable, and this text will generally use just NOT to make the operators as distinguishable as possible.[2] If this feels confusing, take comfort that at least the effects of this operator are more in line with our common usage of *not*: rivers NOT lakes retrieves records that include the term *rivers*, as long as they do NOT also contain the word lakes. Both criteria must be met, in the sense that the first term must be present, and the second term must *not* be present, for a record to be retrieved. The set of records retrieved can be thought of as just the lighter area of the *rivers* circle; anything from the darker *lakes* circle would not be in the results set. Note how the syntax is subtly different (which is further proof that even when a database vendor just uses NOT, what is really going on is AND NOT):

If (rivers) is true (present in a record)

And

If (lakes) is NOT true (not present in the record)

Retrieve the record.

As you would expect, like AND, NOT almost always reduces the number of records retrieved. In general usage, you'll find that you don't often use the NOT operator in commercial databases: the possibility of missing useful records just because they happened to include the "NOTed" out term is too risky. If too many results are coming back, the better strategy is almost always to AND in another term, rather than to NOT out a term.

Order of Boolean Operations

A statement using just one Boolean operator—ducks OR geese—is straightforward. But just as you can write arithmetical expressions with several operators (2+2–3∗9), you can write Boolean expressions with multiple operators. You will encounter plenty of searches that require more complexity than simply (word) AND (word). Again, just as in the arithmetical statements, the Boolean operators have very specific effects, and the order in which they are processed has a powerful effect on what ends up in the results set. When there is more than one operator in a search statement, they are generally evaluated in this order:

- NOT operations are performed first.
- Then AND operations are evaluated.
- Finally, OR.

This is called the *order of operation*. This is the standard order for processing Boolean operators, but some systems simply evaluate statements left to right, the way you read. The results could be very different, depending on which order is used. Although it's important to be aware of the idea of order of operation, luckily, you don't have to figure out what it is on each system you use. There is a simple way to take control and bend the order of operation to your will.

The Power of Parentheses

To control the order of operation, many systems allow you group your ANDs, ORs, NOTs with parentheses: ( ). Just as in arithmetic statements, the use of parentheses is helpful either to just make the order of operation explicit, or to override it. What happens is that the expression in parentheses will be evaluated first, and then the order of operation (standard or left to right) will take over.[3] Throwing parentheses into the mix can change the way the system interprets the search dramatically. For example, the statement:

ducks NOT migration OR geese

produces the same result set as:

(ducks NOT migration) OR geese

because in this case, putting the parentheses around the NOT statement (causing it to be executed first) is exactly the same as what happens in the standard order of operation (NOT first, OR last). The set of documents retrieved would be fairly large, and contain records for ducks (as long as those records didn't mention migration), and any records mentioning geese—even records that discuss geese and migration. OR really opens the door to let things back in, in sometimes surprising ways.

Represented as a Venn diagram, the statement (ducks NOT migration) OR geese looks like Figure 2.4.

The results of this search would include all the records except those represented by the visible dark area of the "migration" circle. Note that records

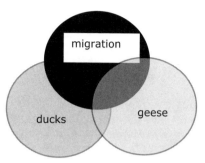

Fig. 2.4. (Ducks   NOT   Migration) OR Geese.

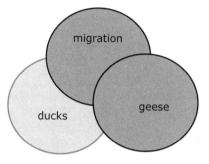

Fig. 2.5. Ducks NOT (Migration OR Geese).

about geese that mention migration *would* be included in the results; the NOT only affects the duck records. However, writing the search statement as:

ducks NOT (migration OR geese)

will produce quite a different result set, much smaller and more focused. These would be records that mention ducks, and only those duck records that don't mention either migration or geese—the lightest area in Figure 2.5. The Venn diagram for this statement is shown in Figure 2.5.

Quick Recap

The Boolean operators are AND, OR, NOT (also expressed AND NOT). Adding terms to a search with AND will reduce the number of results, as will "NOTing" out a term. "ORing" more terms into a search will increase the number of results. Boolean expressions can be represented graphically with Venn diagrams. The standard order of operations for Boolean statements is to evaluate any NOT statements first, followed by AND statements, finally by OR statements. Putting part of the statement in parentheses changes the order of operations, because the parenthesized section will be evaluated first.

Basic Tool No. 2: Controlled Vocabulary

The conundrum of online searching is that "We want to look for concepts, but we are forced to search for words" (Walker and Janes, 1999). Think about it: if you wanted an *overview* of some topic, or a *discussion* of the pros and cons of some action, or especially *one good article on* ... how do you express these squishy notions to a digital search engine? Even if you can search the full text, the item you want might not include in its text "this is an overview" or "here is a discussion" and certainly not "here is the latest best article" on topic xyz. All that you can do, in each of these cases, is to search on words that represent the topic. In the world of commercial, subscription databases, there is an additional, powerful option: the provision of *controlled vocabulary*, also known as *subject headings*, a *thesaurus*,[4] *descriptors*,[5] *authority control*.[6] Controlled vocabulary is one of the added extras, one of the contributions of the companies that put together the databases, and one of the reasons they charge a subscription fee to access them. Remember the indexers from Chapter 1? You are paying for a bit of human analysis on each entry in the database. If done well, this analysis is worth the price of admission for the efficiency that it provides.

Advantages of Controlled Vocabulary

Why is controlled vocabulary so valuable?

- Controlled vocabulary saves you from having to come up with, and then search for, every possible synonym (or alternative spelling) for a term. For example, if all of the articles discussing various kinds of clothing are assigned a subject heading of "clothing," you don't have to worry about looking for all the possible ways clothing might be expressed, for example: dress, raiment, drapery, costume, attire, habiliment, vesture, vestment, garment, garb, apparel, wardrobe, wearing apparel, clothes, designer clothes, outfit, trousseau, suit, togs, day wear, night wear, zoot suit. . . .

  - *Note*: Don't let your synonym neurons atrophy completely, though, because if you try a term in a subject or thesaurus search and get no results, not even a "see" reference, you'll need to think of another term with which to start. And, of course, there is no controlled vocabulary on the Web.

- Theoretically, the use of controlled vocabulary should make your search more complete: if the indexers at the database company have reliably assigned a subject heading of *waterfowl every* time an article mentions geese or goose, duck or ducks, loon or loons, or any other water bird, it should only be necessary to search on that term to retrieve everything.

- It can be used to disambiguate words that have several meanings (e.g., mercury—a planet, a car, a god, or a metal?), aiding in the precision of your search results. (*Precision*, in searching, is an important technical term, rather than just descriptive. See Searching Lexicon 3: Recall versus Precision). For author names, *authority control*[7] provides *one* way to look up an author known by more than one name (e.g., Mark Twain/Samuel Clemens).

- It provides a "safe" and helpful entry point into an unfamiliar subject area. Even if you know nothing about the subject, you have the assurance that the terms in the subject list are correct and appropriate. By browsing in the list and getting a sense of the terms (especially if there are "see" or "see also" references), you can often get ideas and develop or refine a search strategy.

Expressing these points in more formal terms (Walker and Janes, 1999), controlled vocabularies:

- Facilitate the *gathering of like items*
- Help with *comprehensiveness* of results
- Help also with *precision* of results
- Help *broaden understanding* of a topic in an unfamiliar subject area

Basic Tool No. 3: Field Searching

This tool harkens back to the discussion of database structure in Chapter 1: how records in databases consist of a series of fields, each designated to hold a particular value. *Field searching* simply means the ability to restrict your search to a specific field, for example, to search just the *author* field for a particular value (a name). Most databases offer some kind of default set of fields that are searched, so if you're unsure, in a hurry, or just getting a sense of what the database might contain, you can always throw a word or phrase into the first available search box and hit search, just like you usually do on the Web. Taking a few moments to determine what fields are available for searching can be very valuable, however. Field searching focuses your search, and usually makes it more efficient. For example, say that you wanted to search a database of English literature for works by an author named—English! Just searching on the keyword "English" without limiting to the author field would result in hundreds of irrelevant results, because a great many of the records undoubtedly mention the word in a title or abstract, or English might appear in a Language field that gets included in a Default Fields search. The database designers spent all that time deciding what fields to have—so definitely exploit this feature if it is available.

Combining Field Searching and Controlled Vocabulary

The combination of field searching with controlled vocabulary is especially effective; for example, find an appropriate term in the list of subject terms and then search on it, restricting your search to the Subject Terms field. Of course, you will often construct searches combining all three of these initial tools, to produce a search such as:

Hanushek → in the → Author field

AND

Economics of Education → in the → Descriptors Phrase field

AND

1990–2000 → in the → Date field

There are more tools for your Searcher's Toolkit waiting in Chapter 3. Before going on, however, there are some terms in what we'll call the Searching Lexicon that, while they may not make you a better searcher, are useful to know because they give you a way to describe or better understand your search results.

Terms in the Searching Lexicon

Searching Lexicon 1: False Drops

A *false drop* is a document that is retrieved by your search terms, but the terms in the document are not used in the sense you intended; for example, a search on "employment or jobs or careers" that retrieves articles about Steve Jobs. False drops epitomize the problem of wanting to search for concepts but only being able to search for words! They are not *wrong* in a technical sense: the words in the records match the words you typed in—they just aren't being used to express the meaning you had in mind. (To make up for the inconvenience, such results are often quite humorous, if not downright bizarre.) When you get what appears to be a completely off-the-wall result, don't immediately assume that the system is defective or that something is wrong. Now you have a term for such a result; it might simply be a false drop.

Controlled vocabulary and field searching can help avoid the false-drop problem, although even those tools may not make it go away completely. Systems that search large quantities of full text are especially prone to the false-drop problem.

Searching Lexicon 2: Stop Words

Stop words were mentioned in Chapter 1 but are worth revisiting here. Stop words, a.k.a. *noise words*, are those little words that most systems (commercial database or Web search) do not index. Typical choices for a stop word list could include: *an, by, for, from, of, the, to, with, be, where, how, it, he, my, his, when, there, is, are, so, she,* and *her.* There is no standard list of stop words that all databases adhere to, which is good in a way, because it allows for the possibility of a database having a relatively short list of stop words, or possibly even none at all. This means, however (if you determine that stop words might be interfering with your search results), that you'll have to dig around in the database's help files and hope that somewhere they have documented their list of stop words. There will be occasions where the words that a database or search engine has chosen *not* to index are very important, and you'll need to come up with creative ways to get around the problem. (One of the most famous examples is a search on the famous line, "to be or not to be"—can it be done?)

Searching Lexicon 3: Recall versus Precision

Recall and precision have to do with the number and quality of the results retrieved by your search:

- *Recall* refers to retrieving more results—spreading your net as wide as possible, and probably picking up a number of less relevant results along with the "good" results. *High recall* means that you are unlikely to miss any relevant items.

- *Precision* refers to focusing your search down, retrieving fewer, but more perfectly on-target and relevant results. *High precision* means that you are unlikely to retrieve very many, if any, irrelevant results (no false drops).

What might be the pros and cons of each?

- With greater recall the chances are better that you won't miss any relevant materials, but you'll invest more time going through your results, reviewing them after the fact to filter out the irrelevant items (in other words, you might have to wade through an awful lot of junk to find the gems).

- The more precise your search is, the more likely it is that you'll miss some things. There will be items in the database that might well meet your needs, but that your search didn't pick up because your choice of terminology or fields or limits was just a little *too* specific.

Google provides a great example of both ends of the recall–precision spectrum: ultimate *recall* is all the matches to a simple search. Ultimate *precision* is represented by the "I'm feeling lucky" search button, which takes you to just one (theoretically ideal) result.

Should I Aim for Recall or Precision?

Neither one—recall or precision—is intrinsically good or bad; they simply describe an outcome. But recall and precision also provide a useful a way to think about your search, to guide how you go about it: what database or search engine you use, and what search techniques you employ. The outcome desired dictates the search style employed: someone who is testing a choice of Ph.D. thesis topic wants to spread the net as wide as possible, to make sure that no one has looked at their particular problem before. For that situation, high recall is crucial. Similarly, if you believe you're looking for an obscure topic, but you want absolutely everything and anything that can be found about it, you'll want to try for maximum recall. You might start with a Web search, or in an appropriate database, enter a very simple style of search (e.g., no controlled vocabulary, not limited to any specific field). An undergraduate writing a short paper or a community hobbyist investigating a new topic, however, may be perfectly served by a high-precision search that identifies a few recent, relevant articles, even though many more related, or equally relevant, articles remain behind in the database. In that case, choose an appropriate database, check for subject terms, perhaps combine two or more with Boolean operators, and use some field searching.

Quick Recap

Now you have three major tools in your search arsenal:

1. The concept of Boolean logic for combining terms: the operators AND, OR, and NOT, and the use of parentheses to affect the order in which the Boolean operators are processed.

2. The concept of controlled vocabulary: terms that the vendor has applied to help you get all the articles on a topic without having to keyword search every variation or synonym, and to disambiguate among various meanings.

3. The concept of field searching: restricting your search to specified fields to make it more precise and efficient.

You also now know that database indexing programs have lists of certain words they do *not* index, known as *stop words*.

In addition, you have some new language to describe the results of your searches:

- False drops
- Recall
- Precision

Applying the Tools

Let's look at EBSCO's *MasterFILE Select*, a multidisciplinary database, and see how these tools apply there.

MasterFILE Select: Notes and Search Examples

The first challenge with any database is to be able to look at and interpret what is presented in the interface. We're so used to looking at busy Web pages that we look—but we don't really *see*. To turn yourself into a more efficient and effective searcher, however, it is important to be able to look over an interface, and quickly translate what's there into the tools you are looking for:

- Does it use Boolean operators for combining terms?
- Is it possible to search in specific fields, and if yes, which ones?
- Is there any kind of controlled vocabulary available? (Can you browse it?)

Determining Availability of Search Tools

Many databases offer two search modes: *Basic* and *Advanced*. Usually the questions above won't be answered by looking at the Basic search interface, but there should be good information in the Advanced screen. Figure 2.6 shows the Advanced Search interface in *MasterFILE Select*. What do you see? Are your first three tools available?

Check: Boolean operators work here. In fact, there appears to be an alternative way to achieve a Boolean affect: note the *Search modes* area, and the *Find all . . .* and *Find any . . .* options. (You will explore the SmartText option in one of the Exercises at the end of the chapter.) The whole lower area of the screen is devoted to *Limit* options, but we haven't talked about limits yet, so we won't go into those.

Now take a look at Figure 2.7: do we have the option of restricting our search to certain fields?

Check: there are fields available for searching. The list of fields gives a clue, reinforced by the top bar in the interface, that there might be some kind of controlled vocabulary available, and that it can be browsed. See the word *Subjects* in the bar across the top?

Controlled Vocabulary: The Subjects List

Some databases offer separate lists of the terms that have been indexed from various fields (as in the ERIC screen snaps in Chapter 1, where there were separate lists of terms for the Descriptors, and the Descriptors

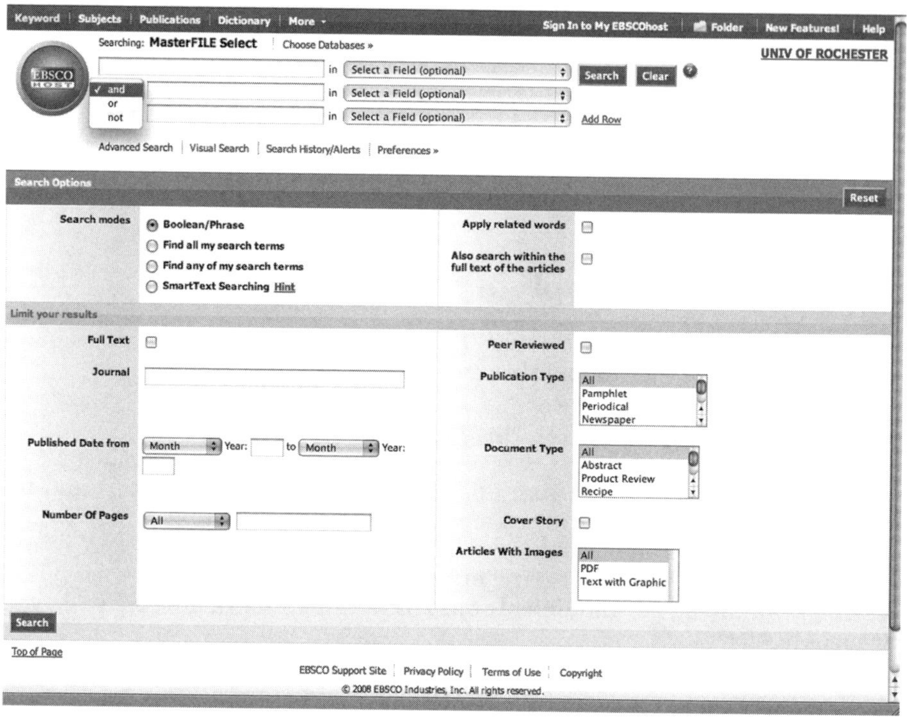

Fig. 2.6. Advanced Search interface, showing Boolean operators, in *MasterFILE Select*. © 2008 EBSCO Industries, Inc. All rights reserved.

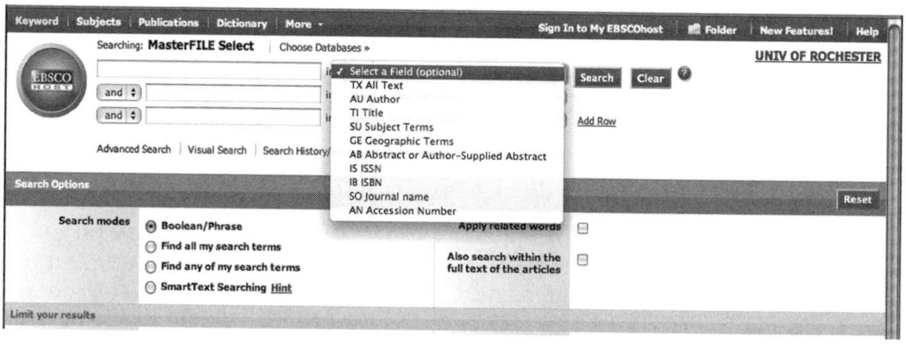

Fig. 2.7. Fields available for searching in *MasterFILE Select*. © 2008 EBSCO Industries, Inc. All rights reserved.

Phrase fields). The *MasterFILE Select* Subjects list is an all-in-one affair: it includes terms from many fields, not just "subjects" per se. You can use it to identify controlled vocabulary, as well as identify titles of books, poems, companies, places, and people—proper names of all kinds. The *MasterFILE Select* Subjects list also provides some nice value-added information: each entry includes the article publication type(s), and how many of each, available for that heading. Sections of the entries starting at the Subject "Mars" demonstrate this well (Figure 2.8a and 2.8b):

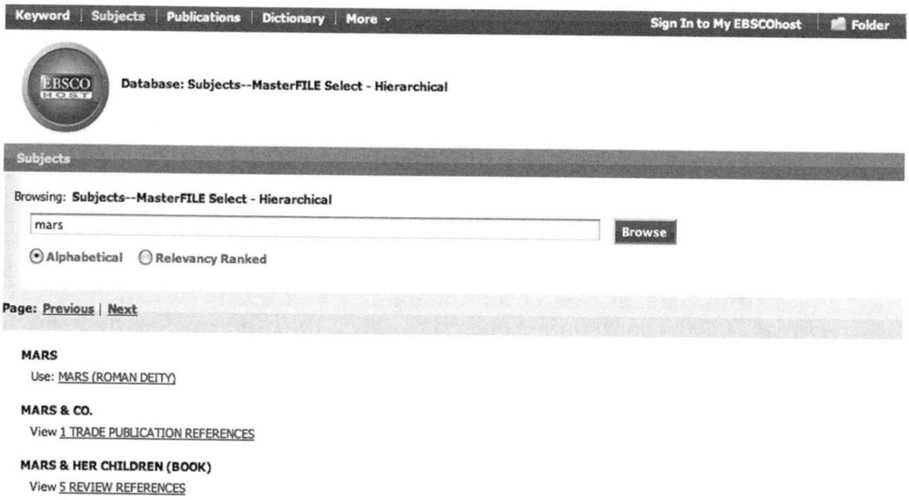

Fig. 2.8a. Beginning of Subject listing for "Mars." © 2008 EBSCO Industries, Inc. All rights reserved.

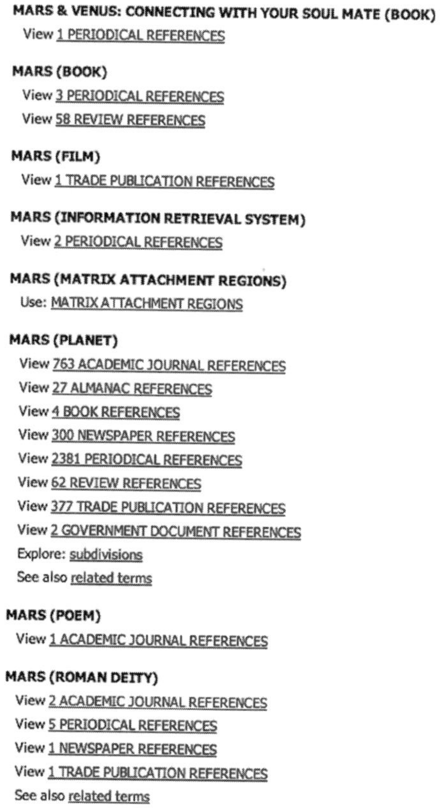

Fig. 2.8b. Farther down in the subject listing for "Mars." © 2008 EBSCO Industries, Inc. All rights reserved.

The *MasterFILE* Subjects list is useful if you are looking for one thing (e.g., person, place, book review, company, etc.), from one sort of publication, for example, academic journal references to Mars (the planet). It makes it very easy to connect directly to the results you intended (minimizing false drops). It does not, however, offer any way to construct a multiple term search, or to view all the articles on a topic, regardless of type of publication.

Multiple Field Searches in MasterFILE

To set up a Boolean search and use known values in specific fields in *MasterFILE Select*, the best approach is to check the Subjects list, determine the correct form of the terms you want to use, then click on Advanced Search and type the terms in yourself, setting the field to be searched to Subject (or Author, etc.). One cautionary note: do not include the parentheses on the terms that have been glossed to distinguish their meaning, for example, Mars (Planet) has to be entered Mars Planet.

Search Example 1

A patron approaches and says: "I want to find some articles about the Mars lunar lander." Something about this doesn't sound quite right to you, but the patron insists on that terminology.

The most simple, literal approach (besides going to the Web) might be to go to *MasterFILE Select*, and simply type in "mars lunar lander," as shown in the upper part of Figure 2.9.

This produces only one result (Figure 2.9)—and a very odd one, at that! (Would you call this a false drop?) You were right to think there was something wrong with the patron's terminology; however, it's always worth taking a look, to figure out why you got something. In this case, by simply mousing over the magnifying glass icon next to the article title, we see a "preview" of the record (Figure 2.10). Right from that, you can see that one of the subject headings in this odd result is *space probes*, indicated by the

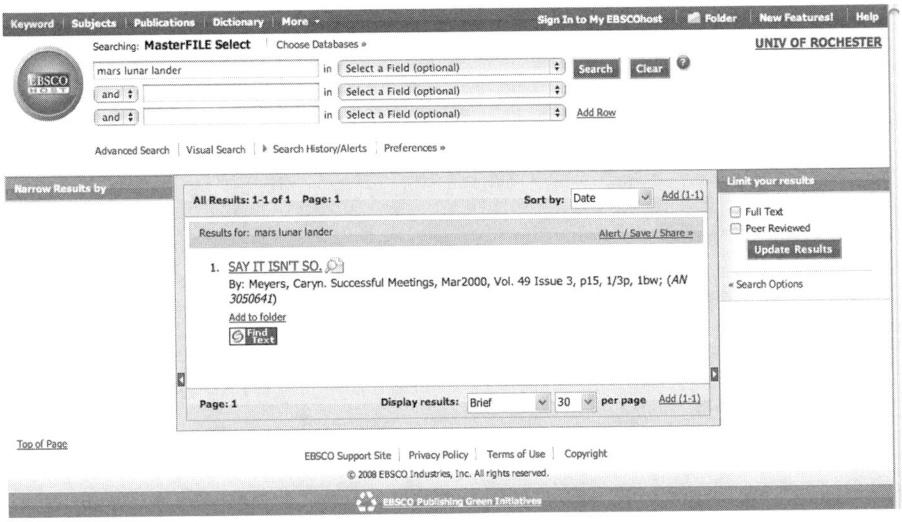

Fig. 2.9. *MasterFILE Select* search for "Mars lunar lander," showing a single result. © 2008 EBSCO Industries, Inc. All rights reserved.

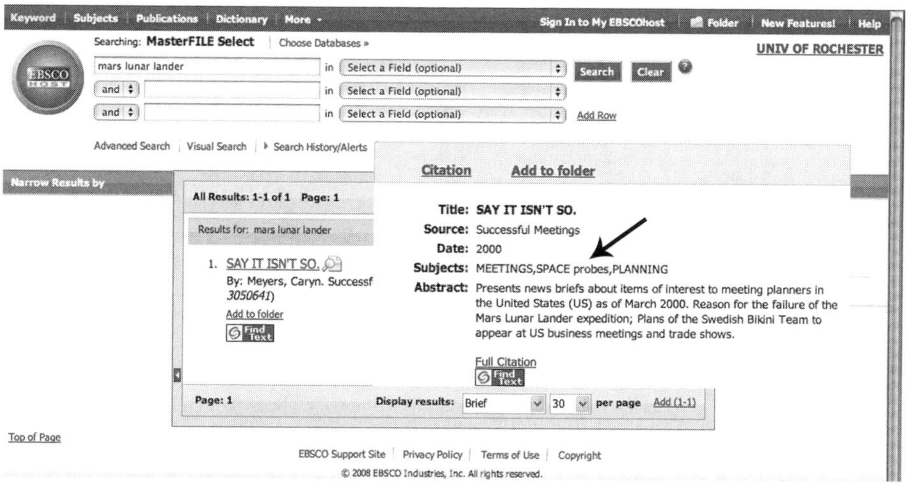

Fig. 2.10. Citation preview feature, with subject headings indicated. © 2008 EBSCO Industries, Inc. All rights reserved.

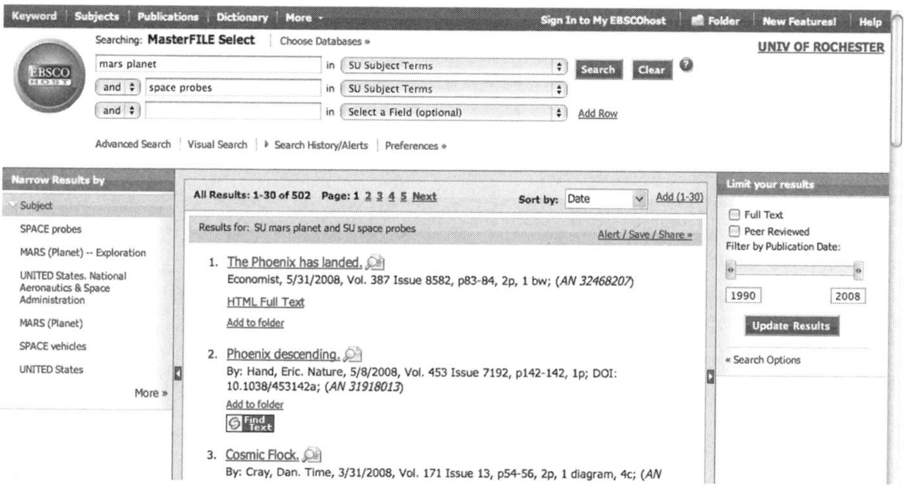

Fig. 2.11. Better results from search strategy using subject terms in *MasterFILE Select*. © 2008 EBSCO Industries, Inc. All rights reserved.

arrow in Figure 2.10. Ah hah! That sounds good. From Figure 2.8b we know there should be lots of entries for the planet Mars. Because the Advanced search screen is right here for us above the results, we can reformulate our search immediately by filling in these two known subject headings and setting their fields to Subject Terms (reflected in the results screen in Figure 2.11).

The results of this search are now on target, with the first few of many showing in Figure 2.11. Suggested additional subject headings on the left confirm that we're on the right track, as well as offering ways to focus the search further. (The patron must have been thinking of a previous Mars Lander or Rover—the "lunar" part was misremembered.) We will be seeing EBSCO's interface again in Chapter 7, where we will go into more of its features in detail.

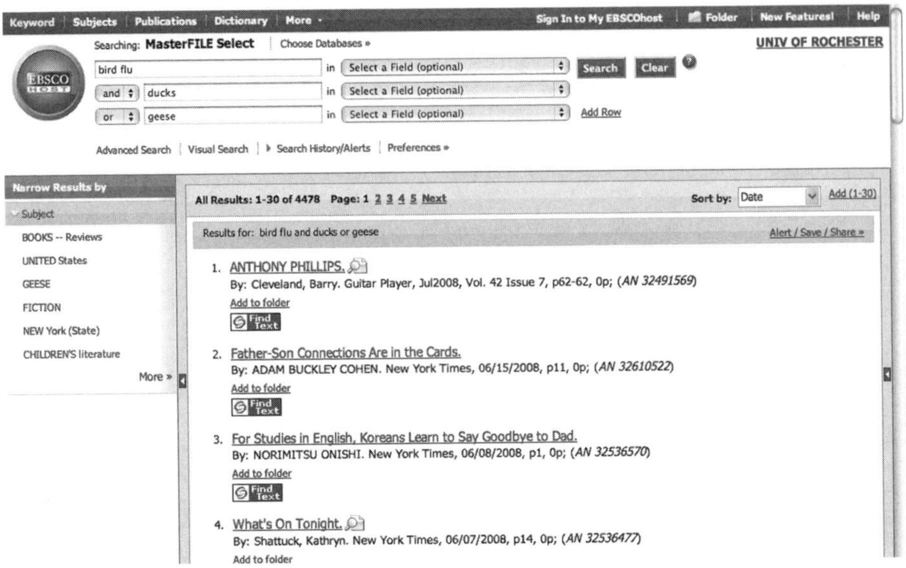

Fig. 2.12. Boolean logic pitfalls in the Advanced Search screen. © 2008 EBSCO Industries, Inc. All rights reserved.

Boolean Logic: Advanced Search versus Basic Search

As a final note to this chapter, unfortunately we have to reveal that there are no comfortable absolutes in this business. The Advanced Search screen may not always be the best answer, as shown in the following two screen snaps. In Figure 2.12, a Boolean search was set up in the Advanced Search screen, using the operators in the drop-down menus. If you can read the small print in the screenshot, notice how the system interpreted the search ("bird flu and ducks or geese"), and how many results it returned (4478).

What the searcher *meant* was bird flu and (ducks or geese), that is, anything about bird flu and its impact on ducks or geese. If the searcher thought to type "ducks or geese" all into the first search field, and then AND in "bird flu," the search would work (or, obviously, typing the whole statement into one field of the advanced search interface would work fine). The interface structure doesn't lead you to think of doing this, however, and so the results are full of false drops.

In the Basic screen, however, it's a snap to do it right, using those powerful parentheses (Figure 2.13). You can immediately tell your search is right by the titles in the results, and the additional suggested subject headings on the left. (In this database, you also get Related Images on the right—how fun!)

This is a point to keep in mind: *basic* doesn't necessarily need to mean simplistic. Since you are now a master of Boolean operators and parentheses, it can be *easier* to do some searches in the Basic mode. (There are even ways to indicate what field to search in the Basic mode, but that can wait.) For quick iterations of a search, testing various terms and combinations, the Basic search box is very useful.

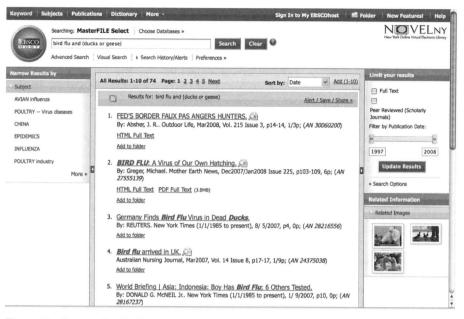

Fig. 2.13. Successful Boolean search statement and results in Basic mode. © 2008 EBSCO Industries, Inc. All rights reserved.

Exercises and Points to Consider

1. Consider these statements:

    ducks OR geese NOT migration

    (ducks OR geese) NOT migration

    (ducks AND geese) OR loons

    ducks AND (geese OR loons)

    (ducks OR geese) AND migration

    (ducks OR geese) NOT migration

    (ducks OR (geese NOT migration)) AND lakes

    Try drawing Venn diagrams for the paired statements to see how (or if) they differ. Then try describing in words what the content of the documents retrieved by these statements would be. Test out the statements in *MasterFILE Select's* Basic search mode.

2. Pick three terms relating to a subject that interests you, and explore searching them in various ways in *MasterFILE Select*. Try a number of Boolean combinations in Basic search mode, try setting up similar searches in Advanced mode, and see if your terms appear in the Subjects list. Even though we didn't discuss them, experiment with the various limits options, both in the search screen and in the results screen.

3. In the *MasterFILE* Advanced Search, try the "mars lunar lander" search again, but this time set the Search mode to SmartText Searching. The results will be very different. In fact, you might not ever realize that there's no such thing as a Mars lunar lander, because the results are so appropriate. Experiment with the SmartText mode for a while. Would you want to set this as the default in your library? Why or why not?

4. In describing the benefits of controlled vocabulary, you will have noticed a consistent use of terms such as *should,* as in "use of subject headings *should* ensure that you retrieve everything on a given topic," rather than the more certain term *will*. What do you think might prevent controlled vocabulary from being a perfect retrieval panacea?

5. If you had part of a citation and were trying to find the rest of the information (a *known item search*), what type of search would you probably try first, one that had high recall, or high precision? Based on your answer, what type of resource (commercial database or Web search), and techniques would you use? What if your first approach didn't work?

Sidebar 2.1. Analyzing Recall versus Precision

Say that there are N relevant items "out there." You have a search engine that retrieves items based on a query. We can make a chart that describes the efficacy of the search, in terms of the four possible types of results (Table 2.1). You can think of actual numbers being substituted for all the types of results.

True positives are search results that indeed are relevant items. You can clearly count these.

False negatives are failures of the search: relevant items that are out there but are not retrieved. If you know there are N relevant items altogether, then this number is N—(true positives). This is called a *Type II* error in statistical hypothesis testing (the test wrongly reports that a true hypothesis is false).

False positives are search results that are useless and irrelevant. You can count these because you're looking at them. This is called a *Type I* error in statistical hypothesis testing (the test wrongly reports that a false hypothesis is true).

True negatives are all of those items not found that indeed you don't care about because they are irrelevant. There are presumably a great many of these unless something is really off in the system. We don't usually use this number.

Considering the NUMBERS of these types of results, we can define:

Recall: the number of relevant items found divided by the number of relevant items out there (N):

recall = (true positives)/((true positives) + (false negatives)) = (true positives)/N.

Precision: the number of relevant items found divided by the number of items found (relevant and irrelevant):

precision = (true positives)/((true positives) + (false positives)).

One error measure is the number of false results divided by the number of relevant items out there (N):

$$\text{error rate} = ((\text{false positives}) + (\text{false negatives}))/((\text{true positives}) + (\text{false negatives}))$$

$$= ((\text{false positives}) + (\text{false negatives}))/\text{N}.$$

So if you have good recall (near 1), you don't wind up with lots of missed but relevant items, but your results could be diluted by lots of false positives, or items that are wrongly retrieved as being relevant when they are not.

If you have good precision, on the other hand, you can be more sure that your results are actually relevant, but you might be missing a lot of other relevant items in your search (you could have a large number of false negatives). Error rate is just the proportion of both types of errors to the total number of relevant items you ideally would like to retrieve.

Self Test

You're looking for information on a guitar maker called David Daily.

Google finds 4,130,000 hits on "Daily Guitars," two of which (the first two, luckily) are relevant. You have reason to know that there are actually two relevant Web sites out there. What are the recall, precision, and error rate for this search?

Google finds 31,500 hits on *hog farm waste runoff problems* (entered without double quotation marks), of which we will declare that 2,600 are relevant. The authoritative document you are consulting says there are "several thousand" relevant items on the Web. What are reasonable ranges for the values of recall, precision, and error rate for this search?

Table 2.1. Retrieval versus relevancy chart

	Retrieved Items	
Actual Items	Relevant	Irrelevant
Relevant	True positives	False negatives
Irrelevant	False positives	True negatives

Notes

1. Boole was a British mathematician and philosopher. "As the inventor of Boolean algebra, the basis of all modern computer arithmetic, Boole is regarded as one of the founders of the field of computer science." This and more details about George Boole are available from the online *Wikipedia*, the free encyclopedia, http://en.wikipedia.org/wiki/George_Boole (accessed February 26, 2005).

2. Strictly speaking, in mathematical logic terms NOT and AND NOT are different. NOT is a unary operator, that is, it can take just one argument: NOT argyle, for example, if you were offered a world of socks and were willing to take anything but argyle. AND NOT is a binary operator, that is, it takes two arguments: pie AND NOT banana cream—you must provide a first set, and then a second set that you wish to exclude. Databases and Web search engines, even when they express the operator as NOT, mean AND NOT. This is subtly conveyed in the advanced search interfaces of databases: the "AND OR NOT" options don't start until *after* the first text input field.

3. You can have multiple levels of parenthetical expressions, a syntax known as *nesting* or *nested statements*, in which case the most deeply nested statement will be

evaluated first, followed by the parenthetical expression around it, and so forth. You may very seldom, if ever, need to construct a nested statement, but it's interesting to know that you can.

4. Thesaurus, plural thesauri. The formal term for controlled vocabulary. Specific to the database discipline, a thesaurus can also describe relationships between the terms, and provide pointers to the best terms to use.

5. Certain databases use the term *descriptors* for subject headings.

6. Most often associated with library catalogs, *authority control* refers to a system of controlled vocabulary specifically for author names.

7. With thanks to the *ARTFL Project: Roget's Thesaurus, 1911*, http://machaut. uchicago.edu/cgi-bin/ROGET.sh.old?word=clothing (accessed February 26, 2005).

3
The Searcher's Toolkit: Part 2

The tools covered in Chapter 2, Boolean operators, controlled vocabulary, and field searching, are the most fundamental. The tools we are adding here are further refinements: additional search functions; a simple search strategy that can be used in any situation, which will enable you to execute ever more sophisticated searches; and finally a list of "mental tools." The intent is always to enable you to get the information you're after more efficiently and effectively.

Searcher's Toolkit: Part 2

Basic Tool No. 4: Proximity Searching

In addition to allowing you to specify that your search results must include certain terms (Boolean AND: ducks AND geese AND loons), most of the subscription database systems also allow you to set up an even more sophisticated search, in which you set a rule for the relationship between those terms. That is, you can state how close to each other, and sometimes in what order, they must appear in the text to qualify for retrieval. This is known as *proximity* searching.

Proximity searching allows you to specify that termA appears within so many words of termB. For example, if you were trying to discover names of consulting firms that work with the food and beverage industry, it's quite possible that such a thing would only be mentioned as an aside—neither concept would be enough to merit a subject heading. Searching "consulting AND (food OR beverage)" would probably result in a large number of false drops, because the words could occur in the documents but have nothing to do with each other (e.g., consulting could show up in the first paragraph and food or beverage in the last paragraph, in a totally different context). The only way that you're going to have any chance of getting something meaningful is if the terms are somewhat close to each other: at least within the same paragraph, and, even better, within the same sentence, within five to ten words of each other. There's also nothing to prevent you from combining the two approaches: termA within five words of (termB or termC).

When your search topic falls below the radar of subject headings (controlled vocabulary), and you have some text to work with (at least an abstract, if not full text), proximity searching is a wonderful way to get greater precision in your results. You will still get false drops, but not nearly as many as you would using only Boolean operators.

Proximity Searching Strategy

In setting up a proximity search, start by trying to envision how the writer might have expressed what you're looking for: in this case, it might be phrases such as "...consultants to the consumer packaged goods, personal care, and food and beverage industries..." or "...a leading food industry consultant..." or "...has chosen ABC, a Boston consulting firm, for their new beverage marketing campaign...." This helps you to decide whether to set the proximity number lower (4 or 5), or higher (8 or 10). In this case it would be good to set it higher, because it's possible that the writer might have listed several industries, as in the first phrase example. Obviously, this presupposes that you are fairly familiar with the literature of the topic at hand. What if you aren't? In that case, simply experiment: start with a proximity of five words, and (as described in "pearl growing," below) learn from the results, increasing or decreasing the proximity number as seems appropriate.[1] There's no rule that you have to get it exactly right the first time!

Proximity Operators

Like a Boolean search, a proximity search is expressed with special operators. Unfortunately, unlike the universal and easily recognized AND, OR, NOT (AND NOT) used for Boolean expressions, proximity operators vary from system to system, so it's harder to produce a nice neat list to memorize. Even the syntax—the operators—can be mysterious looking, using simply N (for *near*) or W (for *within*), and a number to indicate the number of possible intervening words. Some systems, such as EBSCO, even offer two flavors of proximity operator: one for specifying just proximity, the other for dictating both proximity and word order (termA must occur within so many words, and *before* termB). Let's look at some examples.

Proximity Search Examples

ProQuest

ProQuest uses the syntax "W/<number>" for proximity[2] (the command letter does not need to be capitalized):

homeless w/4 teenagers

In response to this search, the ProQuest system will return records where the word *homeless* appears within four words of *teenagers*, regardless of word order. All of the following phrases would meet the search criteria:

...teenagers who have been homeless for more than...

...From Homelessness to College, One Teenager's Journey

...those involving teenagers, prostitutes, and the homeless...

...even teenagers who are not homeless...

...has been homeless ever since he was a teenager...

EBSCO

EBSCO's syntax looks similar, but the effects are slightly different. EBSCO has two proximity operators: N<number> and W<number> (note there is no slash between the operator and the number). They are used as follows:

Near

teenagers N5 homeless

That is, the word *teenagers* must appear from zero to five words away from *homeless* in the text for a document to be retrieved. The terms can be in any order: teenagers first, or homeless first.

Within

homeless W3 teenagers

This means that the word *homeless* must appear within three words of *teenagers*, *in that order* (homeless first), to be retrieved. Note how this contrasts with ProQuest's W operator, which does not specify word order. These subtle variations are the norm, so be prepared to be flexible, and to take a quick glance at each database's Help file for guidance.

Factiva

In another variation on this theme, in *Factiva* you spell out *near* and append a number, such as near5, to set the parameters for your proximity search. If you were looking for information about gourmet or specialty pickles, you'd probably be interested in an article that mentions "...the specialty market now extends to pickles, teas...." The search:

specialty near5 pickles

would pick up this article. The pickle reference is so casual that the subject headings for the whole article give no clue that it might mention pickles. (And trust me: if you are trying to find information about the specialty pickle market without spending a fortune for a market research report, you'll take any reference, no matter how casual.)

Factiva also provides a conceptual rather than numerically bound operator with "same" to specify "in the same paragraph." For example, "Merck same research" retrieves articles in which Merck and research occur in the same paragraph, in any order.

Determining Proximity Operators

Unlike Boolean operators, proximity operators usually don't appear as drop-down menu choices in the database interface. While the use of N or near, and W or within, is fairly standard, the way they are interpreted, and the use (or not) of additional characters such as a slash mark, make each database just a bit different. Given that there are several subtle variations that might be used, it's best not to just guess. To find out whether a database provides proximity searching and the syntax to use, you'll need to explore files such as Help or Examples.

Importance of Proximity Searching in Full-Text Databases

Proximity, although requiring a bit more effort to discover, is becoming an ever more valuable function as vendors strive to provide more and more searchable full text. A database that is just an electronic version of an index simply doesn't offer that many words to search on. The text fields (i.e., author, title, journal name, and abstract) aren't very extensive, so the use of Boolean operators in that situation is just fine (using proximity in such a situation might well reduce your results to zero, in fact). Matches on termA AND termB in the limited realm of index fields are likely to be relevant because the terms are, in a sense, by definition "close" to each other. In a full-text situation you could certainly still restrict your search to just subject headings (if they are available), or a field such as title, and use Boolean operators, but by searching the full text you have the opportunity to get at more deeply buried aspects of an article, to tweeze out nuances and secondary topics that cannot possibly be covered by a few, necessarily broad, subject headings. The more searchable full text a database has, the more important the ability to do proximity searching becomes, because it is the only useful way to really mine all that text for everything it has to offer.

Really Close Proximity: Phrase Searching

Searching on exact phrases can be extremely important in some cases, and the inability of some databases to do this (easily) can really inhibit how effectively you can search. In the commercial database world, the way you indicate to the system "this is a phrase search" can vary considerably.

EBSCO databases and *Factiva* perform phrase searches without quotation marks or indicators of any kind: their search functions assume multiple word entries in the search box should be searched as a phrase. FirstSearch, ProQuest, and the *Web of Science* databases work as the Web search engines do: enclose the terms to be searched as a phrase in double quotes. (ProQuest and LexisNexis will actually treat two-word queries as a phrase by default.)

Uses for Phrase Searching

Phrase searching is useful any time you're searching for things such as the name of a place or an organization (especially if the name is made up of common words), a multiword concept or topic (latch key children, gourmet pickles, missile defense shield), or—especially on the Web—for tracking down more complete information from incomplete fragments. Problems such as the rest of the lyrics, or indeed the real title, of a song whose only line you can remember is "is the moon out tonight?" can be quickly resolved and put in context (and possibly bar bets won) by plunking the quote-bound phrase into Google. In a more academic scenario, say you have a bad or incomplete reference to a thesis or a journal article. If available to you, head for a database such as *Dissertation Abstracts*, or an appropriate subject database, and try a partial phrase from the title, or the author's name and a word from the title, depending on what information you (seem) to have.[3] (If that doesn't work, try only the most distinct words as a title field search, and if *that* doesn't work, go to the Web. You might not find the actual item, but at least you might find a more accurate, complete reference to it from someone else's bibliography.)

Proximity and phrase searching are useful for reducing and focusing your results; they tend to increase the precision of the search. The next tool takes us back the other way, providing a way to broaden the search net (to increase recall).

Basic Tool No. 5: Truncation

"Truncation" is an efficient way of extending your search to pick up many variations on a word without having to (1) think of all the possible variants or (2) input them with endless "ORs." Truncation allows you to search on a word stem and retrieve any word beginning with those letters, for example,

harmon*

to retrieve harmony, harmonious, harmonica . . .

In another database, the syntax and results for the truncation function might be:

employ$

to retrieve employ, employs, employee, employment, employer, employed . . .

Note that when the stem (the letters being truncated) is a word in its own right, that word will be included in the search results. Truncation generally means the word stem, and any number of characters following, from zero on up.

Using Truncation

Truncation is a tool that is equally useful in field searching and in full-text searches in commercial databases. In a field search, for example, truncation is a wonderfully efficient way to pick up several related subject headings at once (searching poet* to pick up poet, poetics, poetry), or variations on author names (with and without a middle initial, for instance, or even with or without a first name being spelled out: Adams, J!). In a full text search, obviously, truncation greatly increases the number of documents that are eligible for retrieval. When you are fishing around for a concept or topic that you think might be rather rare, and that isn't expressed with any set phrases or words, the combination of truncation and a proximity search can be invaluable. The earlier example of trying to

Table 3.1. Truncation and wildcard symbols used by various vendors

Vendor	Truncation Symbol	Wildcard Symbol(s)	Other
EBSCO	*	?	
Endeavor (OPAC)	?	N/A	
FirstSearch	*	#, ?[a]	+[b]
LexisNexis	!	*	
ProQuest	*	?	
Web of Science	*	?	

[a] "#" replaces one character only; ? replaces zero to nine characters; ? used with a number, e.g., ?2 would replace exactly two characters.
[b] "+" finds plural forms using "s" or "es" only.

identify any articles mentioning companies that act as consultants to the food and beverage industry is a prime candidate for this technique:

Consultan* near10 (food or beverage*)

to retrieve consultant, consultants, or consultancy, within a ten-word radius of food or beverage or beverages.

Common Truncation Symbols

Truncation symbols vary somewhat from database to database, but the ones most frequently used are:

- ' * '
- ' ! '
- ' ? '

Factiva uses the symbol "$," which is more unusual, but always strikes me as appropriate for this resource from the financially focused Dow Jones company.

Determining Truncation Symbols

As is the case with the other tools in this chapter, there is likely to be nothing in the initial search interface to indicate whether truncation is supported, and if so, which symbol to use. There are databases that don't offer a true truncation function, but simply search on a limited set of variants (e.g., plural forms) automatically. Some information is supplied in Table 3.1, but if the database in question is not listed, or to check the most current usage (it could change), look for links to "Help" or "Examples" to determine how the database at hand handles truncation.

Wildcards

Closely related to truncation are *wildcard* symbols, in the sense that a symbol is used in place of letters. Unlike truncation symbols, which are used to represent any number of characters, wildcards are used to substitute for characters on a one-to-one basis. Be prepared for confusion: the symbols used for wildcards are the same as those used for truncation, but with the effect changing, depending on the vendor. That is, one vendor may use "!"

for truncation, and "*" for a wildcard, while another exactly reverses those two meanings. For example, LexisNexis uses "*" as their wildcard (one-to-one replacement) symbol, and "!" as their truncation symbol. In EBSCO, ProQuest, and the *Web of Science*, "*" is used as the truncation symbol (any number of characters, at the end of a word), and "?" is used as the wildcard symbol, replacing interior characters on a one-to-one basis.

Using Wildcards

Wildcards are probably most frequently used to replace just one letter, for example:

wom*n

retrieves woman, women, womyn. Multiple wildcards can be used to substitute for an equal number of characters, for example,

manufactur**

will retrieve manufacture, manufactured, or manufactures, but not manufacturing.

A search situation in which single wildcarding can be very helpful is for picking up U.S./U.K. alternative spellings, such as,

labo!r   to get either labor or labour

globali#ation   to get either globalisation or globalization

If you were searching a database that included British publications, and you wanted to be sure you picked up relevant material from them, this use of wildcarding could be very important.

Table of Symbols by Vendor

Some information on common truncation and wildcard symbols used by different vendors is supplied in Table 3.1, but you are always encouraged to consult the database's Help file for the most up-to-date information on what functionalities the database supports, and the appropriate symbols to use.

This probably strikes you as a fairly esoteric capability, and probably you won't need to use such functionality very often. In real life, you're much more likely to stick a truncation symbol on the end of "manufactur" and be done with it. But knowledge is power!

Sidebar 3.1. Department of Confusing Things

In everyday speech, the term *wildcard* is often used to mean truncation. For example, you'll hear the symbol used at the end of a word to retrieve multiple endings expressed as a wildcard. I'm quite guilty of this myself: when working with a student who has never heard of truncation, the easiest course of action is to call the odd thing being demonstrated a wildcard, because almost everyone immediately grasps the sense of that notion. If you are getting serious enough about searching that you're looking at the Help files, however, you should know the technical terms used in the business, and understand that different symbols can have different effects (one replaces only one character, while another is used to replace any number of characters).

Quick Recap

Proximity searching allows you to search for documents containing terms within a given number of words of each other. Proximity searching is particularly valuable for searching full text. Phrase searching is available in commercial databases, and can be very important for retrieving accurate results. Truncation refers to the use of a symbol to substitute for 0 to N characters at the *end* of a word. Wildcards are symbols used to substitute on a one-to-one basis for characters *within* a word. Proximity and phrase searches tend to narrow and focus results; truncation and wildcards help to increase the potential set of results. To determine the symbols or syntax to use, in all cases consult the database's Help or Examples files.

Basic Tool No. 6: Limits to Constrain Your Search

Limits or *Limiters* are preset options in the search interface that can be used to further define your search. They are described here as *preset options* to distinguish them from the words or subject terms that you have to come up with and type in. Limits make use of fields in the database record that are used to store attributes of the record rather than conceptual content: you could say limit fields are about the article, not what the article is about. Limiters usually appear as check boxes or drop-down menus. Typical Limit choices include:

- Scholarly (or *peer reviewed*)
- Publication or article type (book, conference proceeding, review, editorial, etc.)
- Language
- Full text (e.g., in a database that offers some records with full text and some without, this limit will constrain the search to retrieve only matching records offering full text).[4]
- Date

The Date Limit

The Date limit is a bit of an anomaly. In the context of a known citation, you would consider it a "content" field: the date would be part of the unique information identifying that citation (Joe Blogg's 1996 article is not Joe Blogg's 1998 article). However, if you are searching for material published before or after a certain date, or in a particular date range, the date information becomes an attribute used to limit your search results. The way the date option is displayed in the search interface is frequently hybrid as well, offering both a drop-down menu of preset choices, as well as fields for specifying a specific date (or date range).

Basic Tool No. 7: "Pearl Growing": A Useful Search Strategy

This charming expression[5] refers to the process of doing a very simple search first, with the intent of achieving high recall, and then examining the results to find appropriate subject headings or to discover further terms to search on, from the most on-target hits. You then add one or more of these terms to your search strategy to produce a more precise list of results. This is very useful when you are venturing into a new database or unfamiliar subject matter, or when you simply don't have the time or inclination to do formal preparatory work by hunting around in the subject indexes.

A Search Example Using Pearl Growing

For example, let us say that you're an engineer, and are tired of your straight engineering job. A colleague suggests that you look into jobs in engineering sales. Whenever you're working with someone and doing this sort of "career exploration"—What is the work like? How is the pay? Are there openings, or is it a stagnant market?—a good first thing to check is the *Occupational Outlook Handbook* (OOH).[6] If you had come to see me, we'd start there. At the OOH, a keyword search for "engineering sales" produces just one result, for Public Relations Specialists. Huh? Browsing the index under *E* doesn't help either. A search on just "sales" finally does it, and we find that such people are referred to as "sales engineers." This is useful. Let's move on to a database and try for some articles about sales engineers.

Going to a database of business articles, ProQuest's *ABI/Inform*, we can start by seeing if, by chance, "sales engineer" is a subject term. It's not. So then we can try the quick-and-dirty approach: simply searching "sales engineers" in the citation and abstract, hoping to pearl grow from the results. We can prescreen the results a bit by choosing the "Scholarly journals, including peer reviewed" limit. Among the results is an article titled "Control and Autonomy among Knowledge Workers In Sales: An Employee Perspective." Despite the "Knowledge Workers" in the title, the abstract is full of the phrase "sales engineers." This looks useful! From the subject headings: Employee Attitude, Control Sales, Studies, and Human Resource Management, we decide that Sales could be useful, or Employee Attitude. Examining some of the other results, we notice that Salespeople is also a subject term. We go back to the search interface and try:

Employee attitude—in Subject

AND

Sales engineers—in Citation or Abstract

Another variation we can try is:

Sales OR Salespeople—in Subject

AND

Sales engineers—in Citation or Abstract

The ProQuest system also automatically provides helpful, usually insightful search suggestions in the results interface, in this case:

Engineers and Personal profiles (both terms will be searched as subjects).

Engineers and Organizational behavior (both terms will be searched as subjects).

To reiterate, the strategy in pearl growing is to start with a fairly simple, broad search, examine the most likely results, and learn to refine or improve the search based on subject headings or other terminology used in the on-target results. This technique is really only useful in the structured, subject-headings world of commercial databases. On the Web, you may encounter links in search results saying "More like this," which are trying to do the same thing. How well they do it, and what they are basing the similarity on, are open questions.

Quick Recap

Limits are preset options built into a search interface that enable you to search by document attributes such as language, article or document type, peer reviewed, and date. Pearl growing refers to a strategy of starting with a very simple keyword search, examining the results, and discovering useful subject headings or additional terms to search on from the most on-target records.

Your Mental Toolkit

Understanding and being able to use concepts such as Boolean logic, controlled vocabulary, proximity searching, and limits will definitely go a long way towards making you a more effective searcher. In addition, there are certain mental attitudes that will help you a great deal as well. Of course, there are some aspects of mind or personality that you either have or you don't: general curiosity, interest and enjoyment in puzzles, and an ability to think "out of the box," that is, to make connections or have ideas ("lightbulb moments") *beyond* the research request as it is explicitly stated. But there are three mental tools that you don't have to be born with; rather, you can make a conscious effort to develop them. These are tools to employ in any search, which can be just as important to your success as a searcher as your knowledge of search functions.

The mental toolkit:

- *A healthy skepticism*: do not trust anything someone tells you that "they remember," or even anything that is printed in a bibliography.

- *Willingness to let go*: someone may offer a great deal of information, but if the results keep coming up zero, or wrong, *let go*: drop pieces of information, one at a time.

- *Maintain mental clarity and patience*: be systematic about your searching; don't just thrash around rapidly trying this and that. It may seem longer to stop and think and try one change at a time, but in the end it will save time.

To emphasize the second point: one of the biggest pitfalls in searching is not being willing to *not* look for a part of the information provided. In general: be flexible, not fixated.

Summary and Advice

And that's your toolkit. You now have some concepts, some tools you'll use over and over, in various combinations, and some attitudinal tools to use as well. My advice for how to employ this information to the best advantage is fairly simple:

1. Master the concepts.

2. Do not attempt to memorize exactly which databases offer which capabilities. Instead...

3. Train your eyes!

Learn to scan an interface quickly. Look for *Help* or *Search Guides*. (Actually read them, although be prepared: sometimes the *Help* is not updated as quickly as changes are made to the database.) You now know *what* to look for,[7] so simply look for it. Nothing on that screen should be "noise" or ignored. This is the most important thing you can do: LOOK with your trained eyes. Why? Because:

Things can change at any time—and they will change!

Especially now that database vendors have moved their products to the Web, their interfaces have become more fluid. They are more stable than most Web pages, but still, the lure and the ability to change things so easily is hard to resist. Indeed, by the time you see this book, the interfaces shown in the figures here may have already changed anywhere from a little to a lot. You need to be flexible, and able to relearn continually as the interface designers move things around and change their terminology. Let me assure you that you will become good at it, but you need to be alert and ready for change ("oh, now that tab is orange and they've changed the name Advanced Search to More Options. Same thing. OK."). I cannot emphasize this enough:

USE YOUR EYES. They are the best tool that you have.[8]

Exercises and Points to Consider

1. Consider again this search: homeless W/4 teenagers, which produced this result:
   ...has been homeless ever since he was a teenager...

Count the words between *homeless* and *teenager*. Why would the article containing this phrase be retrieved by this search?

2. What do you think would be the best way to search for a personal name, especially if you wanted any article that made any mention of the person? Would you use a phrase or proximity search? What are the pros and cons of each method?

3. Consider again this search: Consultan* near10 (food or beverage*). How might you alter this slightly to make even more documents eligible for retrieval? What might be the pros and cons of doing that?

4. Going back to ProQuest's suggestions when we did the "sales engineers" search:

   Engineers and Personal profiles (searched as Subjects).
   Engineers and Organizational behavior (searched as Subjects).

What would be an elegant way to accomplish both of these searches at once?

5. One major vendor whose syntax wasn't addressed in this chapter was Wilson. Go to a Wilson database, and see if you can find out: does it support proximity searching, and what is the syntax, if so? Phrase searching? What about truncation and wildcards?

Suggested Reading

Tenopir, Carol. "Are You a Super Searcher?" *Library Journal* (March 1, 2000): 36,38. The date might look old, but the discussion of characteristics of what makes a good searcher are just as relevant today as when this article first appeared.

Notes

1. When dealing with a totally unfamiliar subject area, it's also very useful do a Google search, just to get a sense of how people write about the topic.

2. ProQuest also simply treats three-word queries as proximity searches by default, that is, if you entered "total homeless teenagers," ProQuest would automatically search for those three terms in proximity to each other. Phrases such as "...the total number of homeless teenagers..." and "...teenagers who are homeless are not included in the total..." would be retrieved.

3. Reference Desk Rule No. 1: citations almost always have a mistake in them somewhere.

4. Beware, though, that if the database is enabled with a technology for linking to full text in other databases to which the library subscribes, turning on the full text limit could eliminate potentially useful results.

5. Why "pearl growing"? Well, you throw out a small bit (one or two words, say), a seed. Then from all the results, you add layers, the way a pearl adds layers of nacre around a grain of sand. I guess you could call it "onion growing," but it doesn't sound quite so nice! To be honest, this is one of my favorite and most frequently used techniques.

6. Available on the Web at http://www.bls.gov/oco/.

7. Just in case you had a momentary mental lapse, "what to look for" is: Boolean operators, proximity operators, fields you can search, controlled vocabulary you can use, truncation and wildcard symbols, and limits that you can set.

8. Well, they need to be connected to your brain, of course....

4
Social Science Databases

Introduction to Subject Databases

Before plunging directly into the nuts and bolts of the following databases, let's pause for a moment to think about the whole idea of subject-specific databases. The following statement might fall into the "duh" category, but sometimes it's good to start with the absolute basics: a subject-specific database is a searchable, electronic resource devoted to a particular topic. It focuses on a subject area by including only the journals, books, conferences, or other published materials in that discipline. Naturally, there are journals that are useful and interesting to more than one subject area, and you will discover that some journals are indexed in several different databases. In general, however, if you are doing research that falls into an identifiable subject area, working with the appropriate subject databases is the most efficient and effective way to pursue that research. Why is a subject database better than a Web search in this case? A Web search is just that: it will find *Web pages* and various other media that are freely available on the Web, but it is not an organized, structured index of commercially published material. A Web search is by definition "all subjects"—it's anything the search engine's indexing program has picked up. A Web search may well find someone's paper, if they have put it on the Web, or a reference to a paper within another paper that someone put on their Web site. But it is *not* a complete, orderly scan of all the appropriate journals and other published materials in a subject area. That kind of organized, thorough, ongoing effort implies an organization, staff, and money, and is not something anyone is going to give away for free. They are each very powerful in their way, but subject databases and Web search engines are very different animals.

How do you know what databases there are for your subject? Go to the Web site of any major university, find the university library page, and look for links such as "databases," "electronic resources," "subject guides," or "resources by subject." Almost all institutions of higher education at the university (and certainly many at the college level now as well) will have so many of these databases that they will offer a list of them "by subject." Simply roving the alphabetical list, you will probably be amazed at the number and variety of different databases that are out there.

The number and variety of databases on the market is remarkable. But who knew? Even though they are different kinds of things, why don't at least some of these databases have the name recognition of Google? Is it simply the difference between free and fee? Access to the subject databases is all by subscription, but you certainly get value for money. Yet compared with Web search engines, subject databases are almost unknown among the general public, and this is a shame, because they are so good at what they do.

This chapter looks at three databases that support research in the social sciences. There are many more, of course, but these three will make us look at three different interfaces, and are each significant in their own way.

Library Literature & Information Science

Background and Coverage

Since many readers of this book probably are librarians or library school students, it seems only right to start with the original database of librarianship: H. W. Wilson's *Library Literature & Information Science*. Started as a print index in 1921, *Library Literature* has been available online for many years, first through Dialog, and since the movement of databases to the Web, via Wilson's own WilsonWeb. A full-text version has been available since 2000. The WilsonWeb database provides indexing for materials back to the early 1980s, and full text dating from 1997. Although there are two other library science–specific databases (LISA—*Library & Information Science Abstracts*, and LISTA—*Library, Information Science & Technology Abstracts*), and other databases that index some library journals, *Library Literature* still stands out for "its high-quality indexing, full text, complete coverage of the journals that are indexed, and participation of an advisory committee for journal title selection" (Tenopir, 2003). In addition to journal and review articles, *Library Literature* has records for books, book chapters, conference proceedings, library school theses, and pamphlets. Coverage is international.

Notes and Search Examples

Advanced Search Interface

Let's take a look at the Advanced Search interface (Figure 4.1). What are all the parts and what do they do?

- Colored bar[1] across the top provides access to functions: search modes, access to indexes and the thesaurus (controlled vocabulary), search history, and output/citation management functions.

- Directly below function bar: "database selection area"—change database to be searched.

- Central search area (white): text input fields, Boolean operators, a Sort function, and Limit options. Note the Peer Reviewed limit: although you should still employ your own judgment in reviewing the

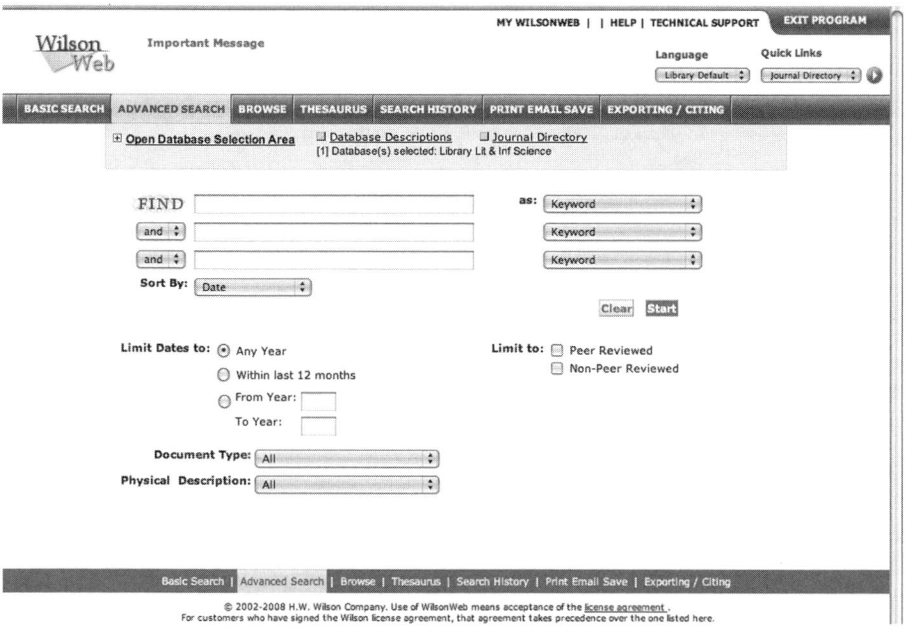

Fig. 4.1. *Library Literature* Advanced Search interface. Reproduced with permission from the H. W. Wilson Company.

results, this limit is intended to filter the results for only scholarly, academic articles. Librarians in academic settings often point out this feature when working with less-experienced students who express a requirement for "scholarly" articles. You can also specify the opposite: "Non–Peer-Reviewed." Other Limits are by *Date*, *Document Type*, and *Physical Description* (helpful for trying to find materials that include graphics, tables, charts, etc.).

• Note the "as" drop-downs—all the search fields this database uses.

• Colored bar across the bottom: echo of the top.

Library Literature Thesaurus

One of the great strengths of the Library Literature database is its *Thesaurus*; a hierarchical guide to the subject headings of this database; in a sense, this is a guide to the language of librarianship. For example, we might go to the Thesaurus and look up OPAC (Figure 4.2), the acronym for Online Public Access Catalog.

Because *OPAC* is one of the "Used for" terms, the Thesaurus system automatically takes you to the subject heading "Online Catalogs," as shown in Figure 4.3. (And if you decided at this point that you wanted to check for other terms in the Thesaurus, the search interface to do another lookup is right there.)

Online Catalogs is the term that the Thesaurus designers have decided will be the subject heading assigned to all articles on this topic, no matter how it is referred to in the article itself. The "Used for" terms represent many possible variants that people might look up (as we just did), and guides them to the one subject heading they need to search on to retrieve all the material on this topic. As noted before in discussing controlled vocabulary, otherwise

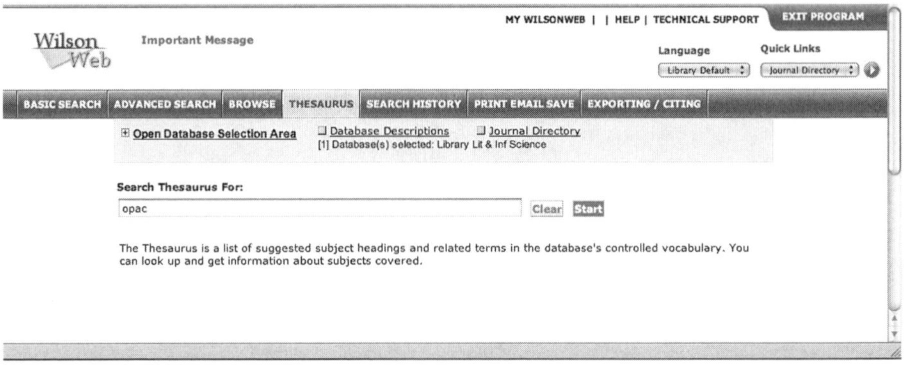

Fig. 4.2. *Library Literature* Thesaurus interface. Reproduced with permission from the H. W. Wilson Company.

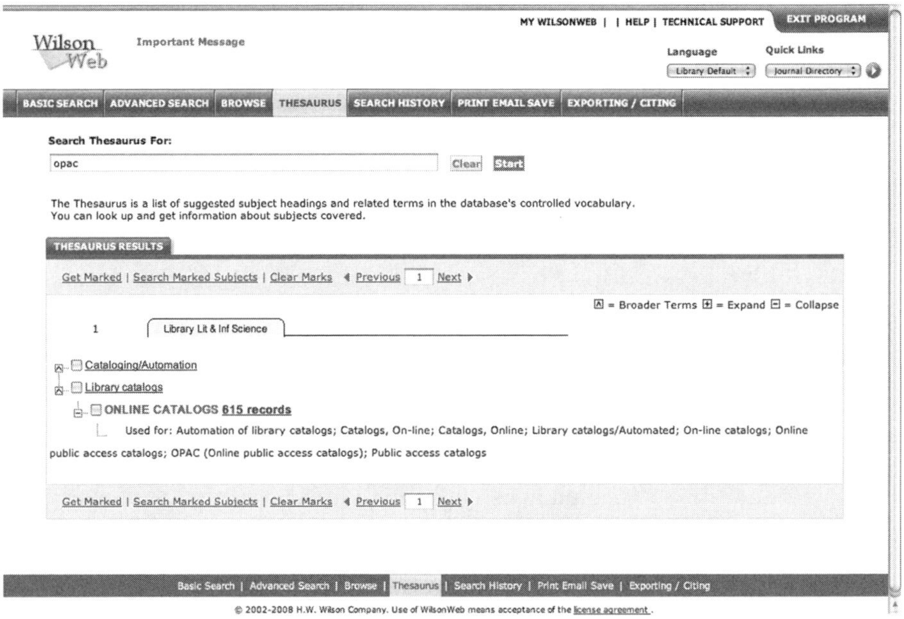

Fig. 4.3. Thesaurus search results. Reproduced with permission from the H. W. Wilson Company.

we might have to think of all these variations and search them all. A good set of subject headings, consistently applied, makes searching so efficient.

Sidebar 4.1. Analyzing Disparities in Subject Heading Results in Library Literature

A small *caveat emptor* regarding the *Library Literature* Thesaurus: although it guides you to the appropriate term or phrase to use, it might not be exactly equivalent (in terms of number of records) to entering the term or phrase, and searching it as a subject in the search interface. Consider the following:

If you look up "information seeking" in the Thesaurus, you are presented with the heading Information Needs, and told that it is "Used for" information-seeking behavior, among other terms. As of May 2008, the Thesaurus states there are 569 records associated with Information Needs. (If you click the link for those 569 records, your search results will show 571 records. That discrepancy was small enough that I decided to ignore it.) If you go back to the Advanced Search interface, however, and enter the search:

Information Needs as: Subject(s)

The system returns 2,286 records! This discrepancy is too large to ignore. What can account for it?

Checking the Browse index begins to show why: if you browse Information Needs as a Subject, you discover that, indeed, "Information Needs" just by itself is associated with 569 records. However, the subject heading Information Needs has a plethora of additional subheadings, both of locations (e.g., Information needs/Afghanistan) and of topics (e.g., Information needs/Case studies). By searching the heading through the Advanced Search interface, it is picking up the phrase wherever it appears in a subject heading, that is, with any subheading (/term or phrase), or even possibly embedded in some other subject heading. The Search Results statement at the top of the screen gives some indication that something different is going on in each case: searched as a subject heading unto itself (by searching directly from the Thesaurus or the Browse index), the syntax is very simple:

571 Records found for Information needs

Searched against the Subject(s) field in the Advanced Search screen, the syntax is:

(Information Needs) <in> Subject(s)

That is, "Information Needs"—somewhere in the Subject.

There is nothing wrong with any of this, *per se*. It is only that since the Thesaurus does not give any indication of all the possible subheadings, you might either: (a) miss some potentially useful articles searching just from the Thesaurus, or (b) be quite surprised by the greater number of results when searching the (apparently) same term by typing it into the search interface as a Subject field search.

In sum, just a cautionary note that although the Thesaurus is very useful, and can really help you sort out the best term(s) to use, it doesn't hurt to also Browse the Subject(s) index, or use what you find in the Thesaurus and enter it yourself in the search interface. It might make an important difference.

Search Example 1: Identifying Terms Using the Thesaurus

We'd like to find articles on how library school curriculum is changing in response to advances in information technology (IT).

Since we know that this database is already focused on libraries and librarians, we might start by typing:

changing curriculum

into the Thesaurus.

Figure 4.4 demonstrates another great feature of this Thesaurus system: if the word or phrase that you type in does not exactly match a subject heading or "used for" term, rather than leaving you high and dry with a "not found" message, it offers suggestions. The suggestions are usually quite useful, and often rather interesting (you wonder what's going on in the "suggestion algorithm" to produce the results).

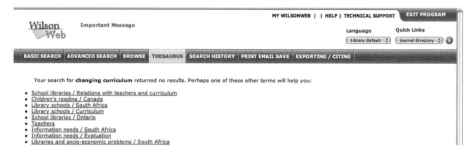

Fig. 4.4. Thesaurus "Not Found" suggestions. Reproduced with permission from the H. W. Wilson Company.

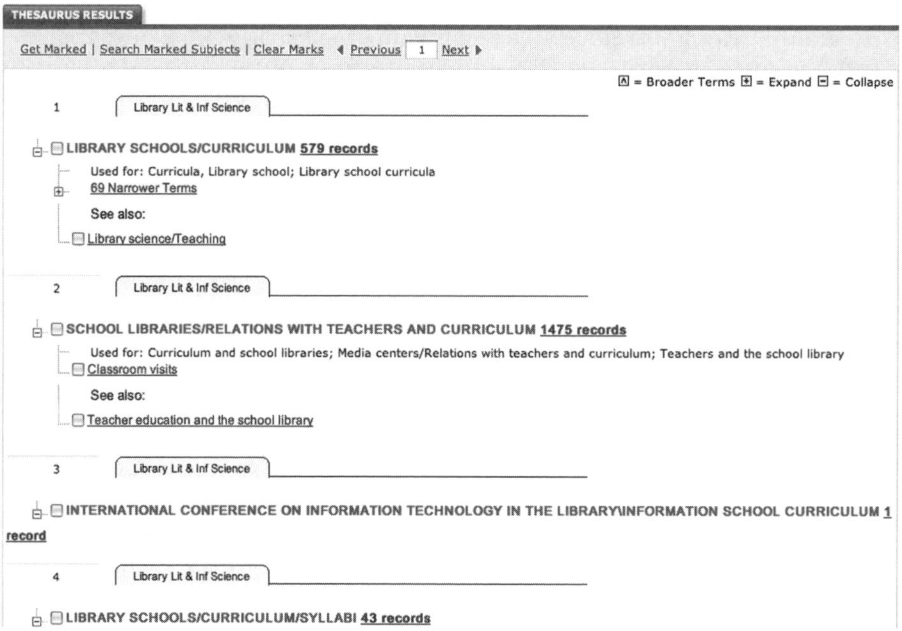

Fig. 4.5. Thesaurus results for "Library Schools/Curriculum." Reproduced with permission from the H. W. Wilson Company.

Obviously the most appropriate suggestion here is the entry for "Library schools/Curriculum." Clicking that brings us to the next screen (Figure 4.5), where there are various useful features.

In Figure 4.5 we are in the Thesaurus at Library Schools/Curriculum. It's useful to know there are 579 records that have been assigned this heading, and that there are 69 (!) "Narrower" terms we might want to explore, as well as a related term ("See also"). Notice that further down the screen there is also the additional, even more specific, subject heading of "Library Schools/Curriculum/Syllabi." At this point there are some things that might not be obvious but that are useful to know:

- Choosing the main heading (Library Schools/Curriculum) does not automatically include all the Narrower Terms. You need to expand (click the "+" sign) the Narrower Terms and choose any of them you want to include in your search.

- You can choose as many Main headings or Narrower Terms as look useful, click "Search Marked Subjects" at the top or bottom of the screen, and all marked items will be "ORed" together in the search results.

- You cannot perform an "AND" search from the Thesaurus.

- Whatever you "Mark" will stay marked, so that if you are doing a series of searches in the Thesaurus, be sure to click "Clear Marks," or the "Get Marked" link, where you can see (and adjust) everything you currently have "Marked."

- At the Results screen, however, you now have many ways to focus the search.

There are all kinds of useful things happening in the Results screen: on the left side is a section called Content Discovery Keys that allows you to run a new search by Subject. (Note that this is a *new* search; your current search will be left behind. This functionality is probably based on the mindset that the user will have started by just typing in some keywords, as one would do in a Web search engine, and that a "new" search by a subject heading will produce more focused results.) Below the Subjects, one can revise the current search with the "Narrow These Results" options: by Author, Subject, or Publication Year. (Below this would appear a list of our recent searches: our search history, to remind us of what we had tried, or enable us to return to some previous results.) Moving back into the section above the results list, we could get back to the search interface using Modify Search, create an Alert or an RSS Feed for the search (to automatically send us a notice when new materials get added to the database), or create a "Link to [this] Search" that could be emailed to a colleague or put in a Web page. Finally, but to my mind one of best features: there is a Find search box in the upper right, set by default to "Search Within Results." This is very useful for ANDing in an additional concept, or set of alternative keywords, as shown in Figure 4.6.

ANDing in: "chang* or new or develop*" reduces the result set from 1398 to 164 (as of June 2008), and includes potentially useful results in the most recent articles. For example, it rapidly becomes apparent that the *Journal of Education for Library and Information Science* is the one to keep an eye on for this topic; you might want to create an Alert or RSS feed to notify you when new articles from this journal are added to the database. Also notice the Peer Reviewed and Non–Peer-Reviewed tabs in the results interface—another example of a post-search limit. The tabs provide an easy and quick way to see only the scholarly (or non-scholarly) results.

Almost all of the features discussed here represent changes from the look and functionality of the Wilson databases in the first edition of this book. In particular, the Content Discovery Keys, Search Within Results, and Peer-reviewed features, are excellent examples of how databases change and develop, frequently for the better, over time. Previously, to combine a Thesaurus search with a keyword (or AND in another subject term), your only option was to observe what the heading was in the Thesaurus, then go back to the Advanced screen, and type in the heading and terms with which you wished to combine it. Being able to choose and search from the Thesaurus and then refine the search is a very useful improvement. Again in the previous version, to limit a search to peer-reviewed articles, you had to notice the checkbox for this option on the search page and select it there. Having Peer Reviewed as a tab in the results makes it more obvious, as well as keeping

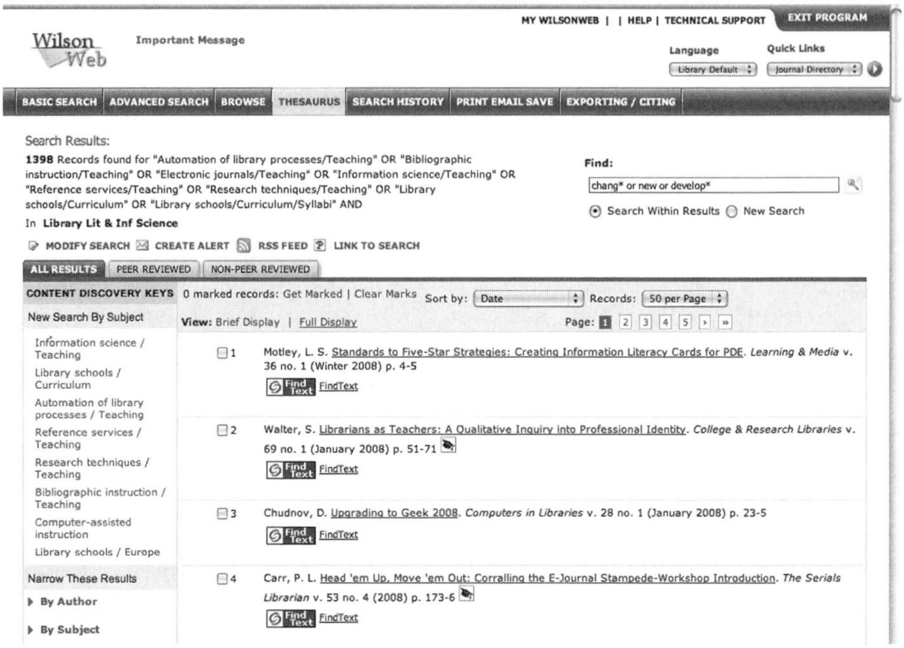

Fig. 4.6. Advanced Search Strategy using Thesaurus entries and keyword. Reproduced with permission from the H. W. Wilson Company.

your options open: you can *look* at the scholarly results, while still retaining the rest.

With the Content Discovery Keys on the left side of the results page, Wilson is participating in a trend in interfaces not to require users to make all their decisions upfront at the search interface, but to change, adjust, or limit their search at the results screen. Keep your eyes out for this functionality—you'll be seeing more of it!

Browsing Library Literature Indexes

The Browse button is your way to see the raw contents of the *Library Literature* index lists (cf. the index browsing in FirstSearch in Figures 1.4 and 1.5 in Chapter 1). It is a strictly alphabetical, "left-anchored" list—you only get terms *beginning* with whatever word you put in. If the term you entered doesn't exactly match anything in the index list that you chose, the message "your term would have been here" appears in the appropriate alphabetical spot.

Browse is a quick way to see if a term is a Subject, to find out if a particular journal is indexed by *Library Literature*, or to check the content of any of several other indexed fields. It is especially handy for checking the spelling of an author's name, and getting an immediate idea of how many articles by that person have been indexed in the database, as shown in Figure 4.7.

For the Document Type and Physical Description fields, the drop-down menus on the Advanced Search page provide an immediate list of all the valid entries. Checking these fields in the Browse interface will show you how many "hits" are associated with each entry type.

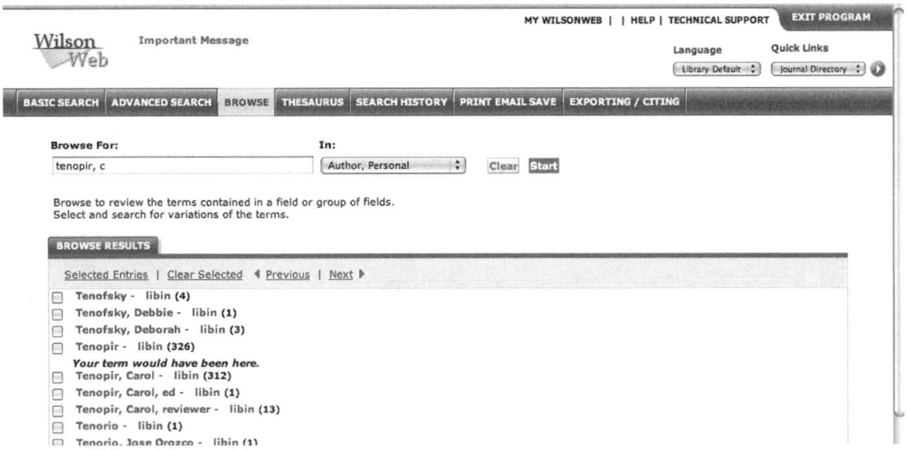

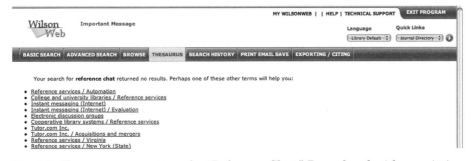

Fig. 4.7. Browsing the Author, Personal index. Reproduced with permission from the H. W. Wilson Company.

Fig. 4.8. Thesaurus suggestions for "Reference Chat." Reproduced with permission from the H. W. Wilson Company.

Browse Exercises

Try looking up "librarians in film" as a Subject in Browse. Use your eyes! Look at the other entries in the list. Even if you don't hit exactly the right wording with what you typed in, often the subject heading you need will be nearby. Now compare the results of looking up "interlibrary loan" by Browsing the Subject Index, and as a term in the Thesaurus. Feeling daunted by all the possible headings? You're not alone, and a perfectly reasonable approach at this point would be to go to the Advanced Search screen, type in "Interlibrary Loans" (ILL) as a Subject(s) (since we learned that this term always expressed in the plural by the *Library Literature* indexers). Now add whichever keyword or phrase that expresses what you're trying to find out about ILL.

Search Example 2

You want to find some information on chat services as part of reference. You start by looking up "reference chat" in the Thesaurus. It suggests "Reference Services/Automation" and "Instant messaging (Internet)" among other things (Figure 4.8)—it's quite smart, this suggestion screen.

You might be tempted to go immediately for the "Instant messaging" entry, since it is obviously on target, but the Reference services/Automation term came up for a reason. Take a couple of moments and try this search in two ways. Follow the Instant messaging (Internet) link into the Thesaurus, choose all the entries that seem to relate or look interesting, and scan those results. Note a couple of things about the results: how many are there in all? Roughly how many are "on target" (estimate from the first couple of screens)? How recent are they, and how quickly do the dates start to get "old"?

Now go to the Advanced Search screen, and set up this search:

Reference Services/Automation—as Subject(s)

OR Instant messaging—as Subject(s)

AND chat—as Keyword.

Compare these results with those of the previous, "instant messaging"–only search. Which set do you feel would work better for you if you were writing a paper on this topic? (There is no right or wrong answer to that question!)

Working with Results: Mark and Output

Marking Selected Results

No matter how good your search skills are, there are bound to be items in your results that are not as useful as the others. The database vendors understand this, and therefore generally offer a "marking" functionality, usually with checkboxes. You click the checkboxes of all the entries in your results list that you want to output from the database. Typical output options are to print, save, or e-mail (send records and/or full text to yourself or someone else), and increasingly database vendors are offering the option to export to a citation manager program as well.

Output Options

Wilson offers the options of: "Print Email Save," as well as "Exporting/Citing." Clicking either option from the results screen provides all the functions in a tabbed display (Figure 4.9). There is a strong emphasis on citing throughout these function screens, but generally they are nicely laid out to display only the information pertaining to the function that you are going to use.

Notice in particular:

- On the Print screen, the Estimate number of printed pages function is very useful.

- You can send just Marked Records or all records or a range of records.

- *Mail to:* allows you to send to multiple addresses using a semicolon in between, like this: me@mine.edu; you@yours.edu.

- You get to fill in the e-mail Subject, as well as your name and any notes. All of these are important, especially if you are sending results to someone else, because a system-supplied subject and the unfamiliar sender e-mail address tends to make such messages look like spam, and cause your recipient to delete them without looking at them.

- Records can be downloaded directly to either RefWorks or EndNote, two of the most popular citation management programs.

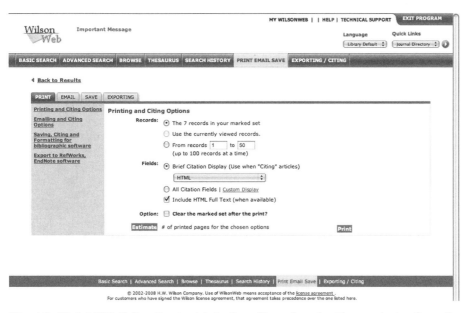

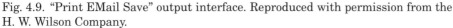

Fig. 4.9. "Print EMail Save" output interface. Reproduced with permission from the H. W. Wilson Company.

Quick Recap

H. W. Wilson's *Library Literature & Information Science* is the oldest and longest running index devoted to the library field. *Library Literature* indexes journal articles, books, book chapters, conference proceedings, library school theses, and pamphlets. Materials are mainly in English, but coverage is international, and a number of other languages are represented. The *Library Literature* Thesaurus is custom built for this database, and is an important tool for discovering subject headings and relationships between headings. Marking terms in the Thesaurus is cumulative throughout a search session; clear the Marked terms before running a different search from the Thesaurus.

The Browse button provides access to the contents of many fields, arranged as alphabetical lists. Browse is useful for seeing all the possible subheadings that have been applied to a Subject Heading, and for discovering all the possible values (with associated record counts) for a field, such as author name. The Advanced Search interface provides several useful limits. The Results screen offers options for focusing a search by Subject, or by adding a keyword, allowing a search to be re-run without having to go back to the Search interface. The H. W. Wilson Output options have a strong emphasis on support for citing and working with citation management software.

ERIC via FirstSearch

Background and Coverage

ERIC, the Education Resources Information Center, is another database with a long history of excellence, but that has gone through some significant changes in its lifetime. ERIC was a "born digital" effort: in 1966, the Department of Education established sixteen "clearinghouses," each with its own educational subject specialty, to "gather, index, and input bibliographic information" (Tenopir, 2004) for journal articles as well as documents known as *grey literature*. Grey literature is material that has not been commercially published, but that has scholarly value: papers presented at conferences, progress reports, working papers, technical reports, lab notebooks, student papers, curriculum guides, etc. One of the great contributions of the ERIC database was the amount of effort put into gathering, evaluating, indexing, inputting, and making available (through a microfiche distribution program) a huge amount of otherwise unpublished and inaccessible, but valuable, grey literature. At over 1 million records, the ERIC database is now the largest and foremost subject resource for education.

But what the government creates, the government can also change. Starting with the Education Sciences Reform Act of 2002, the ERIC effort began to change. In December of 2003, the sixteen clearinghouses were closed, "as part of an effort to revamp, streamline, and centralize" the system (Viadero, 2004). The Education Department's goals were laudable: one centralized, easy-to-use resource, with more full text. What followed, however, was a period of interregnum: the database and the materials already indexed continued to be available, but no new material was being added, even though production continued apace. The issue of this ever-mounting backlog troubled many in the Education community. In March 2004, the Department of Education awarded the contract for their new vision of the ERIC system to Computer Sciences Corporation (CSC). By June 2005, the loading of new materials had resumed, and further agreements with previous and new suppliers of material are in process (Institute of Education Services, 2005). All of these changes were closely followed by the library community. Members of the ERIC User Group, a project of the Education and Behavioral Sciences Section (EBSS) of ACRL/ALA, and the ERIC User Group of the Education Division of SLA, keenly monitor what is happening with the database, communicate with CSC, and pass their findings on to the world by means of The ERIC Development News Web site,[2] all of which ensures the continued viability of this important resource.

Luckily, even when there were sixteen clearinghouses offering various services in support of their educational topic area, there was still only one ERIC database to which they all contributed records. A variety of vendors contract with Computer Sciences Corporation to obtain the ERIC data, and each vendor then offers the database through their own search interface. (In addition to these choices, the Department of Education also provides free access to ERIC through their own Web site.) We'll take a look at the "flavor" provided by OCLC's FirstSearch system. We've already had a preliminary introduction to this search interface in Chapter 1.

Notes and Search Examples

Advanced Search Interface: Functions and Fields

Take a look at Figure 4.10. What do we have here? You'll find many of the same functions as in the WilsonWeb interface, some with different labels, plus some additions. Starting from the top, we have tabs for major locations: Home, Databases (to change to another FirstSearch database), Searching, and Resource Sharing. Since we are in Search mode, the next band offers buttons relating to searching, either to change the type of search (i.e., Basic, Advanced, or Expert), or to review what you've tried so far in the current session: your Previous Searches. Next band: two useful icon buttons,

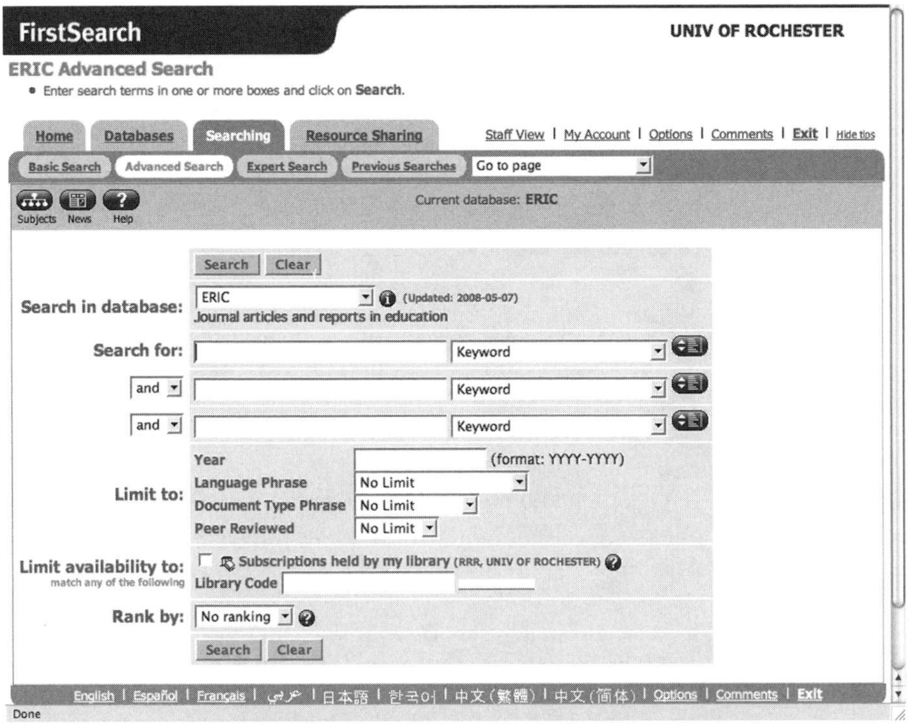

Fig. 4.10. ERIC via FirstSearch®: Advanced Search interface. Screen shots used with permission of OCLC; FirstSearch® and WorldCat® are registered trademarks of OCLC Online Computer Library Center, Inc.

Subjects and Help, as well as News, and a reminder of which database you are currently using. The Subjects button is your access to the ERIC Thesaurus, to which we will return later. This brings us to the main area, devoted to setting up your search and applying limits. The very first drop-down menu, however, is yet another chance to switch databases: you'll find this is a common theme in the interfaces of vendors that supply many databases. But here we are in familiar territory! Search boxes, the opportunity to restrict the search to a particular field, Boolean operators, and limit capabilities. The icons at the end of the text input field selector drop-down menus are the equivalent of WilsonWeb's Browse function: your access to the lists of terms in the database's many indexes (i.e., the black, lozenge-shaped buttons with white up-down indicators). These indexes were first introduced in Chapter 1, Figure 1.3; as noted there, FirstSearch has separate indexes for single words and for phrases.

Limits

In addition to some of the most common types of limits (e.g., year, language, document type, and peer reviewed, as seen in the WilsonWeb interface), FirstSearch offers some very useful "availability" limits, such as the library at your own institution. The FirstSearch databases have a bit of an inside track here, because they are OCLC products. Libraries around the world contribute their catalog records to OCLC, which then, among many other uses, produces from these records the largest union catalog in the

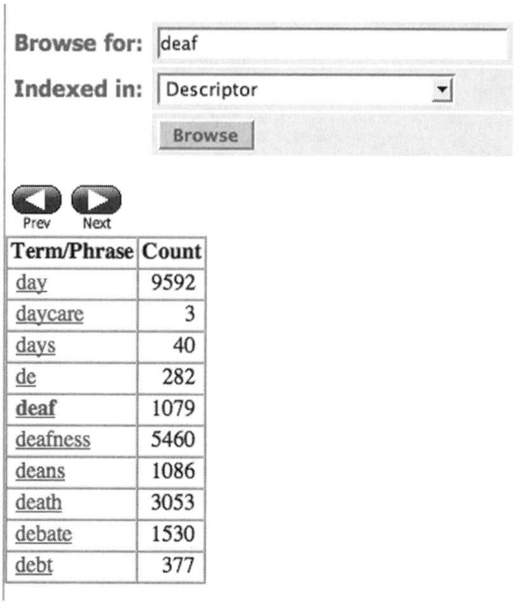

Browse for: deaf

Indexed in: Descriptor ▾

Browse

◀ ▶
Prev   Next

Term/Phrase	Count
day	9592
daycare	3
days	40
de	282
deaf	1079
deafness	5460
deans	1086
death	3053
debate	1530
debt	377

Fig. 4.11. Browsing the Descriptors index for "deaf." Screen shots used with permission of OCLC; FirstSearch® and WorldCat® are registered trademarks of OCLC Online Computer Library Center, Inc.

world (we'll meet this as a database called WorldCat in Chapter 6). They have been able to integrate the information from the catalog records with their article databases, and thus provide a limit based on what they know of your library's (or any "contributing" library's) holdings. It's quite a nice reuse of already existing information.

Ranking

Finally, you can "rank" your results, if you wish, by relevance or by date. Relevance is mainly applicable if you are only doing keyword searches. Making use of subject headings and field searching should ensure that your results are relevant. The default, "No ranking," will display the results in the order in which they were added to the database, which is not quite the same as a strictly chronological list.

Search Example 1

The search example that we'll use for our tour of the ERIC database is to find material on training teachers of deaf students.

As noted previously, FirstSearch uses the label *Descriptors* for a database's subject headings. By clicking one of the black, up-down indicator icons (following each field drop-down menu in the Advanced screen), we can get into and Browse the Descriptors index for "deaf" (Figure 4.11).

Here is a dilemma, however—the index includes both "deaf" and "deafness." Which is more appropriate, or doesn't it matter? If there are two terms, it suggests that it might well matter. The answer can be found in the ERIC Thesaurus, which is accessed via the Subjects icon. (In Figure 4.10, the Subjects icon is located immediately below the *Basic Search* link.)

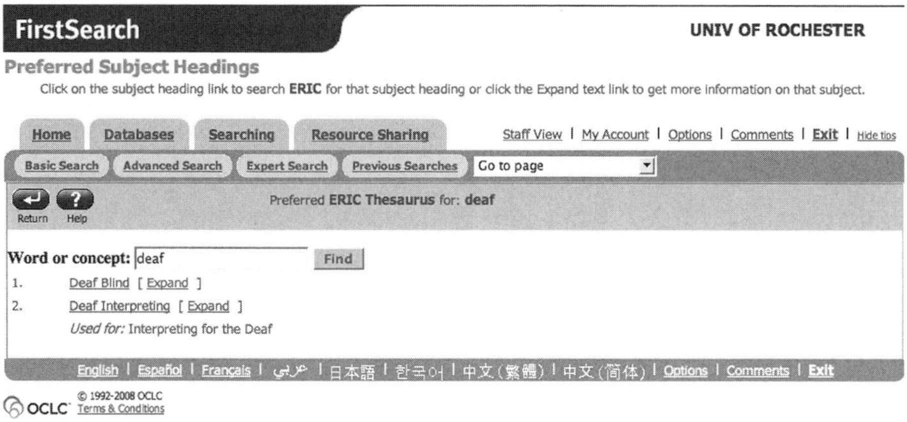

Fig. 4.12. Checking the ERIC Thesaurus (Subjects) for "deaf." Screen shots used with permission of OCLC; FirstSearch® and WorldCat® are registered trademarks of OCLC Online Computer Library Center, Inc.

Fig. 4.13. Expanded ERIC Thesaurus (subject heading) for "deaf blind." Screen shots used with permission of OCLC; FirstSearch® and WorldCat® are registered trademarks of OCLC Online Computer Library Center, Inc.

ERIC Thesaurus

Just as in the *Library Literature* Thesaurus, the system behind the Subjects icon lists all the subject headings used in this database, and displays them in hierarchical, thematic groups. (The field indexes that you can browse are a straight alphabetical list.) Notes are provided to disambiguate meanings, if necessary. Working with this Thesaurus, the indexers then assign descriptors to each document.

If we go into Subjects and type in "deaf," as in Figure 4.12, we discover that deaf is really the first half of "deaf blind." If we then expand that term, we find that "deafness" is a related subject (Figure 4.13).

You may have noticed, when you went in to browse the field indexes, that included in the list were not only Descriptors (single word or phrase) and Subjects (single word or phrase), but also Identifiers (single word or phrase). Oh no! How do you know which to use? What's the difference? Believe it or not, it used to be *more* complex: there used to be both Major and

Minor Descriptors, as well as Identifiers, and the Subject field search was a convenient way to retrieve them all. Now Subjects and Descriptors are approximately equivalent; a rough rule of thumb might be to use whichever field appears to have a higher count for your search term. As for Identifiers, the definition in the Help Glossary is somewhat vague; within the ERIC Development News Web site they are described as "terms related to proper names, geographic area, laws and legislation, tests and testing." Other hints in the same text suggest that the Identifiers are no longer actively being applied (e.g., the "Legacy file will still have Identifiers"). In general, it might be best not to restrict a search to this field. Instead, run your search(es) using the subjects or descriptors fields, or simply as keywords, then observe the contents of the results carefully. If you notice a useful term in the Identifiers section of a record, re-run your search using that information.

Back to the Descriptors Index

Let's not get too wrapped around the axle about this. We'll stick with the plan and search "deafness" as a Descriptor. The other concept that we were after was about training the teachers who work with deaf students. Let's browse for the single term "teacher" in the Descriptors *phrase* index, to see all the possible phrases that begin with the word *teacher* (Figure 4.14).

If you keep browsing forward, there are more and more entries beginning with "teacher" (you can certainly tell this is the "education" database!), and there could be several of these that might be good. What we are really after is "teacher education," however, or "teacher education programs." Using a truncation symbol, we can pick up either of these headings.

Term/Phrase	Count
teacher distribution	221
teacher early childhood education	1
teacher educati on	1
teacher education	32164
teacher education curriculum	3742
teacher education programs	5189
teacher educationcation	1
teacher educator education	609
teacher educators	3008
teacher effecctiveness	1

Fig. 4.14. Searching a single term in a phrase index, several screens into the list. Screen shots used with permission of OCLC; FirstSearch® and WorldCat® are registered trademarks of OCLC Online Computer Library Center, Inc.

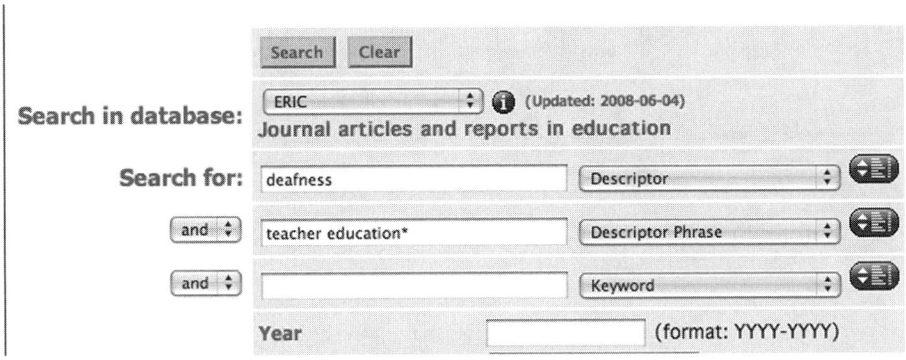

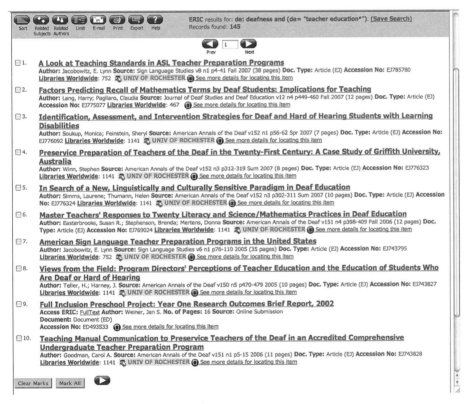

Fig. 4.15. Search strategy for training of teachers of deaf students. Screen shots used with permission of OCLC; FirstSearch® and WorldCat® are registered trademarks of OCLC Online Computer Library Center, Inc.

Fig. 4.16. Deafness and teacher education* descriptor search results. Screen shots used with permission of OCLC; FirstSearch® and WorldCat® are registered trademarks of OCLC Online Computer Library Center, Inc.

Final Strategy and Results

Figure 4.15 shows the strategy that we decided to use for this search. There are 145 citations in the results list, and they appear to be right on target, as indicated by the first screen of entries showing in Figure 4.16.

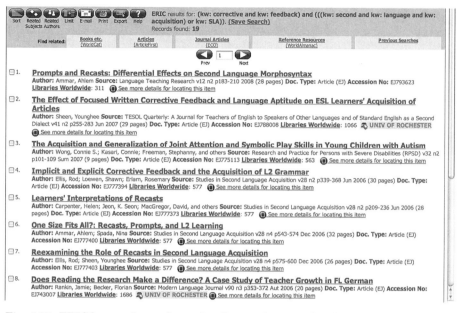

Fig. 4.17. ERIC keyword search results. Screen shots used with permission of OCLC; FirstSearch® and WorldCat® are registered trademarks of OCLC Online Computer Library Center, Inc.

Note the ninth item in the list: it differs from the rest in a couple of ways. Rather than Source and the name of a journal, it has "Access ERIC" and a FullText link, and its Accession No. begins with "ED." This is an example of an *ERIC Document*, one of those pieces of grey literature mentioned in the Background and Coverage section for this database.

Search Example 2

Keywords and Pearl-growing Strategy

Sometimes (in fact, most of the time), you don't have time for a very structured approach, where you carefully check the indexes and thesaurus entries before deciding on your search terms and setting up the strategy. When a busy graduate student is at the desk asking for resources on corrective feedback in second language acquisition (SLA), you are absolutely allowed to go to ERIC and simply type in what she's told you:

corrective feedback—as Keywords

AND

second language acquisition or SLA—as Keywords

This strategy seems to work quite well: she is particularly delighted with the second result (Figure 4.17). You might be concerned, however, since this search returned only nineteen results. But here is a great tip: remember the pearl growing strategy introduced in Chapter 3? Well, it's not just for focusing or reducing results; it can also be used to "grow" results from a

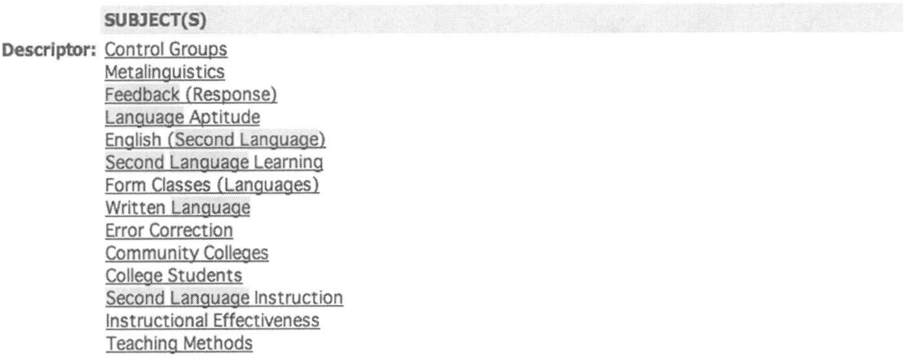

SUBJECT(S)

Descriptor: Control Groups
           Metalinguistics
           Feedback (Response)
           Language Aptitude
           English (Second Language)
           Second Language Learning
           Form Classes (Languages)
           Written Language
           Error Correction
           Community Colleges
           College Students
           Second Language Instruction
           Instructional Effectiveness
           Teaching Methods

Fig. 4.18. Subject headings in Record 2. Screen shots used with permission of OCLC; FirstSearch® and WorldCat® are registered trademarks of OCLC Online Computer Library Center, Inc.

	Search	Clear	
Search in database:	ERIC ⬢ ℹ (Updated: 2008-06-04) **Journal articles and reports in education**		
Search for:	corrective feedback	Keyword ⬢	🔲
and ⬢	second language*	Descriptor Phrase ⬢	🔲
and ⬢		Keyword ⬢	🔲
Limit to:	**Year** [ ] (format: YYYY-YYYY)		
	Language Phrase No Limit ⬢		
	Document Type Phrase No Limit ⬢		
	Peer Reviewed No Limit ⬢		

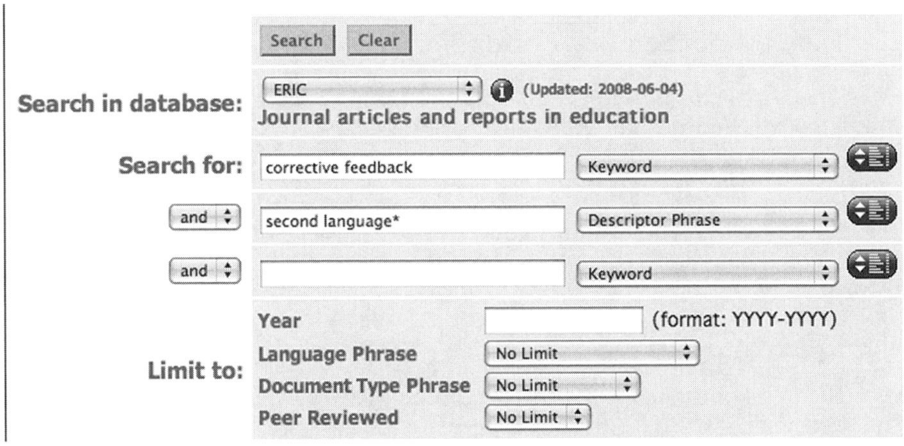

Fig. 4.19. Search strategy for Example 2 revised by pearl growing. Screen shots used with permission of OCLC; FirstSearch® and WorldCat® are registered trademarks of OCLC Online Computer Library Center, Inc.

perhaps overly specific search. Thus, immediately on hearing the patron's expressions of interest about that "ideal" record, you should open it up and take a look at the descriptors, which are pictured in Figure 4.18.

Ah! Second Language Learning—or Second Language Instruction! They both look like perfect headings. It's very tempting to click on a linked subject heading, but beware: if you do you'll get *all* the records with that heading—but the rest of the context of your current search (the "corrective feedback" part) will be left behind. To use this information, you'll need to return to the Searching interface, and type in the phrase (or copy and paste from this page). Since either heading could be good for this patron's research, and she is really focused on a specific kind of feedback, the revised search might look like Figure 4.19.

This search strategy yields a stronger fifty-three results, while remaining nicely on target.

Fig. 4.20. Functions available in the Results List display. Screen shots used with permission of OCLC; FirstSearch® and WorldCat® are registered trademarks of OCLC Online Computer Library Center, Inc.

Working with Results: Mark, Functions, and Output

Mark

As you can see in Figures 4.16 and Figures 4.17, each record in your results list has a checkbox associated with it, so that you can mark the records you wish to output.

Results Screen Functions

There are a number of functions available in the Results list display, as indicated by the icon bar shown in Figure 4.20.

Sort

Sort is what you would expect: you can sort your results in various ways. Note that the Sort function will not appear for results sets of over 500 records.

Related Subjects

Be somewhat wary of the *Related Subjects* option: all of the subjects that you check are "ORed" together, which might not be the effect you had intended. On the other hand, you could make that work to your advantage: you could mark several subjects, search them, and then click back on the Searching tab from the results list. Then you could AND in a new term (ERIC will have transferred the search syntax for the string of ORed terms into the first search field), and focus your search back down.

Related Authors

Related authors shows a list of all the authors represented in the current results list. The ones at the top of the list are those with the most articles; thus, these are the names that may be important to you as you continue your research.

Limit

Limit provides the opportunity to add limits to your search without having to return to the main search screen.

E-mail, Print, Export, and Help

E-mail and *print* are the usual useful output options. *Export*, as in WilsonWeb, is the function for downloading citations directly into applications such as EndNote or RefWorks, or to produce a text file that can be imported into Reference Manager or ProCite. All of these applications are used for creating correctly formatted footnotes, endnotes, and bibliographies. And if you're in doubt about anything—there's the *Help*!

Quick Recap

ERIC, the Education Resources Information Center, is produced under the aegis of the U.S. Department of Education. It is the premier database for education, and dates back to 1966. ERIC indexes journal articles as well as *grey literature*—scholarly works that have not been commercially published. The ERIC database is offered by many different vendors, as well as being freely available at the Department of Education's Web site. ERIC via FirstSearch offers many searchable fields, and browsable single word and phrase indexes. The indexes are accessed by an icon following each text input field in the advanced interface. The hierarchy of ERIC subject headings (the ERIC Thesaurus) can be browsed using the Subjects icon in the upper left area of the interface. The field name for subject headings in First-Search is Descriptors. The *Advanced Search* interface offers year, language, and document type limits, as well as an availability limit ("my library" or another specific library) that is unique to FirstSearch databases. (This is made possible because the vendor, OCLC, also offers the WorldCat database of library holdings records.)

PsycINFO from Ovid

Background and Coverage

PsycINFO is the online version of the American Psychological Association's venerable *Psychological Abstracts*, a print abstracting and indexing service dating from 1927. *PsycINFO* is probably the largest, and most well-known, index of the literature of psychology and the behavioral sciences. In addition to journal articles, document types indexed in the database include books and book chapters, dissertations, and electronic collections. The American Psychological Association (APA) draws on international sources, with journals in more than twenty-seven languages, and English language books and book chapters from all over the world (OCLC 1998). The *Thesaurus* terms (subject headings) used to index entries in the *PsycINFO* database are developed and applied by APA indexers.

One of the truly remarkable features of *PsycINFO* is the range of time it covers. *PsycINFO* has abstracts of books and journal articles dating from as early as 1806, although most journals are from the 1880s to the present, and most of the books are from 1987 to the present. The database is updated weekly, and the latest updated week is reflected in the search interface (Figure 4.21). As noted in the APA's PsycINFO *Fact Sheet* (2008) "more than 129,000 records" were added to the database in 2007, a demonstration of what a vibrant and growing resource this is. (The URL for the *Fact Sheet* is provided in the References; it includes a great deal of useful information.)

Like ERIC, the *PsycINFO* online database is available from quite a few different vendors. Depending on which vendor and what backfile option your institution has chosen to subscribe to, you may have access to the complete file in one database, or the file may be divided in various ways, and you may have access to all or only to the most recent file.

Extensive Set of Search Fields

Another aspect of the *PsycINFO* database that demonstrates what an expertly crafted product it is (and it is, literally, crafted by experts in the field), is the set search fields used in the record structure. In 2005, the database designers made a number of changes in the field structure, field names, and field content values (PsycNET Guide, 2005), something that this book has indicated is not a task to be taken lightly—thus, a significant event. The following list of fields has therefore changed quite a bit from the one in the first edition of this book.

Abstract	Correction Update Record*	Population
Affiliation	Country of Publication*	Publication Type
Age Group	Document Type	Publication Year
Audience Type (book and chapter records only)	DOI (Digital Object Identifier)	Publisher
Author	Grant/Sponsorship	Release Date (aka Update code)
Author Correspondence Address	Index Terms (aka descriptors, thesaurus terms)	Reviewed Item (journal and electronic collections records only)
Author E-mail	ISSN / ISBN	Source
Auxiliary Material	Keywords	Table of Contents* (book records only)
Book Type	Language	Tests & Measures
Cited References	Location	Title
Classification Code	Methodology	Unique Identifier

* Indicates display-only field.

Some of the fields listed in the table deserve some commentary:

- Cited references (the article's bibliography; very important in tracing the development of research)

- Auxiliary material (indicates that there is additional material such as audio, video, Web sites, tables, data sets, etc., separate from the source document.)

- DOI (to help users link to full text, and provide a stable URL for the item)

- Tests & Measures (a field indicating if a test was used in the methodology of a study or featured as the subject of discussion)

Why Look at Ovid's *PsycINFO*

We're going to take a look at *PsycINFO* as offered by the database vendor Ovid. The Ovid interface differs from the previous two that we've seen so far in a couple of interesting, and to me, quite useful ways:

- It has a built-in map-to-subject-heading feature that tries to offer you the best subject heading choices based on what you type in.

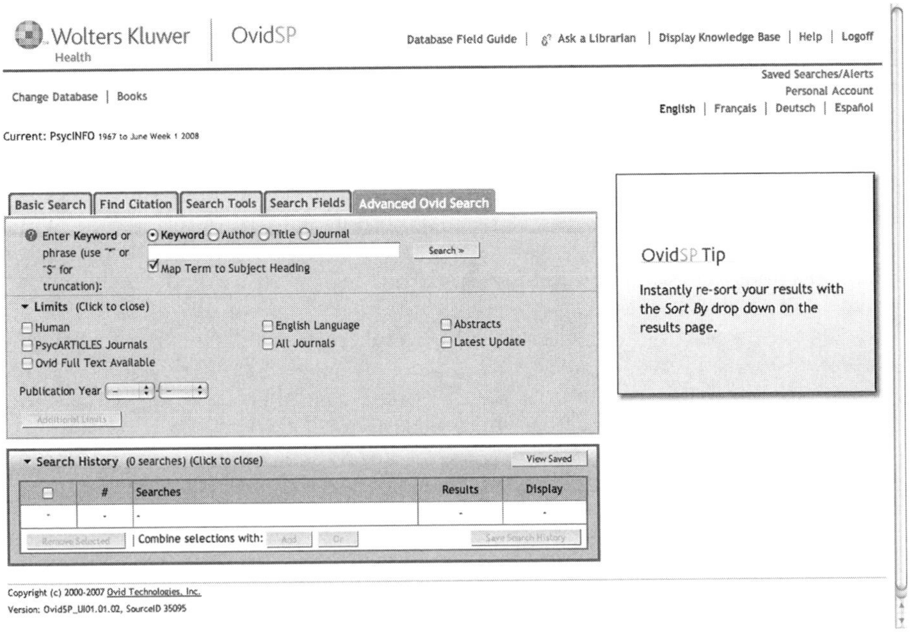

Fig. 4.21. *PsycINFO* Advanced Search interface. *PsycINFO* screen shots are reprinted with permission of the American Psychological Association, publisher of the *PsycINFO* database, all rights reserved. OVID interface © OvidSP, 2008 Wolters Kluwer Health | Ovid.

- It encourages you to build your search one concept at a time, which turns out to be very handy because when you have all the conceptual pieces, it is then very easy to experiment with putting them together in different combinations.

Notes and Search Examples

What do you notice about the interface shown in Figure 4.21? The first thing that strikes me is a slight sense of compression, but also of strong focus: your eye is drawn immediately to the search area. Although it only has one text entry box (unlike those of Wilson and FirstSearch, which have three), it is surrounded by tabs, radio buttons, and check boxes. The Tip in the large box on the right is obviously meant to be helpful, but one does wish it didn't take up quite so much prime real estate on the page. If it weren't there, the search interface might not feel quite so squeezed. However, don't let your eyes start to "screen out" all the options—there is great usefulness here, and power.

Advanced Search Interface

Let's work through the areas of the Advanced interface, from top to bottom. The topmost area contains the vendor's branding logos, and a set of very clear and useful links: the Database Field Guide, the option for real-time assistance (Ask a Librarian), Help, and so forth. Just below the line delineating that area, you are provided with a link to change to another Ovid-provided database (as is often the case with vendors that offer many databases), or to jump into an online collection of full-text books (an interesting new addition). This is also where you can access any saved searches or "alerting" searches you have set up. Just below that you find the usual database identification information, to make it very clear what database (and dates) you are searching.

Then we have the search interface region. There is only one text entry field, and the "Map Term to Subject Heading" option is turned on by default. The keyword search mode is the default, but if you want to search for an author's name, the title of a work, or for a particular journal (e.g., to see if it is indexed in this database), the radio buttons above the search box make it easy to switch search modes. If you knew that you wanted to search just within a certain field or fields, the Search Fields tab[3] takes you to a screen where you enter your term in a search box, and restrict your search to a particular field by clicking its checkbox. (This is quite different from the drop-down menu approach.) The Search Tools tab provides direct search access to the supporting materials, such as the Thesaurus and scope notes (definitions of subject headings), which govern the content of *PsycINFO*.

The Limits area is directly below the search box area. The standard limits you might want to invoke are ready and waiting (once a search has been performed, the "Additional Limits" button offers other, more detailed limits). Note that a standard limit in this subject area is "Human" (to rule out articles about tests or studies on animals).

Finally, in its own, differently shaded box, is the Search History table, which becomes very important as you work in this database. As mentioned above, the most effective way to use this interface is to build your search one step at a time, with the results of each step recorded in the Search History display. These individual search elements can then be combined in various ways, as we shall see.

Here is what the Ovid interface is like to use.

Search Example 1

We'd like to search the psychological literature for material on the "effect of peer pressure on self esteem."

We'll start by typing into the search box:

peer pressure

and pressing return. This brings up the Mapping Display screen, shown in Figure 4.22.

The Mapping Display

Because the "Map Term to Subject Heading" feature was turned on, the system automatically tries to match, or "map," what you type in against its Thesaurus, the hierarchical list of subject headings for *PsycINFO*. The results can be quite fascinating, because even in the case of an exact match (as we have here: Peer Pressure is a subject heading), the system also offers all the other headings that have a thesaurus relationship to this heading, that is, they are broader, narrower, or "related." The immense amount of thought the Thesaurus designers put into their product can make your searching life so much easier, suggesting relationships and lines of thought that otherwise might not have occurred to you.

Each heading has two options: *Auto-Explode* (if you scroll down, the interface explains that this will pick up the heading and any narrower headings, ones indented below it in the hierarchy), and *Focus*. *Focus* means

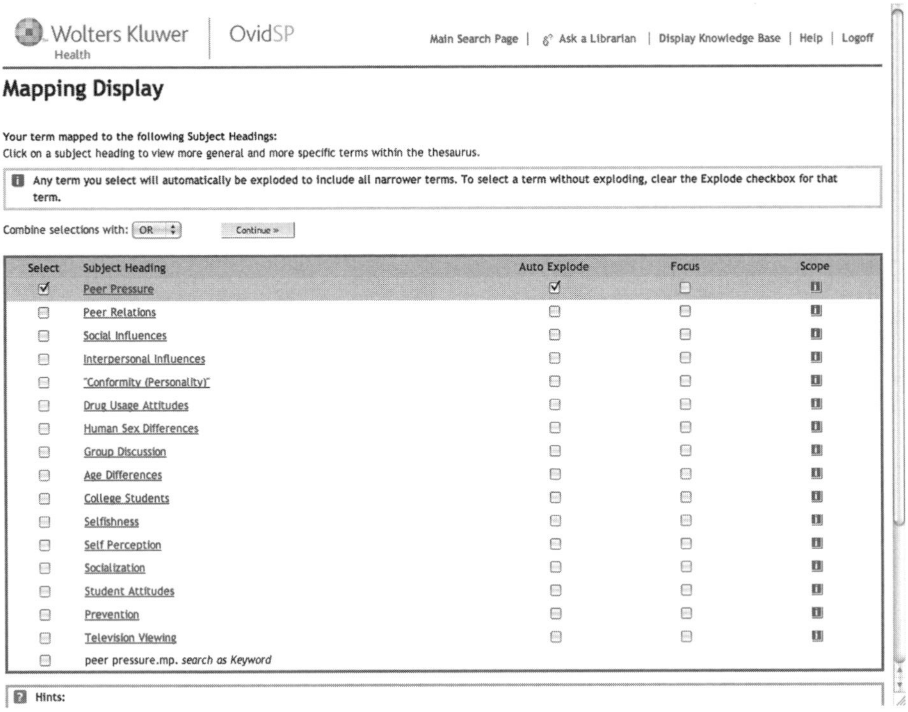

Fig. 4.22. *PsycINFO* Mapping Display for Peer Pressure. *PsycINFO* screen shots are reprinted with permission of the American Psychological Association, publisher of the *PsycINFO* database, all rights reserved. OVID interface © OvidSP, 2008 Wolters Kluwer Health | Ovid.

that the indexers decided that the heading was a main aspect, or focus, of the article. Only a few of the subject headings assigned to an article will be designated as a Focus, so you may want to use it sparingly in the initial phases of your search.

For the current search, we'll leave Auto-Explode on, but won't check Focus—we'll leave it a little more open. Clicking the *continue* button returns us to the main search page, which now displays the interface to start another search, our search history, and the beginning of our results list, as shown in Figure 4.23.

Building the Search

Now to add the second concept of our search, by typing:

self esteem

into the search box. Again, this maps exactly to a subject heading.

As shown in Figure 4.24, this time we'll click the Focus box, because we really want the main theme of these articles to be about self-esteem. There should be over 13,000 results for this search.

Combining Search History Sets

Now we will combine the results of these two searches. In the Search History box, we could check off both searches and use the "Combine

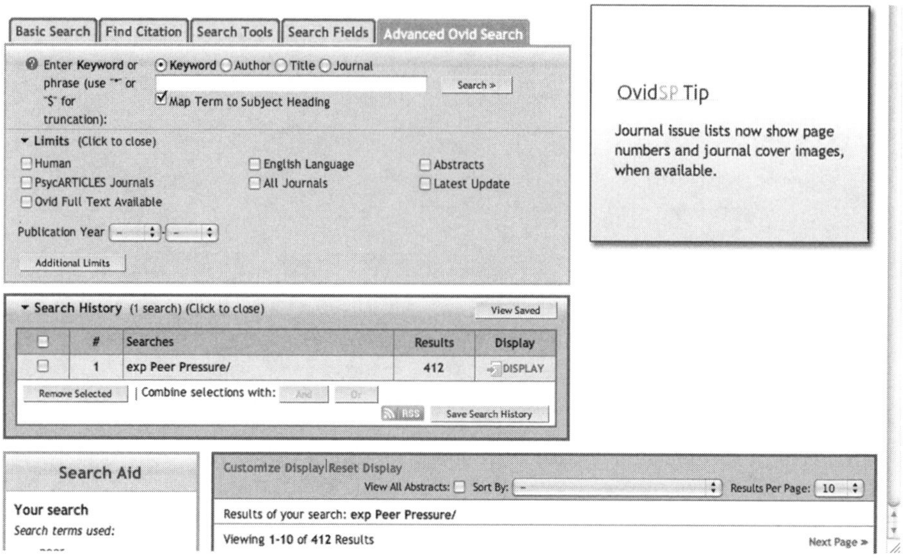

Fig. 4.23. Return to main page: Search interface, Search History, and Results. *PsycINFO* screen shots are reprinted with permission of the American Psychological Association, publisher of the *PsycINFO* database, all rights reserved. OVID interface © OvidSP, 2008 Wolters Kluwer Health | Ovid.

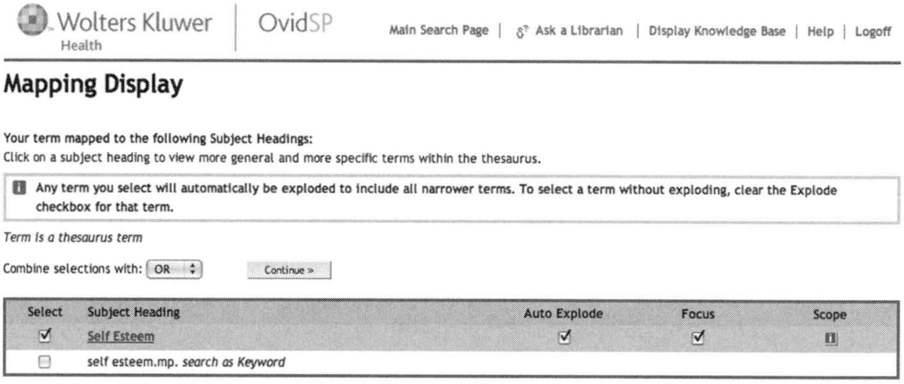

Fig. 4.24. Mapping display for "self esteem," Focus checked. *PsycINFO* screen shots are reprinted with permission of the American Psychological Association, publisher of the *PsycINFO* database, all rights reserved. OVID interface © OvidSP, 2008 Wolters Kluwer Health | Ovid.

Selections with" AND button. Note, however, that each search in your history is numbered: an insider's shortcut is that you can simply type:

1 and 2

into the search box, as shown in Figure 4.25 (or whatever numbers correspond to the searches in your search history that you wish to combine).

You can use any of the Boolean operators, and parentheses for making nested statements, to combine Search History set numbers in this way. Each variation will, of course, produce a set of results that differs to a greater or lesser extent. If you have built up a series of searches, this is a very

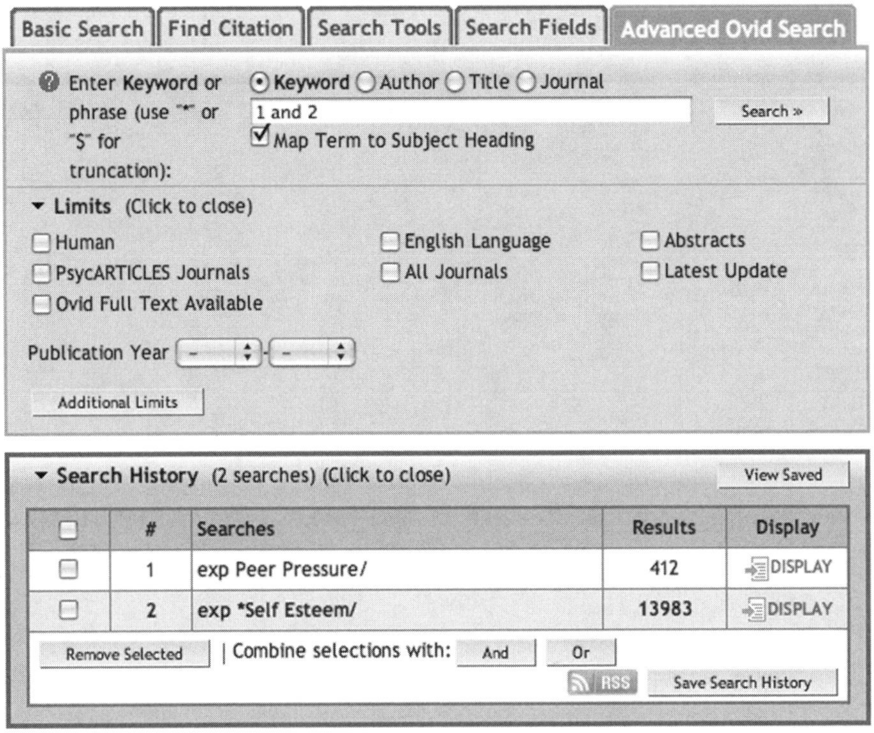

Fig. 4.25. Combining sets using search numbers and a Boolean operator. *PsycINFO* screen shots are reprinted with permission of the American Psychological Association, publisher of the *PsycINFO* database, all rights reserved. OVID interface © OvidSP, 2008 Wolters Kluwer Health | Ovid.

fast and easy way to experiment with them, to arrive at an optimal set of results.

Results

Presto: our combined sets result in fourteen articles, as indicated both in the *History* box, and at the beginning of the results list, in Figure 4.26. This is a useful feature of the Ovid interface, that it allows us to see the search history, search interface, and results all on the same page. These results seem on target and fairly useful, but fourteen isn't a lot. How might we get more?

Search Example 1 Redone

Getting More with OR

Let's do this search again. We'll type "peer pressure" into the search box again. This time in the Mapping Display, let's select some more terms in addition to Peer Pressure. Note the "Combine selections with" drop-down at the top of the page. It's set to OR, which is what we want. After picking several headings and ORing them together, yes, the number of results is enormous (search set 4 in Figure 4.27).

Don't panic.

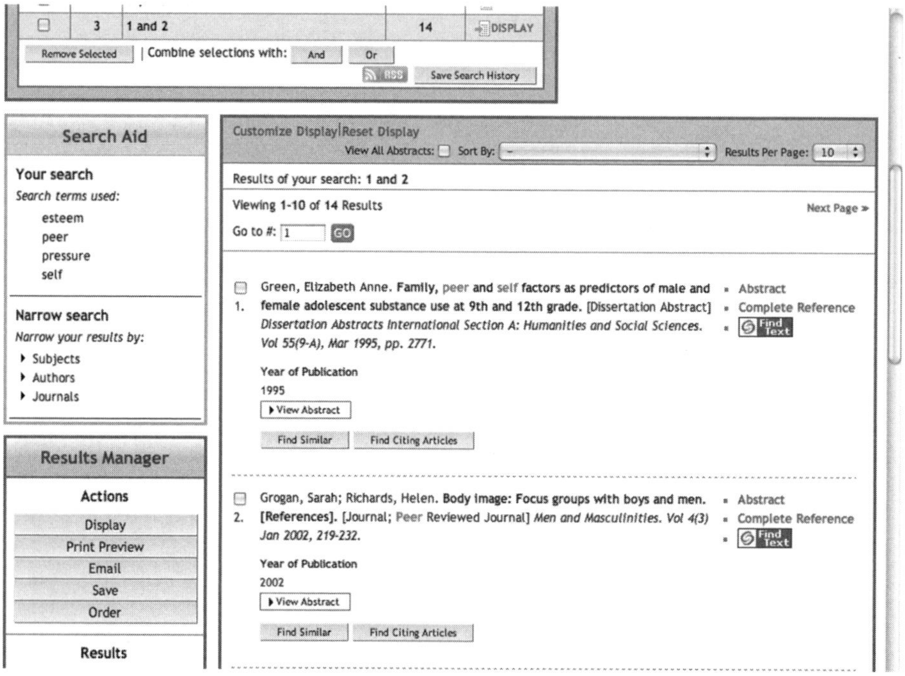

Fig. 4.26. Result of combining sets 1 and 2: fourteen articles. *PsycINFO* screen shots are reprinted with permission of the American Psychological Association, publisher of the *PsycINFO* database, all rights reserved. OVID interface © OvidSP, 2008 Wolters Kluwer Health | Ovid.

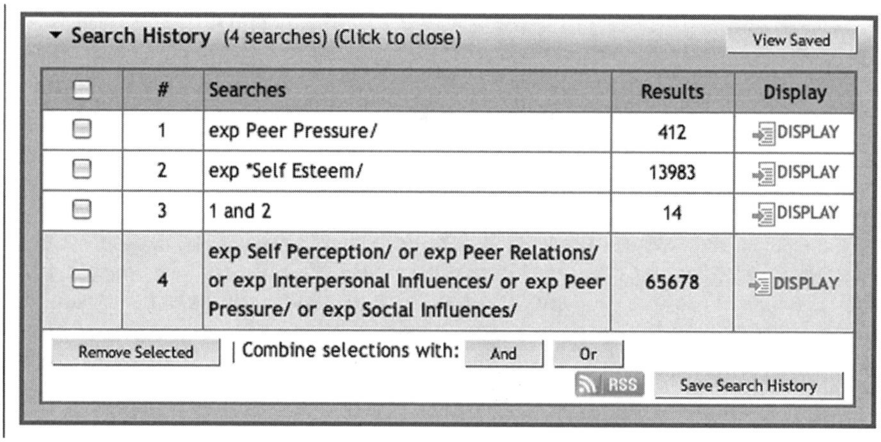

Fig. 4.27. Result of selecting several subject headings related to Peer Pressure. *PsycINFO* screen shots are reprinted with permission of the American Psychological Association, publisher of the *PsycINFO* database, all rights reserved. OVID interface © OvidSP, 2008 Wolters Kluwer Health | Ovid.

Combining from the Search History

There were LOTS of hits for self esteem when we searched it before, so let's re-use that search, and combine it with our new set of "peer" topics (here is the beauty of quickly and easily reusing previous sets). Simply type

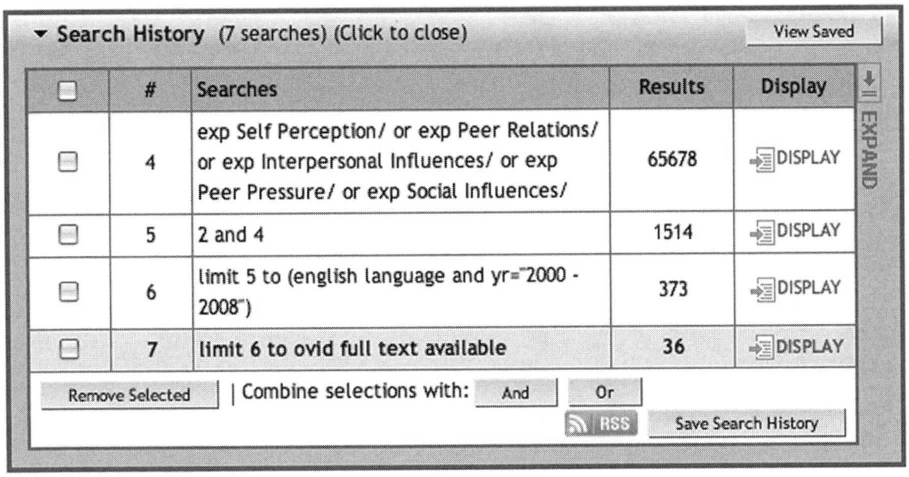

□	#	Searches	Results	Display
□	4	exp Self Perception/ or exp Peer Relations/ or exp Interpersonal Influences/ or exp Peer Pressure/ or exp Social Influences/	65678	DISPLAY
□	5	2 and 4	1514	DISPLAY
□	6	limit 5 to (english language and yr="2000 - 2008")	373	DISPLAY
□	7	limit 6 to ovid full text available	36	DISPLAY

▼ Search History (7 searches) (Click to close)   View Saved

Remove Selected | Combine selections with: And   Or

RSS   Save Search History

Fig. 4.28. Applying limits to reduce numbers of results. *PsycINFO* screen shots are reprinted with permission of the American Psychological Association, publisher of the *PsycINFO* database, all rights reserved. OVID interface © OvidSP, 2008 Wolters Kluwer Health | Ovid.

the numbers of the sets that you want to combine into the search box, in this case:

2 and 4.

Applying Limits

OK, it's still a fairly big set of records, but still, don't panic. Let's make use of some of those limits that are so easily provided in the interface: English Language, and Publication Year. If the results list still seems daunting, there are a couple of options. You could try another limit: Ovid Full Text Available. Simply select the Limits that you want to use, and click the Search button. It feels odd, because there is nothing in the input field above the Search button, but the system understands that you are applying limits. The other option appears right next to the results list, where the Ovid interface now offers three ways to "Narrow" your search: by Subjects, Authors, or Journals, as shown in Figure 4.26. The lists for each provide the most frequently occurring entries from the total results list; thus, you might decide to look only at the articles from the journal that had the most articles on this topic, or by an author that publishes on the topic frequently.

Using just the checkbox limits, we whittle down the results to thirty-six. Now that's a manageable set of results (Figure 4.28).

More Search History Advantages

The Ovid "piece-by-piece" approach to searching is also helpful if you decide to change direction as you're working. If you get a new idea, you simply start that new thread, and then experiment with combining it with previous searches. You can delete searches if you're really sure they aren't useful (the Remove Selected button in the Search History box), but you can also just keep adding new ones. Although the interface will default to

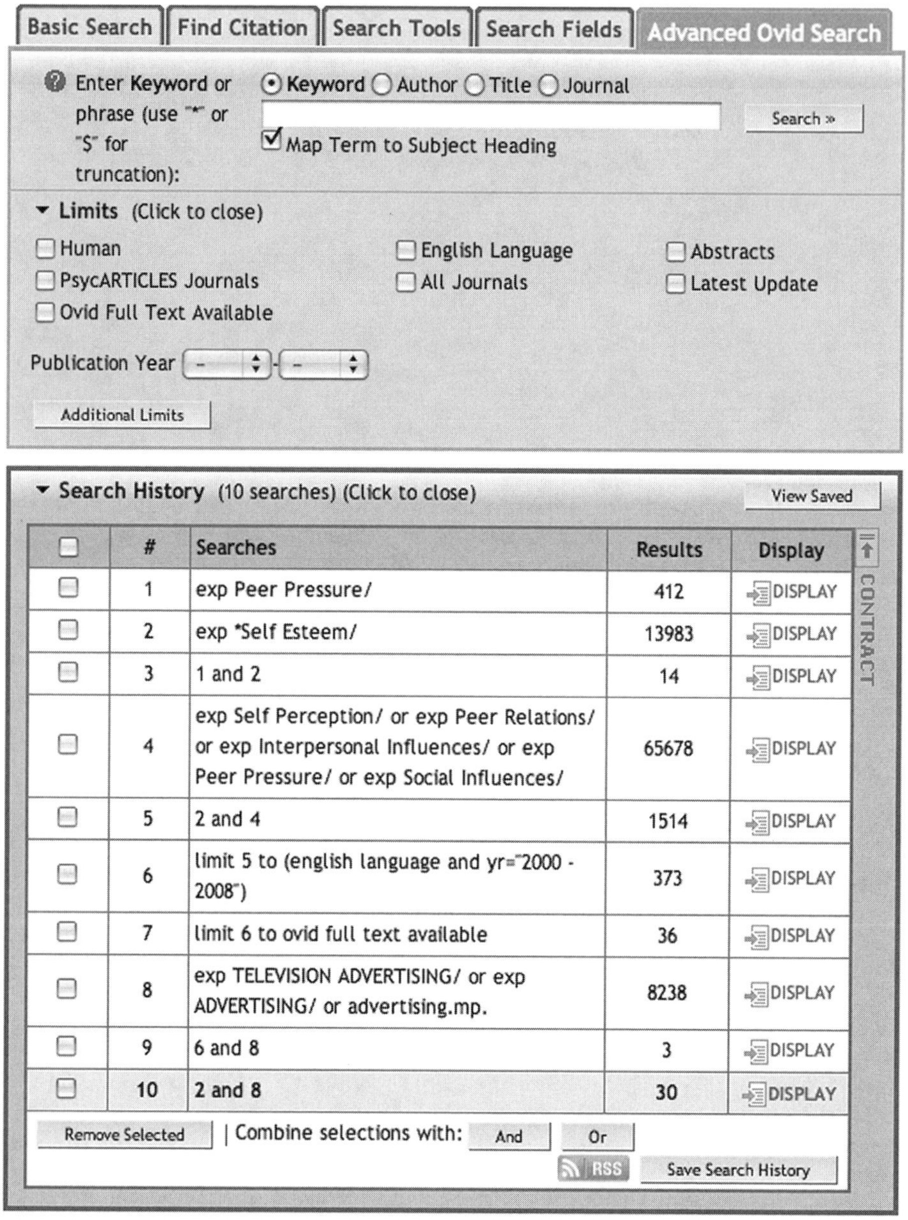

| Basic Search | Find Citation | Search Tools | Search Fields | Advanced Ovid Search |

Enter **Keyword** or phrase (use "*" or "$" for truncation):

⦿ **Keyword** ◯ Author ◯ Title ◯ Journal

[   ] Search »

☑ Map Term to Subject Heading

▾ **Limits** (Click to close)

☐ Human
☐ PsycARTICLES Journals
☐ Ovid Full Text Available

☐ English Language
☐ All Journals

☐ Abstracts
☐ Latest Update

Publication Year [– ▾]-[– ▾]

[Additional Limits]

▾ **Search History** (10 searches) (Click to close)   [View Saved]

☐	#	Searches	Results	Display
☐	1	exp Peer Pressure/	412	⬛DISPLAY
☐	2	exp *Self Esteem/	13983	⬛DISPLAY
☐	3	1 and 2	14	⬛DISPLAY
☐	4	exp Self Perception/ or exp Peer Relations/ or exp Interpersonal Influences/ or exp Peer Pressure/ or exp Social Influences/	65678	⬛DISPLAY
☐	5	2 and 4	1514	⬛DISPLAY
☐	6	limit 5 to (english language and yr="2000 - 2008")	373	⬛DISPLAY
☐	7	limit 6 to ovid full text available	36	⬛DISPLAY
☐	8	exp TELEVISION ADVERTISING/ or exp ADVERTISING/ or advertising.mp.	8238	⬛DISPLAY
☐	9	6 and 8	3	⬛DISPLAY
☐	10	2 and 8	30	⬛DISPLAY

[Remove Selected] | Combine selections with: [And] [Or]

[🔊 RSS] [Save Search History]

Fig. 4.29. More search history combinations. *PsycINFO* screen shots are reprinted with permission of the American Psychological Association, publisher of the *PsycINFO* database, all rights reserved. OVID interface © OvidSP, 2008 Wolters Kluwer Health | Ovid.

showing you only the four or five most recent searches, note the small Expand tab on the upper right of the Search History table.

Figure 4.29 shows an example of adding a new search (for material about advertising), and seeing the results of combining it with previous searches. We find that the new search set 8 produces only three results when ANDed with search set 6, so we might simply try combining set 8 with the large set on self esteem, set 2. This combination results in thirty citations, a very comfortable number.

Working with Results: The "Results Manager"

The first ten results of the latest search are always listed on the main search page, starting below the Search History box (cf. Figure 4.26). As with the other databases that we've been looking at, you mark the citations of interest by clicking their checkboxes. Along the left side of each page, the "Results Manager" Table (Figure 4.30) offers many options for handling your results: marked items can be printed, e-mailed, saved, or exported to a bibliographic software application. (The latter is not entirely obvious: choose Direct Export as the format, and then the Save button. From there on it's clear what to do.) You can choose exactly which fields to include, and even sort the records in a particular way. A nice, subtle feature is that as you mark records, your list is immediately reflected under Selected Results in the Results Manager, as shown in Figure 4.30.

Additional Feature: The *PsycINFO* Thesaurus

You can directly access the *PsycINFO* Thesaurus by going to the Search Tools tab, selecting the Thesaurus, and entering a term. You can also access it from the Mapping Display screen in the course of a search, by clicking on any of the linked subject headings. (Figure 4.22 shows a good example of a list of linked subject headings in a Mapping Display.) In either case, you'll get taken to the Thesaurus display for that term. This allows you to see how the term fits into the hierarchy, what "narrower" terms will be included if you leave the Auto-Explode box checked, what terms are broader, and what terms are related, as indicated in Figure 4.31. It can be quite interesting to wander around in the Thesaurus for a bit.

Quick Recap

PsycINFO is the online version of *Psychological Abstracts*. The online database provides journal indexing back to 1806. *PsycINFO* is the pre-eminent index to psychology literature, and covers journals, books, book chapters, technical reports, dissertations, published conference papers, bibliographies, and more. Sources are international. Using *PsycINFO* through the Ovid interface takes advantage of the Ovid "Map to Subject Heading" functionality, which automatically provides a list of suggested terms from the *PsycINFO* Thesaurus for any word or phrase typed into the search field. Specialized functions in the Subject Heading Mapping Display are Auto-Explode, that is, automatically search the indicated term and all narrower subject headings, and Focus, that is, restrict the search to records in which the indicated term is a major aspect (or focus) of the article. The optimal search style to use in the Ovid interface is to build a search one concept at a time, and then combine sets from the search history. This is very different from the other databases considered so far. The most commonly used Limits appear in the Advanced Search interface, and many more are accessible by means of the Additional Limits button. In addition, options for narrowing a search by Subject, Author, or Journal are available in the results interface.

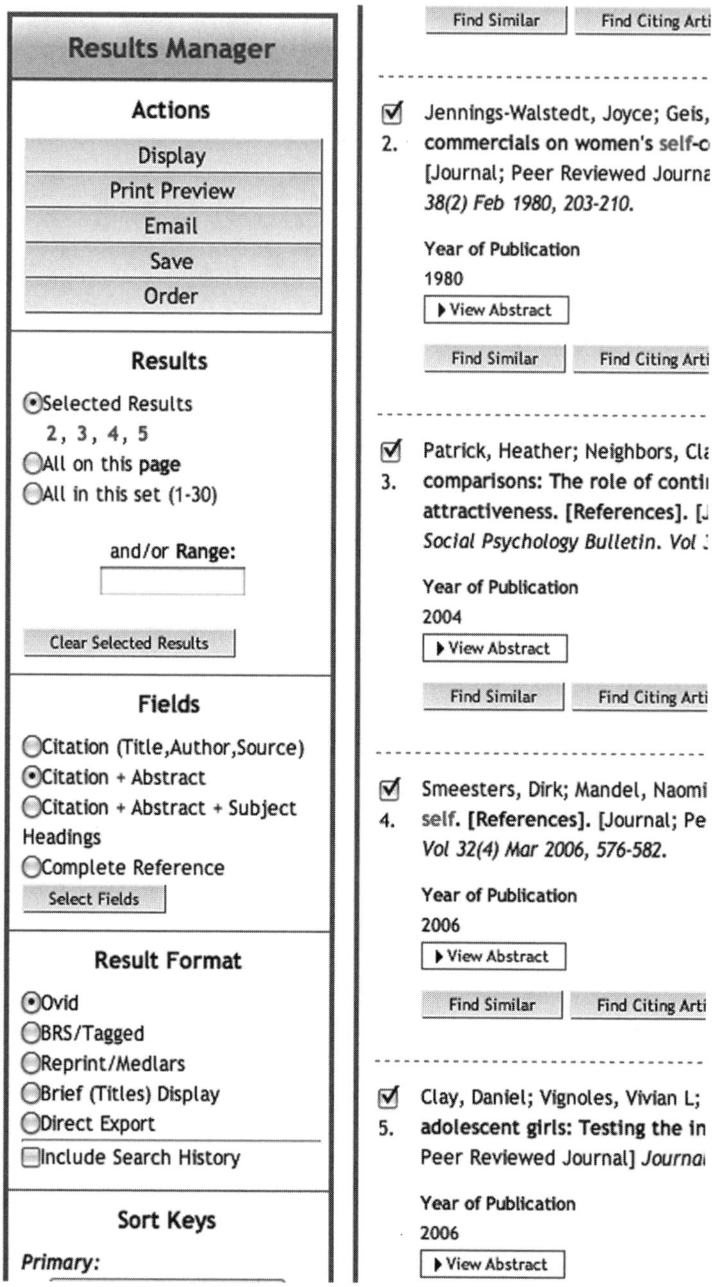

Results Manager

Actions

Display
Print Preview
Email
Save
Order

Results

⦿ Selected Results
   2, 3, 4, 5
◯ All on this **page**
◯ All in this set (1-30)

and/or **Range:**

[   ]

[Clear Selected Results]

Fields

◯ Citation (Title,Author,Source)
⦿ Citation + Abstract
◯ Citation + Abstract + Subject Headings
◯ Complete Reference

[Select Fields]

Result Format

⦿ Ovid
◯ BRS/Tagged
◯ Reprint/Medlars
◯ Brief (Titles) Display
◯ Direct Export

☐ Include Search History

Sort Keys

Primary:

[Find Similar] [Find Citing Arti]

- -

☑ Jennings-Walstedt, Joyce; Geis,
2. commercials on women's self-c
    [Journal; Peer Reviewed Journa
    38(2) Feb 1980, 203-210.

    Year of Publication
    1980
    [▸ View Abstract]

[Find Similar] [Find Citing Arti]

- -

☑ Patrick, Heather; Neighbors, Cla
3. comparisons: The role of conti
    attractiveness. [References]. [.
    Social Psychology Bulletin. Vol .

    Year of Publication
    2004
    [▸ View Abstract]

[Find Similar] [Find Citing Arti]

- -

☑ Smeesters, Dirk; Mandel, Naomi
4. self. [References]. [Journal; Pe
    Vol 32(4) Mar 2006, 576-582.

    Year of Publication
    2006
    [▸ View Abstract]

[Find Similar] [Find Citing Arti]

- -

☑ Clay, Daniel; Vignoles, Vivian L;
5. adolescent girls: Testing the in
    Peer Reviewed Journal] *Journa*

    Year of Publication
    2006
    [▸ View Abstract]

Fig. 4.30. The "Results Manager." *PsycINFO* screen shots are reprinted with permission of the American Psychological Association, publisher of the *PsycINFO* database, all rights reserved. OVID interface © OvidSP, 2008 Wolters Kluwer Health | Ovid.

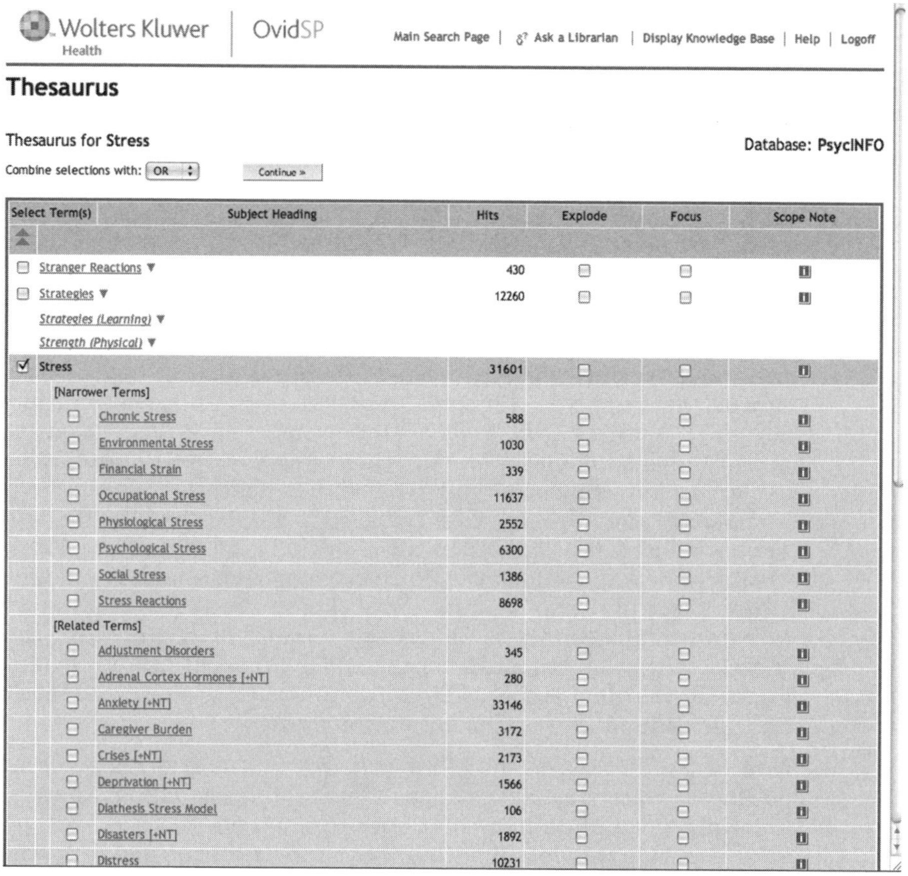

Fig. 4.31. The *PsycINFO* Thesaurus at heading "Stress." *PsycINFO* screen shots are reprinted with permission of the American Psychological Association, publisher of the *PsycINFO* database, all rights reserved. OVID interface © OvidSP, 2008 Wolters Kluwer Health | Ovid.

Exercises and Points to Consider

1. I've heard there's a bibliography of movies that had librarians in them—surely *Library Literature* would be the place to find out? This time, instead of Browsing the Subject Index, go to the Thesaurus, and search for: librarians in movies. What do you get? What happens if you try this without the Thesaurus? Try some other approaches for this search, as if you were a typical patron. (And note the dates on your results—maybe you could compile the updated filmography.)

2. Search Example 2 in *Library Literature* was about chat services as part of the Reference function. Go to the database, reproduce that search, and then compare the results with what you get by simply typing in: Reference chat as a Keyword search. There are several things to notice about this. For one thing, you learn that Wilson does not automatically search multiple word entries as a phrase: it simply looks for both words, in any order, and not necessarily

together. To take a devil's advocate role here: aren't these results just as good as the ones we retrieved with a much more elaborate search? Carefully compare the results—are there any records not found in the second set (the keyword search) that really would have been bad to miss? Not to undermine the more sophisticated techniques that this text has been encouraging you to learn, but the reality is that most people simply keyword search, and in some—perhaps many—cases, that approach does the job. When it doesn't work, you need to be ready with better techniques. Message: don't get rigid, either about what you're seeing, or what you're doing.

3. Say that you want to catch up on what's being written about information literacy classes in either college or school libraries (whichever you are more interested in). Rather than using the Thesaurus, you simply do an Advanced search on "information literacy" in Keyword, AND "college" [or "school"] in Subject, and let *Library Literature* do the work of informing you about appropriate subject headings by observing what comes up in the "New Search by Subject" and "Narrow These Results" by Subject in the Results screen. What is the Thesaurus term for this kind of teaching? Pick a subject heading under the Narrow suggestions and see how it affects the number of results. Now choose the same heading as a "New" search, and note again the number of results. Use the "Search within these results" box to add a keyword, such as "evaluation," to your last search. Finally, go into the Thesaurus and look up "information literacy." What do you find?

4. One last quick search in *Library Literature*: a growing topic in database searching is the idea of federated searching, that is, searching several databases at once through one Google-box-type interface. One wonders if such a thing will mean the end of teaching people how to search. See what *Library Literature* has to offer on federated searching and teaching.

5. In the first Search Example for ERIC, we used a very structured approach, carefully checking the indexes and Thesaurus entries before deciding on our search terms and setting up the strategy. Compare that with the following much less structured approach. Try simply searching:

    Teaching the deaf—as Keywords

    This search results in a great many more records (more than 1,000). Look over the results; some of the results are on target, but others probably aren't. While our search recall has gone up, the precision of our search has gone down. If you had started with this search, what would you immediately start doing to cut down and focus the results?

6. Your sister recently had a baby, and is upset because the baby's sleep patterns aren't settling down at all. She wonders if the baby has some kind of sleep disorder, and if it's going to affect her (the baby's, not the mother's!) development.

    You start by going to *PsycINFO* and typing in "sleep disorders."

    That maps directly to a subject heading, but you're curious about what might be included "under" it, or near it in the Thesaurus list. Click the subject heading to find out.

Now look down through the list. Hmm—"Sleep Onset"—that's kind of the problem. What happens if you click that? Hey—look down there! "Sleep Wake Cycle"! That sounds good. Select that (deselect Sleep Onset), and click its Explode box. Click the Continue button (top of screen).

Next term: type "infants" in the search box, and see what comes up on the Mapping Display.

"Infant Development"—that looks good. Select that and Continue.

Now combine those two searches by ANDing their search set numbers together.

Do you like the results?

7. A friend has a child with Aspergers syndrome (a form of autism) and is worried about how this could affect his verbal and writing skills, that is, his language development. In *PsycINFO*, what happens if you search and then combine Aspergers Syndrome and Language Development? (You don't get very many.) Maybe we could "widen our net" on the "Language" aspect of the search. Type in the broad term Language, and see if the Mapping Display offers more subject headings we could use. Choose several. Now combine this new (very large!) set with the Aspergers Syndrome set. It should result in more results than before.

8. As you compare what is discussed about these databases with what you see on your screen, you will undoubtedly spot additional features or functionality not mentioned here. Figure out what these other features or functions do, and ask yourself why they were included. Think about "which users would most benefit from [feature X]?," and how you might market it to them (i.e., get them to use it). Discussing this as a class or in small groups will help to generate more ideas as you bounce things off one another.

Consider this Exercise as applying to every chapter that discusses specific databases in this book.

Notes

1. As of June 2008, users can choose from four color schemes for the Wilson interface: blue (the default), red, green, and orange.

2. http://www.lib.msu.edu/corby/education/doe.htm. Should this site become inactive, a Web search on "EBSS and ERIC" should find its new home fairly quickly.

3. If you do this in the Ovid interface, you'll find that the list of fields is far longer than the list provided at the beginning of the discussion of *PsycINFO*. This list represents the searchable field structure devised by Ovid; to be totally honest, I can only make a reasonable guess that a "mapping" process must take place to make the data supplied by the APA work with this structure.

5
Databases for Science and Medicine

The databases in this chapter, besides being intrinsically interesting and well-crafted systems, provide a view into their respective disciplines that goes beyond their content. Obviously, medical databases index medical material, and science databases index scientific publications. But the two subject databases considered here are functionally quite different, and I believe that the difference reflects a basic tenet of each discipline.

Every discipline or profession has its own language: a specialized vocabulary is one of the things that unites and defines a profession (think of all the jargon we use in libraries). In almost no area is this truer than in medicine: a major part of the study of medicine is mastery of its language. The language is crucial, and *the* medical database, MEDLINE (see later for description of MEDLINE), reflects this. One of the key components of MEDLINE records is their detailed system of subject headings and subheadings for *terms*, painstakingly applied by trained professionals. The "Mapping" functionality of the Ovid interface to MEDLINE reflects this emphasis on subject terms: whatever word or phrase you enter, the "Map to Subject Headings" function will do its best to steer you to the appropriate subject headings. Consider this, and see if you agree: the basic tenet here as a focus on *"what."* Medical terms represent *"what:"* what organ, what condition, what symptoms, what drugs, and what outcome.

In contrast, the approach taken by the scientist who developed the *Science Citation Index* (and later similar indexes for the other disciplines), was that the *citations* were of paramount importance: the references associated with scientific papers. To me, this represents *who.* Who was cited? *Who* was citing? Although used in other organizations, the *Science Citation Index* is a very *academic* product, and in academia, a great deal rides on who you are (which you establish by publishing your work), and who has recognized your work (by citing it). You will find that the *Web of Science* citation indexes do not use subject headings (in the sense we've seen so far) at all.

Another way this difference in emphasis (terms or what versus who) is reflected in the functionality of each database is the way they arrive at "Related records." In PubMed, an algorithm based on words (what) identifies related records. In the citation indexes, shared citations (who) identify related records.

As you work through this chapter and become familiar with these databases, keep this idea in the back of your mind: that medicine is focused on what (terms), and the citation indexes are focused on who. See if you spot additional aspects of the databases' functionality to support it.

MEDLINE and PubMed

MEDLINE

It's easy to know where to start a consideration of medical databases: it has to be with the MEDLINE database from the National Library of Medicine. The difficulty is knowing where to stop: MEDLINE is a huge, immensely detailed, highly specific, and sophisticated resource for an elite professional field. Let me declare right here: this text is not going to attempt to teach you how to search MEDLINE. If you get a job in a medical library, you will receive thorough training from professionals in the field. Instead, in the spirit that you can achieve *something* reasonable, no matter what the subject area, by employing the same basic strategy (i.e., engaging in a reference interview, using your searching techniques, and keeping your eyes open), what follows will be a demystifying look at MEDLINE as offered through the database vendor Ovid. We'll then take a look at a freely accessible version of MEDLINE on the Internet, where it is available through a resource called *PubMed*. This situation is almost unique in the database world, in that the same high-quality content is available both by subscription and for free, and thus definitely merits our attention.

About MEDLINE

MEDLINE (Medical Literature Analysis and Retrieval System Online), is a product of the U.S. National Library of Medicine (NLM), which describes it as their "premier bibliographic database" containing "approximately 13 million references to journal articles" in the life sciences, with a focus on biomedicine. Date coverage is generally from 1966 to the present, although some older material is also available. MEDLINE is a journal citation database (many citations offer links to full text, but the database itself does not contain full text), and international in scope: it selectively covers "approximately 5,200" journals from all over the world, in thirty-seven languages. The NLM enhances records from non–English-language journals by supplying translated article titles; English translations of abstracts are dependent on the article authors supplying them. The database is updated daily, from Tuesday through Saturday, with the addition of "between 2,000–4,000" new citations each day. (Additions "each day" does not mean, however, that the contents of a journal published yesterday will be indexed and added today. The kind of detailed processing required to create full MEDLINE records does take some time.) In 2007 alone, over 670,000 references were added to the database. This phenomenal effort is the result of a distribution of labor among the NLM, its international partners, and collaborating institutions (U.S. National Library of Medicine 2008, *MEDLINE Fact Sheet*).

A key distinguishing feature of MEDLINE is its carefully crafted thesaurus, known as *MeSH*, for *Medical Subject Headings*. (Think of it as the Library of Congress Subject headings [LCSH] for the medical world.) This highly developed, hierarchical system of subject headings is also the work of the NLM, which has a whole branch devoted to continuous maintenance, revision, and updating of the MeSH vocabulary. The impression one gets is that this is a dynamic system, continually growing and changing in response to developments in scientific and medical research and practice. Statistics about MeSH are impressive: the 2008 MeSH contained 24,767 subject headings, augmented with 97,000 *see* references, and more than 172,000 other entry points (U.S. National Library of Medicine 2007, *Medical Subject Heading (MeSH) Fact Sheet*).

As with any thesaurus, of course, these terms are employed by highly trained indexers to describe and provide entry points for each article. As a user of this database, one important thing for you to remember is that indexers are instructed always to choose the most specific terms available. Although the MeSH system is hierarchical,[1] with broad terms such as "Digestive System Diseases" at the most general level, if an article is discussing a specific malady, such as Crohns Disease, only the more specific term will be applied as a heading. All the layers of headings between Digestive System Diseases and Crohns Disease (e.g., Gastrointestinal Diseases, Gastroenteritis, and Inflammatory Bowel Diseases) would *not* appear as additional subject headings.

Accessing MEDLINE

The MEDLINE database is leased to several different vendors, including OCLC's FirstSearch, Ovid, and Cambridge Scientific Abstracts (CSA). At one institution, you may well find you have several "flavors" of MEDLINE available to you. In addition, the MEDLINE database is also available as part of PubMed, a free Web resource at http://pubmed.gov, which we will look at in the next section. Since we are looking at MEDLINE through the Ovid interface, which we saw in Chapter 4 for *PsycINFO*, the initial search screen should look very familiar (Figure 5.1).

As in *PsycINFO*, the limit options represent the most frequently used types of limits, such as articles dealing with human (rather than animal) subjects, English language, articles with abstracts, or full text. A couple of the limits for MEDLINE are specific to the database: the option to limit to Core Clinical Journals, or to Review Articles, indicating the importance of these types of publications to this subject area. Many more options are available on the full Limits screen, accessible via the Additional Limits button (grayed out in Figure 5.1 because no search has yet been performed).

Stepping through a MEDLINE Search

The search topic for our walk through MEDLINE is: prevention and control of heart attacks in women who are adults, but not yet classified as middle aged (e.g., ages 19–44). We'll start by simply entering "heart attack"

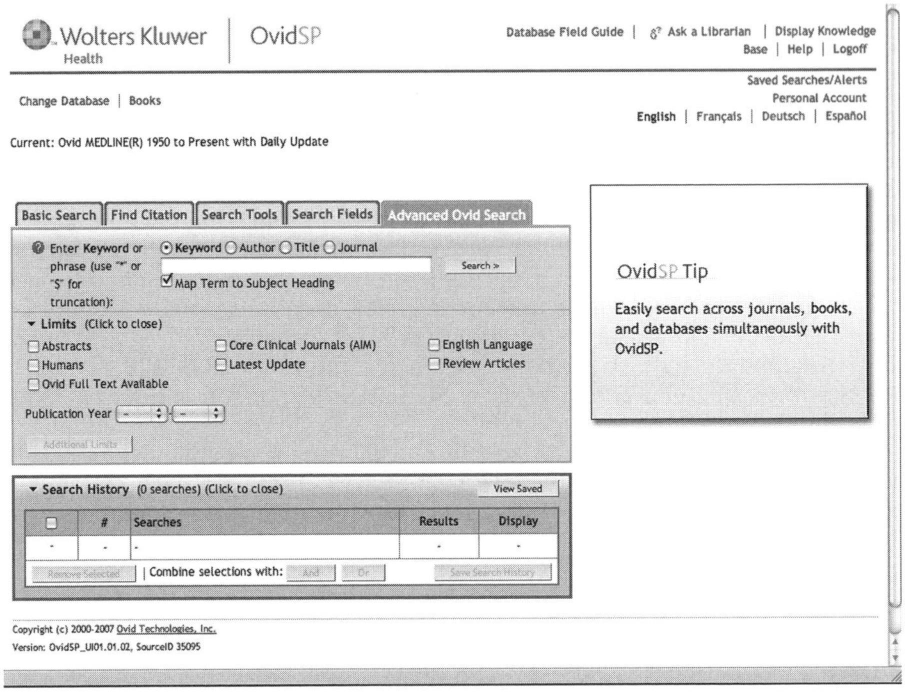

Fig. 5.1. Ovid MEDLINE, initial advanced search screen. OVID interface © OvidSP, 2008 Wolters Kluwer Health | Ovid.

as our search—not a very professional term, but again the excellent "map to subject headings" feature will take care of us.

Select a Subject Heading

A heart attack is, of course, known in the medical profession as a *myocardial infarction*. We'll choose that term (and try not to be distracted, as usually happens, with the other interesting and related terms), and mark both the Explode and Focus options (Figure 5.2). (These options were explained in the discussion of *PsycINFO*, and also appear in the Hints section of this screen.) We'll choose not to Include All Subheadings at this point, and Continue. By not including all the subheadings, we'll get offered the Subheadings screen to choose the ones of interest.

Select Subheadings

The Subheadings screen is something new that we didn't see in *PsycINFO*, and it provides a wonderful and fascinating glimpse into the medical worldview. The subheadings system is a standardized list of terms that reflect all the facets of how the medical profession approaches tasks or topics: does it have to do with blood? Is it a complication? A therapy (by diet or drug or in general)? Is it about epidemiology? Genetics? Mortality? Surgery? All the possible aspects are provided for in the subheadings system, but what is displayed in this screen represents only those subheadings that can be meaningfully used with the current MeSH heading (in this case, Myocardial Infarction). You can learn a great deal by simply studying the list (Figure 5.3).

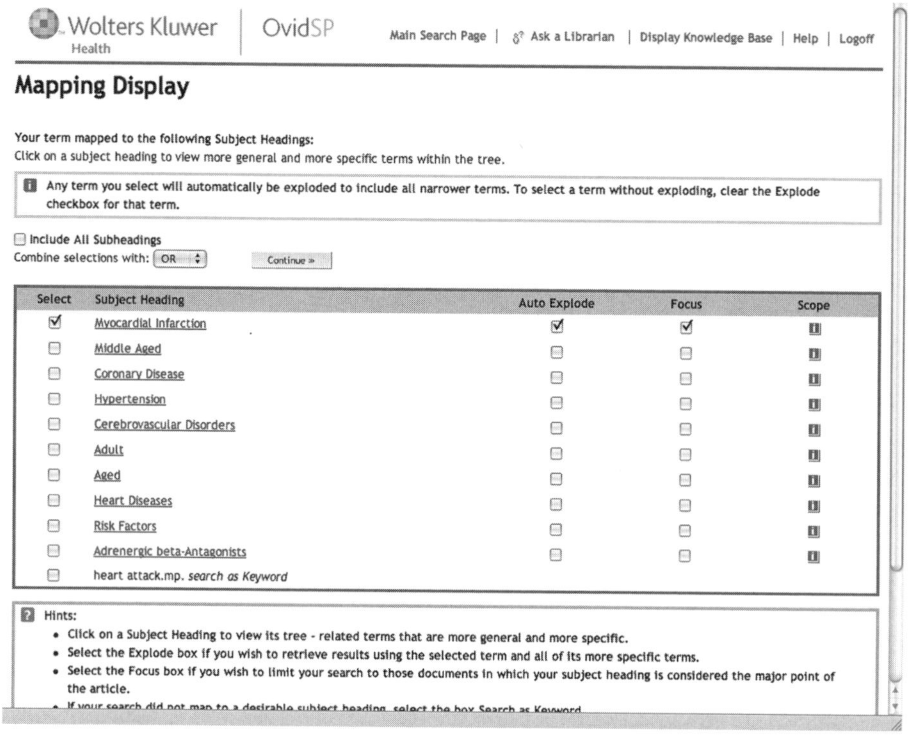

Fig. 5.2. Ovid Mapping Display: suggested MeSH subject headings for "heart attack." OVID interface © OvidSP, 2008 Wolters Kluwer Health | Ovid.

The main intent of the subheadings system is to provide a very efficient way to get at precisely the aspect of a topic you might be looking for, such as "Prevention & Control." Without doing a second search on the "prevention" idea, we can, in one search, retrieve only those articles that deal with prevention and control of myocardial infarction. (Note that you can also choose multiple subheadings, to retrieve several aspects of your main search term at once.)

Apply Limits

We get our results (over 3,000 of them), but we haven't gotten at the "adult females" aspect of our search yet. Time to visit the Additional Limits screen, where we can choose Female, and Age Group Adult (19 to 44 years; Figure 5.4). Although it's tempting immediately to limit to English language, try to hold off until you've looked over the results. Titles are offered in translation, and if the perfect article happens to be in German, surely in our globalized, multicultural world, you can find someone who can translate for you? In any event, don't eliminate the possibility without looking through the results first.

As you can see, the Limit screen is quite long: the screen shot in Figure 5.4 is a partial shot, to show just those limits we used ("Female" toward the top of the figure, and "Age Groups" below on the left). While you're at this screen, note also all the other limits, such as "Clinical Queries,"[2] so specific to this database. Handily, your Search History box is included on this Additional Limits display, to remind you of what you are limiting

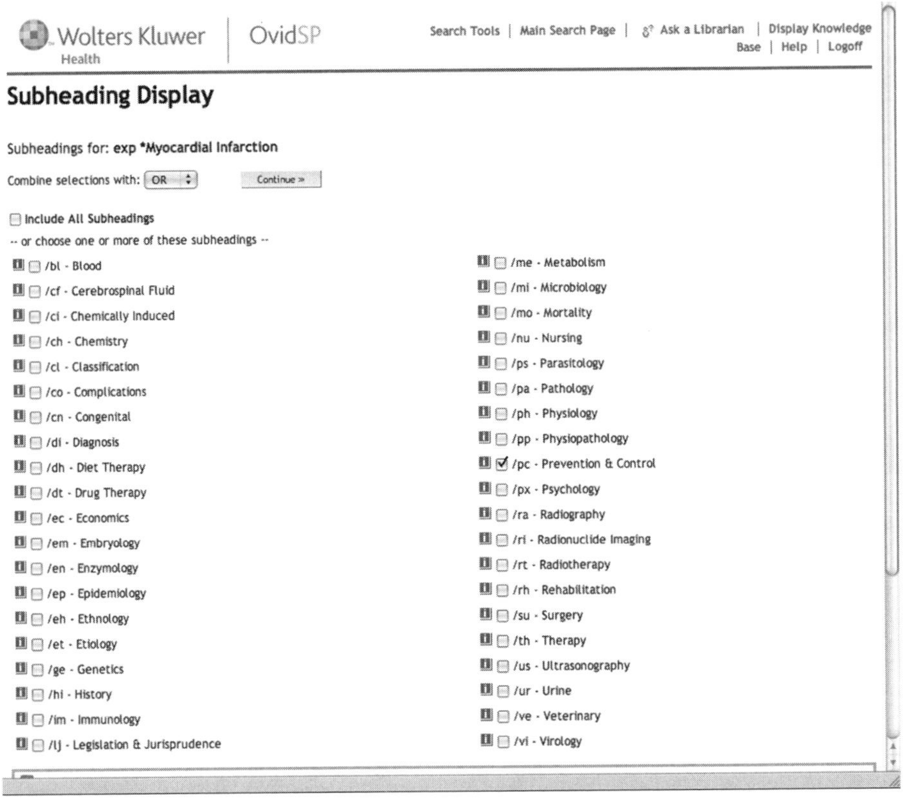

Fig. 5.3. Subheadings display for "Myocardial Infarction." OVID interface © OvidSP, 2008 Wolters Kluwer Health | Ovid.

(as your short-term memory begins to go, you appreciate touches like this).

Results

After limiting, our results are down to a somewhat more manageable 272. As you can see even in the first few results, while all of them are scholarly, the technical level of the sources varies. Some of these articles definitely will be accessible only to specialists (e.g., number 3), and others, such as the one from the *Journal—Oklahoma State Medical Association* (number 4), are more likely to be understood by an educated lay audience (Figure 5.5).

Overall, however, the results make clear that MEDLINE is very much a professional tool. Medical librarians can go through weeks of training, learning all of its functions and what they mean. As mentioned at the beginning, this brief introduction is simply meant to give you exposure to one of the most sophisticated databases on the market (both in functionality and in content), and to show that if you really had to, you could certainly go in and perform *some* kind of search here. For general consumer health queries, however, there are better choices: subscription databases such as *Health Reference Center* (from Gale-Cengage Learning), or free government Web sites such as MedlinePlus.gov (also a product of the NLM).

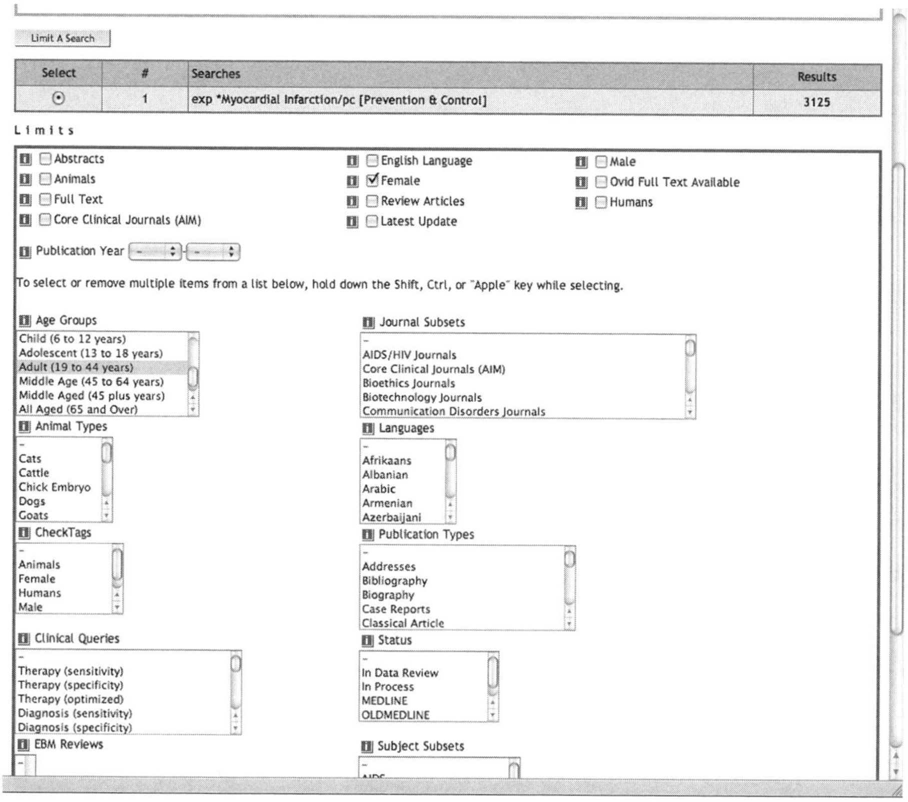

Fig. 5.4. Partial view of the Additional Limits screen. OVID interface © OvidSP, 2008 Wolters Kluwer Health | Ovid.

PubMed: More than MEDLINE

On to PubMed (http://pubmed.gov). As a database of medical citations, you could think of PubMed as what you'd get if databases were like hamburgers: "give me MEDLINE—and super size it!" MEDLINE is the main component of PubMed, but PubMed offers a number of groups of additional material, notably:

- Older (pre-1966) citations, known as OLDMEDLINE.

- Citations for articles in MEDLINE journals that were not selected for indexing in the medical database due to their non–life sciences content.

- "In-process" citations: records that have not yet had full MeSH indexing applied (U.S. National Library of Medicine 2008, *What's the Difference*).[3]

PubMed is much more than a super-sized database of medical citations, however. It is a portal to databases from the National Center for Biotechnology Information (NCBI)—of gene sequences, molecular structures, etc.—and to "Services" such as citation matchers and a special interface for clinical queries, as well as "Related Resources" such as Clinical Trials and Consumer Health information. It's huge, first-class, professional information,

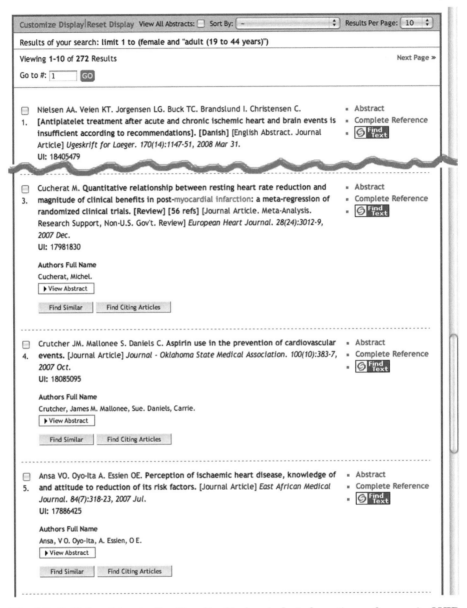

Fig. 5.5. Initial entries in the Results display (selected portions of screen). OVID interface © OvidSP, 2008 Wolters Kluwer Health | Ovid.

and it is freely available on the Web. As with MEDLINE, I'm afraid we won't do more than touch the surface of the possibilities here, but at least you'll now know that it exists, and you can explore further when and if the need should arise.

Introduction to the PubMed Interface

Let's take a look (Figure 5.6).[4]

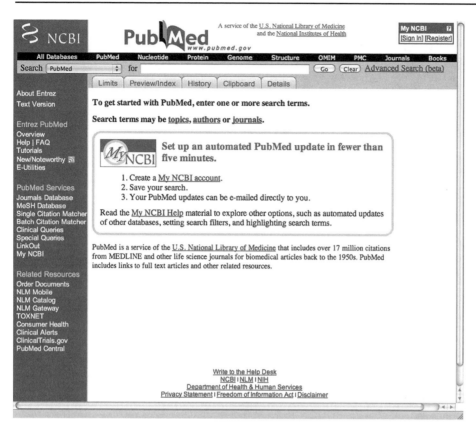

Fig. 5.6. Initial PubMed screen, as of June 2008.

Sidebar 5.1

Beware the trap of expectation that because PubMed is a free Web resource, it will somehow be "easier" than MEDLINE; that the content will be "easier." Not in the slightest. As noted in the opening discussion of this section, PubMed contains the MEDLINE database content, plus additional journals not indexed by MEDLINE, and links to advanced scientific resources such as the NCBI genome databases. In other words, despite the fact that this is a free Web resource that is open to the world, this is probably not the place for the average mortal to try and find an answer to a medical question. If you are working with a health professional, researcher, or student in the health sciences, yes, this is the place. If you want to help your mom or your neighbor find some health information, go to MedlinePlus.gov.

Similarities to Ovid's MEDLINE

If you look around, many of the features in Ovid's MEDLINE can be found here. Under the Limits tab is the opportunity to limit to a particular Author or Journal title, as well as the Full Text or abstracts options, Dates, Humans or Animals, Gender, Languages, Subsets, Type of Article, and Ages (Figure 5.7). The Preview/Index tab provides the ability to search

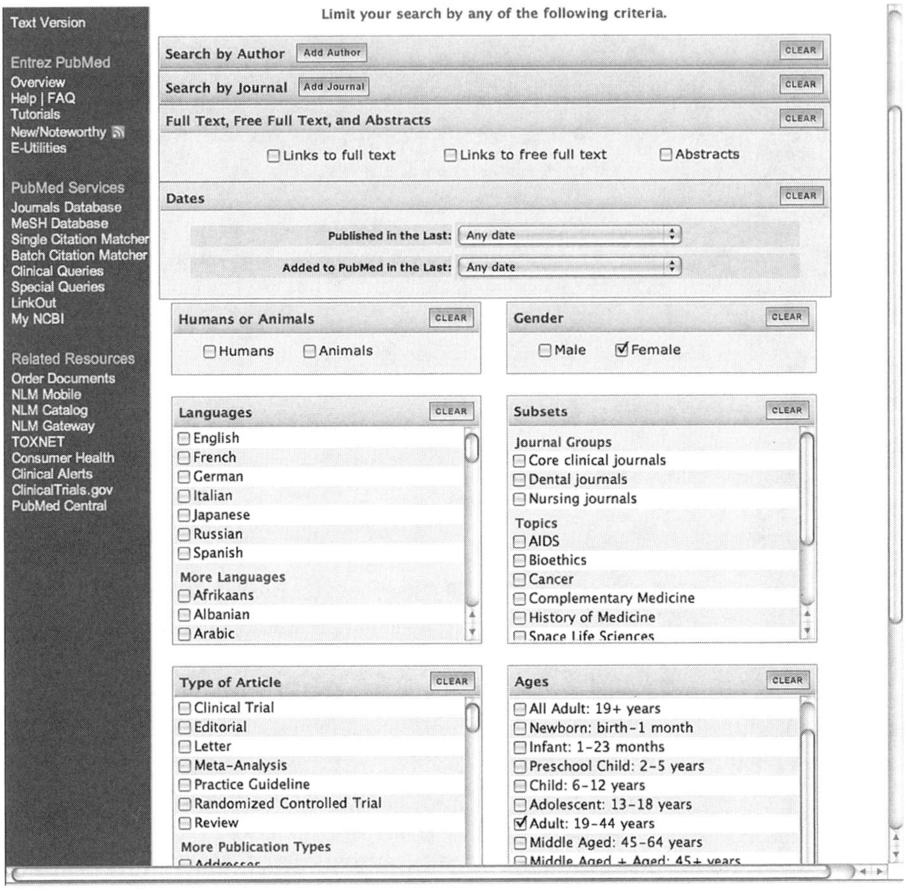

Fig. 5.7. Limits in PubMed, as of June 2008.

in a particular field, and the History tab provides a list of previous searches, similar to the Ovid interface. In the drop-down list of Search options (above the Limits, Preview/Index, and other tabs), and linked on the sidebar under PubMed Services, is access to the MeSH Database, giving you access to the thesaurus to explore terms and their relationships.

Unique PubMed Features

Other features are unique to the PubMed interface and are quite handy, such as a spell-checking feature that "suggests alternative spellings for PubMed search terms that may include misspellings" (NCBI PubMed, 2008). In the results lists, there are additional links to Related Articles and Links (these vary depending on the article, but take advantage of the other NCBI resources whenever possible). The Related Articles feature in PubMed makes use of a word-analysis algorithm, which is very effective: the results are almost always quite useful. In the second half of this chapter, when we look at the *Web of Science* citation databases, we'll see a different way of judging and retrieving "related" articles.

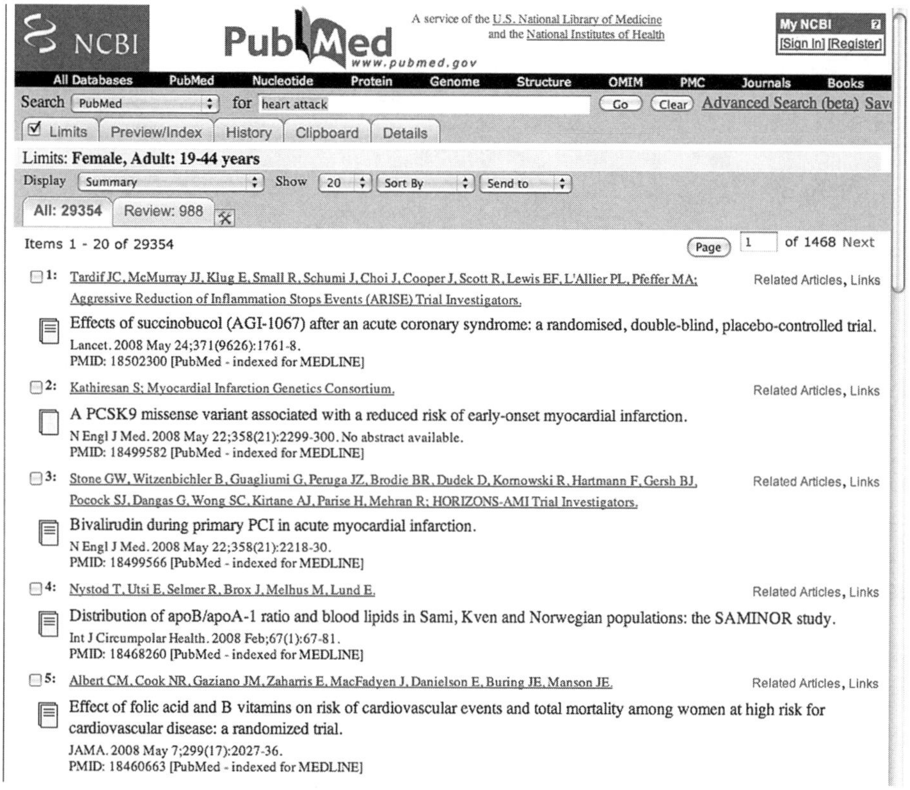

Fig. 5.8. Search results in PubMed, as of June 2008.

Running the Same Search in PubMed

Let's try our same search again: "prevention and control of heart attacks in adult women." We can basically set up the same search in PubMed, using the Limits tab to select our age group and gender limits. Then, because we are laypeople who don't know any better, we still search on the layman's term "heart attack." Because PubMed performs "automatic term matching,"[5] the same process that we saw explicitly in Ovid's MEDLINE is carried out here as well, behind the scenes, so that all of our results are, seemingly magically, exactly on the appropriate professional term "Myocardial Infarction," which is automatically exploded to include the more specific terms Myocardial Stunning and Shock, Cardiogenic. However, PubMed also searches the terms "heart attack," and "myocardial infarction" in several other ways, which has a significant effect on the size of the result set: this search has retrieved close to 30,000 hits—a daunting number (Figure 5.8). Information on the Details tab and a careful reading of the Help assist in explaining why.

Search Details

The Details tab provides a "query translation," an explicit rendition of how your search was executed (although you may still need the Help to translate the "translation"!) In this case, five variations of the search were "ORed" together:

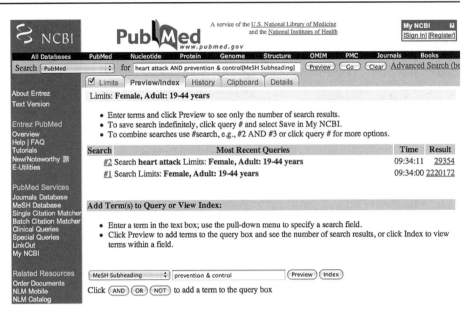

Fig. 5.9. Using the Preview/Index tab to add a Subheading, as of June 2008.

1. Myocardial infarction was searched as a MeSH subject heading.

2. The individual terms *myocardial* and *infarction* were searched as a Boolean AND search in "All Fields," that is, any text field.

3. The phrase "myocardial infarction" was searched in "All Fields."

4. The terms *heart* and *attack* were searched as a Boolean AND search in "All Fields."

5. The phrase "heart attack" was also searched in "All Fields."

The effect of all these ORed searches probably accounts for most of the dramatic increase. We also weren't led through the screens of subject headings (see Figure 5.2) and subheadings (see Figure 5.3), we didn't have the opportunity to "Focus," or to choose just one subheading: "Prevention & Control." But because we now know something about how the MEDLINE database is set up and have an idea of what MeSH Subheadings are, we can at least apply our one desired subheading.

Applying a Subheading in PubMed

The subheading functionality lives under the Preview/Index tab: we can go there, select the appropriate field, and put in an appropriate value (Figure 5.9).

Limiting to Review Articles

Applying the one subheading definitely cuts down and focuses the number of results. The Review tab also helps: it shows only the results that are review articles, leaving us with 158 results (Figure 5.10).

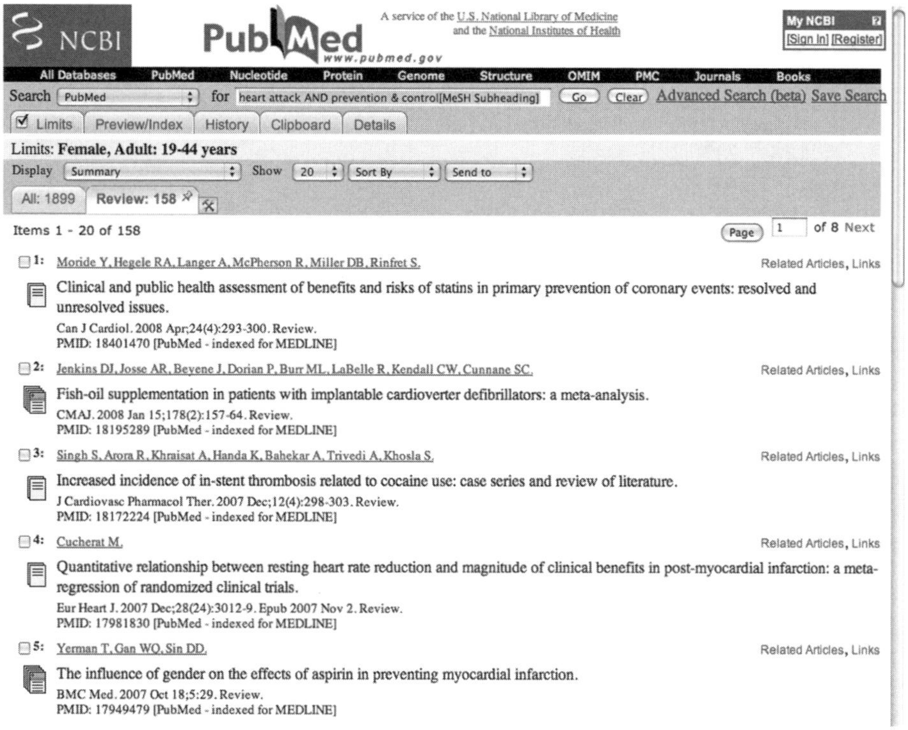

Fig. 5.10. Revised result set, as of June 2008.

Larger Result Sets in PubMed

The total number of results (1,899) is still higher than the number we retrieved in Ovid's MEDLINE. The records with MeSH headings and subheadings have been reduced, but the ORed text word searches are still driving the overall results up. It is possible to achieve something more like our MEDLINE search and results numbers by employing more Limits, as you'll see in the Exercises, but it's useful have an "everyman" experience first, and experience the database as ordinary users would. PubMed is more than MEDLINE, as this example has amply demonstrated.

Concern about Large Results Sets

My only (old-fashioned?) concern is that medical professionals will simply accept these huge numbers of (possibly) not the most precise results, because of their experience with Web search engines: thousands of results, that's the way it is. Will medical professionals notice, or bother to learn how to make use of, these filtering and refining features? Usually they are not trained as searchers; they are trained as doctors and nurses. Our medical librarians report that PubMed is increasingly popular, however, so evidently users are finding it satisfactory. One might speculate that mastery of the language of medicine, and usually knowing what they are looking for (rather than a broad, exploratory search such as a layman might do), are key factors that allow medical professionals to compose effective searches without sophisticated search techniques. For the layman, adding more terms to the query (e.g., simply entering a word search on "heart attacks and women and

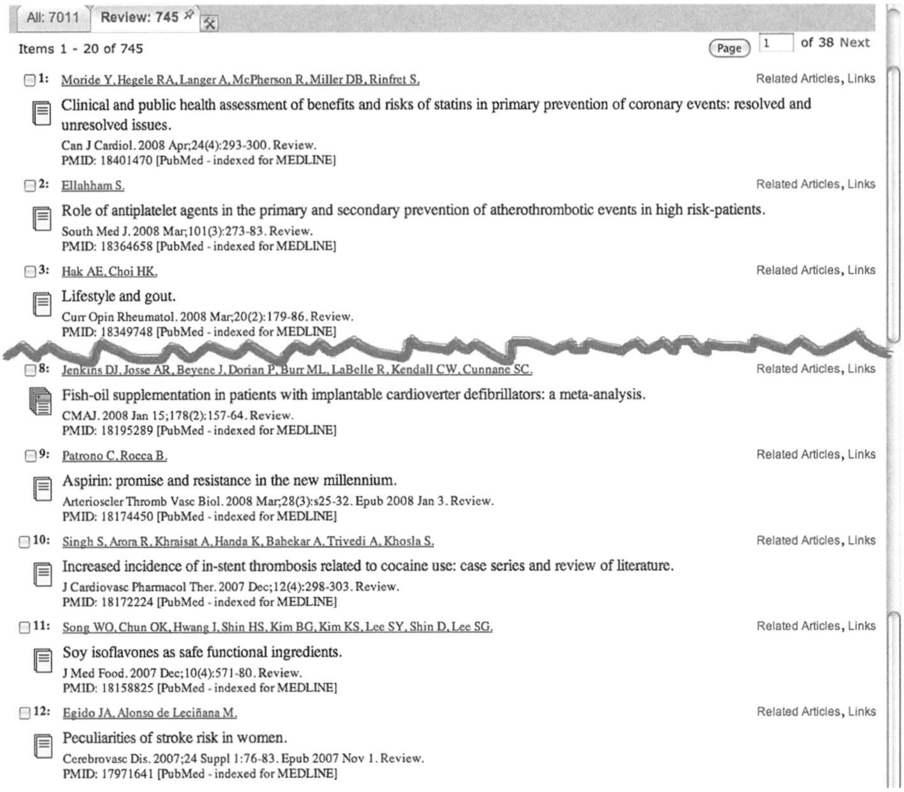

Fig. 5.11. Doing the search without using features, by ANDing terms in the search box, as of June 2008.

prevention") still produces results sets of staggering size (recall), but acceptable precision, especially if you focus on the first couple of screens of Review articles (Figure 5.11).

Output in MEDLINE and PubMed

Ovid Results Manager

The Ovid version of MEDLINE has the same Results Manager that we saw in the discussion of *PsycINFO*, with the same functionality: formatting for printing, e-mail, save, and order (through the local library's Interlibrary Loan unit).

PubMed: Send to and Order

PubMed is similar, with the *Send to* drop-down in the Results display offering choices such as text, file (save-type functions), printer, clipboard, e-mail, a nifty RSS feed option, and order. *Order* is where things can get interesting. Although it is now possible for libraries to create customized access to PubMed, if such access has not been set up, or a user still uses the public URL to go to PubMed, the Order function will take the user to an NLM function known as Loansome Doc (cute or what?), which has nothing to do with the local library and will charge the user for document delivery. About here is where librarians get rather anxious about users' preference for PubMed: although it is now possible to integrate PubMed with local customized link resolvers (e.g., SFX), this kind of personalized access is dependent on people using a special URL. If the "right" URL isn't used (and "pubmed.gov" is pretty easy to remember and type in), even though the user may be sitting right in the library not 10 feet from the Interlibrary Loan office, there is no way for the non-customized PubMed to convey the information that a local, lower or possibly no-cost, Interlibrary Loan service is available.

Getting to the Full Text

Full Text in Ovid MEDLINE

Many subscription databases that do not provide full text themselves now work with "bridging" services such as *SFX*, a link resolver that will make the connection between the citation database and other local resources. Added to the bibliographic database, these services offer a menu of choices, depending on availability, such as another database that does provide the full text, the local catalog (for hard copy), or a link to the local Interlibrary Loan system. The Ovid databases can be integrated with SFX.

Full Text in PubMed

Accessing full text in PubMed raises some of the same issues as Interlibrary Loan. The non-customized version of PubMed provides as many links as it can to full text, some of which are free (titles in the collection called PubMed Central and other free full text), and others that are subscription based. If subscription based, PubMed will link directly to the publisher's Web site for the journal (via the "Links—LinkOut" link). If this is how the local library also accesses the electronic version of that particular journal, and the user is onsite, access from the library or organization is thus "recognized" by the site, and the user will get the article he or she needs. If the library accesses that journal through an aggregator service, however, there is no way to convey that information in the non-customized PubMed, and the user would be misled into thinking that either the material was not accessible, or only available at a cost. If the library has set up customized access, citations will include links to the local "bridging" service, providing users with as much functionality as the subscription version of the database. Now *that's* food for thought, indeed.

Quick Recap

MEDLINE is the pre-eminent journal citation database of medical literature and is the product of the U.S. National Library of Medicine (NLM) and its collaborating partners. Date coverage is generally from 1966 to the present, although some older material is also available. Over 5,000 journals from all over the world, in thirty-seven languages, are covered. A key component of MEDLINE is its thesaurus, known as "MeSH" (*M*edical *S*ubject *H*eadings). MEDLINE indexers always choose the most specific terms available from MeSH. The MEDLINE database is available through many different commercial database vendors; the Ovid version, discussed here, encourages the use of subject headings, subheadings, and limits, as well as providing refining features on the results pages. MEDLINE data is also freely available on the Internet, as part of PubMed.

PubMed is part of a portal to databases provided by the National Center for Biotechnology Information (NCBI). PubMed includes additional material not found in MEDLINE. This additional material, the way searches are interpreted, and an interface that makes some search functions less apparent, tend to make PubMed result sets much larger than MEDLINE's. Most of the MEDLINE functionality (limits, thesaurus, field searching, etc.) can be found in PubMed if you know where to look. PubMed also has a spelling suggestion feature and Related Articles links not found in MEDLINE. PubMed offers its own fee-based document delivery service and links to full text. This worries librarians at institutions that provide Interlibrary Loan and online journal subscriptions, because users may not realize that they have the same services available to them at no charge. It is possible to customize PubMed so that it provides linking services to local resources, but users must then access PubMed using the institutional link, which can be hard to train users to do.

The *Web of Science* and the Citation Indexes

Now we're going to take off the stethoscope, and get into the mindset of the scholarly academic researcher. Think of yourself as Joe(sephine) Bloggs, Ph.D. When you write a scholarly paper, it almost always involves a literature review, or at least a process of consulting previous articles that you can quote to support various points throughout your paper. You are drawing on past knowledge in this way, building on the ideas of previous researchers and taking them further, or moving tangentially. If we look at your list of references, we can trace the "lineage" of your ideas back in time. For J. Bloggs, undergraduate, this is still a common and accepted way to get started writing a paper: to find a recent work that is related to what you want to write about and trace its references. This is fairly easily done, because the references provide the information about the other articles (accurately, you hope). However . . . there are works in every field that achieve the status of classic papers, which are cited by subsequent authors over and over again. What if you wanted to trace that evolution, that is, all the people who had *cited* a particular paper or book? A professor could hand you a classic work from 1965, and tell you "that's the authoritative work in this area." What do you do with that? A place to start would be to see who has cited the work recently, and in what context. You want to trace the evolution of those ideas *forward* in time. How in the world could you do that?

History of the Citation Indexes

The concept of tracking and indexing not just articles, but the references associated with those articles, was the brainchild of Dr. Eugene Garfield, founder of the Institute for Scientific Information (ISI). From a concept first outlined in a 1955 article in *Science*, the oversize, print, multivolume sets known as the *Science Citation Index* (1963–), the *Social Science Citation Index* (1965–), and the *Arts & Humanities Citation Index* (1976–), have been providing researchers with a unique and powerful way to trace the evolution and impact of ideas over time. As Carol Tenopir (2001) put it: "The power of citation searching lies in the capacity to take a seminal article and uncover who the author was influenced by (who was cited) and go forward in time to discover how that seminal research affected newer works (who is citing it)." Now it was possible, albeit somewhat physically challenging (because of the size of the volumes: huge—and the size of the print: tiny) to trace "who is citing whom." As technology progressed, the Citation Indexes moved to CD-ROM, and then to the Web. If ever a tool benefited from going electronic, it is this one. The whole concept of what a citation index allows one to do seems much easier to grasp and to explain to others in an online realization. It also makes possible many enhanced features, which we'll explore as we work through the database functionality.

Citation Indexes in the *Web of Science*

In 1992, ISI was acquired by The Thomson Corporation, which has continued to take the citation index concept from strength to strength. The Science, Social Science, and Arts and Humanities Citation Indexes are now all part of the *Web of Science*, which itself is one element in an overall *ISI Web of Knowledge*—the total suite of research tools offered by Thomson, now Thomson Reuters.

Web of Science Content

In all, the *Web of Science* indexing and abstracting tools cover more than 10,000 research publications from around the world, with the addition of 700 regional journals in May 2008 (Thomson Scientific Press Room, 2008). More and more years of backfiles have been added to the database, steadily expanding coverage both back in time as well as forward, with weekly updates. Depending on the subscription package, coverage can go back as early as 1900 for the Science Citation Index, and 1956 for the Social Sciences. The institutions in my purview have opted for the "1973-to-present" package. What this date cutoff refers to is how far back the records for the *journal articles* go; under a "1973 to the present" subscription, you can still search a *cited reference* from any time period, but you will only be allowed to see records for articles citing that reference that were published from 1973 to the present. Keep remembering that this database has a dual nature: the cited references records, which can be from any date, and the journal article records, which are restricted depending on the subscription.

As you might imagine (if you haven't, you should), an undertaking of this size and complexity involves thousands of workers, incredible feats of programming, etc. It is big, and frankly, it's expensive. You are likely to find it only at major research libraries, but it's worth being aware of as part of your overall understanding of how research works, and how our current knowledge builds on past work. If you work in an academic environment, this is part of understanding the scholarly animal.

An Index Focused on Citations

The unique feature that the citation indexes introduced was to load the list of cited references—the bibliography—for each article, in addition to the bibliographic record (author, title, journal, year, etc.). The cited references are associated with their articles, but each reference is also recorded in the database as an independent, "cited reference" record, which can be searched and used in various ways. Note too that although the type of source material indexed in the *Web of Science* databases is only journal articles (i.e., not books, technical reports, etc.), the references associated with a source article can be drawn from any type of material, and thus cited reference records can be articles, but also books, reports, unpublished papers, or whatever the author has cited. (If your brain is starting to hurt, don't despair: it's actually surprisingly clear and easy once you get into the database.) Again, note the dual nature of this database: source article records, and cited reference records for items referred to by the source articles. What can you do with all this information?

Regular Topic Searches; Tracing *Back* by Means of Citations

You can use the *Web of Science* databases just like any other indexing and abstracting product: to perform a keyword search to find articles on a particular topic, to find articles by a particular author, or to track down a specific article when you have only partial information. The added twist is that having identified one or more articles, you can also see the list of references from each article, and by looking at this bibliography, you can, if the items are linked (to other journal article records in the database), immediately start tracking the ideas in a current article *back* in time.

Tracing Forward and Tracking Citations for Tenure

In addition, because you can search cited references, you can see which subsequent articles have cited a particular work. As mentioned previously, you can track the development and influence of an idea from when it was first published, to now—a way to bring research forward, from old to new. In addition to helping students and scholars in the process of writing papers, citation indices also provide important—even crucial—functionality. Researchers can use this database to find out who is citing their work, and in what context. The crucial element is that in the "publish-or-perish" scramble for academic tenure in the United States, faculty who are up for tenure can use these databases to show how many times their papers have been cited by others, which can be a key factor in proving their eligibility for tenure.

Relating Records by Citations

As mentioned previously, in electronic form, the data captured by the citation indexes can be exploited in new and useful ways that are impossible in the print version. The *Web of Science* databases have built in a feature called *Related Records*. Related records are articles that have at least one cited reference in common. Articles that share four, five, or more references are likely to be discussing the same topics. This is a completely different way to locate relevant papers on a topic; material that might not have been found with a traditional author or subject search. Think of it: this is about as close to "searching by concept" as opposed to "searching by words" as you can get. True, you start with a word search (to produce the initial results), but then, based on shared references—shared *concepts*—you can move into related intellectual territory. This is a powerful concept and tool.

Additional Differences in Available Fields

Present: The Address Field

The article records in the *Web of Science* databases also include an Address field, used to record where each author works. This is useful in several ways. From a librarian's perspective, it provides a quick way to get a sense of the total output of a particular department or person (if they publish in journals covered by the *Web of Science*), and what sorts of things they write about. Used in conjunction with the Analyze function (discussed as an advanced feature at the end of this chapter), it can be used to determine where your institution's faculty publish most frequently, and thus which journals to lobby hardest for during a serials review. For an academic or corporate researcher, it allows him or her to track what a colleague (or a competitor!) at a specific institution is publishing. The researcher could search on just author name, or author name combined with address (to disambiguate common names) to track known people. Using a keyword(s) and address search, the researcher could track the output of a department or unit at another institution, without knowing any specific names at all.

Absent: Subject Headings Fields

Finally, there is one thing that hasn't been mentioned about these remarkable databases. Did you notice? Having just discussed MEDLINE, where subject headings are crucial and heavily emphasized, here at the *Web of Science* we haven't mentioned them at all, because . . . the citation indexes don't use subject headings! Yes, it's true. All the databases we've looked at up to this point have used some kind of subject indexing, and I've made a big point of emphasizing it. Now we come to a set of databases that don't use added subject terms at all, but that are every bit as powerful and compelling (if not more so), than the previous databases. The determination not to employ subject indexing was another part of Dr. Garfield's vision. The labor-and thought-intensive process of having humans analyze each article and apply subject terms slowed the production of the indexes down too much for the needs of the scientific research community. He realized that as "retrieval terms, citations could function as well as manually indexed keywords and descriptors" (Thomson Scientific, 2005). (There is also the advantage that in the sciences, paper titles tend to be more descriptive and express the true content of the work, thus providing a richer source of keywords for searching.) So, you will not find indexer-applied subject indexing here.[6] But I can almost guarantee you won't miss it. Let's take a look.

Searching the *Web of Science*: Main Search Interface

Figure 5.12 shows the initial search screen for the *Web of Science* databases (the details will depend on your subscription, but this should be close).

As you can see, this screen allows you to set up your search simply but with many options in the dropdown menus, while below are two sets of limits: Timespan, and which of the Citation Databases you wish to search (i.e., one, two, or all three). We're going to start with a search on a "scientific" topic, so we'll leave only the *Science Citation Index Expanded* checked.

You can get a sense of some of the Boolean operators and other elements of our Searcher's Toolkit that are available here from the examples provided right in the interface. See the Sidebar for more details. When we get to the Results pages, you'll find additional opportunities to employ limits, to "Refine" your results. Note too the emphasis on customization: "My . . . x" and "My . . . y," in the links across the very top and in the text panel on the right side. The Thomson Corporation did a lot of user research, and determined that personalizing the search experience as much as possible might be the answer to meeting the needs of their very diverse universe of users.

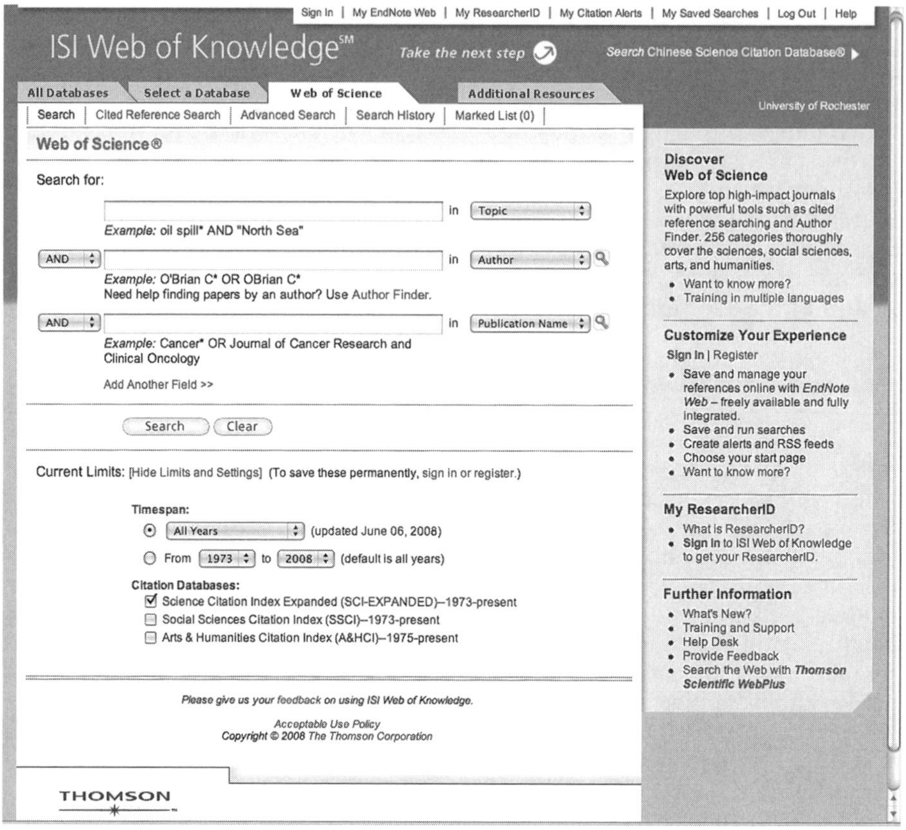

Fig. 5.12. *Web of Science* initial search screen. Data from *Web of Science,*® produced by the scientific business of The Thomson Corporation.

Sidebar 5.2

Here's a quick inventory of your Searcher's Toolkit for the Citation databases:

- Boolean operators: AND, OR, NOT

- Proximity operator: SAME

- Order of precedence: SAME, NOT, AND, OR. Use parentheses to change the order.

- Enclose phrases in double quotes.

- Truncation/wildcards:

  - *—zero to "many" characters

  - ?—substitutes for characters on one-to-one basis, for example, ?—one character, ??—two characters, etc. Can be used within a word, or at the end

  - $—zero or one character only, for example, labo$r to get labor or labour

- Limits for Language, Document Type incorporated in the drop-down menus for the search fields

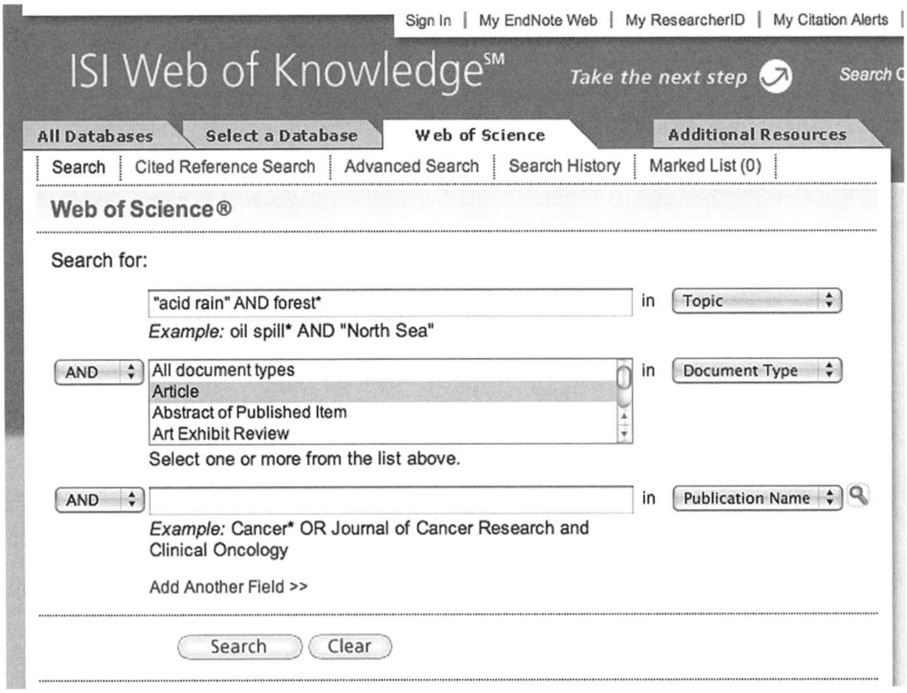

Fig. 5.13. A first, simple topic search. Data from *Web of Science*,® produced by the scientific business of The Thomson Corporation.

Search Example 1: A Topic Search

We'll get our feet wet with a simple search (Figure 5.13):

"acid rain" AND forest*—as Topic.

Select Article after choosing Document Type from the drop-down menu.

Search Results

The results screens in the version of the *Web of Science* as of June 2008 are incredibly powerful and informative, thanks to the Refine Results panel. Not only does it provide a chance to immediately "refine" your results by applying any of the sorts of limits listed, by providing the hit counts for each one, but you also get a sense of "who writes on this topic most frequently? Which journals are most important? Which institutions are most interested in this area?" You don't need to know which limits you might want to use up front; you can decide afterwards, and easily choose the ones that seem most promising. You can also immediately Analyze the results, or create a Citation Report (icons just above the results list). With this database's emphasis on citations, it's no surprise to see that each result record includes a line for Times Cited, so you can see immediately what kind of impact they are having on their field. (There hasn't been time for the newest articles to get cited, obviously.) This is no longer any ordinary results screen: it's a powerhouse (Figure 5.14).

From the results, we'll explore the one by Burns DA, Blett T, Haeuber R, et al. (Figure 5.15). How many references does it have? At the time this screen snap was taken, this article was so new that it hadn't been cited yet, but note again how Times Cited appears in the brief results list, and

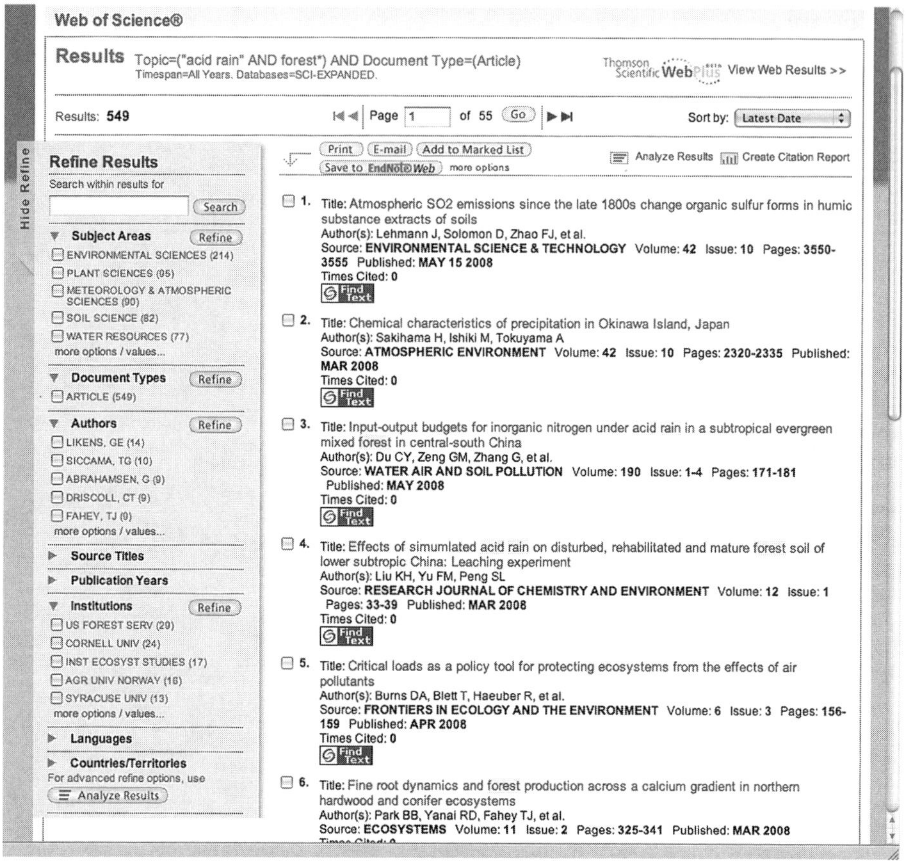

Fig. 5.14. Initial results for the "acid rain" search; with the Refine panel. Data from *Web of Science*,® produced by the scientific business of The Thomson Corporation.

its prominent place in the full record display.[7] Take a look at the Related Records (Figure 5.16). Do they seem related or useful to you? And again, you can refine these results.

Search Example 2: An Author Search

Another example: say that you were familiar with Stephen Hawking's books, but wanted a list of journal articles by him. We'll set the search field to Author, and, as the interface indicates, enter the name as Hawking S* (no comma, and do not spell out the first name).[8] How many S Hawkings can there be? But we can add Cambridge and set the search field to Address to be sure that it's the one we want (Figure 5.17).

The results for this search indicate that Stephen Hawking is a prolific author, and that almost all of his articles are frequently cited, as well. If you can access this database, note too that usually he is listed as Hawking SW, but sometimes as Hawking S—so it was good to use the wildcard symbol to be sure that we retrieved both.

Cited Reference Searching

On to the special functionality of this database: searching a *Cited Reference*. Wherever you are in the database, notice the search function links

Fig. 5.15. Full record from the "acid rain" search results. Data from *Web of Science*,® produced by the scientific business of The Thomson Corporation.

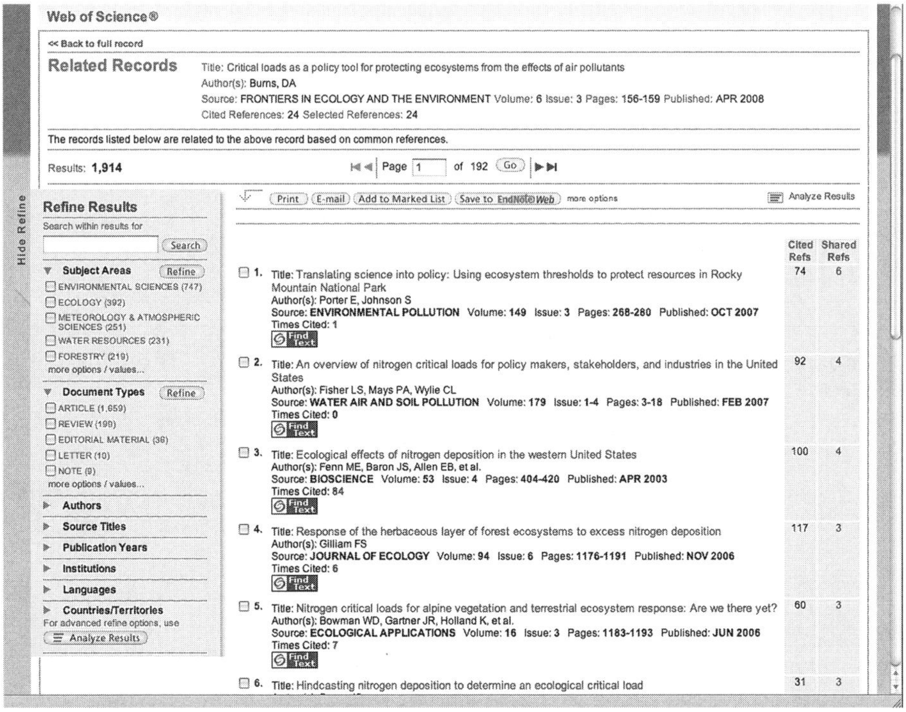

Fig. 5.16. Related Records, based on shared citations, for the Burns article. Data from *Web of Science*,® produced by the scientific business of The Thomson Corporation.

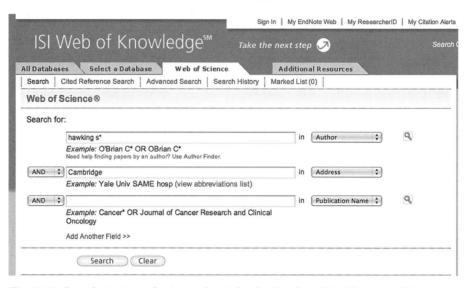

Fig. 5.17. Search strategy for journal articles by Stephen Hawking—partial screen. Data from *Web of Science*,® produced by the scientific business of The Thomson Corporation.

at the top stay with you, allowing you to change direction at any time (e.g., see Figure 5.15). To change search modes, click the Cited Reference Search link at the top of the screen.

Cited Reference Search Example 1

Now let us say that you are interested in the classic book by James Watson, *The Double Helix*, in which he described the discovery of DNA. How many times has it been cited? Is it still being cited by current authors? In what contexts? As mentioned in the introductory notes for these databases, here is an interesting thing: we can search for articles that have cited a work that is both outside the year coverage (1973–current), and outside the material type (book rather than journal article), of the database. The work itself does not have to be retrievable as a record in the database; it just has to have been cited by others. You can do a cited reference search on really ancient material, as long as people are still citing it. Ponder that for a couple of minutes. We're not used to working with material that is outside of the stated year span of the database.

Cited Reference Search Input

In this case, we will make use of all the fields provided in the cited reference search screen, and boldly type in the information as given. Later on, we'll work on an example that isn't as tidy or straight forward.

As shown in Figure 5.18, type in

Cited Author: Watson J*

Cited Work: double helix

Cited Year(s): 1968

This produces a list from the Cited Reference Index, as shown in Figure 5.19.

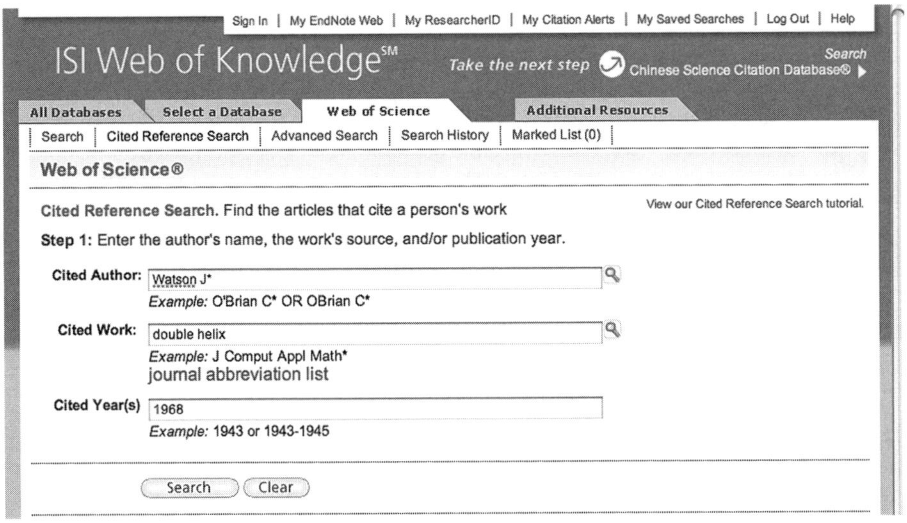

Fig. 5.18. A cited reference search. Data from *Web of Science*,® produced by the scientific business of The Thomson Corporation.

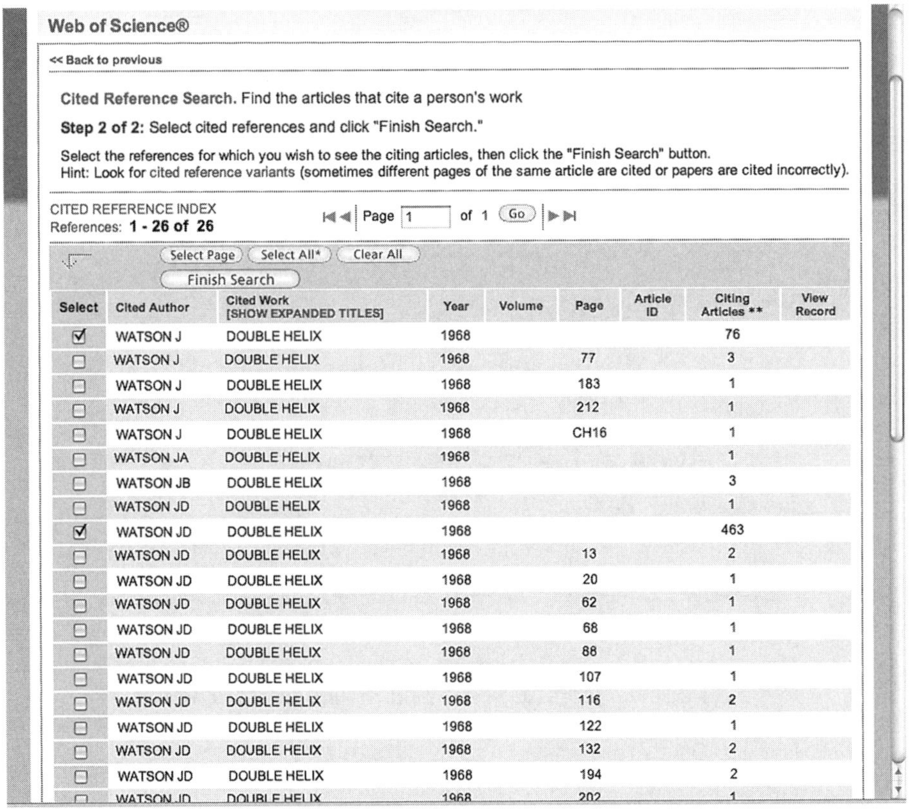

Fig. 5.19. "Cited Reference Index" produced by a cited reference search. Data from *Web of Science*,® produced by the scientific business of The Thomson Corporation.

Cited Reference Index Results

Yikes! A million variations! Is this all the same thing? Unfortunately, yes. This represents all the ways that people have cited this work in their bibliographies. Every time somebody writes a reference a little differently (or even incorrectly!), that reference gets its own entry (note the "Hint" in the list of instructions just above the results). Although Thomson Scientific does do a lot of clean up and "normalization" of references, it would be impossible to check and fix every reference for every article, and still maintain the rate at which new material is added to the databases to keep them current. As a result, papers that are frequently cited produce results lists like this one. Don't panic; now you know why.

Getting to the Articles Doing the Citing

In real life, you would probably want to use the Select All* button if you wanted to be comprehensive. For example purposes, however, we'll select (checkbox) the two entries with the most "hits" on this page, and click the Finish Search button. Now we presented with the articles that have cited this classic work, with the most recent ones listed first, as in the earlier Figure 5.14.

Here are ten articles selected from the first two pages of results. Note the variety of disciplines referring to this work, and the international range of journals.

1. Glynn J
   Rosalind Franklin: 50 years on
   NOTES AND RECORDS OF THE ROYAL SOCIETY, 62 (2): 253–255 JUN 20 2008

2. Le Comber, SC
   A natural appetite
   JOURNAL OF ZOOLOGY, 274 (3): 205–206 MAR 2008

3. Viney, M
   A classroom strategy
   AMERICAN BIOLOGY TEACHER, 69 (9): 525-+ NOV 2007

4. Singer, F
   Dualism, science, and statistics
   BIOSCIENCE, 57 (9): 778–782 OCT 2007

5. Lesnikowski, ZJ
   DNA as platform for new biomaterials. Metal-containing nucleic acids
   CURRENT ORGANIC CHEMISTRY, 11 (4): 355–381 MAR 2007

6. [Anon]
   Modeling in biomedical informatics: Pastime or necessity? A dialogue on lessons from the past and directions for the future
   ARTIFICIAL INTELLIGENCE IN MEDICINE, 38 (3): 319–326 NOV 2006

7. Drew, N
   Bridging the distance between the objectivism of research and the subjectivity of the researcher
   ADVANCES IN NURSING SCIENCE, 29 (2): 181–191 APR–JUN 2006

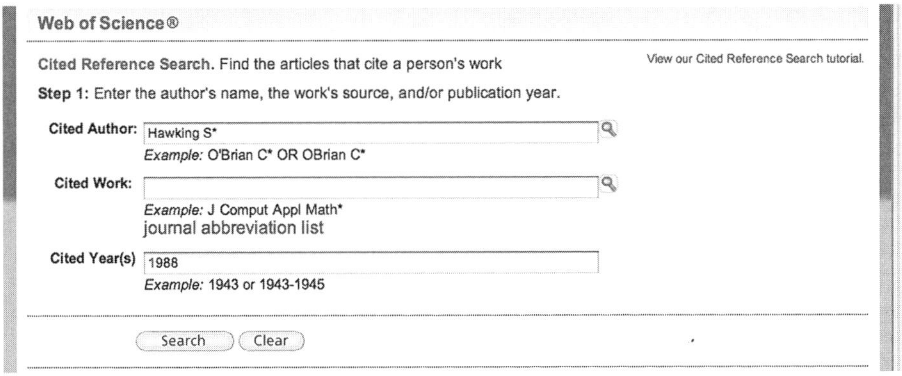

Fig. 5.20. Cited reference search for Stephen Hawking's book published in 1988. Data from *Web of Science*,® produced by the scientific business of The Thomson Corporation.

8. Kryazhimskii, FV; Bolshakov, VN
   Superorganismal systems in human ecology
   RUSSIAN JOURNAL OF ECOLOGY, 36 (3): 143–149 MAY–JUN 2005

9. Manchester, K
   Denaturation of DNA and the concept of secondary structure
   SOUTH AFRICAN JOURNAL OF SCIENCE, 100 (11–12): 509–511 NOV–DEC 2004

10. Stauffer, JE
    Nutrigenomics
    CEREAL FOODS WORLD, 49 (4): 247–248 JUL–AUG 2004

We'll get to how this selected set of records was produced in a moment, when we address how to output results from the Citation Indexes. First, however, another cited reference challenge. . . .

Cited Reference Search Example 2

Getting back to Stephen Hawking, say that you'd like to see who has been citing his book *A Brief History of Time* recently. (The book was published in 1988.) This is basically like the previous cited reference search. We would start at the Cited Reference search screen and enter the author's name in the correct way, and the year the work was published (Figure 5.20).

Title Abbreviations and the Cited Work Index

Now you might be wondering why the Cited Work field was left blank. In the previous example it was given to you (*Double Helix*). But wasn't it given to you here? The book is called *A Brief History of Time*, right? Well, yes, and it also has a subtitle: *From the Big Bang to Black Holes*. The issue here is that we have a Work title that is potentially many words longer, and this database is very big on abbreviations. Very big. They have to be, to fit all the information in. The point is that almost every cited reference title will be abbreviated in some way, and it's a very, very bad idea to try to *guess* the abbreviation. (Although you might use truncation successfully.)

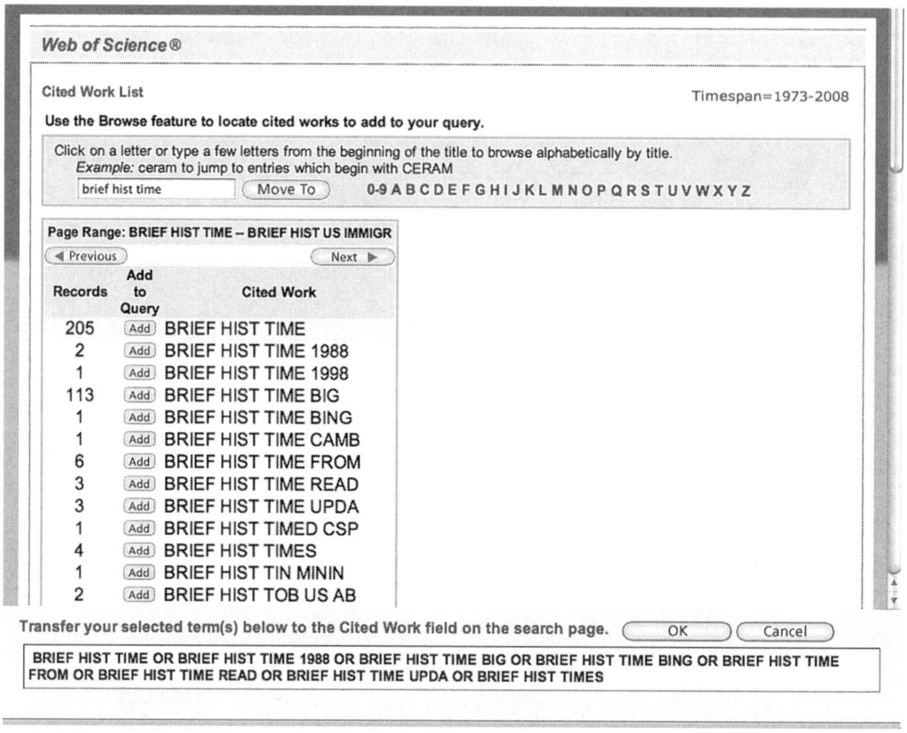

Fig. 5.21. Using the Cited Work List to select variants on a title. Data from *Web of Science*,® produced by the scientific business of The Thomson Corporation.

Note the helpful links associated with the Cited Work field: to the journal abbreviation list, and the magnifying glass icon at the end of the input field lets you "access the search aid." This turns out to be the access point for Browsing all the values in the Cited Work List. We know that this is not a journal, so we'll use the cited work index. Because I know how this story comes out, here is a hint: the favorite way to abbreviate History in this case is "Hist." The cited work index very nicely allows us to type in the beginning of what we're looking for and jump to it in the list. If we jump in the index to "brief hist time" (because there are a great many other "brief hist's," as it happens) we find a list as pictured in Figure 5.21.

We'll choose the variations with more than one record count,[9] and what a handy system: we can simply click the ADD button for each one, and it appears in the selection field below, intelligently ORed together (Figure 5.21). A click of the OK button inserts this whole string into the appropriate field in the search screen. Performing the search now results in another amazing list of variations on a theme, as indicated in Figure 5.22.

Results: Example 2

Note how people citing this work have listed Hawking sometimes with just his first initial, S, sometimes as SW, and some people think he has a different middle initial altogether. The title of the work appears in various ways (the subtitle is sometimes part of it), and people sometimes include the chapter or page number in their citation. As mentioned before, basically

CITED REFERENCE INDEX
References: **1 - 43 of 43**

Page 1 of 1 (Go)

(Select Page) (Select All*) (Clear All)

(Finish Search)

Select	Cited Author	Cited Work [SHOW EXPANDED TITLES]	Year	Volume	Page	Article ID	Citing Articles **	View Record
☐	HAWKING S	BRIEF HIST TIME	1988				143	
☐	HAWKING S	BRIEF HIST TIME	1988		65		1	
☐	HAWKING S	BRIEF HIST TIME	1988		107		1	
☐	HAWKING S	BRIEF HIST TIME	1988		139		2	
☐	HAWKING S	BRIEF HIST TIME	1988		140		1	
☐	HAWKING S	BRIEF HIST TIME	1988		148		1	
☐	HAWKING S	BRIEF HIST TIME	1988		174		1	
☐	HAWKING S	BRIEF HIST TIME	1988		1355		1	
☐	HAWKING S	BRIEF HIST TIME	1988		CH8		2	
☐	HAWKING S	BRIEF HIST TIME BIG	1988				76	
☐	HAWKING S	BRIEF HIST TIME BIG	1988		103		1	
☐	HAWKING S	BRIEF HIST TIME BIG	1988		155		5	
☐	HAWKING S	BRIEF HIST TIMES	1988				1	
☐	HAWKING SA	BRIEF HIST TIME BIG	1988				2	
☐	HAWKING SH	BRIEF HIST TIME BIG	1988				2	
☐	HAWKING SW	BRIEF HIST TIME	1988				148	
☐	HAWKING SW	BRIEF HIST TIME	1988		9		8	
☐	HAWKING SW	BRIEF HIST TIME	1988		24		5	
☐	HAWKING SW	BRIEF HIST TIME	1988		25		1	
☐	HAWKING SW	BRIEF HIST TIME	1988		38		1	

Fig. 5.22. Partial first screen of the Cited Reference Index for Hawking's *Brief History of Time*. Data from *Web of Science,*® produced by the scientific business of The Thomson Corporation.

what appears at the end of an author's article is what goes into the database. Remember Reference Desk Rule No. 1: citations are *never* quite accurate. If you don't believe that yet, try this: look up Hawking S* as a cited author (without any other fields filled in). Browse forward through the screens until you get to the Cited Works beginning with *Breve Hist Temps* (ah ha—this book was translated into French). Note the many variations in titles, and year (probably different editions), and this is only the Hawking S section of the list! Imagine what might be waiting when you get to the two-initial part of the list.

Pause and Think

Again, take a moment to ponder this: all of these entries represent articles that *cited* this book. There is no general record for this book in this database, because it doesn't index books. No record for the thing itself, but endless records that refer to it. Isn't that rather interesting? Exploring the world of scholarship is lovely, but ultimately, of course, you want to identify some records and do something with them. On to output options.

E-mail, Print, Save, or Export Results

Marking and Outputting

The process for outputting records from the *Web of Science* is similar in many ways to the other databases that we've looked at so far, but with

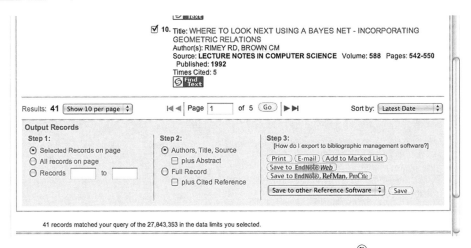

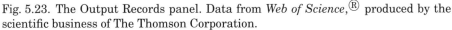

Fig. 5.23. The Output Records panel. Data from *Web of Science*,® produced by the scientific business of The Thomson Corporation.

some twists. If you can determine which records you want to print, e-mail, or export to bibliographic management software from the information given in the results list, you simply checkbox those records, and then choose what to do with them using the quick Output Records panel at the bottom of each result screen (Figure 5.23).

Should you move off that results screen by going to the next page of results or by looking at a full record, the system will retain any records you have check boxed so far by adding them to the Marked List. Such records will then appear with a new icon in the results list, and are no longer "recognized" by the Output Records panel on the results screen. You must go into the Marked List to output them. (When viewing a full record, the only option for marking it is to use the Add to Marked List button, shown in Figure 5.15; therefore you have to go into the Marked List to work with them.)

Output From the Marked List Screen

The link to the Marked List appears with the links to Search, Cited Reference Search, etc., toward the top of the screen (see Figure 5.18). This screen gives you some more detailed choices for fields to include in the output, but the functionality is otherwise similar to the Output Records panel (Figure 5.24):

- The many checkboxes in the middle of the screen give you the exact choice of additional fields to include with the records. The default is author, title, source, and ISSN.

- The e-mail function is good: it lets you put in your address for return address and add a note to explain why you're sending the information. If you are sending results to someone else, using your e-mail as the return address, rather than a strange system e-mail, makes the message look less like spam.

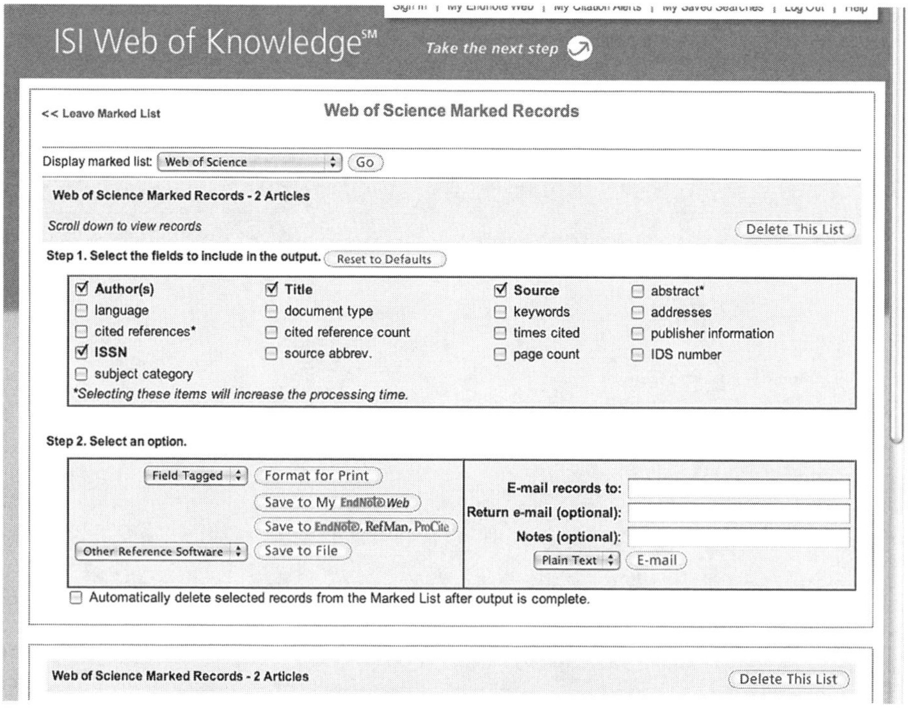

Fig. 5.24. The Marked Records screen. Data from *Web of Science,*® produced by the scientific business of The Thomson Corporation.

Other options are to format for printing, save to file, or "Save to End-Note" or other types of citation management software. The list of marked articles begins at the bottom of the screen.

Advanced Features: Advanced Search and Analyze

Advanced Search

The Advanced Search screen offers options for you real search hackers out there: searching with field codes and detailed syntax, or manipulating sets from your search history, as shown in the lower half of the screen (Figure 5.25). (Specific access to the search history for simple manipulations of previous search sets is also available by means of a link in the search function series across the upper part of the interface.)

Analyze

In everyday usage of searching for articles and tracing citations, you probably won't find yourself using the Analyze function that frequently. However, for tracking publication patterns, or doing general research on scholarship (e.g., Who is doing it? Where, that is, in what country, by which organizations? What journals are they publishing in? What subject categories does this multidisciplinary department publish in?), the Analyze function provides a fascinating tool.

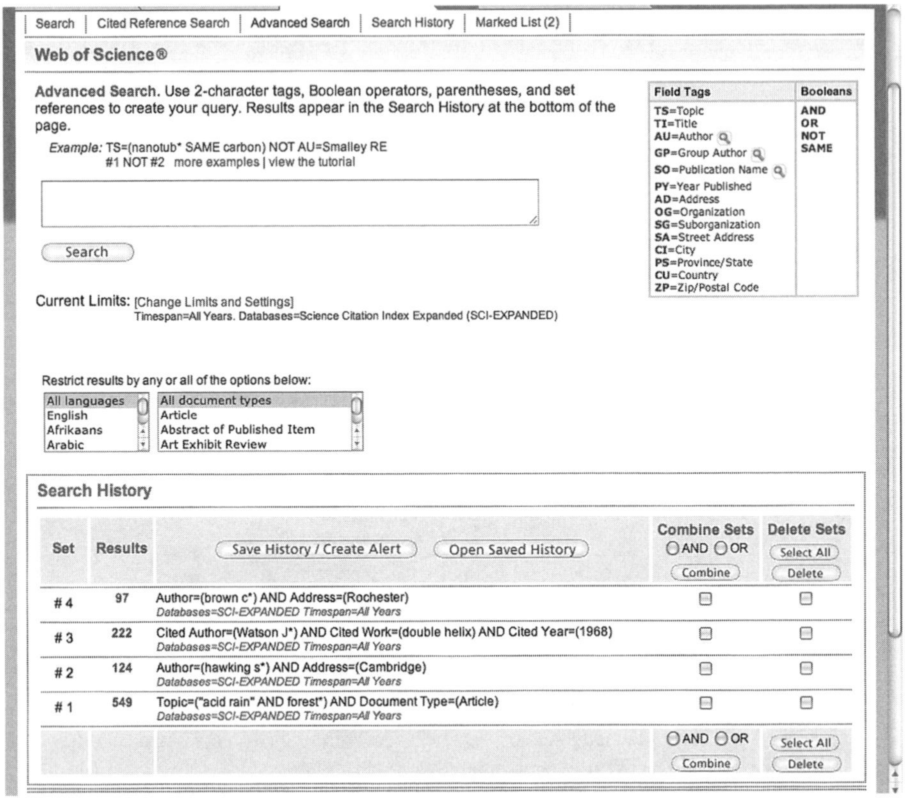

Fig. 5.25. The Advanced Search screen. Data from *Web of Science*,® produced by the scientific business of The Thomson Corporation.

Searching for "Cog* Sci, Rochester, NY" in the address field retrieves articles published by members of the Department of Brain & Cognitive Science at the University of Rochester. This is a highly interdisciplinary department, so it is interesting to Analyze the results to see what journals they publish in most frequently (Figure 5.26), or to what subject categories those journals are assigned.

Quick Recap

The *Web of Science* citation indexes have a dual nature. They allow you search and identify articles by keywords (topic searches), by author, journal title, or by the author's address. The citation indexes do not have added subject headings; topical searches are dependent on the content of the article titles, abstracts, and author-supplied keywords. The other side of the citation indexes' dual nature is that they allow you to search by cited reference information, to find articles that have *cited* a particular work from the past. The original cited work can be any material type, not just journal articles, and can be from any date. Article records include a list of all works cited by the article. These citations are in a highly abbreviated format, and it is important to use the built-in lookup indexes to pull up citations (and variations) correctly. Each article record has a link to related

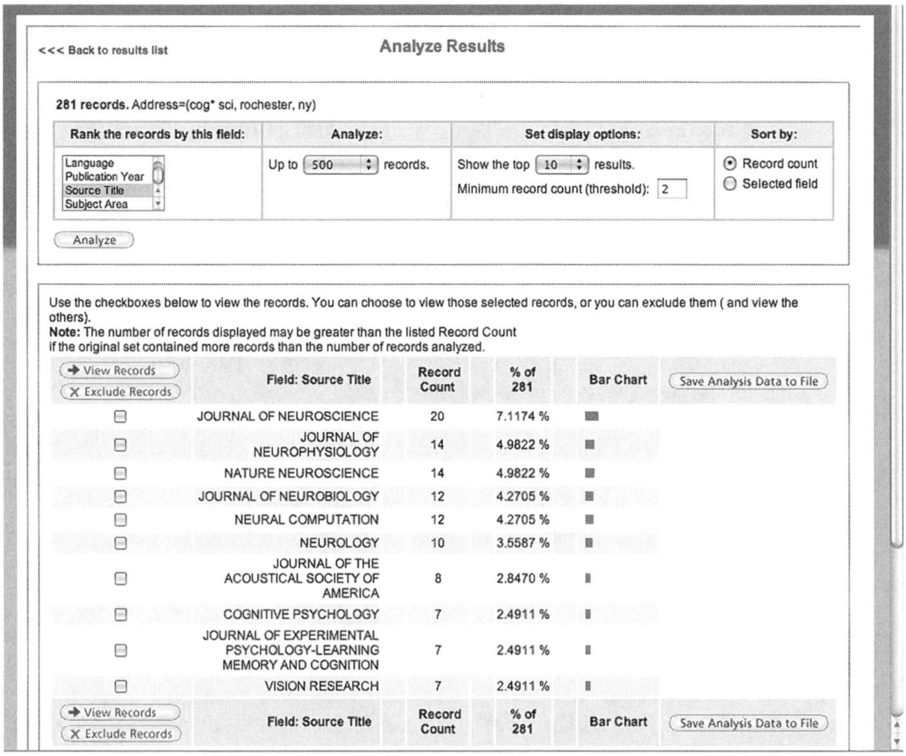

Fig. 5.26. The Analyze interface. Data from *Web of Science,*® produced by the scientific business of The Thomson Corporation.

records, which are identified based on the number of cited references they share.

Exercises and Points to Consider

1. It was mentioned that by using more Limits in PubMed, it was possible to reduce the number of results to counts similar to those that we obtained in Ovid's MEDLINE. Go to PubMed, and set up the "heart attack" Limits as in Figure 5.7. In addition, look at the Subsets drop-down: why, there's a "MEDLINE" subset! That should fix it, right? Choose this subset, put in "heart attack," and search. Look at the information on the Details tab afterward, to see what was searched.

    Back to the Limits screen. Click on the drop-down menu with the default of All Fields—change this to MeSH Major Topic. (This is the equivalent of Focus in Ovid.) Search again.

    Finally, visit the Preview/Index tab, to add the MeSH Subheading: prevention (cf. Figure 5.9). Choose MeSH Subheading from the drop-down menu, type prevention in the box, and click the And button below the box to add it to the search.

    The number of search results, especially those on the Review tab, should now be about what you'd get in MEDLINE.

2. Think about all the work you did in PubMed to replicate the MED-LINE results. Do you think anyone besides librarians would ever master all that? On the other hand, does it matter? What if users treat PubMed as a sort of medical Google, and simply look at the first few screens of huge results sets? On a scale of 1 to 10, where 1 is "OK" and 10 is "a disaster," how would you rate this?

3. Ovid MEDLINE versus PubMed continued: for features that are the same, but implemented slightly differently (checkboxes versus drop-down menus, for example), which style of implementation do you prefer? Why? Overall, which database do you find more user friendly?

4. While you're looking at PubMed, try some of the Related Articles links. If you have access to the *Web of Science*, do a search there, and take a look at some Related Records links. Going solely by the titles produced in each case, what is your impression of how well the different databases' "relatedness" function works? PubMed relates articles by a word algorithm, and *Web of Science* does it by number of shared citations. Does either approach seem to produce more related results than the other? (Gut impression only, no research required.)

5. For fun and amazement: at PubMed, click on the All Databases link. (In the PubMed screen shots, it's the first item in the narrow black bar across the top. If the interface has changed, look for it.) This takes you to the "Entrez cross-database search page." Put in our old friend, "heart attack," or any other term you want (diseases are good). You'll see the number of hits in each database for your term. Even if you have no idea of what most of these resources represent, this is fascinating! (You can always click the "?" to get a fairly understandable description of the database content.)

6. A search scenario: You are applying for the position of librarian for physics and astronomy at the (name of university here). You want to make points when you meet the astronomy faculty, and a good way to do that is to find out what they've been writing about. In the *Web of Science* you search:

   Topic: galax*

   Address: (part of school name) same astron* (same state abbreviation, if needed to distinguish).

7. In the *Web of Science*, look up Hawking S* as cited author again. Note the remarkable number of variations, lots of different years, in French, etc. Select only those entries where the cite seems to be odd or incorrect in some way, then "Finish" the search and look at the articles produced—interesting titles!

8. Do a search on an author with a fairly common name, such as Brown C*. Then use the Refine options in the results screen to differentiate the results: by subject area, by name, etc. Experiment and familiarize yourself with all the possible options.

9. Now that you've finished this chapter, what do you think about the opening premise: that the medical database is about *what*, and the science database is about *who*. Do you find this valid? Did you see further evidence to support this theory?

Notes

1. To eleven levels of specificity! (MeSH *Fact Sheet*).

2. *Clinical, clinician*: to do with patient care (e.g., in the clinic), a medical professional who is primarily involved in treating patients (as opposed to doing research).

3. Fact Sheet includes additional added materials and a list of other PubMed services.

4. Note that when this screen shot was taken, what was being highlighted was the "MyNCBI" service (and by the time this book gets to your hands, the look and feel of this Web site will probably have changed again). Just a little reminder that the details will always be changing in this business, and you need to be ready to map the new information onto your basic search principles.

5. Note: if you use truncation (*) in your query, the automatic mapping feature is disabled.

6. Alert readers may notice in Figure 5.15 a field called Keywords Plus, and Subject Category. Does this mean the *Web of Science* is getting into subject headings? In a word, no. Keywords Plus terms are automatically generated terms, representing words or phrases that show up most frequently in the titles of an article's *references*. Subject Category is the subject category of the *journal* that the article appeared in, a value decided once and then applied automatically every time a record is added from that journal. Finally, in other records you may notice "Author Keywords." These are exactly that: author-supplied terms, a useful addition, but the addition of these terms did not slow down the process of getting the record into the database, and there is no controlled schema for them—they are simply whatever the author provided.

7. Just for curiosity's sake, I used the Citation Report function to see which article in this set of results had been cited most often. It turns out to be Likens GE, Driscoll CT, Buso DC. Long-term effects of acid rain: Response and recovery of a forest ecosystem. Science 272 (5259): 244–246. April 12, 1996. It had been cited 340 times!

8. You don't *have* to use the wildcard; you can also use initials for both first and middle names, if you're sure that the author always uses the middle initial. Not sure what Hawking's middle name is? Google for "Stephen * Hawking" —you'll be able to verify his name (and anything else about him) in no time.

9. My favorite is "Brief Hist Time Bing"....

6
Bibliographic Databases

From the beginning of this book, we have been focusing on "article" databases that serve an abstracting and indexing (A & I) function: databases that provide a means to identify (and often to supply), articles from periodical publications. In this chapter, our focus shifts to "bibliographic" databases, which we define as resources that provide information (mainly) about books. While A & I databases provide information about the contents of journals, and may include book chapters, conference papers, or other materials, bibliographic databases provide information about the contents of a particular library, or many libraries, or any collection of book titles (e.g., *Books in Print*, Amazon.com). Put another way, an A & I database is like being *inside* a collection of journals or books, seeing all the contents, while a bibliographic database is like being on the *outside*, running your eyes down the spine titles of everything (book, bound journal, video, etc.) sitting on the shelves of a library or other collection.

You have undoubtedly used a bibliographic database many times already as a student or as a regular library user: every library's online catalog is a bibliographic database. The Online Public Access Catalog (OPAC) is how you find out about the contents of that particular library. If you think about it for any time at all, it's easy in today's networked, everything-is-on-the-Web world to see that it would be even more interesting if you could find out about the contents of other libraries, without having to go to each of their catalogs and search. It would be incredibly useful to gather the records from many libraries and provide them as one massive "union" catalog. Such things were at one time published in hard copy, but an electronic database version would obviously be far more powerful and useful. It would provide all the contents of all the libraries, searchable through one interface. This sounds like a totally natural idea now ... but can you imagine having this vision in 1967? That is when Frederick G. Kilgour and university presidents in Ohio founded the Ohio College Library Center (Jordan, 2003), in order to "share library resources and reduce costs by using computers and technology" (Helfer, 2002). The original idea was to establish an online shared cataloging system, which OCLC introduced in 1971, and an Interlibrary Loan system, which was introduced in 1979 (Helfer, 2002). OCLC introduced the FirstSearch interface and access to several databases, including the union catalog, dubbed WorldCat, for use as a reference tool in 1991 (Hogan, 1991). OCLC (the acronym now stands for *Online Computer* Library Center) was a brilliant idea, way ahead of its time.

Most of this chapter is devoted to an exploration of WorldCat and to its free web version, WorldCat.org. We'll conclude with some suggestions and reminders about what to look for in your own local catalog.

WorldCat: The "OPAC of OPACs"

In the online Help for WorldCat, OCLC rather modestly describes their product as a catalog of books and other materials in libraries worldwide. WorldCat is far beyond just a union catalog, however. The OCLC Web site pulls no punches, describing it as a "global catalog," and a "window to the world's libraries"—the world's largest bibliographic database. As of June 2008, there were 60,000 libraries represented in the database, representing 112 countries (OCLC, 2008). How was it, and is it, possible to put together and maintain such an enormous resource?

Background and Coverage

Note: in the following discussion, although it is always the same body of information being referring to, *how* it is referred to differs depending on the library context. To Cataloging and Interlibrary Loan departments, this database is usually known simply as OCLC. To librarians and library users, the database information is presented via WorldCat. (The cataloging and ILL interfaces and programs for interacting with the database are very different from WorldCat.) When the discussion concerns Cataloging or ILL, the text refers to this resource as the OCLC database. In the context of a database used by reference librarians and patrons, it is referred to as WorldCat. Again, it is all the same body of information.

Part of the brilliance of OCLC's vision for creating this far-reaching union catalog was to make it a distributed, cooperative effort, and one that had immediate benefit for those supplying the effort. The business model here is that libraries pay annual fees to be members of OCLC, as well as activity fees to search the database and download records for use in the library's local catalog. OCLC manages the contributed data, and provides many services and benefits based on the database information. A key factor in the business model, however, is that whenever a cataloger at a member library contributes a new record or improves an existing record, the library receives *credits*. The more the library contributes, the more credits it receives.[1] While an actively contributing library is usually also an actively "using" library (thus incurring more service fees), receiving the credits does help to keep the financial relationship from being entirely one sided. Thus the OCLC database is built by catalogers at member libraries, already experts in their field, who would need to create records for their library's holdings anyway. By contributing their work, these member library catalogers offset the costs of searching and downloading records supplied by *other* member libraries. Everyone benefits, in terms of time, effort, and efficiency. One of the great benefits is that this huge bibliographic database is made available to reference librarians and patrons in the form of WorldCat.

The scope of WorldCat is dazzling: as of this writing, the number of records in WorldCat has passed the 100 million mark, representing works dating from before 1000 BC to the present, in nearly 500 languages. As a collaborative, contributed effort, the database is updated constantly: according the OCLC Web site, on average a new record is added to WorldCat every 10 seconds.[2] The records in WorldCat represent the whole gamut of material types, everything that the contributing libraries have cataloged: books, serials, manuscripts, musical scores, audiovisual materials (i.e., videos, DVDs, audio tapes, and other "sound recordings"), maps, electronic resources (i.e., Web sites, electronic journals, e-books, etc.), and these are just the common formats. There is, literally, everything from stone tablets to electronic books, and more.

A Tool for Many Parts of the Library

The OCLC database is both a creation and a tool of the *cataloging* department. Original catalogers create new records that get added to the local OPAC and to the OCLC database, while copy catalogers download preexisting records for the local OPAC, as well as adding the local library's holdings to existing OCLC records (a process known as *tagging*). As you might imagine, the OCLC database is also integral to the *Interlibrary Loan* function. OCLC supplies several services that help to speed and streamline resource sharing by ILL departments.

As a *reference* and *collection development* tool, librarians can use WorldCat to:

- Explore new or unfamiliar topics presented in reference questions; get a sense of what is available in a subject area.

- Find resources in an area that your library is limited in.

- Find resources in a particular format.

- Find everything written by a particular author.

- "Test the waters" before encouraging a patron to request an Interlibrary Loan; see how many libraries own the item, and where they are located.

- Identify government documents.

- Verify citations (for titles of books, journals, etc.), check publication dates, serial start dates, etc.

- Provide an interim solution if your catalog is down (but your holdings are in WorldCat).

- Develop a collection: see what's out there on a topic, what other libraries own, and what you might want to buy.

Note that records for serial publications in WorldCat can include holdings records, that is, the dates of the journal run owned by the library. It has always been possible to use WorldCat to see if another library owned a particular journal, but until holdings records were added to the WorldCat records, there was no way to tell if that subscription was current, or stopped in 1964. This is very useful for ILL staff, as well as at the Reference Desk.

Fig. 6.1. WorldCat® Advanced Search screen. Screen shots used with permission of OCLC; FirstSearch® and WorldCat® are registered trademarks of OCLC Online Computer Library Center, Inc.

Notes and Search Examples

Let's get into the database and start looking for our Searcher's Toolkit items, and get a sense of how this database differs from the article databases. We have several lighted-hearted searches to try here in World-Cat. We'll go straight to the Advanced Search screen (Figure 6.1) to begin.

Advanced Search Screen

We've seen the FirstSearch advanced interface before when we looked at ERIC in Chapter 4, but the WorldCat interface has several significant differences that reflect its role as an access point to the contents of libraries. The immediately visible differences have to do with Limits and Ranking possibilities. In ERIC, we could limit by Year, Language, Document Type, and by library ("Limit availability to:"). Here in WorldCat, we can also limit by Year and Language, but rather than a drop-down menu of Document Types, we have a whole section of the screen devoted to choosing *material* types (Books, Serials, Archival Materials, etc.). A new drop-down menu has been added that limits the search by the "Number of Libraries" that own the item: the choices are 5 or more, 50 or more, or 500 or more. (Think about this one for a moment: what is the implication here? Why might you want to use this limit?)

We also have new Subtype limits to define our audience, content, and format. Under audience, we can specify Juvenile or not Juvenile. Under content, we have options for Fiction, not Fiction, Biography, Thesis/dissertation, Musical recording, or Non-musical recording. The format options are Large print, Braille, Manuscript, Microform, not Microform, CD audio, Cassette recording, LP recording, VHS tape/Videocassette, and DVD Video/Videodisc. These "subtypes" say a lot about WorldCat as both a reflection of the content and a tool for *public* libraries, which also distinguishes this database from the article databases in this book. Not that academia doesn't use World-Cat constantly, it does. But WorldCat is equally useful in any other kind of library too: a database of all the libraries, for all the people. Quite an achievement!

Next on the screen we see the same "Limit availability to" function found in ERIC (i.e., the library that you are in, or another library that you would indicate by an alpha code), followed by a "Rank by" setting. The "Rank by" options are slightly different from ERIC's: rather than No Ranking, Relevance, or Date, the WorldCat options are Number of Libraries, Relevance, Date, or Accession Number. This is another reminder that this database is all about the holdings of libraries.

More differences become apparent when we compare the fields available for searching (the drop-down menus associated with the three text input fields in the "Search for" section). The list of searchable fields in ERIC is heavily focused on indexes to subject term fields, having one-word and phrase indexes for Descriptors, Identifiers, and Subjects. Fields such as Source (and Source Phrase), Report Number, and Abstract also reflect ERIC's function as an abstracting and indexing database, rather than a bibliographic database. In contrast, the searchable fields in WorldCat are all about identifying books and other complete items that you would find on library shelves, or, increasingly, digital items owned by libraries. There are many variations on Author (nicely gathered together and indented under *Author*), along with Publisher and Publisher Location, and specific Standard Number choices: ISBN and ISSN. We have an opportunity to search by Material Type in more detail (e.g., "book not URL"), or types of Musical Compositions (overtures, part-songs, etc., or phrases such as folk music, gospel music, etc.). WorldCat certainly has subject-related search fields, but subjects here are rather different: in addition to Subject, Subject Phrase, and Descriptor, we have Genre/Form, Geographic Coverage, Named Corporation and Conference, and Named Person.

"Subject" is an excellent way to start exploring WorldCat, however, in conjunction with some limits.

Search Examples

Search 1

You'd like to find some cookbooks for your friend's Korean mother, who doesn't speak English. Although your natural inclination in this case might be to use the term given, "cookbooks," or perhaps "cooking," if you browse the Subject index it turns out the overwhelming majority of records use the term

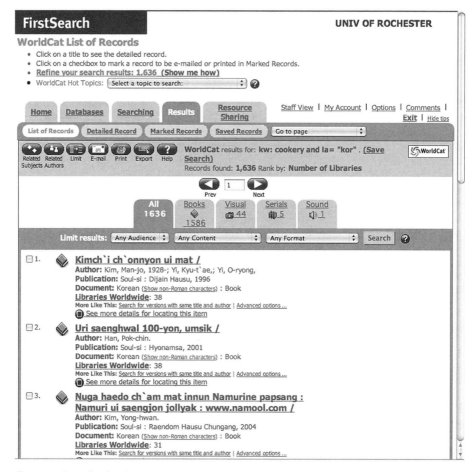

Fig. 6.2. Results for Subject: Cookery and Language: Korean. Screen shots used with permission of OCLC; FirstSearch® and WorldCat® are registered trademarks of OCLC Online Computer Library Center, Inc.

"Cookery" for this Subject. Clicking "Cookery" in the Subject index pastes it into the search screen, and we can then use our Language limit to limit to materials about Cookery in Korean.

Notice the tabs above the result list, shown in Figure 6.2, indicating the number of results for each type of media. Note too that there are over 1,600 records for cookbooks in *Korean*—isn't that incredible? (In case you're curious, the Sound file is an instructional cassette tape.) Remember that the results are sorted, or ranked, by the number of libraries that own the item.

Search 2

Your kids are beginning to show an interest in cooking, and you'd like to see if there are some cookbooks written for children.

Returning to the search screen (the Searching tab is a good way to do this), we already have "cookery" set as our Subject. Any limits that you set previously will also still be in effect, so remember to change the language back to English. This is the perfect occasion to use the first Subtype limit:

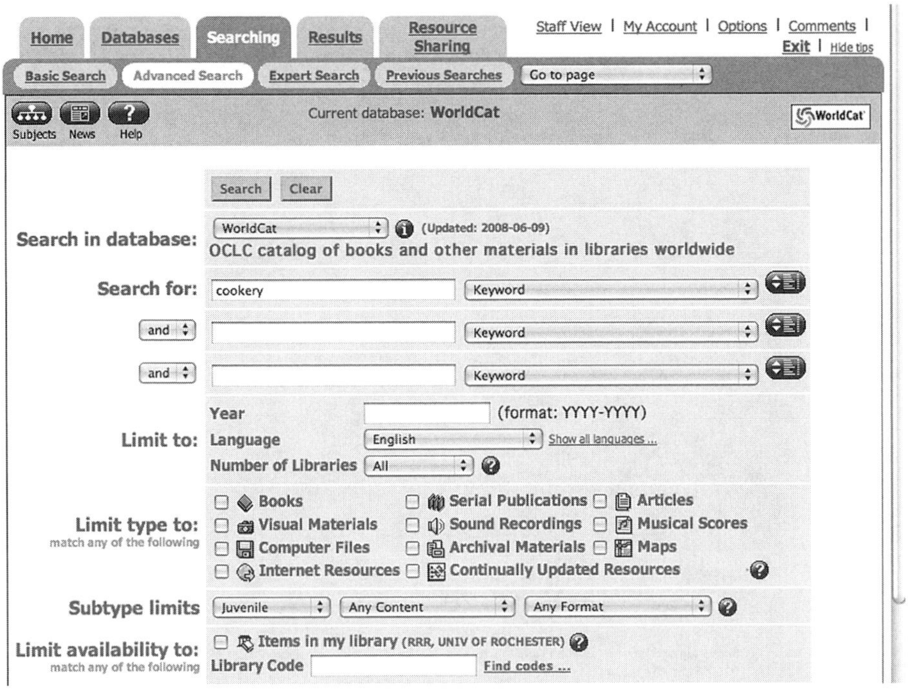

Fig. 6.3. Cookbooks for kids search strategy. Screen shots used with permission of OCLC; FirstSearch® and WorldCat® are registered trademarks of OCLC Online Computer Library Center, Inc.

audience, to specify we want materials for a "Juvenile" audience. Figure 6.3 shows this search ready to be run.

There are plenty of options to explore, as indicated by the number and variety of formats shown in the results screen in Figure 6.4.

Note that there is even one entry on the "Musical Scores" tab—how peculiar! Whenever you see an odd result, don't immediately assume it's a mistake. Take a good look at the record and find out why. In a carefully crafted database like this one, where your search has been set up only in terms of subjects and field search values (rather than as a keyword search), it is highly unlikely that an odd result will be a false drop. By looking and figuring out why, you'll add to your understanding of database lore in general, and discover interesting and bizarre things that may bring a smile to your face (and remind you why this profession is so much fun).

Here is why our search retrieved this "Musical Score." It's a book of children's songs and activities, including recipes, for Halloween. See the Descriptors and Notes fields in Figure 6.5.

Search 3

Continuing in a similar vein, now we'd like to find some mystery novels with a cooking theme.

Returning to the Search screen, we'll keep "Cookery" as our Subject term and add another field search: mystery in the Genre/Form field. We'll also want to change our "Audience" subtype to "not Juvenile."

In the results, an author named Diane Mott Davidson seems to lead the pack in terms of these cooking mysteries. Figures 6.6a and b give us a

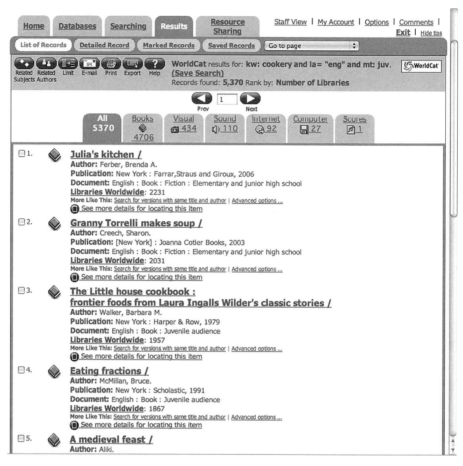

Fig. 6.4. Results for Subject: Cookery and Audience: Juvenile. Screen shots used with permission of OCLC; FirstSearch® and WorldCat® are registered trademarks of OCLC Online Computer Library Center, Inc.

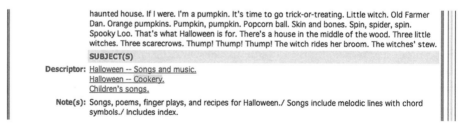

Fig. 6.5. Explanation of the "Musical Scores" result. Screen shots used with permission of OCLC; FirstSearch® and WorldCat® are registered trademarks of OCLC Online Computer Library Center, Inc.

view into a full record: note the "Amazon.com-like" feature of providing the book cover and a brief blurb. In fact, the one record is really being offered two ways: the upper, generally eye-catching, easy-to-grasp-quickly section (Figure 6.6a), and then the lower, nitty-gritty, all the details section (Figure 6.6b). Even when an image of the "cover art" is not provided, the basic citation information is set off in this upper section.

Fig. 6.6a. Upper part of a full record display.

Availability:	**Check the catalogs in your library.**
	• Libraries worldwide that own item: 1678
	• Search the catalog at University of Rochester Libraries
External Resources:	• Miner InterLibrary Loan
	• Sibley InterLibrary Loan
	• River Campus InterLibrary Loan
	• Cite This Item
	FIND RELATED
More Like This:	Search for versions with same title and author I Advanced options ...
Title:	**Dark tort /**
Author(s):	Davidson, Diane Mott.
Publication:	New York : William Morrow,
	Edition: 1st ed.
Year:	2006
Description:	312 p. : ill. ; 24 cm.
Language:	English
Standard No:	**ISBN:** 0060527315; 9780060527310 **LCCN:** 2005-44912
	SUBJECT(S)
Descriptor:	Bear, Goldy (Fictitious character) -- Fiction.
	Women in the food industry -- Fiction.
	Lawyers -- Crimes against -- Fiction.
	Caterers and catering -- Fiction.
	Cookery -- Fiction.
Genre/Form:	Humorous fiction.
	Mystery fiction.
Geographic:	Colorado -- Fiction.
Class Descriptors:	**LC:** PS3554.A925; **Dewey:** 813/.54
Responsibility:	Diane Mott Davidson.
Vendor Info:	Ingram Baker & Taylor Baker and Taylor YBP Library Services (INGR BKTY BTCP YANK) 24.95
	Status: active
Material Type:	Fiction (fic)

Fig. 6.6b. Screen shots used with permission of OCLC; FirstSearch® and WorldCat® are registered trademarks of OCLC Online Computer Library Center, Inc.

Using WorldCat for Citation Verification

WorldCat is also invaluable for resolving citation problems, such as determining what the *real* title of a work is, or its publication year, author, etc. You can use it to fill in information on books and other formats, or determine what material type a title really is (i.e., a monographic series? A conference report? A serial publication?). WorldCat can be particularly useful for resolving questions about serial publications, especially esoteric titles, or titles that have ceased (and that don't appear in a periodicals directory). If we know that something existed at some time, then it is likely that *some* library,

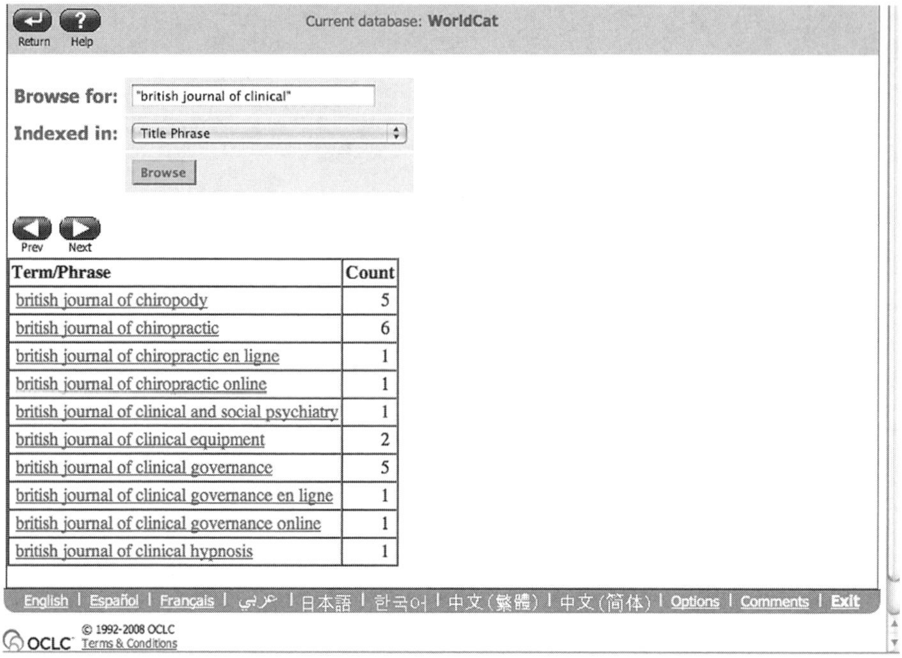

Fig. 6.7. Browsing the Title Phrase field index. Screen shots used with permission of OCLC; FirstSearch® and WorldCat® are registered trademarks of OCLC Online Computer Library Center, Inc.

somewhere, owns it, and chances are good that that library also contributes records to WorldCat.

Search 4

A student comes to the Reference Desk and says: "My professor said I should look at some journal—it's the British journal of clinical something-or-other, I can't remember...but she said she knows the Health Sciences Library at Buffalo gets it...."

In doing any kind of citation verification or completion in WorldCat (or in an article database), the Searcher's Toolkit tools that you'll want to make good use of are the field indexes and truncation symbols. If at all possible, especially in tracking down journals, try to come up with the ISSN for the publication (or ISBN, for books). Words are fuzzy and easily mistaken, but numbers don't lie. There is only one identifying number for every publication (exceptions exist, of course, but as a general principle you can depend on this). It's much more efficient and accurate to search by number than by name.

However, because we are unsure of the journal name, we can't determine an ISSN and look it up that way. Checking the Title Phrase field index for "British journal of clinical" we find the following (Figure 6.7).

Since there are obviously quite a few *British Journal of Clinical...* titles, rather than choosing anything from the index list, we'll simply return to the Advanced Search screen and enter:

British journal of clinical*

as a Title Phrase search.

Fig. 6.8. "Find an OCLC Library" search screen. Screen shots used with permission of OCLC; FirstSearch® and WorldCat® are registered trademarks of OCLC Online Computer Library Center, Inc.

The patron has also told us this journal is available at the Health Sciences Library "at Buffalo." We could refine our search by finding the "Library Code" for the Health Sciences Library and entering it in the "Limit availability to" section (see Figure 6.1). Clicking the "Find codes ..." link opens the "Find an OCLC Library" search in a new window. While "at Buffalo" usually refers to the State University of New York at Buffalo, it's hard to know how that name might be abbreviated, and so we'll play it very safe, and simply search Buffalo as the City, and "health" in the name of the Institution (Figure 6.8).

This search gives us five results, from which it is fairly easy to pick out the appropriate institution (State Univ of New York, Health Sci Libr). Note that the symbol for each institution appears in the first column, on the left side of the screen (Figure 6.9).

We'll note the symbol, SBH, then close this window and return to the search screen. Our "mystery journal" search is now ready to run (Figure 6.10).

Upon seeing the results (Figure 6.11), the student decides it must be the first title, because it's for a Psych class.

The student might also want to know "is the Health Sciences Library's subscription current?" And it would be even more convenient if the journal were here, at the University of Rochester, so she wouldn't need to drive to

Symbol	Institution type	Institution name and address	Regional Service Provider	Member Status	MARC21 Code
SBF	Corporate/Business	LIBRARY CONSOR OF HEALTH INST BUFFALO BUFFALO, NY 14214 United States	Nylink	Active	
SBH	Academic	STATE UNIV OF NEW YORK, HEALTH SCI LIBR BUFFALO, NY 14214-3002 United States	Nylink	Active	NBuU-H
UC1	Corporate/Business	HEALTH CARE PLAN, BUFFALO BUFFALO, NY 14202 United States	OCLC Misc	Inactive	
VTO	Corporate/Business	BRY-LIN HOSP, HEALTH SCI LIBR BUFFALO, NY 14209 United States	Nylink	Active	
VUK	Corporate/Business	HEALTH SYST AG WNY LIBR BUFFALO, NY 14203 United States	Nylink	Active	

Fig. 6.9. "Find an OCLC Library" search results. Screen shots used with permission of OCLC; FirstSearch® and WorldCat® are registered trademarks of OCLC Online Computer Library Center, Inc.

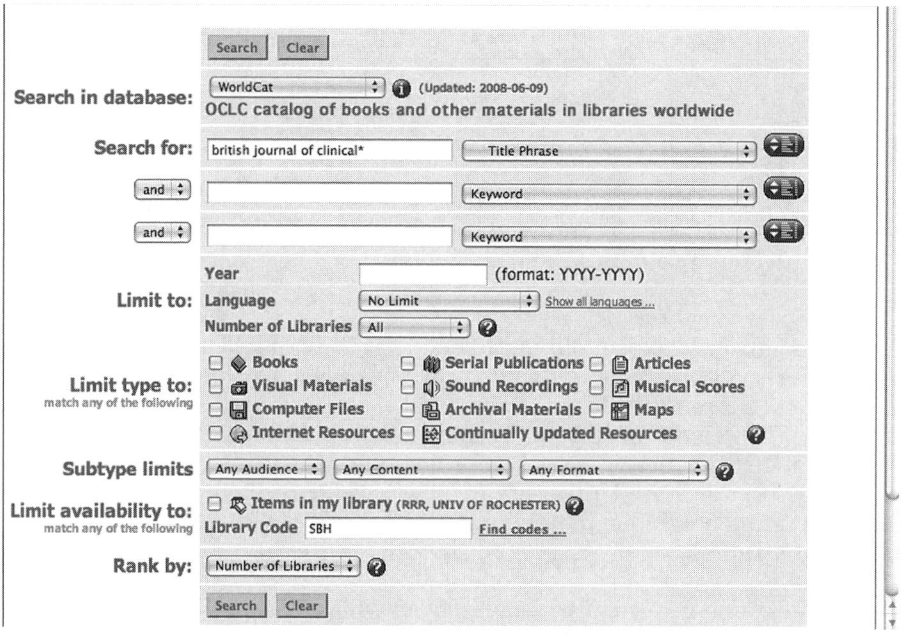

Fig. 6.10. Search strategy for *British Journal of Clinical** titles restricted to Library Code SBH. Screen shots used with permission of OCLC; FirstSearch® and WorldCat® are registered trademarks of OCLC Online Computer Library Center, Inc.

Buffalo—or best of all, if she could simply access it online. There is an immediate tip-off here in the results screen: the first *The British Journal of Clinical Psychology* entry includes a small icon, with the notation "Univ of Rochester," indicating that the title *is* held locally. But are the local holdings up to date? Clicking the "Libraries worldwide" link for any of these records

Fig. 6.11. Results from *British Journal of Clinical** titles restricted to Library Code SBH. Screen shots used with permission of OCLC; FirstSearch® and WorldCat® are registered trademarks of OCLC Online Computer Library Center, Inc.

reveals a very useful feature noted above, in the *A Tool for Many Parts of the Library* section. Many serial records in WorldCat now include holdings information, that is, in addition to which libraries own the title, the years and volumes owned are available as well (Figure 6.12). The local holding library is helpfully listed first.

This is all very nice, but what really catches the student's eye is the link to an electronic version, both from the record for the print, and as its own record (the third one in Figure 6.11). That will probably be her preferred way to "look" at the journal.

Quick Recap

WorldCat is different from all the other databases in this book. Rather than being an index to journal articles or statistical publications, it is a database of the contents of all kinds of libraries: public, academic, and corporate. The range of materials included and audiences that might be served by the information contained here are thus incredibly broad.

WorldCat is the largest union catalog in the world, comprised of records for books and many other material types from thousands of member libraries. The database is a distributed effort, built by catalogers at contributing libraries. As a reference tool, WorldCat can be used in many ways, such as topic exploration or collection development, finding resources in a particular format, verifying citations for books or other materials (not articles),

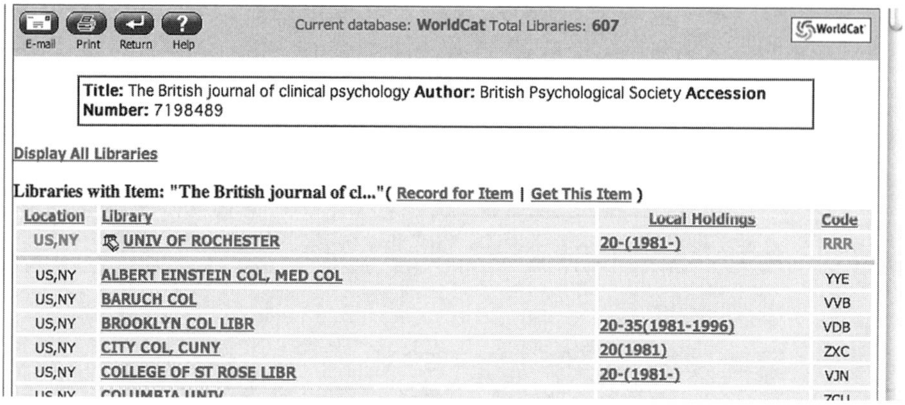

Fig. 6.12. Holdings information screen. Screen shots used with permission of OCLC; FirstSearch® and WorldCat® are registered trademarks of OCLC Online Computer Library Center, Inc.

or discovering where materials that your library does not own are available (e.g., which other libraries own them). The WorldCat Advanced Search interface has several additional Limits (for material types) and Subtype limits (for audience, content, and formats) not found in other FirstSearch databases. The Results screen is tabbed to allow users to see all the results, or to view records by material type (serials, Internet resources, maps, etc.). Every record includes a "Libraries worldwide" link to view the list of libraries that own the item. (One can also restrict a search to a particular library.)

WorldCat.org

When the National Library of Medicine provides the entire contents of MEDLINE (and more) for free on the Internet in the form of PubMed, or similarly the Department of Education gives us ERIC, it's wonderful, it's amazing, but after all, these are government-produced resources: in the United States, these are our tax dollars at work. So while these are very important additions in terms of information sharing, they aren't *completely* unexpected. In contrast, when OCLC, a private, for-profit organization, decided to provide the WorldCat database for free on the Internet as WorldCat.org, it was, to me at least, a breathtaking move. WorldCat had only ever been offered through OCLC's FirstSearch platform (which makes sense), it was the result of thousands of contributing member libraries' efforts, and building it had involved a great deal of money sloshing back and forth over the years. To decide to "give it away" must have involved meetings and discussions and struggles beyond the powers of my imagination.

Background: The Path to WorldCat.org

OCLC didn't immediately produce the current WorldCat.org: starting in December 2004, they first experimented with a program dubbed Open WorldCat, which only inserted "Find in a Library" pages into the results from Google and other search engines. Open WorldCat also let the search engines have access to only certain subsets of the total WorldCat database,

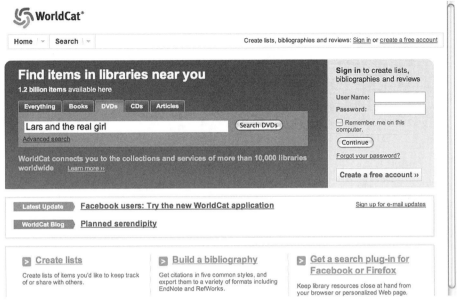

Fig. 6.13. WorldCat.org "home" search screen set to search for a DVD, as of June 2008. Screen shots used with permission of OCLC; FirstSearch® and WorldCat® are registered trademarks of OCLC Online Computer Library Center, Inc.

and operated under a number of other constraints as well (Hane, 2006). Although limited in many ways, Open WorldCat evidently convinced OCLC that they could go further, and the appearance in August 2006 of World-Cat.org, a "destination Web site," was greeted very positively by librarians (Flagg, 2006; Hane, 2006). At last, anyone who could get online could search the entire WorldCat database, using a simple, friendly interface. Each search result is linked to a "Find in a Library" information page, where the user can enter geographic information (e.g., zip code), and receive a list of nearby WorldCat libraries that own the item. Users can also link right to a library's online catalog record to initiate circulation activity or access electronic content directly ("OCLC Launches," 2006).

Developments and Change

Since its launch, WorldCat.org has been enthusiastically adding both technical and social features to appeal to all sorts of audiences. In 2006, you could add a WorldCat.org search box to your personal or institutional Web pages, or download Web toolbars or plug-ins for your favorite browser. RSS feeds from WorldCat.org were also available, as well as the ability to add reviews and notes on individual items ("OCLC Launches," 2006). By early 2007, WorldCat.org records offered links out to related "Web Resources," faceted browsing, a Chinese-language interface, and automatic geographic location sensing based on IP address ("WorldCat.org Adds," 2007). By August 2007, WorldCat.org was offering personalization with "My WorldCat" accounts, allowing users to build and share lists of materials as well as a personal profile ("WorldCat.org Adds List-Building," 2007). Since then, OCLC has added the ability to limit results by format, and to be kept up to date on the contents of other people's (public) lists by means of RSS feeds. To

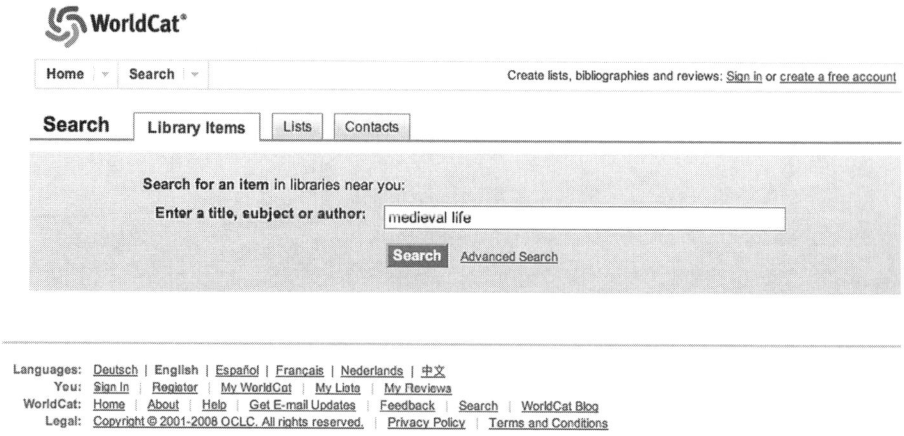

Fig. 6.14. WorldCat.org "basic" search screen set up for search example 1, as of June 2008. Screen shots used with permission of OCLC; FirstSearch® and WorldCat® are registered trademarks of OCLC Online Computer Library Center, Inc.

aid students and other writers in their quest for easier bibliography creation, WorldCat.org can format citations in any of five common styles, and lets you export them to RefWorks, EndNote, or other bibliographic management software. (Want to learn how to do it? The tutorial is a video, only 1:47 minutes long, on YouTube.) And what would modern life be without Facebook and Google? To further its intention to be where the users are, OCLC provided code to Facebook to allow users to add WorldCat.org as an application there, so that you can have a WorldCat.org search box on your Facebook page. OCLC is also working closely with Google Books, exchanging data and links. Google Book Search will provide links to WorldCat.org, and WorldCat records will get links to digitized books (Murphy, 2008). WorldCat.org even has its own blog. It will be interesting to see what new features have been added by the time this book is available.

Notes and Search Examples

As of June 2008, the WorldCat.org home screen offered one search box, five tabs, and various announcements and invitations to log in (Figure 6.13). If you want to search "everything," you can, and refine your results afterwards. Or, if you know you're looking for a DVD to while away the evening, this search screen lets you specify that, or one of the other most common formats people tend to search for.

Note that this is "home" for WorldCat.org. The Search link just below the logo offers the options to Search for Library Items, Search for Lists, or Search for Contacts. You might expect that Search for Library Items interface would be the same as on the home screen, but it turns out to be even more minimalistic (Figure 6.14). Let's think of it as the basic search.

Both the home and the basic search screens also link to an Advanced search (Figure 6.15), which provides just enough additional sophistication to make it efficient but not overwhelming.

Every results page and record display page includes a "Search for items:" search box, along with a link to the Advanced search, at the top of the page.

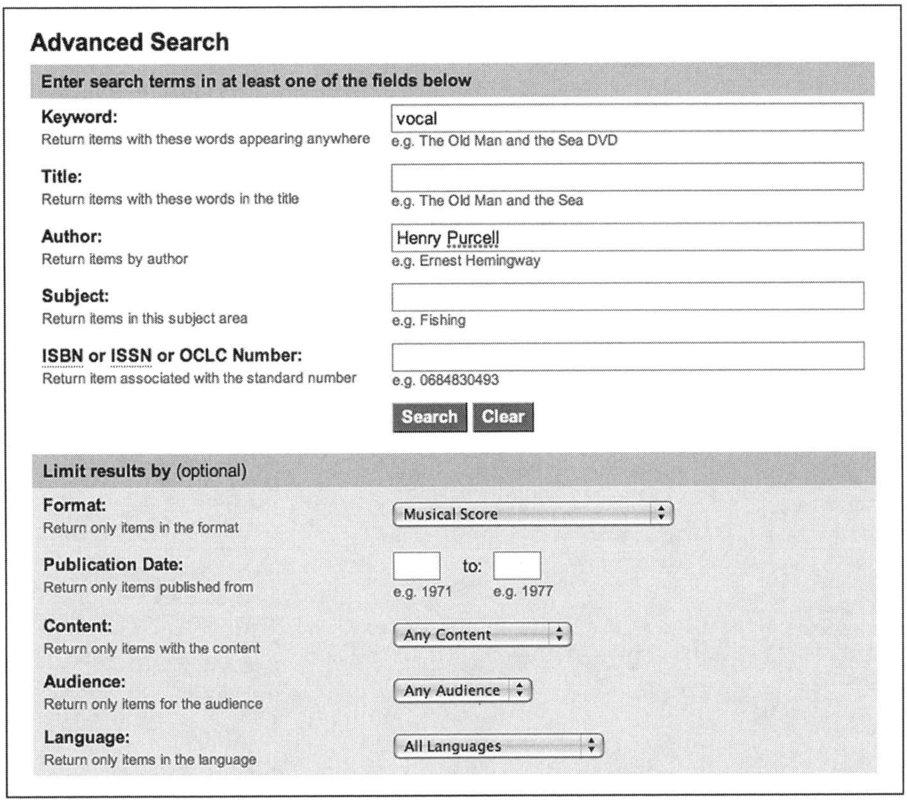

Advanced Search

Enter search terms in at least one of the fields below

Keyword:
Return items with these words appearing anywhere

vocal
e.g. The Old Man and the Sea DVD

Title:
Return items with these words in the title

e.g. The Old Man and the Sea

Author:
Return items by author

Henry Purcell
e.g. Ernest Hemingway

Subject:
Return items in this subject area

e.g. Fishing

ISBN or ISSN or OCLC Number:
Return item associated with the standard number

e.g. 0684830493

[Search] [Clear]

Limit results by (optional)

Format:
Return only items in the format

Musical Score

Publication Date:
Return only items published from

[ ] to: [ ]
e.g. 1971   e.g. 1977

Content:
Return only items with the content

Any Content

Audience:
Return only items for the audience

Any Audience

Language:
Return only items in the language

All Languages

Fig. 6.15. WorldCat.org Advanced search screen set up for search example 2, as of June 2008. Screen shots used with permission of OCLC; FirstSearch® and WorldCat® are registered trademarks of OCLC Online Computer Library Center, Inc.

Search Examples

Here are just a few ideas for getting into WorldCat.org and exploring its features. Since it is freely available and also very likely to keep changing, screen shots here are kept to a minimum, but features to look for are described.

Search 1

Say that you are a student taking a course on medieval history, and you have to write a paper on some aspect of the period that interests you. A pretty broad mandate, and frankly, you're not sure if you're that interested in *any* aspect of medieval times, at least not enough to write a paper on it! Maybe if you can see a lot of results, however, something will get your attention. At the Home screen or the "basic" interface, you type in:

Medieval life

as shown in Figure 6.14. Wow! Plenty of results . . . and observe, the feature that we are seeing more and more of, the opportunity to "Refine Your Search" in the panel on the left (in Figure 6.16, this long narrow area has been broken into three columns in the interests of space).

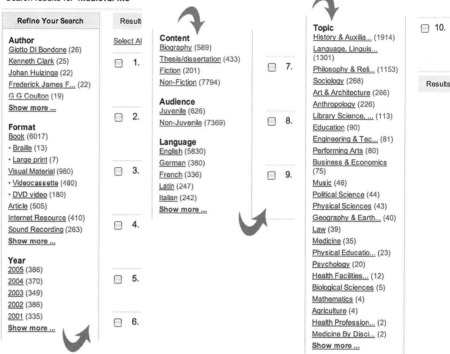

Fig. 6.16. "Refine Your Search" panel for the "medieval life" search, rearranged to save space, as of June 2008. Screen shots used with permission of OCLC; FirstSearch® and WorldCat® are registered trademarks of OCLC Online Computer Library Center, Inc.

If one of the titles doesn't catch your eye immediately, the most helpful way to "Refine" your search in this case might be the last option, by Topic.[3] Clicking "Show more..." in this case reveals a fascinating list of topical areas for "medieval life," and surely one of them will be interesting enough for a whole paper's worth of writing.

Search 2

A Master's in Vocal Performance student is home on break and preparing for a midyear vocal recital. She wants to do an all-Purcell program, but knows that her school's library isn't strong on that period. Going to World-Cat.org, she simply types in:

Purcell music

and is stunned at the number of results; what a jumble of types and authors are represented. Sadly, she misses the "Refine Your Search" area on the left, but does notice the Advanced Search link at the top. In the Advanced Search screen, she knows that her Author is Henry Purcell, and after looking at the Format dropdown for a moment, she recognizes just what she wants: "Musical Scores," as shown in Figure 6.15. At the last minute, she adds "vocal" as a Keyword, having noticed material on "keyboard" compositions in the earlier results. Ah! These results are more manageable. In fact, one

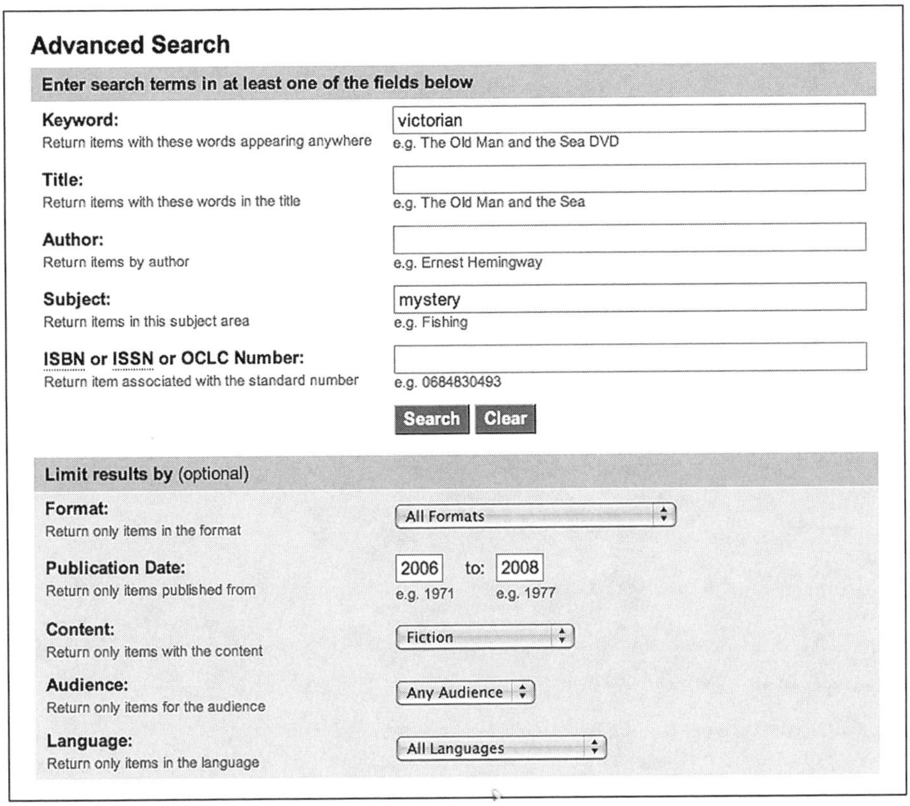

Advanced Search

Enter search terms in at least one of the fields below

Keyword:
Return items with these words appearing anywhere

victorian
e.g. The Old Man and the Sea DVD

Title:
Return items with these words in the title

e.g. The Old Man and the Sea

Author:
Return items by author

e.g. Ernest Hemingway

Subject:
Return items in this subject area

mystery
e.g. Fishing

ISBN or ISSN or OCLC Number:
Return item associated with the standard number

e.g. 0684830493

[Search] [Clear]

Limit results by (optional)

Format:
Return only items in the format

[All Formats ⬍]

Publication Date:
Return only items published from

[2006] to: [2008]
e.g. 1971   e.g. 1977

Content:
Return only items with the content

[Fiction ⬍]

Audience:
Return only items for the audience

[Any Audience ⬍]

Language:
Return only items in the language

[All Languages ⬍]

Fig. 6.17. WorldCat.org Advanced search screen set up for search Example 3, as of June 2008. Screen shots used with permission of OCLC; FirstSearch® and WorldCat® are registered trademarks of OCLC Online Computer Library Center, Inc.

of the book-CD sets looks so useful, she decides not to bother with ILL, and instead makes use of the "Buy This Item" panel in the full record screen to order it from OCLC's "Buy It Now" service. (It's nice that a portion of her purchase will benefit libraries.) For the others, she creates an account and starts putting together her list.

Search 3

A friend mentioned that she was reading a great recently published mystery, set in Victorian times, which really conveyed what daily life was like then (and made her awfully glad not to have had to live through the Victorian era). Of course, she told you the title, but a couple of weeks pass, and this is all you can remember about it. You could e-mail her and admit that you have no short-term memory, or see if WorldCat.org could provide any ideas. In the Advanced screen, you set up a search as in Figure 6.17.

Specifying "Subject—mystery" and "Content—fiction" seems rather redundant, but because this is all you have to focus your search, you do it anyway. Amazingly, you spot the two most likely possibilities right away in the results list: *Kept, a Victorian Mystery* and *Death on the Lizard*[4] (Figure 6.18). (Your friend isn't the type for series books, which rules out the *Mrs. Jeffries* . . . titles immediately.) Going into the full records for each of

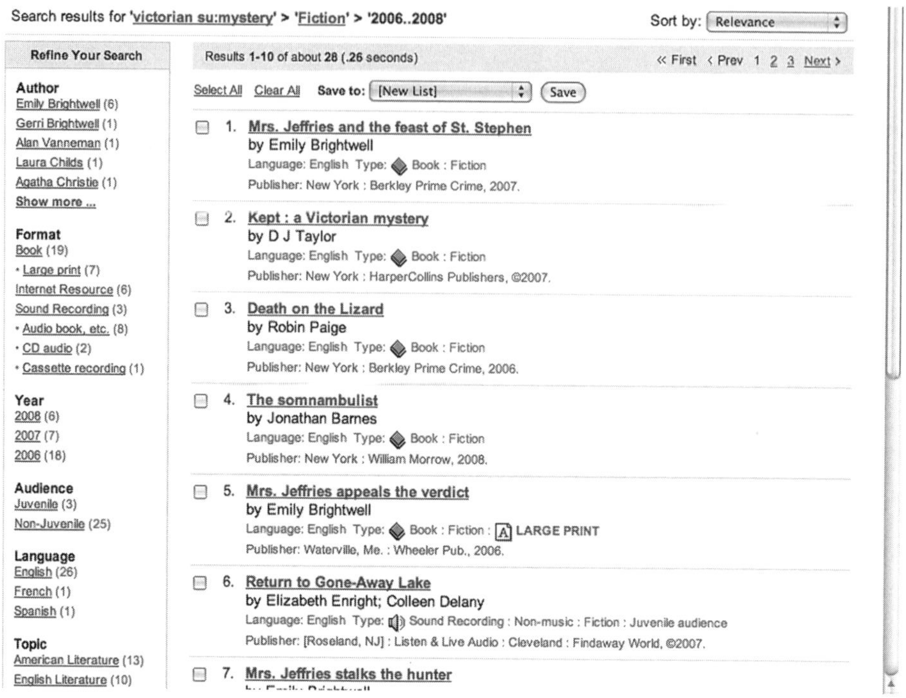

Fig. 6.18. Initial results for search Example 3 in WorldCat.org, as of June 2008. Screen shots used with permission of OCLC; FirstSearch® and WorldCat® are registered trademarks of OCLC Online Computer Library Center, Inc.

the likely ones, under the Reviews tab the comments pulled in from Amazon.com help out further: *Death on the Lizard* turns out to be another series novel, but *Kept* appears to be more serious and thoughtful. That could well be it!

WorldCat.org: A Bold Stroke in the Case for Libraries

Librarians are increasingly anxious that their profession and their institutions will be made redundant by products such as Google, but with WorldCat.org, OCLC is making a resounding counterattack. Their stated goal in providing WorldCat.org is to "make library resources more visible to Web users and to increase awareness of libraries as a primary source of reliable information" (Flagg, 2006). The methodology is direct: put the content of the WorldCat database directly into the hands of everyone online, at a brief, easy-to-remember Web address, and let the site grow and participate in whatever new Web developments come along. It's a breathtaking concept!

Quick Recap

WorldCat.org provides free access on the web to the entire contents of the WorldCat database, with the aim of helping users discover and use library content. It is designed for easy use by any Web user, in both the "one search box" versions on the homepage and the "Search for Library

Items" page, and the Advanced search page. The extensive "Refine Your Results" options that appear on the Results page provide many ways to focus a search, and are particularly valuable for broad keyword searches. When a record for an item is displayed, WorldCat.org displays a list of libraries that own the item, geographically arranged from nearest to farthest. The geographical detection is done either automatically based on the IP of the user, or by the user entering a zip code. WorldCat.org works with partners such as Amazon.com and Google Books Search to enhance what it provides, and offers features for personalization (e.g., lists, personal profiles, notes), alerting (i.e., RSS feeds), and citation management (e.g., exporting to RefWorks and EndNote).

Revisiting Your Local OPAC

Even though WorldCat is a (huge) union *catalog*, I always think of it as a *database*. On the other hand, I always think of my institution's online catalog as—a catalog, not a database. Now, why is that? Is it because WorldCat comes to us through the FirstSearch interface, as do many article databases, and our library catalogs come from other vendors, vendors who specialize in online public access *catalogs*? My feelings about WorldCat.org are the same: it's a database, not a catalog. Whether you have the same reaction or not, go now and revisit whatever library catalog you use most often. Try to look at it as if it were a new database. Examine it with the Searcher's Toolkit in mind: what fields does it offer? What limits? Does it offer a basic and an advanced search mode? Are there even other modes? Does it support Boolean searching, wildcards, or truncation? Are there stop words? What are the default search settings? Are there any special features that have been customized for *your* library?

Now compare searching your OPAC with WorldCat and with WorldCat.org. Does one seem "more transparent" (in terms of how it works) than the other? Look up an item owned by your library, and then find the record for it in WorldCat,[5] and in WorldCat.org. How do the record displays compare? Think about what factors might be driving the needs of a remote, *union* catalog as opposed to the local catalog for one library (or library system). WorldCat.org figures somewhere in the middle of the two: it is the huge WorldCat catalog, but it is also trying very hard to be local. How well does it succeed?

In general, you may find it easy to fall into using the local OPAC just as a title look-up device, forgetting what a sophisticated search engine it really is (or, perhaps, it isn't). It's worth taking a few moments and reacquainting yourself with this local resource, which you probably think that you know so well.

Exercises and Points to Consider

1. In the section called "A Tool for Many Parts of the Library," we mentioned a couple of ways that you might use WorldCat at the Reference Desk. What other uses can you think of?

2. Find some books on fast food (what's the best way to get books really on "fast food," and not about food you can prepare fast?)

3. Half-remembered reference problem: a patron comes in trying to describe some books she has enjoyed. She remembers the author's

name was "something-something smith," and the books are mysteries, about a female detective in Africa somewhere. Try just searching the author field for Smith, and the Genre/Form field for mystery, and see if you can identify this series of books.

4. If you have a favorite author or genre, see if you can use WorldCat to find all the records for those works in your local public library branch. (Tip: use the code look-up screen.)

5. WorldCat claims to have records for everything from stone tablets to electronic books. See if you can find examples of both ends of this spectrum. (Hints: in each case, use a combination of keywords and Limits. For the stone tablets, note the "Visual Materials" Limit, and that the "Material Type" for this sort of thing is "real object." For electronic books, you'll want to use the "Internet Resource" Limit.)

6. WorldCat results are sorted, or ranked, by the number of libraries that own the item. There are three other options, but ranking is often set as the default. Why, do you think? What would be the advantages and disadvantages of other results display options?

7. Now try the searches in Exercises 2 to 5 in WorldCat.org. What are the advantages and disadvantages of searching using the First-Search interface vs. the WorldCat.org interface?

8. Last, think about this approach to cultural research, introduced to me by a faculty member in Anthropology. You can use World-Cat to track longitudinally how new concepts emerge and grow, as reflected in their publication counts. Try this: in WorldCat.org, search: globali#ation (you won't find a peep about something as geeky as the wildcard symbol for one internal letter in the WorldCat.org Help, but anything you can do in FirstSearch, you can do here)—to pick up both the U.S. and U.K. spellings of the term. Now use the Refine Your Search—Year option, and click the "Show more . . ." link once or even twice, to show publishing volume for materials with this keyword year by year. You'll see that starting in 1986, this term starts appearing with ever-increasing frequency, up to the watershed year of 2003, after which its appearance tapers off somewhat.

Notes

1. Not all member libraries can or do contribute records, of course. Many small libraries simply pay to be able to search and download records for their local catalog, as it is still more efficient and economical than employing cataloging staff.

2. Visit the "Watch WorldCat grow" page at http://www.oclc.org/worldcat/newgrow. htm. It is absolutely fascinating.

3. In the image of the Refine list, you might wonder about the initial list of years provided to "refine" by: it might make you think nothing has been published about "medieval life" since 2005, because it is a straight consecutive list from 2001 to 2005. Clicking "Show more . . ." explains it, however: there are materials published on this topic every year, but just by happenstance, it turns out that 2001 to 2005 were banner years for publishing on medieval life. The years 2001 to 2005 simply had the highest "hit counts," and thus were the system's choice of Years for display in the initial Refine panel.

4. The "Lizard" refers to the southernmost tip of Cornwall, in England.

5. Check the "Libraries worldwide" link to make sure that you get the version of the record with which your library is associated. Although the ideal might be one record per title in WorldCat, the reality is that there are often several records for the same title, because participating libraries have cataloged the item slightly differently.

7
Humanities Databases

Although people come to librarianship with all kinds of different backgrounds and with many different undergraduate degrees, from purely anecdotal evidence it seems to me that there is still a preponderance of people with undergraduate degrees in the humanities who enter the library field (or am I imagining that large sigh of relief among you readers, now that we've arrived at the Humanities chapter?). In any event, it's likely you'll find the two databases considered here, *America: History and Life*,[1] and the *MLA International Bibliography*, to be interesting, easy to use, and a fascinating window into their respective disciplines.

As with MEDLINE and the *Web of Science* in Chapter 5, in *MLA* we have an excellent example of a database structured specifically for its subject matter. What is uniquely important to *MLA* and its users are attributes of written (and other forms of) communication: genres, themes, influences, etc., all of which are supported in *MLA* records, and very clearly reflected in the version of the *MLA* database described here. In *America: History and Life*, we have a real-world example of a database that has gone from a unique, special-purpose interface (under its previous vendor, ABC-CLIO, as presented in the first edition of this book), to the EBSCO platform, in which a fairly similar interface is used for many databases. Has the database lost its unique identity or any useful functionality in the move? I believe we will decide that it hasn't, and has even gained functionality in the move.

We will observe some "disciplinary" differences between the two resources in their approach to languages and dates. In the history database, it is sufficient to have the usual single field for language of publication. In the literature database, however, language of publication and language as the *subject* of the publication are equally important and are supported by two distinct fields. For historians, this kind of distinction arises around dates: *when* something happened is part of a publication's content and needs to be distinguished from when the item was published. Thus, two fields: a special-purpose field to specify the historical period discussed in the publication, the other the usual date-of-publication limit field. The *MLA International Bibliography* also has the usual publication date limit field, and a separate field for the period being discussed, but their set of "Period" values (a browsable index list) reveals a rather different mindset about dates. As in Chapter 5, while we work through these two resources, in addition to absorbing information about functionality and content, try to be alert to aspects of each database that seem specially designed to support its subject discipline.

America: History and Life

Background and Coverage

America: History and Life, and its complement, *Historical Abstracts*, were the flagship products of ABC-CLIO, a family-owned company devoted to history and social studies reference products. In 2007, these two databases were acquired by EBSCO, and by July 2008 were available solely through that interface. *Historical Abstracts* indexes materials on world history, while *America: History and Life* focuses on American and Canadian history. We will work with the latter database, but what you learn about searching *America: History and Life* can be applied to *Historical Abstracts*.

As described in an ABC-CLIO Product Information Sheet (Speck, 2002), *America: History and Life* first appeared in print in 1964, but the index covers materials back to 1954, which is a somewhat unusual treat in the indexing world. The online version contains all the content of the print versions, for example, 1954 to the present, making it a "date-deep" resource. According to the EBSCO Help screen, in 2006 *America: History and Life* began adding retrospective coverage for the most important historical journals in JSTOR. When complete, the indexing for these journals will extend the database's coverage back to the late-nineteenth century.

The historical scope of coverage, however, goes back to prehistory: that is, articles, book and media reviews, conference papers, and dissertations, discussing any period of American and Canadian history from prehistory to the present are eligible for inclusion. Journal articles are drawn from a worldwide scan of almost 1,700 journals. The database is updated monthly, and approximately 16,000 entries are added per year.

America: History and Life is a true indexing and abstracting service: it contains citations, some with abstracts. The abstracts are frequently followed by a name or initials in square brackets, indicating that abstracts in *America: History and Life* are written by individuals, rather than being machine-generated. Although *America: History and Life* does not contain any full text, it integrates closely with JSTOR and can be configured to help users get to other sources of full text by link resolvers such as SFX. A combination of these history indexes, a subscription to the full text journal archive service JSTOR, and a linking technology would be very powerful and convenient for users.

Notes and Search Examples

If you subscribe to both *America: History and Life* and *Historical Abstracts,* you can configure your EBSCO links to search both databases at

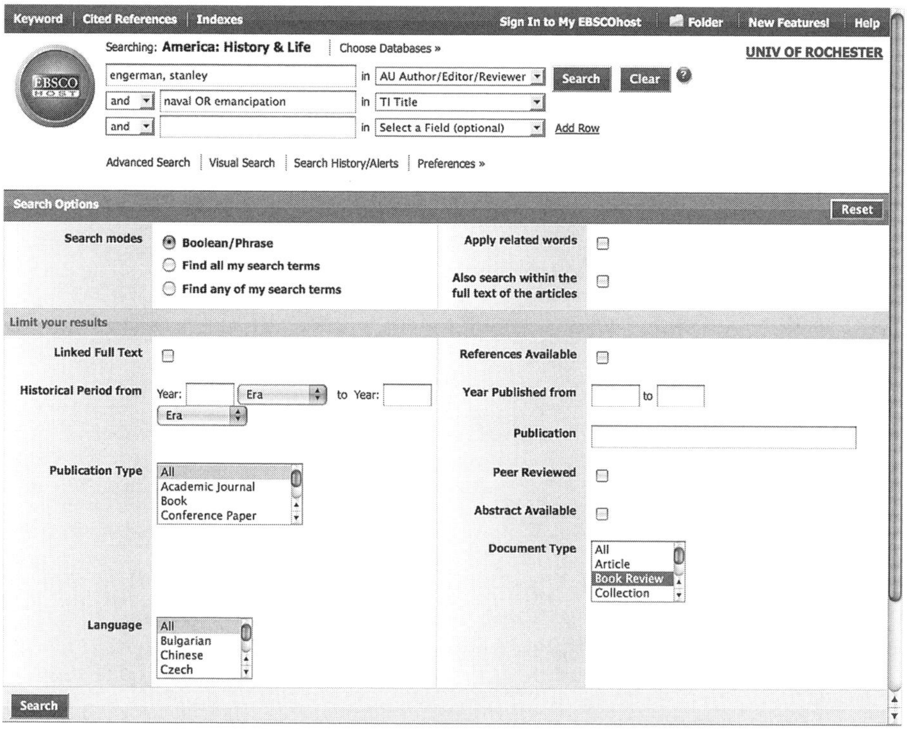

Fig. 7.1. Advanced Search screen, showing search strategy to find book reviews.
© 2008 EBSCO Industries, Inc. All rights reserved.

once, or each one separately. The following scenarios are based on searching
America: History and Life by itself.

Advanced Search Interface

The Advanced Search screen (Figure 7.1) should look familiar, because
it is similar to the interface for *MasterFILE Select* introduced in Chapter 2.
Running through our usual mental checklist of the Searcher's Toolkit,
it's easy to see we have field searching, Boolean operators, and limits—
including several special purpose limits we didn't see in the *MasterFILE*
interface. Looking back up at the very top of the screen, rather than one
combined list of Subjects as in *MasterFILE*, in this database we have access
to Indexes. We can infer that we will be able to browse the values for several
distinct fields, as in ERIC or *Library Literature*. Figure 7.1 is set up to run a
simple search that demonstrates one of the common uses of this database.

Search Example 1: Finding Book Reviews

In this search example, we'd like to find reviews of Stanley Engerman's
two recent books, *Naval Blockades in Peace and War*, and *Slavery, Eman-
cipation and Freedom*. We can simply enter his name directory style (last
name, first name) in the Authors/Editors/Reviewers field, add keywords
from the two titles we are interested in (OR'd together), and select "Book
Review" as our document type from the Limits area. Our search is ready, as
shown in Figure 7.1.

Fig. 7.2. Results for book review search (partial screen). © 2008 EBSCO Industries, Inc. All rights reserved.

Our results appear to be right on target, judging by the six records shown in Figure 7.2 (the left and right side result screen panels have been closed in this shot, to fit all six records into one image).

Some things to understand about this search: in the case of a book review, "Title" always refers to the title of the work being reviewed. "Authors/ Editors/Reviewers" is literally any of those roles: a search against that field retrieves records for a person as author (of the book being reviewed), or as a reviewer of other peoples' books. Although the addition of a keyword from the title of the work being reviewed generally ensures that you'll get the former (e.g., reviews of Stanley Engerman's books), if that title keyword happens to match a record where Engerman was the *reviewer*, you'll get those results as well, as record 6 shows. Searching only an author name (e.g., John Bloggs), limited to book review as document type, retrieves both reviews of works by John Bloggs and reviews by Mr. Bloggs of other people's works. Don't let this throw you. (If you do this for Professor Engerman, you'll find he's both a prolific author and reviewer.) Finally, notice in result 6, where you can see the reviewer's full name, that he uses the middle initial L. If you were to go through the preceding five records, you'd see the same thing: Engerman, Stanley L. You could go into the Indexes, look up the name in the author index and select all the variations—but you don't need to. The search engine is smart enough to do the right thing and not to throw in false drops, at least for fairly distinct names. Of course, to get the works of the correct John Smith, remember to consult and choose from the Author Index.

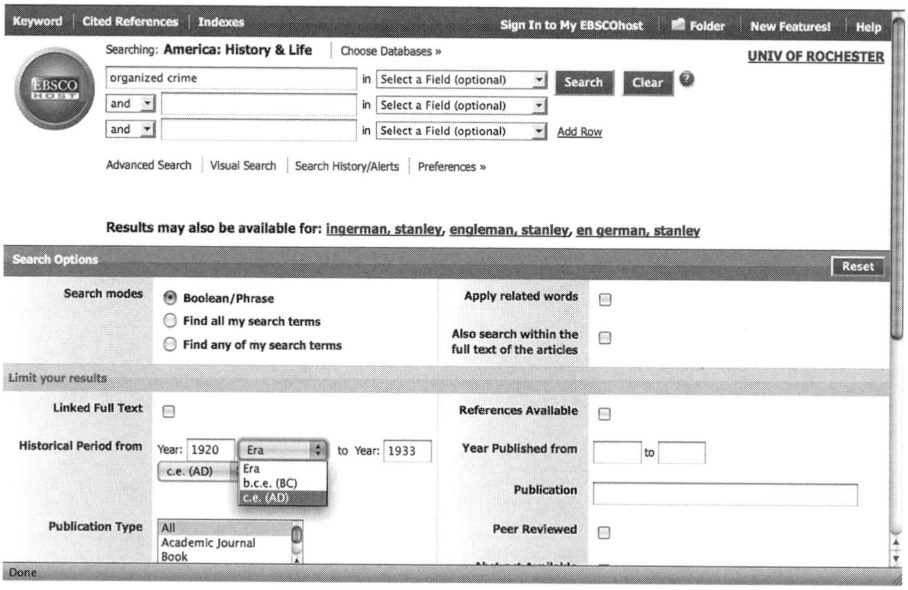

Fig. 7.3. Search Example 2, showing the Historical Period limit menu. © 2008 EBSCO Industries, Inc. All rights reserved.

Search Example 2: Finding Material about a Topic in a Particular Period

In this search, we want to produce a list of references to works about organized crime during Prohibition, that is, the period from 1920 to 1933 when the Volstead Act was in effect. Now we get to use the Historical Period limit field, with its "Era" drop-down menu for specifying "b.c.e. (BC)" or "c.e. (AD)."[2] Figure 7.3 shows the search screen set up for this search.

In the results screen for this search (pictured in Figure 7.4a with both the left and right panels open), we have many options for further adjusting our results. On the left side, we can Narrow the results by Source Type, such as Academic Journals, and/or by adding a Subject heading to the original search ("Crime and Criminals (organized)"). In both cases, if you didn't like the new results, it's very easy to get back to your original list: the Source Types list retains the option of All Results, and any Subject terms can be removed from the search string by just clicking the X box associated with them (Figure 7.4b).

In the list of results, you'll see that the ones that are articles have the handy "full citation preview" feature we saw in *MasterFILE* in Chapter 2, indicated by the magnifying glass icon. Simply mouse over the icon to read the abstract and see some of the subject headings for the record, without leaving the results screen (cf. Figure 2.10). (Document types such as dissertation or book review do not offer this feature.) The article results include the number of Cited References in the article; clicking the linked number displays the references (shades of the *Web of Science*!). In the panel on the right, we could add limits to restrict our results to records with "Linked Full Text," and/or those with "References Available," that is, articles with a bibliography of cited references, by clicking the appropriate checkboxes and the Update Results button. Just below that button is a very elegant feature: a link called *Search Options* (with the notation that we already have some

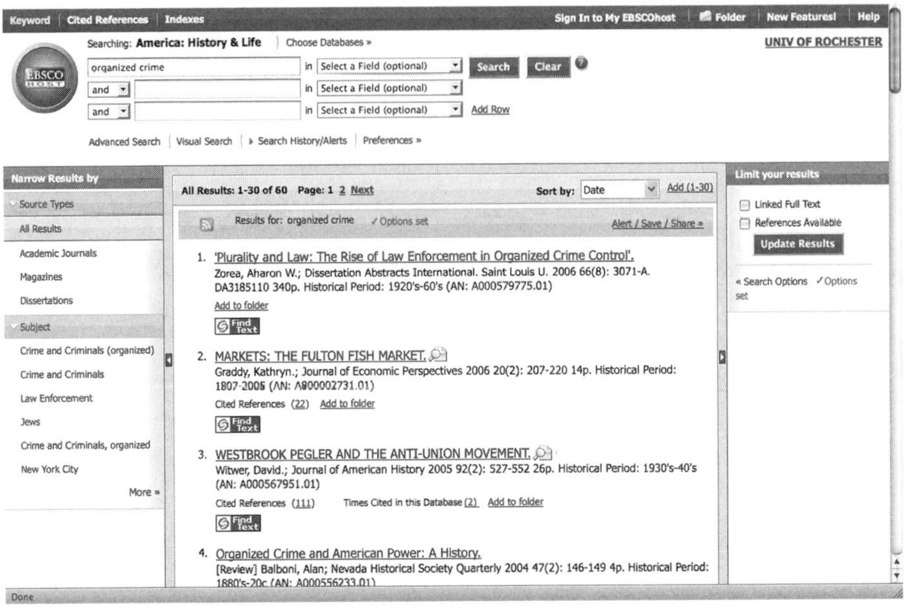

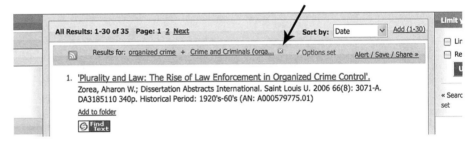

Fig. 7.4a. Initial results screen for Search Example 2. © 2008 EBSCO Industries, Inc. All rights reserved.

Fig. 7.4b. Results list for Search Example 2 altered on the fly; arrow points to icon for removing the additional search term. © 2008 EBSCO Industries, Inc. All rights reserved.

"Options set"). Clicking Search Options superimposes the Limits screen over the current results screen (Figure 7.5), allowing you to change any other limit and re-run the search, without going back to the search interface.

Search Example 3: Searching Cited References

The ability to search cited references ("who has cited Joe Blogg's classic paper lately?") is new with EBSCO's hosting of *America: History and Life*. Citations are as important to historians (e.g., record 3 in Figure 7.4a has 111 Cited References) as to the scientists in Thompson Reuter's *Web of Science*, and it's exciting to see another database vendor tackling this labor-intensive issue.

Our example for this search: we'd like to see publications that have cited Doris Kearns Goodwin's *No Ordinary Time: Franklin and Eleanor Roosevelt: the Home Front in World War II*, published in 1994. Clicking Cited References in the top bar, we get the search interface shown in Figure 7.6.

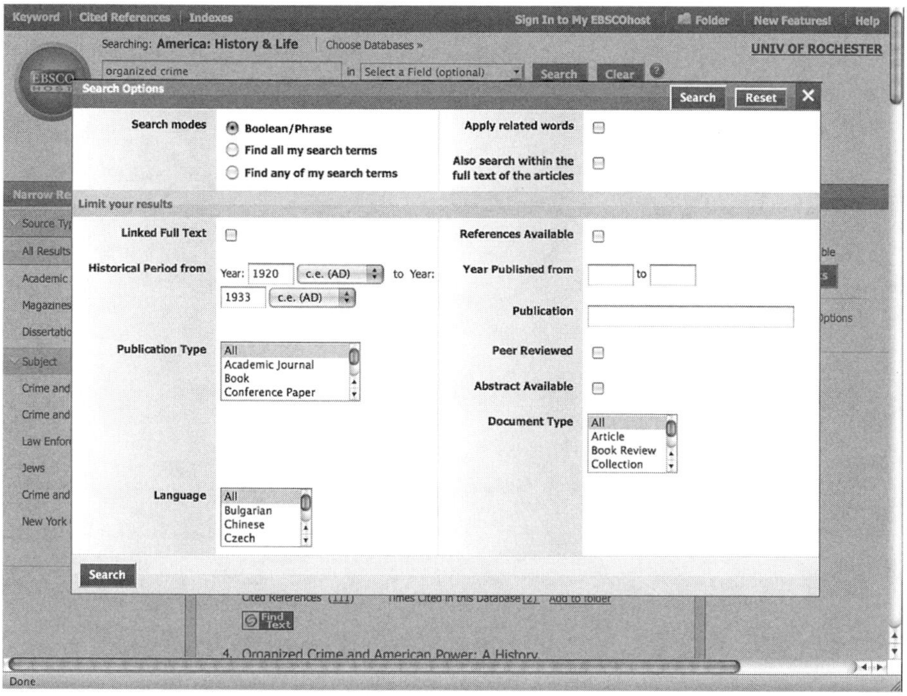

Fig. 7.5. Invoking Search options from the results screen; superimposed limits window. © 2008 EBSCO Industries, Inc. All rights reserved.

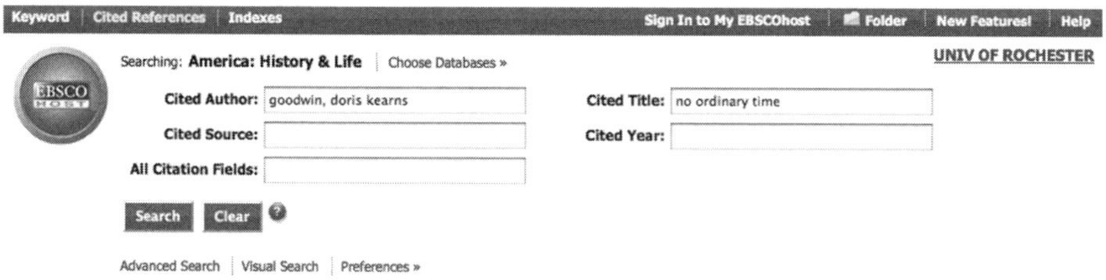

Fig. 7.6. Cited reference search interface, set to run Search Example 3. © 2008 EBSCO Industries, Inc. All rights reserved.

The interface is set up to run our cited reference search with Goodwin, Doris Kearns in the Cited Author field, and the beginning of her book's title in the Cited Title field.

This search already feels very different from the Cited Reference searching in the *Web of Science*—no constraints on how the name is entered, no agonizing about how a title (referring to a book or an article title) or a Source (which could again be a book title or the name of a journal), are abbreviated or entered: simply enter the initial words, or even a keyword. Now look at the results, most of which are pictured in Figure 7.7.

We can enter full words because the citation records contain full words. But some things don't change: as in the *Web of Science*, these references appear to be loaded into the database exactly as the author recorded them, so that we have some records in which the publication date is given as 1995 and others as 1994. In record 5, even the citing author's typo of "Worm War II" is faithfully recorded.

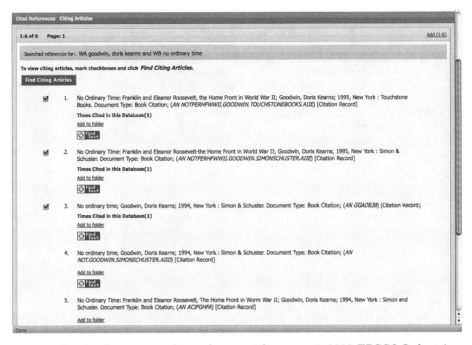

Fig. 7.7. Cited reference search results, partial screen. © 2008 EBSCO Industries, Inc. All rights reserved.

Using the checkboxes to select all the records that have citing articles, we click the Find Citing Articles button and arrive at a screen of four results, shown in Figure 7.8. We are reminded of how the whole process started by the presence of the search interface at the top of the screen, and the reminder in the shaded bar just above the records: "These records cite: WA goodwin, doris kearns and WB no ordinary time." (WA and WB are field codes.) We can toggle back to the Cited References if we want by clicking those words in the bar where the arrow is pointing.

It's time we stopped to look at a full citation, to see how one citation can lead us to other records, and how to collect and output records for our own research and bibliographies.

Related Records, Folder, and Output Options

Related Records

The upper part of a full record display is shown in Figure 7.9. Carried over from the results list display, we have information about the number of Cited References (32), as well as Times Cited in this Database (3). On the right, under Related Information, we are offered three "Similar Results" that do indeed look right on topic. We can assess the usefulness of these records by reading their abstracts using the citation previewer function (mouse over the icon associated with each related record). We might decide we "want" all four records, the main one and the three related records.

The Records Folder

In EBSCO databases (at least as of June 2008), you collect the records that you're interested in by adding them to a "folder." Your opportunities

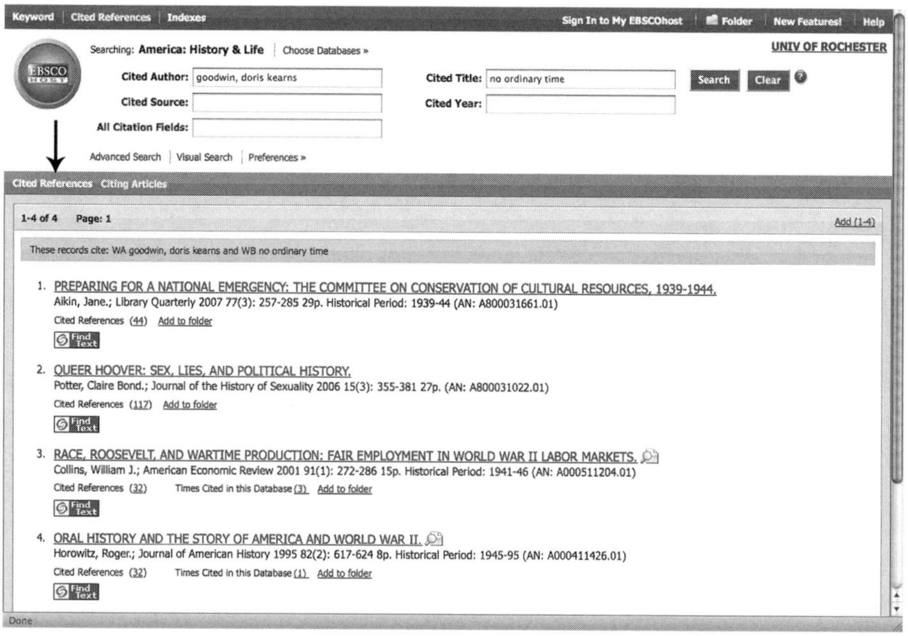

Fig. 7.8. The Citing articles for Search Example 3. © 2008 EBSCO Industries, Inc. All rights reserved.

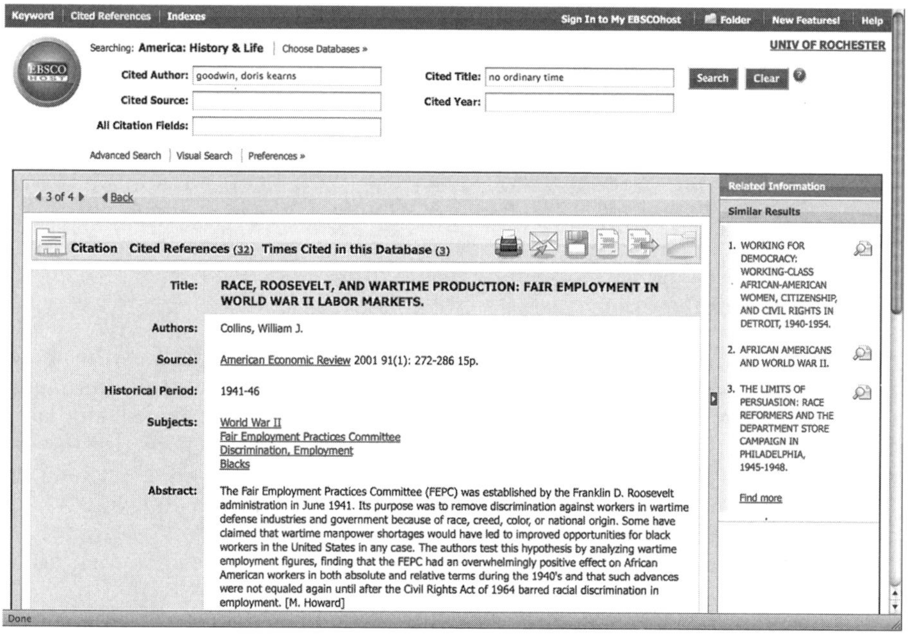

Fig. 7.9. Full record display for an article, showing Similar Results. © 2008 EBSCO Industries, Inc. All rights reserved.

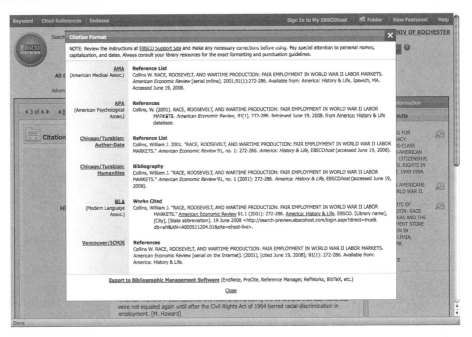

Fig. 7.10. Invoking the "how to cite" function, another use of the superimposed screen technology. © 2008 EBSCO Industries, Inc. All rights reserved.

for adding items to the folder are everywhere: in the results screen, each result has an Add to Folder link, or all the records on the page can be added using the "Add (1-<number>)" links at the top or bottom of the list (see Figures 7.4a, 7.7, or 7.8). In the citation previewer window there is an Add to Folder icon and text link, and in each full record a folder icon appears in the header and footer of the record display, as in Figure 7.9. As you add items to the Folder, the latest three added are displayed in the right-hand panel, under the bar marked "Folder has items." A screen shot and what you can do from the Folder are provided under Output, our next topic.

Output Options

On the individual full record screen, you can print, e-mail, save, see how to cite (in six popular formats), or export the record to a citation manager program, as indicated by the icons in Figure 7.9. The Cite icon, second from the end, again uses a technology that superimposes a new screen over the current one, as shown in Figure 7.10. This technique saves a great deal of "screen loading/refreshing" time, and leaves you right where you were when the superimposed screen is closed. Besides showing the current reference in different citation formats, there is a link to export the record to a citation manager (e.g., EndNote, RefWorks, etc.).

To output a group of records, you'll want to have collected them in the Folder and work from the Folder view (Figure 7.11). The Folder is accessed by the link in the right panel on the results screen, or from any screen using the icon in the topmost bar of the interface. There are three options for Sorting records in the Folder, and as in most of the databases we've seen, you can print, e-mail, save, or export to a citation management program.

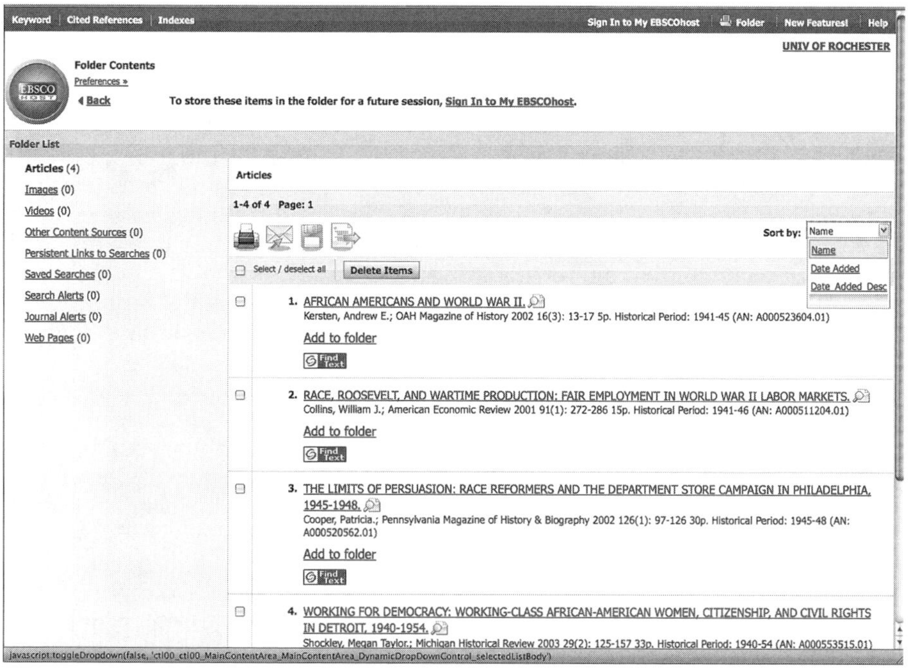

Fig. 7.11. The Folder interface, showing the Sort options. © 2008 EBSCO Industries, Inc. All rights reserved.

The Folder includes detailed information about the materials that you've put in it (on the right), and you can retain your Folder items from session to session by creating a "My EBSCOhost" account.

Last, a word about the e-mail function. The e-mail interface lets you send to multiple recipients, specify the Subject line and add comments. In addition, you can choose a standard format, a specific citation format, or create your own format by choosing exactly which fields you wish to send. The only drawback with the e-mail program as of the time of this writing is that it does not allow you to fill in the "from" field; it is fixed at the vendor's address.

Quick Recap

America: History and Life (AHL), and its complement, *Historical Abstracts*, are the leading indexes to the literature of history. AHL provides citations, some with abstracts, for articles, conference papers, book and media reviews, and dissertations that discuss any period of American and Canadian history from prehistory to the present (*Historical Abstracts* covers the rest of the world). The Advanced Search interface offers field searching and limits, including the special purpose "Historical Period" limit. AHL offers a Cited References search that is friendlier to use but smaller in scale than the *Web of Science*. There is also an interesting Visual Search function (not discussed here). There are many options for changing the search from the Results screen, all easily reversible. Full records for many citations offer links to Similar Results. Records are collected into a "Folder," for mass output processing. The output options are well developed, including good e-mail features and output-to-citation management programs.

MLA International Bibliography

Background and Coverage

The *MLA International Bibliography* is produced by the Modern Language Association of America, and is one of the longest running indexes still in existence. The Association itself was founded in 1883 and began publishing a printed index in 1921. (Materials in the online database, however, date back to 1884,[3] another example of an electronic product that has expanded beyond its print counterpart.) In a situation similar to that at the National Library of Medicine, the staff of the MLA's Department of Bibliographic Information Services work with outside bibliographers from around the world to produce the *Bibliography*. It is a huge cooperative effort.

The *MLA International Bibliography* (MLA IB) is vast in many ways: the scope of topics included, sources, document types, number of records, and publication dates. Topical coverage is described broadly as "all forms of human communication": literature, folklore (including music and art), the study of linguistics and languages, literary theory and criticism, the dramatic arts, and the history of printing and publishing. Coverage of the "history, theory, and practice of teaching language, literature, and rhetoric and composition," from 1998 onward, was added to the scope of the *Bibliography* in 2000 (MLA, 2007). Over 100,000 subject-indexed records, representing the entire runs of the journals in JSTOR's Language and Literature collection, have been added to the *Bibliography*, which extends coverage of journals such as *Modern Language Notes* and *Publications of the Modern Language Assocation* (PMLA*)* back as far as the 1880s (ProQuest, 2008). As indicated in the title, sources from all over the world are reviewed for entry into the database. (The "Language of Publication" thesaurus list is probably the longest and most esoteric you will ever encounter.) Document types covered include types that you would expect, such as books, book chapters, and journal articles, but also indexed are reference works, published working papers, conference papers and proceedings, citations for dissertations listed in *Dissertations Abstracts International*, electronic publications, and works related to teaching: handbooks, textbooks, anthologies, etc. Note, however, that one common type of document that is *not* included is reviews (ProQuest, 2008).

The "numbers" for the *Bibliography* are equally impressive: there are over 2 million records in the database, and new additions total about 66,000 records per year. Subject terms used to describe records come from the *MLA Thesaurus*, which includes over "49,000 topical terms and 327,000 names" (ProQuest, 2008). A database about literature is, obviously, very concerned with names: the names of writers and of characters.

The MLA IB is the first database since Wilson's *Library Literature* that we've encountered in this book that is purely an index. Full records are quite long owing to the number of fields included, but there are no abstracts,[4] and no full text. As we have seen in other databases, however, the *Bibliography* is OpenURL compliant: it supports full-text linking technologies. It is also possible to run the MLA IB in concert with, or as a module in, a full-text database called *Literature Online* (LION), as described briefly below.

Relationship to Other Literature Resources

Any discussion of the *MLA International Bibliography* should also mention two other major literature resources: the *Annual Bibliography of*

English Language and Literature (ABELL), and the previously mentioned *Literature Online* (LION). ABELL has a somewhat smaller scope than MLA IB in that it focuses on just English language materials and literature in English. ABELL also includes book reviews, unlike MLA IB. LION, the only full-text database in the three, also focuses on English literature, and provides the texts of over 350,000 literary works, along with criticism and reference resources. At this time, Chadwyck-Healey, the specialist humanities imprint of ProQuest, is the sole publisher for LION and is also a supplier of ABELL. With the addition of the MLA IB to the set of Chadwyck-Healey databases, it is now possible for subscribers to all three databases from this vendor to opt for integrated access: the use of LION as the single point of access for all three literature databases. For the purposes of this chapter, however, we will consider the MLA IB as a stand-alone database.

Notes and Search Examples

Any consideration of "humanities databases" needs to look at the MLA IB, but the question then is: from which vendor? At the time of this writing, there are five major database vendors offering the MLA's database. (The MLA provides a very informative and helpful chart about the distributors of their database at http://www.mla.org/bib_dist_comparison.) I have chosen to look at the Chadwyck-Healey version, because the interface seems to have been nicely tuned to the subject matter,[5] and the possible integration with other databases (described earlier) is quite compelling. Let's take a look.

Standard Search Interface

The MLA IB as offered by Chadwyck-Healey provides three search interfaces: Standard, Advanced, and Directory of Periodicals. We'll work with the first two here; notes about the Directory of Periodicals appear under "Additional Feature" later in this chapter. The Standard Search (Figure 7.12) offers support for the kinds of searches users might need most often: a straight topical search (using Keyword[s], Title Keyword[s], or Subject—All), the ever-popular search for literary criticism or interpretation (Author as Subject, Author's Work), and the need to fill out a citation from incomplete information (using a combination of Keyword, Article Author, Journal, and Publication Year). If we are mentally ticking things off on our Searcher's Toolkit list, the ability to use Boolean operators is not obvious, although we assume that it's there. The "Help" confirms this, along with supplying information about the other "tools" we're used to looking for, such as proximity operators and wildcards. There is an implied AND between fields on a page. A set of document types appears as an explicit "Limit," as well as fields that act in a limit capacity: Language of Publication and Publication Year.

Search Example 1

Our first search example is a topic that has received continuing attention from the literary community: examples of the use of cross-dressing in the works of Shakespeare. Figure 7.12 shows our search ready to be run.

Just the first five results for this search (Figure 7.13) start to demonstrate the breadth of coverage, in terms of document types and international reach, of this database. Represented are a book, an article from a German film journal, two chapters from edited books, and an article from a theatre

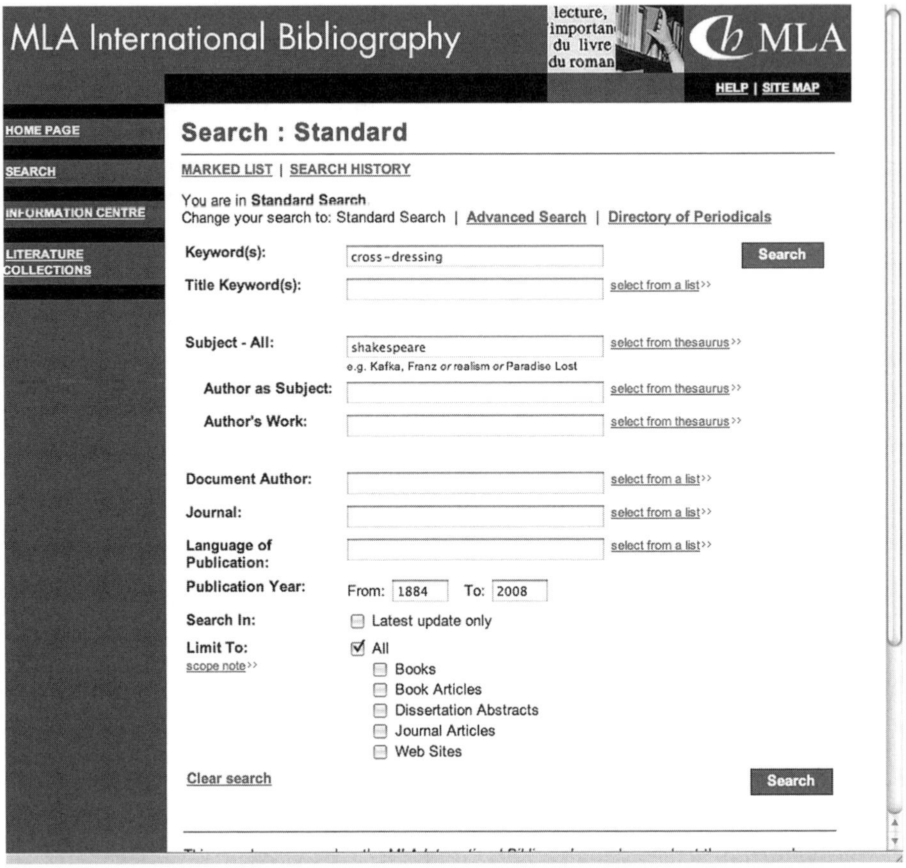

Fig. 7.12. Chadwyck-Healey MLA Standard Search Interface. Copyright © 2004–2008 ProQuest LLC.

journal. Farther down the list you would see a dissertation, an electronic journal article, and articles from Romanian and Spanish journals.

Two additional points to notice about the results screen are:

- First, several of these results have been selected in the usual way, by clicking their checkboxes. These entries are automatically added to the Marked List; if you view a full record or page forward in the results, you won't lose your marked items.

- Second, the system reports that the search retrieved "49 entries," but "61 hits." The entries count refers to the total number of citations, or records. The second, larger "hits" count measures the number of times that search terms appeared in records. A record in which a search term appears more than once causes the hit count to increase.

The Full Record display in Figure 7.14 should begin to give you a sense of the detailed indexing performed on records in the MLA IB, and the degree to which the record structure in this version of the database supports and makes explicit the subject fields. In this record alone there are fifteen subject fields, including six Literary Theme fields, and two Author as Subject and Author's Work fields.

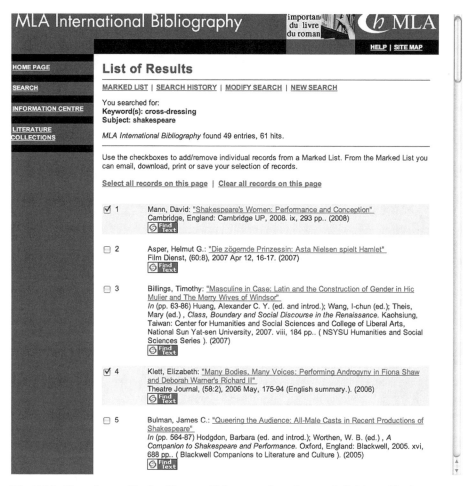

Fig. 7.13. Search results for Keyword(s): cross-dressing and Subject: Shakespeare. Copyright © 2004–2008 ProQuest LLC.

Two Additional Search Samples

Returning to the Standard Search screen, we see an example of a type of search that students frequently need to do, but frequently do incorrectly, in the partial screen shot in Figure 7.15. Students are used to searching for authors as authors, but when they need to find analysis or discussion *about* an author, they often fail to grasp that they must now search the author's name as a Subject. The "Author as Subject" field in the Standard Search screen is helpful for addressing this need.

Figure 7.16 is very similar, demonstrating a strategy for finding materials that discuss a specific work by an author. It also provides the opportunity for a discussion of non-English names.

Non-English Names in the *Bibliography*

As has been pointed out several times, the scope of the *Bibliography* is international, and among those 370,000+ names in the Thesaurus are thousands of names from scores of nationalities, including names transliterated from non-Roman alphabets. For example, the MLA indexers use the spelling

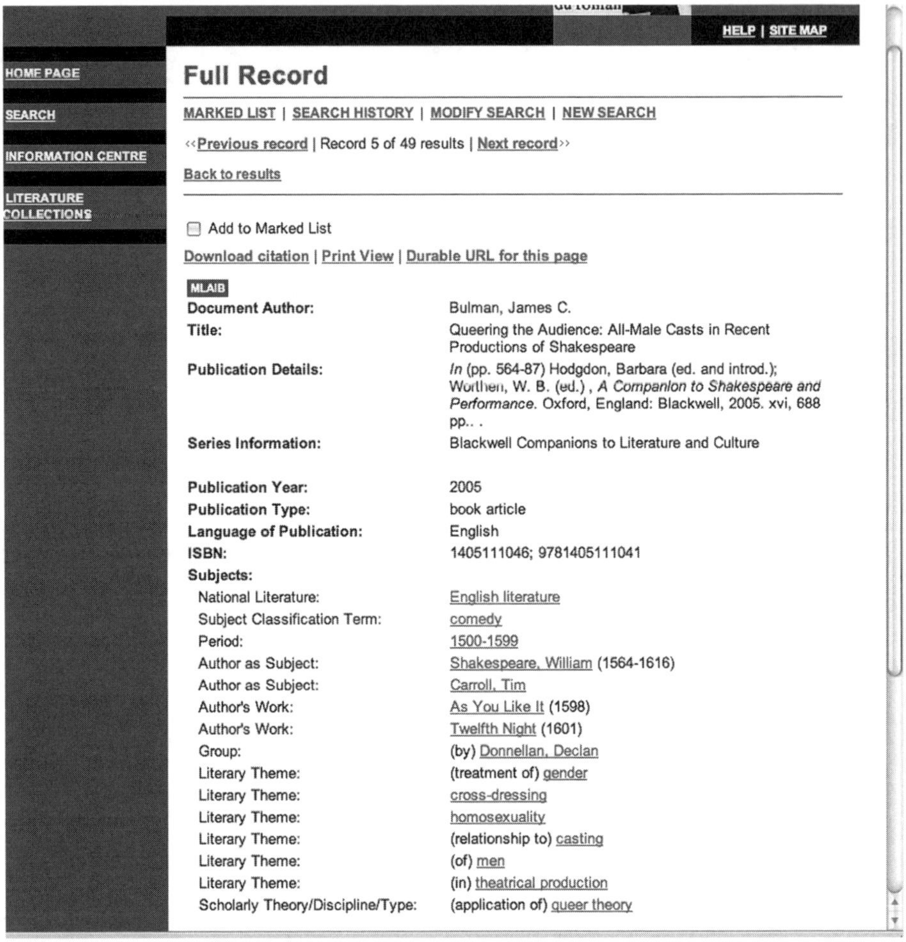

HELP | SITE MAP
HOME PAGE
SEARCH
INFORMATION CENTRE
LITERATURE COLLECTIONS
Full Record
MARKED LIST | SEARCH HISTORY | MODIFY SEARCH | NEW SEARCH
<<Previous record | Record 5 of 49 results | Next record>>
Back to results
Add to Marked List
Download citation | Print View | Durable URL for this page
MLAIB
Document Author: Bulman, James C.
Title: Queering the Audience: All-Male Casts in Recent Productions of Shakespeare
Publication Details: In (pp. 564-87) Hodgdon, Barbara (ed. and introd.); Worthen, W. B. (ed.) , A Companion to Shakespeare and Performance. Oxford, England: Blackwell, 2005. xvi, 688 pp.. .
Series Information: Blackwell Companions to Literature and Culture
Publication Year: 2005
Publication Type: book article
Language of Publication: English
ISBN: 1405111046; 9781405111041
Subjects:
National Literature: English literature
Subject Classification Term: comedy
Period: 1500-1599
Author as Subject: Shakespeare, William (1564-1616)
Author as Subject: Carroll, Tim
Author's Work: As You Like It (1598)
Author's Work: Twelfth Night (1601)
Group: (by) Donnellan, Declan
Literary Theme: (treatment of) gender
Literary Theme: cross-dressing
Literary Theme: homosexuality
Literary Theme: (relationship to) casting
Literary Theme: (of) men
Literary Theme: (in) theatrical production
Scholarly Theory/Discipline/Type: (application of) queer theory

Fig. 7.14. Full Record display from the cross-dressing search. Copyright © 2004–2008 ProQuest LLC.

Subject - All:
select from thesaurus>>
e.g. Kafka, Franz or realism or Paradise Lost
Author as Subject:
Bellow, Saul
select from thesaurus>>
Author's Work:
select from thesaurus>>

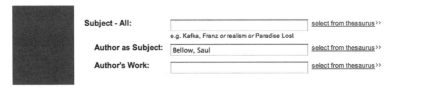

Fig. 7.15. Use of the Author as Subject field. Copyright © 2004–2008 ProQuest LLC.

Subject - All:
select from thesaurus>>
e.g. Kafka, Franz or realism or Paradise Lost
Author as Subject:
tolstoi
select from thesaurus>>
Author's Work:
"war and peace"
select from thesaurus>>

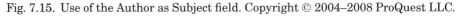

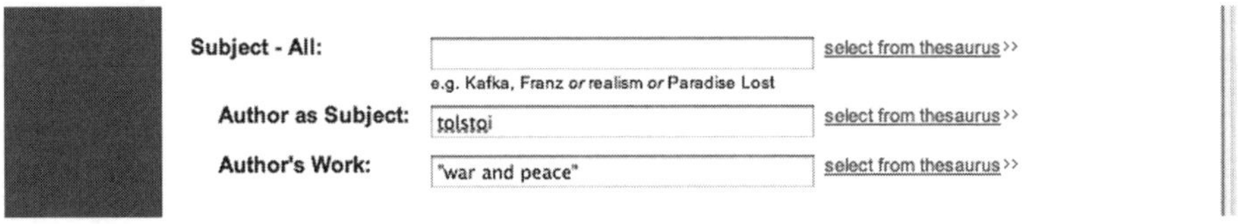

Fig. 7.16. Use of the Author as Subject and Author's Work fields. Copyright © 2004–2008 ProQuest LLC.

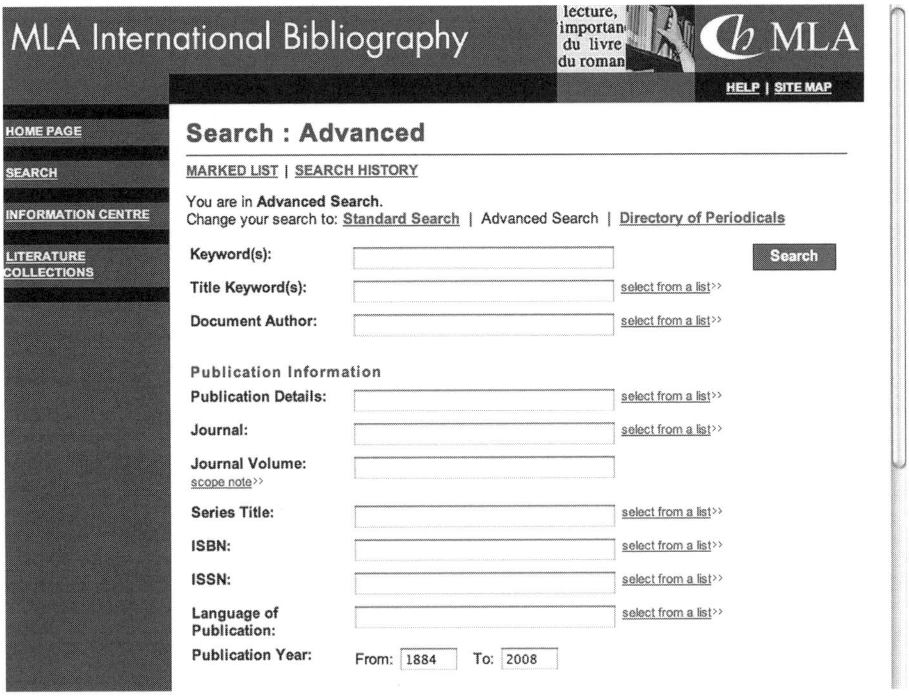

Fig. 7.17a. Advanced Search interface, upper half. Copyright © 2004–2008 ProQuest LLC.

Tolstoi, not *Tolstoy*, for the author of *War and Peace*. The only problem is that if you look up Tolstoy in the Thesaurus, there is no "see" reference to guide you to the other spelling. Working with Eastern European, Russian, and Chinese names (including place names) can be particularly tricky. For example, the controlled heading for the former leader of Communist China is *Mao Zedong*, not *Tse-tung, Mao*, or *Zedong, Mao*, forms and spellings that Westerners might be likely to try. If you can figure out the correct heading in the Thesaurus, *then* a Related Terms button is available and will show you the "Non-preferred Term(s)"—such as *Mao Tse-tung*, but the non-preferred entries are not searchable in the Thesaurus.

When working with names, be prepared to be flexible: use the Thesaurus if possible, but if the answer still isn't clear and you're getting frustrated, try searching the form of the name you're familiar with as Keyword(s), search parts of the name, or use truncation. You are likely to find records containing the information you need quickly, and you can then "pearl grow" from there.

Advanced Search

Let us move on to the Advanced Search screen. Chadwyck-Healey has made a deliberate decision to display all the searchable database fields in a list rather than using drop-down menus. The advantage is that the number and names of all the fields are obvious at a glance; the disadvantage is that it does make for a rather long screen! Figures 7.17a and Figure 7.17b provide the complete picture.

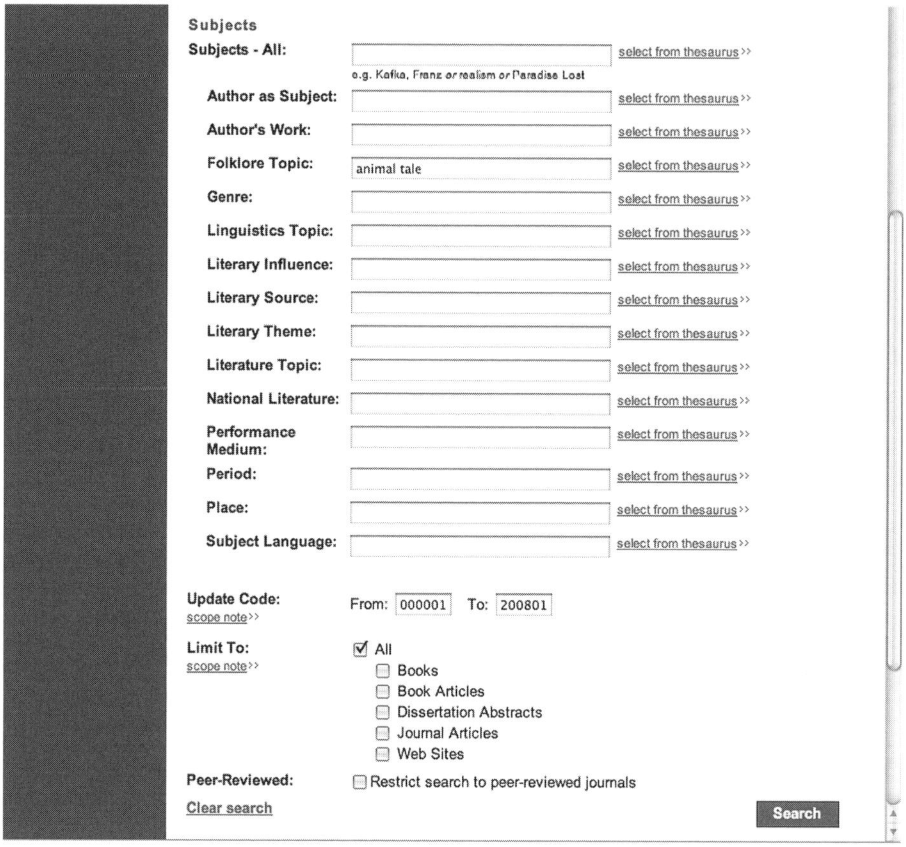

Subjects		
Subjects - All:		select from thesaurus >>
	e.g. Kafka, Franz or realism or Paradise Lost	
Author as Subject:		select from thesaurus >>
Author's Work:		select from thesaurus >>
Folklore Topic:	animal tale	select from thesaurus >>
Genre:		select from thesaurus >>
Linguistics Topic:		select from thesaurus >>
Literary Influence:		select from thesaurus >>
Literary Source:		select from thesaurus >>
Literary Theme:		select from thesaurus >>
Literature Topic:		select from thesaurus >>
National Literature:		select from thesaurus >>
Performance Medium:		select from thesaurus >>
Period:		select from thesaurus >>
Place:		select from thesaurus >>
Subject Language:		select from thesaurus >>

Update Code: scope note>>   From: 000001   To: 200801

Limit To: scope note>>   ☑ All
☐ Books
☐ Book Articles
☐ Dissertation Abstracts
☐ Journal Articles
☐ Web Sites

Peer-Reviewed: ☐ Restrict search to peer-reviewed journals

Clear search   [Search]

Fig. 7.17b. Advanced Search interface, lower half. Copyright © 2004–2008 ProQuest LLC.

What a wealth of fields: every possible aspect of a publication has a searchable field, and now we see some of the other topical areas of this database being brought out, such as Folklore, Linguistics, and Performance. (I've left a search in the Folklore Topic field; we'll see a couple of results from that search later on.) Note that you can search by "Language of Publication," but in keeping with the Linguistics aspect of this database, there is also a field to search by "Subject Language," that is, the language being discussed in the article. For example, you could find articles written in French, on the Kumak language. Another Limit, for identifying Peer-Reviewed materials, also appears on the Advanced Search screen in this version of the database.

Advanced Search: Period Field

There is also a Period field that deserves a brief discussion. If you go into the Thesaurus for the Period field, your initial reaction is likely to be "*what* is going on here? How in the world are they defining *period*?" Many of the entries look quite strange (especially compared with the regularity of the time period index in *America: History and Life*). For example, year spans that are huge: 1–500 AD, 1–1499, 100–1999, 1699–1200 BC, and also not as huge but very specific: 196–220, 1699–1792, 1700–1737, 1700–1820. There are month spans: 1–30 September 1990, February 1999; and specific

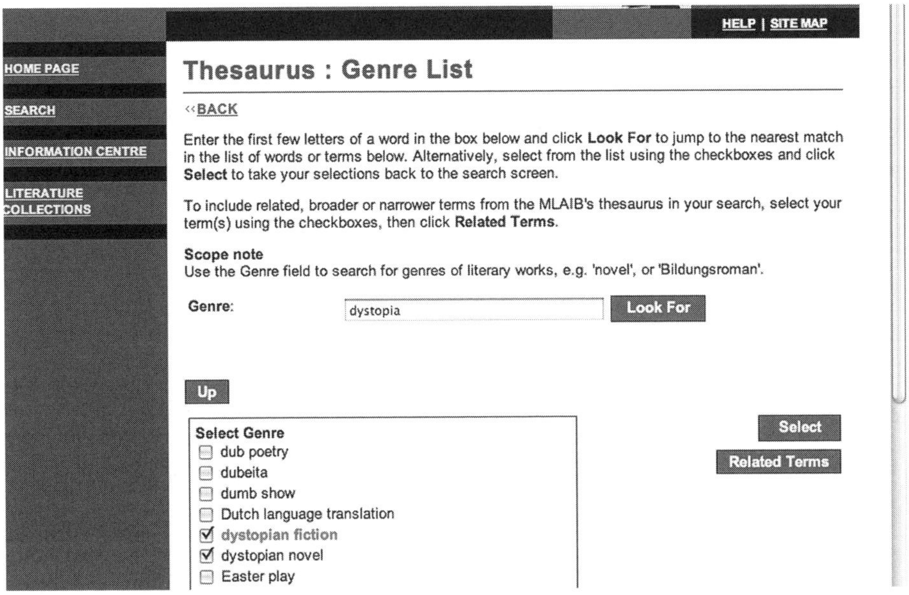

Fig. 7.18. The Genre List Thesaurus. Copyright © 2004–2008 ProQuest LLC.

dates: 2 September 1849, Sept. 18, 1981. There are also the kinds of year spans or descriptive terms that you might expect: 1800–1899, 1700–1899, Belle Époque, fin de siècle, Showa period, and Ming Dynasty. What *is* going on here? It turns out that the MLA indexers use the Period field in several ways. Any dates specifically mentioned in a work being indexed get added as Period entries, which explain the unusual time periods. In a full record display, these appear as a Period field, with the gloss (date) before the value. In addition, such records almost always have a second Period field, with one of the broader, "controlled" types of time values, such as 1900–1999. Thus, a record for the citation of an interview with Spalding Gray that took place in February 1999 has two time period fields:

Period: 1900–1999

and

Period: (date) February 1999.

MLA places great emphasis on recording information exactly as given by an author, but also works to put the materials being indexed into some kind of broader context. In literature, the broader context seems to be spans of one or more centuries, or occasionally a well-recognized "named" period.

Search Example 2

Our search objective now is to find some materials discussing dystopias in the literatures of various countries. We could just type "dystopian" into the Genre field, but it's interesting and useful to see all of the possible headings that appear in the Thesaurus (Figure 7.18).

There we find "dystopian fiction" and "dystopian novel," which are both good. After check marking the desired headings, the Select button transfers the information to the Search screen, appropriately ORed together. Because

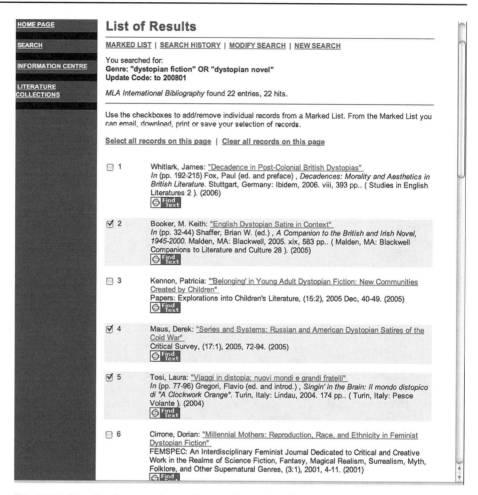

Fig. 7.19. Results for search on Genre: dystopian fiction or dystopian novel. Copyright © 2004–2008 ProQuest LLC.

the patron is interested in how dystopias are depicted across cultures, we will simply search for this Genre and see what this very international database can give us.

The first six of our twenty-two results for this search appear in Figure 7.19. In this screen, some entries have again been selected to add to the Marked List, which already has some records from various other searches not depicted in the text. Let's see what that Marked List has accumulated.

The Marked List and Output

The first eight entries in my Marked List appear in Figure 7.20a. The first five are from the most recent search on dystopian literature. The next three are from a Folklore Topic search on "brewing" (not mentioned in the text), exemplifying the broad topical reach of the database, into culture (food) and history.

In Figure 7.20b, the rest of the Marked List, the first three records (numbers 9–11) are from the Folklore Topic search on "animal tales" shown

HELP | SITE MAP

Marked List : MLA International Bibliography

NEW SEARCH | MARKED LIST FOR THE DIRECTORY OF PERIODICALS

Back to results

Your selected records are displayed below.

Email records | Print view | Download citations

Remove all records from list

1	Dalton-Brown, Sally: Signposting the Way to the City of Night: Recent Russian Dystopian Fiction The Modern Language Review, (90:1), 1995 Jan, 103-19.	Remove from list
2	Albinski, Nan Bowman: A Survey of Australian Utopian and Dystopian Fiction Australian Literary Studies, (13:1), 1987 May, 15-28.	Remove from list
3	Booker, M. Keith: African Literature and the World System: Dystopian Fiction, Collective Experience, and the Postcolonial Condition Research in African Literatures, (26:4), 1995 Winter, 58-75.	Remove from list
4	Tosi, Laura: Viaggi in distopia: nuovi mondi e grandi fratelli In (pp. 77-96) Gregori, Flavio (ed. and introd.), Singin' in the Brain: Il mondo distopico di "A Clockwork Orange". Turin, Italy: Lindau, 2004. 174 pp.. (Turin, Italy: Pesce Volante).	Remove from list
5	Maus, Derek: Series and Systems: Russian and American Dystopian Satires of the Cold War Critical Survey, (17:1), 2005, 72-94.	Remove from list
6	Meacham, Sarah Hand: 'They Will Be Adjudged by Their Drink, What Kinde of Housewives They Are': Gender, Technology, and Household Cidering in England and the Chesapeake, 1690-1760 Virginia Magazine of History and Biography, (111:2), 2003, 117-50.	Remove from list
7	Haid, Oliver: Early Tourism and Public Drinking: The Development of a Beer-Drinking Culture in a Traditional Wine-Producing Area (Meran, South Tyrol) In (pp. 105-24) Jacobs, Marc (ed.); Scholliers, Peter (ed.), Eating Out in Europe: Picnics, Gourmet Dining, and Snacks since the Late Eighteenth Century. Oxford, England: Berg, for International Commission for Research into European Food History, 2003. xii, 411 pp..	Remove from list
8	Asher, Andrew D.: Beer Bottles an[and] Bar Signs: Brewing Identity in Postsocialist Poland Anthropology of East Europe Review, (21:1), 2003 Spring, 139-47.	Remove from list

Fig. 7.20a. Marked List, beginning. Copyright © 2004–2008 ProQuest LLC.

9	Malotki, Ekkehart (ed. and translator); Toelken, Barre (introd.): Hopi Animal Stories Lincoln, NE: U of Nebraska P, 2001. xxxi, 261 pp..	Remove from list
10	Teuton, Sean: Talking Animals: An Interview with Murv Jacob American Indian Culture and Research Journal, (26:2), 2002, 135-50.	Remove from list
11	Gold, Ann Grodzins: The Long-Tailed Rat Asian Folklore Studies, (63:2), 2004, 243-65.	Remove from list
12	Kim, Hwa-Seon: [Viola's Pursuit of Subjectivity through Crossdressing in Shakespeare in Love] Feminist Studies in English Literature, (12:1), 2004 Summer, 81-103 (In Korean; English summary.).	Remove from list
13	Chu, Hsiang-chun: 'The Master Mistress of My Passion': Cross-Dressing and Gender Performance in Twelfth Night SEDERI: Journal of the Spanish Society for English Renaissance Studies, (12), 2001, 181-91.	Remove from list
14	Klett, Elizabeth: Many Bodies, Many Voices: Performing Androgyny in Fiona Shaw and Deborah Warner's Richard II Theatre Journal, (58:2), 2006 May, 175-94 (English summary.).	Remove from list
15	Mann, David: Shakespeare's Women: Performance and Conception Cambridge, England: Cambridge UP, 2008. ix, 293 pp..	Remove from list

MLA International Bibliography. Copyright 1963-2008, The Modern Language Association of America. All rights reserved.

Fig. 7.20b. Marked List, continued. Copyright © 2004–2008 ProQuest LLC.

Fig. 7.21. E-mail output interface. Copyright © 2004–2008 ProQuest LLC.

in Figure 7.17b. The last four are from the first "Shakespeare and cross-dressing" search. Take a moment to appreciate the range and international variety of sources and authors represented in these results.

Note: if you are wondering about the order of the results, the entries accumulate in the exact sequence in which they were checked off in a Results screen. Thus, in the results screen for my first search, you can see that I chose the first, most recent record ("Shakespeare's Women...") first, and two more in order as I looked down the list—but then decided to add one back toward the top of the list ("[Viola's Pursuit...]") after those three. Thus, they don't appear in chronological order in the Marked List, but rather exactly as I selected them. If you revisit some previous search results using the Search History, any additional records you mark will be added to the "top" of your Marked List; that is, they won't be automatically grouped with the earlier marked records from that search. There is nothing wrong about this, but it is worth mentioning because it might be somewhat confusing the first time you look at the Marked List.

Records in the Marked List, as indicated by the links across the top, can be e-mailed, printed, or downloaded. The output interface for the e-mail function is shown in Figure 7.21, and includes a particularly nice feature: you can add an annotating note to *each* record in the list. The links associated with each citation point back to the corresponding record in the database.

The "Download citations" function is very bibliographic-management-software savvy. There are options to export directly to RefWorks, or to ProCite, EndNote, or Reference Manager, to download a file compatible with importing into any of these four programs, or to download short or long versions of the citation records, in plain text format.

Cautionary Note

Although this section of the chapter is obviously enthusiastic about the many subject-specific search fields available in the Advanced Search screen, at the same time, do not hesitate to fall back on a simple keyword search if a field search doesn't seem to be working. For example, a search on "women" as a Folklore Topic and "animals" as a Keyword made sense to me, but this retrieves no results. (Reversing the terms doesn't help.) Searching "women and animals" as Keywords, however, retrieves many results, which can then be browsed for the most on-target citations. (Information from those citations might then be used for pearl growing a slightly better search.) The MLA indexers are governed by many principles in choosing and assigning terms for entries, as indicated in the overview provided on the MLA Web site (MLA, 2004), but an overarching theme is that the indexing depends on *explicit* content. That is, a term will not be assigned to a record unless it is specifically mentioned in the content of the item. As the MLA indexers have seen the materials and you haven't, being too specific can lead to frustration. Always be ready to throw your net wider by simplifying your search.

Additional Feature: Directory of Periodicals

The third search option in the MLA IB is the Periodical Directory. (This is implemented in various ways by different database vendors: sometimes the Periodical Directory content is integral with the rest of the database, and sometimes it is necessary to search it as a separate database.) The Periodical Directory provides extensive, detailed information on over 7,100 journals and book series. The information provided is aimed both at users as *readers*—fields such as topical scope (subject), types of articles included, and subscription address—but even more at users as *writers*, as indicated by the extensive series of fields devoted to instructions for authors: charge for submission, preferred editorial style, copyright holder, time from submission to decision, and time from decision to publication, to name just a few. If you were a graduate student specializing in Renaissance literature, the Directory of Periodicals would provide a very easy way to produce a list of journals or book series to which you might submit your work for publication. If you were an established scholar, you could quickly refresh your memory of the submission guidelines for the journal(s) in which you usually publish. Take note especially of all the new Limit options in Figure 7.22: they all have to do with the user as a writer.

Quick Recap

The *MLA International Bibliography* (MLA IB) is produced by the Modern Language Association of America. The topical scope of the *Bibliography*

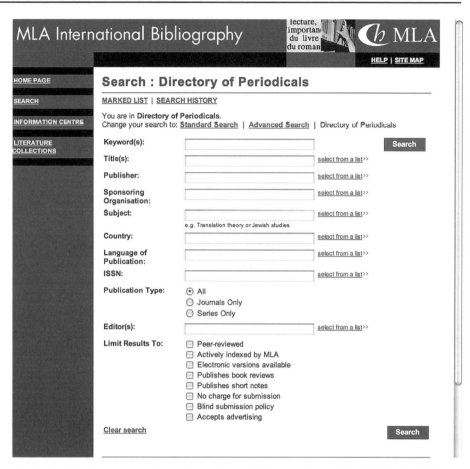

Fig. 7.22. The Directory of Periodicals Search interface. Copyright © 2004–2008 Pro-
Quest LLC.

is very broad, encompassing almost anything that could be described as
"human communication," for example, from literature and linguistics to
folklore, dramatic arts, and teaching. Types of materials indexed include
journal articles, books, book chapters, reference works, conference papers,
dissertations, electronic publications, and works related to teaching, such
as handbooks. Book reviews are *not* included. The MLA IB database is
available from several different vendors; the version considered here is from
Chadwyck-Healey, the specialist humanities imprint of ProQuest. This version supports special purpose search fields such as Author as Subject, and
Author's Work (as subject) in the Standard interface. The Advanced Search
interface offers a long list of discipline-specific search fields, including Literary Influence, Literary Theme, Genre, and Performance Medium. An unusual feature in the e-mail output option is that a "Notes" field is supplied
for *each* record being sent, allowing the user to individually annotate the
citations. An additional feature of the MLA IB is the Periodical Directory,
which contains detailed publication, subscription, and submission information for over 7,000 journals and book series. Authors seeking to publish their
work can use the Periodical Directory to identify appropriate publications
and obtain submission instructions.

Exercises and Points to Consider

1. In the version of *America: History and Life* described in the previous edition of this book, much emphasis was placed on looking up and selecting terms from the Indexes. In EBSCO's version, this has become much less important and was barely mentioned in this chapter. Look in the database Help, and see if you can figure out why. (Hint: you are looking for something about how EBSCO handles phrases.)

2. If you also have access to the *Web of Science* citation databases, try the cited reference search for Doris Kearns Goodwin's *No Ordinary Time* there. Compare the overall experience, specific capabilities, and the results with Search Example 3 in *America: History and Life*. (Hints: search just on the author's name, and for year, fill in: 1994–1995.)

3. What are some archival sources being used by current historians that can provide a *Mexican perspective* on the U.S. war with Mexico (1846–1848)? Think about this carefully for a few moments: How are you going to get at that "Mexican perspective" part of the search? See the Endnotes for a Hint.[6]

4. A faculty member comes and asks for some titles of U.S. military history journals that would be likely candidates for a scholarly article on Gen. George S. Patton, Jr. How many possible sources can you discover in *America: History and Life*? (Additional information is posted on the companion Web site for this book: http://lu.com/bellsearch/index.cfm.)

5. There were many features of EBSCO's *America: History and Life* that did not fit into this discussion: find, explore, and discuss them. Which ones would you have included that I didn't?

6. Compare the version of MLA described here with the version at your school, if available (and different). What are advantages/disadvantages of each?

7. In the MLA Subject list (Thesaurus), how is the author of *Huckleberry Finn* listed? As Samuel Clemens, or his pseudonym, Mark Twain? Compare this to your OPAC—which name is used there?

8. Consider the name of this Spanish author who was active in the late sixteenth and early seventeenth centuries: Lope Félix de Vega Carpio, often referred to simply as "Lope de Vega." Try searching "Lope de Vega" as Keyword(s)—how many results are there? Then choose a record, and see the form of his name used by the MLA indexers. Search on that, and compare the number of results with your previous search. (The Search History link is very handy if you forget to write down the number from the previous search.)

9. How many people have written their dissertations on Tolstoi's *War and Peace*?

10. Look up Saul Bellow as an Article Author, then as the Subject of other people's articles, and observe the difference in the number of results. Explore the longer list, and come up with a way to focus your search.

11.   The searches above focused on "classic" authors. What can you find about a modern author, Terry Pratchett, and his Discworld novels? Has anyone written a dissertation on them yet?

Notes

1. Note that it's not "America*n*:...." This is a mistake people frequently make.

2. b.c.e. stands for "before the common era"; c.e. stands for "common era." Political correctness comes to history.

3. The MLA deep-date coverage isn't just lip service, either: if you search simply the date range 1884–1885, there are fifty-nine entries (as of June 2008)!

4. Having written that, of course I just encountered the first instance I've ever seen of an MLA IB record with an abstract. I can't find any explanation at the MLA Web site, in the literature, or on the Web; we'll have to just accept it as an anomaly for now.

5. Each vendor, of course, has its own user interface that is based on that vendor's field structure, which can make the experience of searching the same database from different vendors vary a great deal. If your institution subscribes to MLA from a different vendor, you will see distinct differences between that version and the one described here. For example, other versions may not offer as many document types or as many search fields, such as the specialized search for "Author as Subject." Another difference you might notice is that other vendors implement field searching as drop-down menu choices (e.g., FirstSearch), rather than listing out all the fields. Be ready for differences, and use them as a constructive exercise: which implementation seems to work better, either for specific types of searches or overall?

6. Hint: If you were writing about something from the Mexican perspective, in what language would you probably be writing? Search "Mexican War" as a Subject and limit it by language.

8
Numerical Databases

This chapter takes us into some very different territory. Rather than citations to textual materials, we're going to explore the idea of searching for numerical information: data, statistics—*numbers* about things. There are very few commercial databases that have tackled the issue of providing numerical information, but a great many Web sites have done so. We'll look at one of the major players in the commercial world, LexisNexis *Statistical*, and two free government Web sites, American FactFinder (from the Census Bureau), and the Bureau of Labor Statistics. Before leaping into the databases, however, let's set the stage with some thoughts about finding numbers.

Finding Numbers

If you are not a specialist with years of experience—and even sometimes when you are—reference questions that involve finding statistics or data are probably the most challenging ones that you'll face. Let's be honest: for most of us, numbers are scary! There was a reason we weren't math majors. Don't be discouraged, however. Numbers questions don't always have to give you that "deer in the headlights" look: as with all of the other subject areas, my intent in this chapter is to try to give you some basic tools to help you to approach the question in an informed fashion, and to increase your chances of connecting the patron with the information requested. To begin with, I'm going to share with you my worldview about some basic "number" concepts: what determines the collection of numbers, how they can be categorized, who does the collection, and what sources to try for various categories.

Sidebar 8.1. Numerical Terminology

Data refers to individual numbers, for example, the original computer file of all the numerically coded responses to a survey, which usually looks like just a series of numbers. This is a *data* file, usually called a *data set*. Data are actual values. One value in a data set is a data point. When you process data, grouping like data points and expressing them as percentages, then you have:

Statistics, which are groups of numbers, usually expressed in terms of percentages. The data (number) and the statistical percentage it represents both appear in the sentence: "Almost 9 million (data) young Americans, or about 15 percent (a statistic) of all children, are overweight."

In my experience, people who are not in "numerically oriented" fields (e.g., economics, business, sociology, etc.) tend to use the terms *data* and *statistics* almost interchangeably: they will ask for *data* about something, when they are really interested in statistics. (This is good, because statistics are usually easier to find.) If a person really does want a series of values to analyze, then he or she really does want a data set. A person in this position usually is quite aware of the difference between data and statistics, and you should be, too.

Concepts about Numbers

Collection of Numbers

First and foremost in working with a numerical question is to consider whether it will have been worth someone's time and effort to collect the information, and to make it available in the way the user desires. "Numbers" take a lot of time and effort to collect: real effort, often by real people. For example, the year 2000 Census cost a total of $4.5 billion, or $15.99 per person counted (Gauthier, 2002). The first reports based on census data only began to appear in March 2001, because collecting the numbers is only the beginning. Next, the data have to be analyzed and formatted into some kind of useful reports that either benefit the collecting organization (e.g., for planning or allocating), or that are interesting enough to outside parties that they'll pay money for them.

In my experience on the job as a "data librarian," I am frequently faced with people who feel they have an absolutely reasonable and rational numerical request, and that "certainly the information should be 'out there.'" And while what they're looking for might sound reasonable and rational to me too, it doesn't mean that the information actually is out there, or that it exists in exactly the way they envision. If the government doesn't have it (our best free source), and a non-profit organization such as the Inter-university Consortium for Political and Social Research (ICPSR) or possibly a trade organization[1] doesn't have it, then it means it would have to be information collected by a for-profit organization. Obviously, it was collected to help the company make that profit, so they have no incentive to disseminate it for free while it is still relevant. If the information isn't strategically vital or tactically important, and the company thinks that they can sell the data (or reports based on the data) for more than the cost of collecting and analyzing the information, then those "numbers" might be available (for a fee). Again, as stated at the beginning of this section: if it's not worth somebody's time and effort, it probably won't be counted, and then exactly *because* it's worth time and effort, it might not be freely available.

Categories of Numbers

It can be helpful to think of collected numbers as falling into three broad categories: people, business, and financial. Numbers that get collected about People are things such as population counts, demographics (e.g., race, income, etc.), and vital statistics (e.g., births, deaths, etc.) Business numbers include broad information *about* business, such as numbers of companies, production, and workers in various industries, as well as numbers related to *doing* business, for example, market research or sales figures for a particular company. There are certainly "business numbers" that are financial (e.g., historical stock prices), but my third category, financial numbers, has to do with money or monetary equivalents (e.g., stocks) in a broader sense: information such as gross domestic product (GDP), banking data (total currency in circulation, total value of money in savings accounts, etc.), exchange rates, and aggregate numbers associated with the stock market, such as the Dow Jones Industrial Averages.

Fitting a "numbers question" into one of these categories helps to organize my plan of attack, because the categories tend to be associated with certain kinds of collection agents. This means that I'll get some ideas of where to look first, and that I'll have a sense of whether the information might be freely available or fee based.

Who Collects Numbers

In the United States, the U.S. government is probably the largest collector and publisher of "numbers." This can probably be said of other developed countries as well. These organizations are termed the *public sector* and usually the information that they make available is free (your tax dollars at work).

At the opposite extreme, we have the "private sector": trade or business organizations, professional associations, market research companies, and polling and surveying organizations. Usually information produced by a private sector organization isn't free, although some trade and professional groups may provide some statistics on their Web sites. In general, however, numerical information collected by the private sector ranges from possibly affordable (say, from $20–500, which would probably be acceptable to a small business owner or to a library buying a reference book), to prices meant for large corporations (e.g., $4,000 market research reports).[2]

Between the public and private sectors is the nonprofit area of academic researchers. Mentioned earlier, the ICPSR was organized specifically to gather and archive the data collected in the course of social science research conducted by scholars across the United States. ICPSR is probably the largest social science data archive in the world. Your institution must be an ICPSR member for you to download their data. The membership fees reflect the magnitude of their organization and offerings (but for high-volume users, the cost per dataset becomes quite inexpensive). If your institution is a member, it is likely that you will have a data librarian on staff, and ICPSR probably is his or her first or second most frequently used resource for serious "number" requests (i.e., for raw data that needs statistical processing, usually for advanced research). Although ICPSR is always working to make its resources more understandable to non-expert users, it is still an "advanced" resource, and not as commonly found on institutional subscription lists as most of the databases in this book. Because I wish to keep the discussion at the beginning to intermediate level, using resources that are fairly common, I won't go into more details about ICPSR here. If you are interested in finding out more, their Web site is very helpful and informative: http://www.icpsr.umich.edu.

Try the Public Sector for ...

When a reference question involves numbers having to do with people, my first move would be to try a government source (as long as the question is about people as *people*, and not as *consumers*). A government exists to govern people, and governing bodies are quite interested in information about their constituents. Governments are also very interested in the businesses in their countries: these companies are, after all, what keep the country solvent. For questions involving numbers of businesses, shipments of product X, employment, etc., try government sources. There are public sector sources for some financial numbers questions as well: for questions involving monetary figures in a nationwide sense, try the Federal Reserve Bank, or for economic data, the Bureau of Economic Analysis.

Try the Private Sector for ...

As mentioned previously, the government is my first choice for questions about people as people (heads that get counted). If someone wants to know about people as consumers, however, or what people are thinking, then it's more likely that the answer will come from a private sector source: a market resource report, a survey report from a company such as Harris Interactive, or perhaps a Gallup Poll. (It will probably also cost money.)

Questions about numbers for specific businesses almost always come from private sector sources: trade organizations or publications that specialize in a particular line of business. Who cares most about home appliance manufacturing? The Association of Home Appliance Manufacturers (AHAM). Hosiery? The National Association of Hosiery Manufacturers (NAHM). Oil, airlines, and milk: they all have trade associations devoted to (among other things) collecting numbers pertinent to their mission, purpose, etc. Certain private sector publishers specialize in trade reports: Crain Communications (thirty trade publications), Ward's Communications (*Ward's Automotive Yearbook*), and Adams Media (beer, wine, and liquor handbooks). For any line of business, remember to consider associations as a source of information. This is perhaps especially true for service businesses; that is, any line of work that does not involve producing a product: be sure to check for a related professional organization, because this might be the only source of statistics about the profession.[3] (For example: want to know what butlers earn? Try the Web site of the International Guild of Professional Butlers at http://www.butlersguild.com/.)

There are two types of "business numbers" that are, surprisingly, freely available on the Web. One is stock quotes for particular companies: current quotes are available from any of several Web sites, and Yahoo! Finance offers a remarkably deep historical stock quote reporting system (the catch is that it works only for companies currently in business and trading on U.S. stock exchanges). Also accessible on the Web are the financial statements of public companies, which must be filed with the Securities and Exchange Commission (SEC), and are public documents. This information is available in a number of places, including the SEC's Edgar system (http://www.sec.gov/edgar.shtml), and the company's own Web site,[4] where the figures appear in the company's Annual Report.

Financial number questions that probably involve a fee-based source tend to be ones that require a series of historical values (e.g., an exchange rate for a particular currency over a 30-year period), or financial information for another country, or a combination of the two (e.g., a table of 20 years of debt values for Nigeria). The sources for such information are often organizations such as the United Nations or the World Bank (not commercial in the ".com" sense), but they still can't afford to give away their data for free.

Quick Recap

It takes time and effort to collect, format, and publish data or statistics. Without a financial or other strong motivation to prompt the process, data are unlikely to be collected. If information has been collected, it may not be available for free. In the United States, the government (the *public sector*) is probably the largest collector and provider of freely available data about people, industries, and economics (national-level financial information). Numbers relating to business that can also be found at no charge on the Web are financial statements (e.g., balance sheet, income statement, etc.) for public companies, and current stock quotes. Information that is rarely if ever free includes market research, and data about specific businesses, which are most likely to be collected by survey companies, trade associations, or trade publishers (the *private sector*). One exception is trade associations, which occasionally make data related to their organization available on their Web sites.

A Comment about Searching for Numbers

One of the frustrating things about searching for numbers is that all too often, whatever the person asks for, the numbers that you can find won't be exactly the ones that the patron wants:

You: "Here are some great figures about spotted hyenas!"
Patron: "Oh. Thanks, but I really wanted *striped* hyenas . . . ."

Remember that this does not represent a failure on your part: if you have done a rigorous search, it probably means that no one has cared enough yet about striped hyenas to collect and publish numerical data about them. Don't be discouraged. It is amazing, on the other hand, the numbers that you *can* find! Let's learn about the first of the three sources that we'll cover, LexisNexis *Statistical*.

LexisNexis *Statistical*

Background and Coverage

Originally known as "Statistical Universe," this database was first reviewed in 1998 by Mary Ellen Bates. She described it as a "recently created" joint effort by LexisNexis and Congressional Information Service, Inc. As Bates says, the new database addressed "the need for value-added access to Web-based information" (Bates, 1998). Indeed, LexisNexis saw how useful it would be if the wealth of statistical material produced by the many agencies and offices of the U.S. government could be brought together under one search interface, enhanced with indexing, and the tables provided in a format that would keep their integrity intact (e.g., GIF images rather than ASCII renditions). Even though much of this information is freely available on the Web, the task of locating it amid the plethora of government Web sites can be frustrating and difficult. In addition, the need to preserve and continue to provide access to earlier editions of files is not consistent across all government Web sites. Putting the materials into a database increases the chances of preserving an historical series of reports. A print indexing and abstracting service for U.S. government statistics already existed: the Congressional Information Service *American Statistics Index* (ASI). By adding GIF images of the tables cited in the index, the service gives users immediate access to the information. Adding in selections from the Congressional Information Service's two other statistical A & I subscription series: *Statistical Reference Index* (SRI, which indexes statistical information published by state governments, private sector publishers, and universities), and the *Index to International Statistics* (IIS, which covers international intergovernmental organizations, e.g., the United Nations, World Bank, and OECD), adds depth of coverage and takes the concept even further. Most of the materials indexed by ASI, SRI, and IIS are available in their attendant microfiche collections, thus a database product incorporating the information from these A & I services could provide an electronic index to the wealth of material locked up in endless drawers of fiche. Truly, this was an excellent idea whose time had come.

LexisNexis *Statistical* is still, as of this writing, the most broadly based "numerical" database on the market. Tom Kmetz (2003) mentioned Gale's TableBase as the only similar product of which he was aware in 2002. In early 2006, Cambridge University Press published the *Historical Statistics of the United States Millennial Edition* in both print and online formats; this is a wonderful resource for very long time series of strictly American data, in fairly broad topic areas (it is based on Census data)—a wonderful tool, but not a substitute for *Statistical*. Also in 2006, a free web resource called DataPlace appeared, which also aggregates data from federal sources to make them easier to find, as well as providing tools to help in analyzing and presenting the data. Mick O'Leary gives it a very favorable review, but admits that DataPlace "has little or nothing on some important subjects, including prices, finance, economic sectors, politics, and any foreign data" (O'Leary, 2006). Again, this is no substitute for LexisNexis *Statistical*, unless you have no other (financial) choice.

Several other sources for international information exist, but they tend to be more narrowly focused than LexisNexis *Statistical*. (Gail Golderman and Bruce Connolly provide an excellent review of the current resources for "international numbers," including LexisNexis *Statistical*, in the Spring 2005 *Netconnect*.) *SourceOECD* is a broad-based source of international data, but is more of an "expert-user" product, and financially beyond the reach of many institutions.[5]

Subscription Options

There are three subscription options for LexisNexis *Statistical*: you can choose the Base Edition or Research Edition collection, and purchase the Abstracts modules as add-ons to either one. The Base Edition draws mainly on materials from ASI, but some materials from state governments and intergovernmental organizations (e.g., SRI and IIS contents) are included as well. The Base Edition is the equivalent of a full-text article database for numbers: all records provide a table, and the number of tables keeps expanding:

in 2002 the Base Edition included "around 30,000 tables" (Kmetz, 2003). In accordance with the database's stated aim of growth, the number of tables in the Base Edition had risen to over 160,000, with 40,000 new and updated tables being added each year, according to product literature available in June 2008.

The Research Edition comprises all the material in the Base Edition, with 400,000 additional titles and their associated tables drawn from all three indexes (ASI, SRI, and IIS). Materials from private sector sources indexed by SRI represent the most significant content "upgrade" in the Research Edition. Again, it is "instant gratification," because every record includes a table.

The "Abstracts modules" represent the full ASI, SRI, and IIS index and abstract books in electronic form. These are a real boon to libraries that subscribe to one or more of the A & I services and to the microfiche collections that can accompany them: finally, an *electronic* index to the microfiche. A library with a subscription to the ASI, SRI, and IIS volumes and fiche sets might choose only the Base Edition and the Abstracts modules, since the library has even more full-text back up (the fiche collections) than is provided in the Research Edition. The only challenge in this situation is that getting to the sources (the microfiche) isn't quite as convenient.

Date Coverage

Date coverage has somewhat different connotations in a numerical database than it does in a bibliographic or citation database. The range of *publication* dates—how "far back" the database goes—is not necessarily as important, because in the world of numbers it's very common to find recently published material that deals with the distant past, for example, "crop losses . . . 1948–1997" (published in 1999), or "acres harvested . . . 1930–1994" (published in 1997). There may be times when someone needs "numbers published in a particular historical time period," but often it doesn't matter so much *when* the document was published as long as it has the right data. That said, to make the description of this database consistent with the other chapters, we'll note that date coverage (in the sense of when the materials were published) in the Base and Research Editions is generally from 1995 onward (Bates, 1998). Those materials can contain information that is much older, however, so that if you need the price of corn in 1970, this is the place to go. The Abstracts modules include the full date coverage of the hard copy indexes, that is: ASI, 1973–, SRI, 1980–, and IIS, 1983–. Again, these represent the total possible depth of *publication* dates; the dates of the information covered in the publications can be much older (gold prices back to 1815, anyone?). Even the way the Publication Date limit field works recognizes this difference: you can set it to, for example, 1930–1940, and the publication dates in your results may range from 1960 to the present, because the information *in* the publication meets the date requirement that you set. This is a far cry from the typical date limit field in a citation database, so pause and ponder it for a few minutes.

Notes and Search Examples

The version of LexisNexis *Statistical* used in the following discussion follows the subscription model described earlier: a combination of the Base Edition and Abstracts modules.

Search Options

The initial search screen for the "Search Tables Base Edition" of Lexis-Nexis *Statistical* is shown in Figure 8.1. Search Tables is our instant grati-fication mode, because it provides tables right in the records. As mentioned previously, the Search Tables Base Edition subscription is drawn mainly from U.S. government statistical publications, including my perennial fa-vorite, the *Statistical Abstract of the United States*.

On the left are links to the other "Statistical Search Forms," in this case Search Abstracts and Links. The Search Abstracts mode is the one that functions as a full electronic version of ASI, SRI, and IIS. As the title implies, and reflecting the content of the print A & I volumes, results in this mode only offer abstracts (although some may provide links to online tables). LexisNexis offers a customizable "Locate a Copy of This Publication In Your Library" link for the Search Abstracts mode, however, so that libraries can direct users to microfiche collections or other local resources for obtaining the tables.

If you would still rather "go to the source" and look around for infor-mation yourself, the Links page provides a useful, annotated, set of links to selected government, university, and non-government Web sites that are good for "numbers." Although there are now some other good "portals" and search engines for government sites,[6] this list, especially because it includes some nongovernment sites, provides a nice, controlled, and less overwhelm-ing way to approach the plethora of statistical Web sites.

Search Tips for the Base Edition

Records in the "Search Tables Base Edition" section of LexisNexis *Sta-tistical* contain brief bibliographic citation information, a GIF image of a table of figures, and Subject Descriptors added by the LexisNexis indexing staff. The tables have also been scanned with an optical character recogni-tion (OCR) program, so that words in column and row headings can be in-dexed and are keyword searchable. Taken altogether, this amounts to many words to search on, but the overall experience is subtly different from a database of articles or article citations. We are in a different place: we are finding numbers, not literature. The following suggestions represent basic strategies that are useful for getting the most out of LexisNexis *Statistical*:

- Choose broad terms to search on, if possible. Choosing from the Sub-ject List can help, but don't be afraid *not* to use the Subject List too. For example, the only way to find tables with information about "eye glasses" is by Keyword searching that phrase. The Subject heading used for a table with this kind of data in it is "Medical supplies and equipment."

- Then refine the request by choosing one or two limits from the many check boxes.

- If you really want or need to put a pretty specific term in the search box (e.g., eye glasses), hold off on adding elements from the limit check boxes until you see what your results are like.

- As always, if you get zero hits, eliminate search limits or terms one at a time until you start getting something. If you get too many hits, be equally methodical about adding limits or terms.

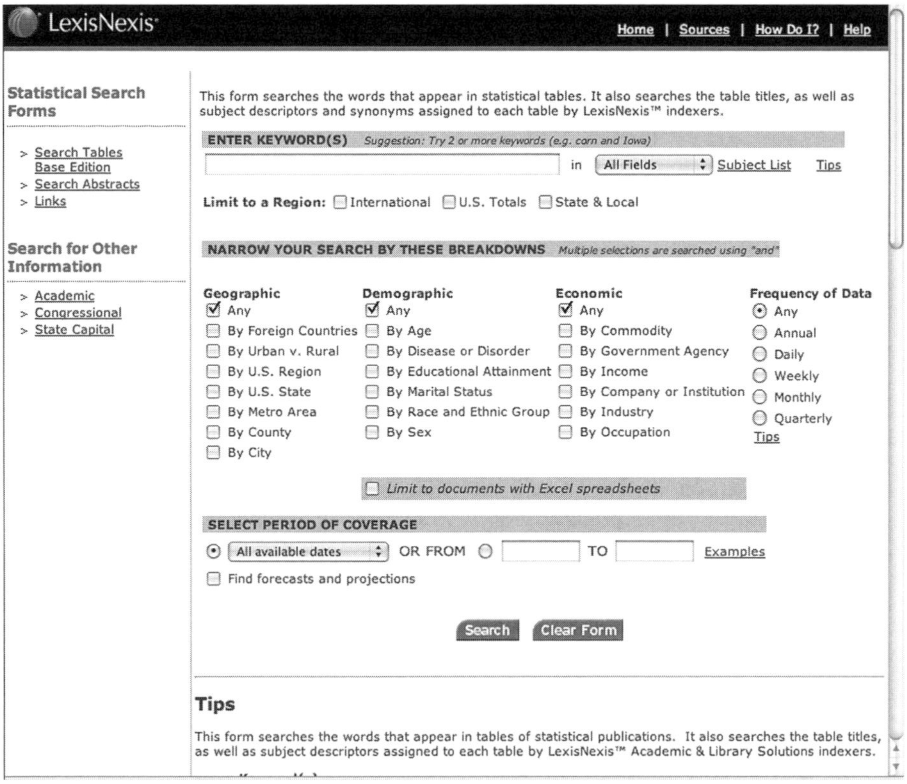

Fig. 8.1. Search Tables Base Edition search interface. Copyright 2008 LexisNexis, a division of Reed Elsevier Inc. All Rights Reserved.

Let's go ahead and get a feel for what searching for numbers is going to be like.

The Base Edition Interface

As you can see in Figure 8.1, instead of an emphasis on text fields, as we have seen elsewhere, the emphasis here is all on limits. We do have one text input field, which we can set, if desired, to search in one of four specific fields (Table Title, Subject Terms, Table Text, or NAICS Code). There is also a link to the Subject List, and therefore we know that a set of controlled vocabulary is available, and we can browse the list. The "Enter Keyword(s)" bar also includes a search suggestion: "Try 2 or more keywords (e.g. corn and Iowa)," alerting us that Boolean operators can be used here. What are particularly exciting and helpful here, however, are all the possible limits, offered as checkboxes.

Limits

The "Limit to a Region" options actually represent sources: "International" is material from IIS, "U.S. Totals" is material from ASI, and "State & Local" refers to information from SRI. As the interface most frequently used by patrons, the terminology used here is much more accessible than referring to the sources by their names. The "Narrow Your Search by these

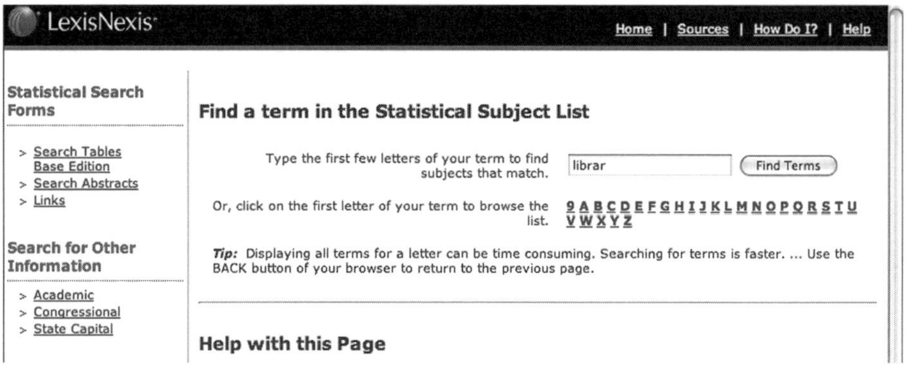

Fig. 8.2. Looking up a term in the *Statistical* Subject List. Copyright 2008 Lexis-Nexis, a division of Reed Elsevier Inc. All Rights Reserved.

Breakdowns" limits reflect how statistics tend to be published, thus subtly guiding you into the right frame of "search mind." This is exactly how you want to be able to search for numbers. Note there is even an option to "Limit to documents with Excel spreadsheets." The Excel files are sometimes offered in addition to the GIF image of the table, and are useful for users who want to experiment with manipulating the data themselves. The familiar Date limit is also available, either as a set of values in a drop-down menu (ranging from "previous year" to "previous twenty years," or "all available dates"), or by setting a date range of your choosing. LexisNexis is very accommodating in terms of date formats: this field will accept dates in almost any format (e.g., 07/24/97, Jul 24, 1997, 07/97, July 1997, or 1997). It's a small detail, but I always appreciate not having to remember and follow one particular date format.

Search Example 1

What "numbers" can we find about librarians?

Using the Subject List

Let's start by checking the Subject list. We can type in the beginning of a word (e.g., "librar" as shown in Figure 8.2), and jump into the hierarchical list of terms at that point (Figure 8.3).

Note the many helpful *see also* and *use* references in Figure 8.3, as well as information on *Broader / related* terms. Always be willing to take an extra few seconds to run your eyes over a list like this, because it can help extend your knowledge of a topic, or provide new options if your original strategy isn't working. You can choose the term(s) you wish to use, and the "paste to search" button enters them into the search form (Figure 8.4).

Using Geographic Limits

The search shown in Figure 8.4 has been set to retrieve tables that organize their data "By U.S. State," which returned fifty-two results at the time of this writing. Changing the Geographic limit back to "Any" and choosing the limit for Region "U.S. Totals" changes both the number and nature of results: it produces 183 results, and reflects a broader set of topics (including "Occupations With a Greater-than-Average Number of Workers Aged 45 Years and Older, 1998–2008"—sigh).

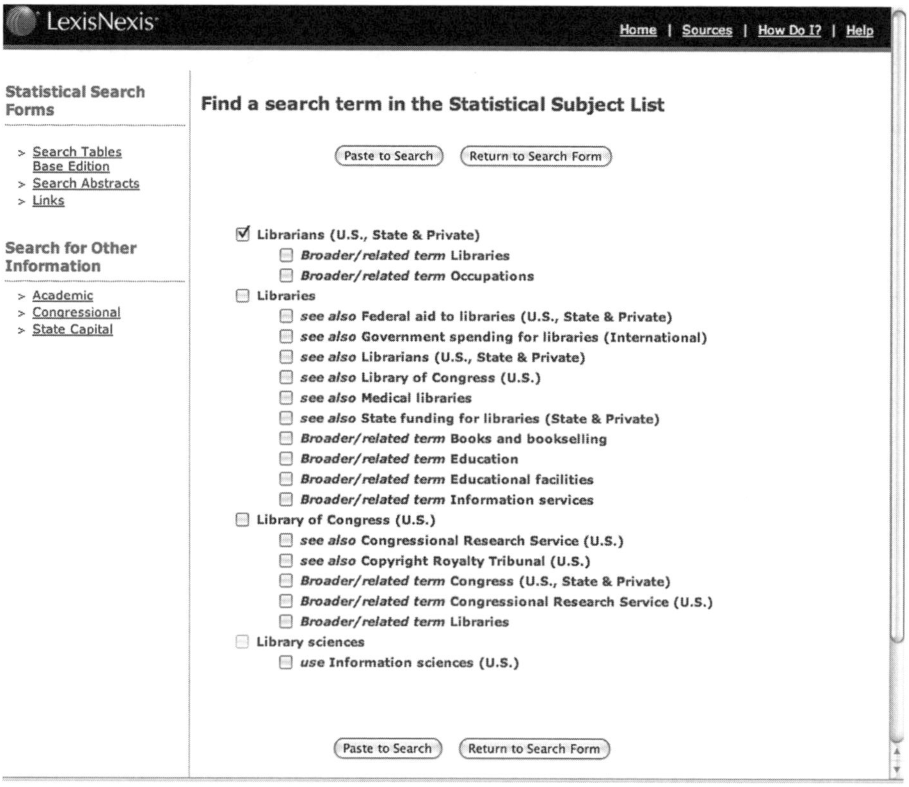

Fig. 8.3. *Statistical* Subject List results. Copyright 2008 LexisNexis, a division of Reed Elsevier Inc. All Rights Reserved.

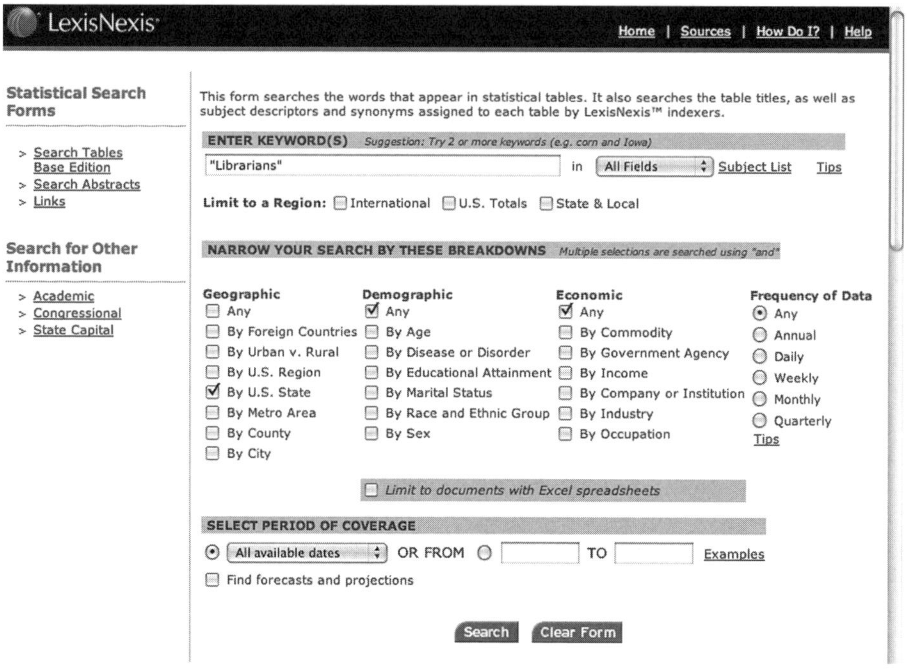

Fig. 8.4. Search form with Subject term, one limit. Copyright 2008 LexisNexis, a division of Reed Elsevier Inc. All Rights Reserved.

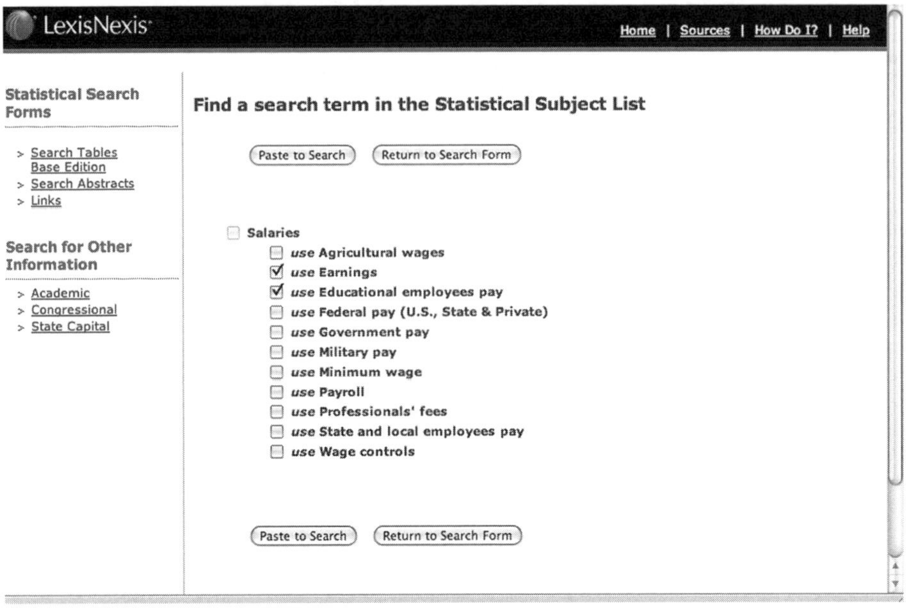

Fig. 8.5. Guidance to other terms in the *Statistical* Subject List. Copyright 2008 LexisNexis, a division of Reed Elsevier Inc. All Rights Reserved.

Iterative Use of the Subject List

Let us say you wanted to focus only on salaries for librarians. Look up "salaries" in the Subject List, and you'll find that LexisNexis instructs you to use other terms. You can choose as many as you want (reminiscent of the "Map to Subject Heading" screens in the Ovid interface), and "Paste" them to your search (Figure 8.5).

Sidebar 8.2

If you look up "salary" in the Subject List, the search produces no results: there are no exact matches for "salary" (singular). You'll be told that no matches were found, but the only button provided is the "Return to Search Form" button. To try another Subject List search, you'll need to use the browser's Back button. What would be ideal would be a choice: Try another Subject Search *or* Return to Search Form.

Anytime you iteratively choose terms from the Subject List and paste them to the search screen, LexisNexis will default to putting "OR" between the terms. Simply change the operator to AND if that is what you want to do, and employ some parentheses to make the search engine do the right thing—*Statistical* can handle it. In this case, we want: "Librarians" AND ("Earnings" OR "Educational employees pay"). Figure 8.6 shows the initial results from this search.

Results Page Options

Take a moment to study the results display in Figure 8.6; there are several useful features here. If our search had returned a large number of

Fig. 8.6. Results: Librarians AND (Earnings OR Educational employees pay) search. Copyright 2008 LexisNexis, a division of Reed Elsevier Inc. All Rights Reserved.

results, we could immediately "focus" the search by adding another keyword here, without having to return to the search screen. (Note that if your search is going to return more than 1,000 results, the system tells you this, and will not provide results until you've devised a more focused search.) If you do want to get back to the search screen, however, there is the Edit Search link. Print and Email options, which we will cover a little later, are right there. One of the most interesting features, however, is the "Table View" tab: going to Table View lets you page through the full records, which in this case, means each table. It's a wonderfully quick way to scan and compare these graphically presented results.

Search Example 2

This example is actually an interactive exercise. It depends on your having access to LexisNexis *Statistical* and being able to get online and experiment. The suggested search statement to use as a starting point is: "Earnings" (a Subject term) OR salar!, in case there is pertinent material out there, only accessible by the keyword "salary" or "salaries." (The indexers are good, but you don't want to miss any possibilities.)

Time to Experiment

With the suggested search statement, try checking various options under the Geographic, Demographic, Economic, and other limits. Can you find earnings by City? By Metro Area? What happens if you try it by County? Does any organization track earnings by Educational Attainment? Marital status? How about forecasts and projections for earnings? If a limit (or

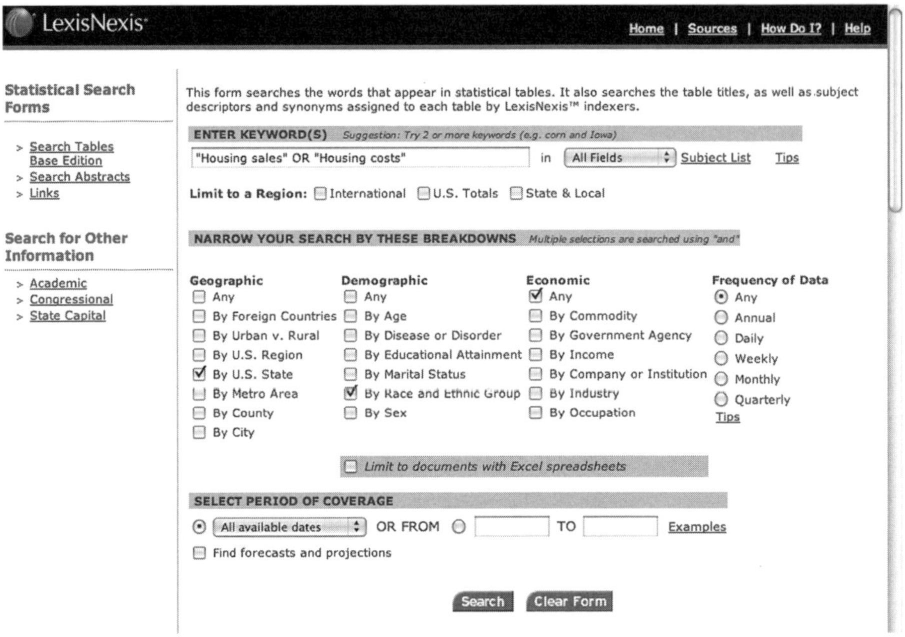

Fig. 8.7. Two-term OR search with two limits. Copyright 2008 LexisNexis, a division of Reed Elsevier Inc. All Rights Reserved.

combination of limits) produces no results, simply try another, or switch that category back to "any." If you are getting too many messages that say, "This search has been interrupted because it will return more than 1,000 documents," either add more limits, or remove the OR'd term from the search.

Multipart Reports in Results

Figure 8.7 shows a new search, which is looking for information about "Housing sales" OR "Housing costs" (Subject headings) by State and Race and Ethnic Group. Look at the results in Figure 8.8 carefully: at first they almost look like all the same thing. What is different? What do these results represent? What you are seeing is typical for searches limited by geography: the results frequently appear as multipart reports. Thus, there will be several hits that represent consecutive sections of one large report, broken down into Part 01, Part 02, etc. Each part represents a section of the alphabetical list of whatever the geographic unit is; in this case, it is states: Alabama to California, California to Delaware, Florida to Georgia, and so forth.[7]

Search Example 3

Now suppose we really wanted to find the average commute time (travel time to work) in various U.S. cities. Still in the Base Edition, we could try looking up "commute" in the Subject List. By truncating the term to "commut," we would find that commuting is a subject. "Travel time" is too specific, however, and there are no matches. Trying:

"Commuting" AND work

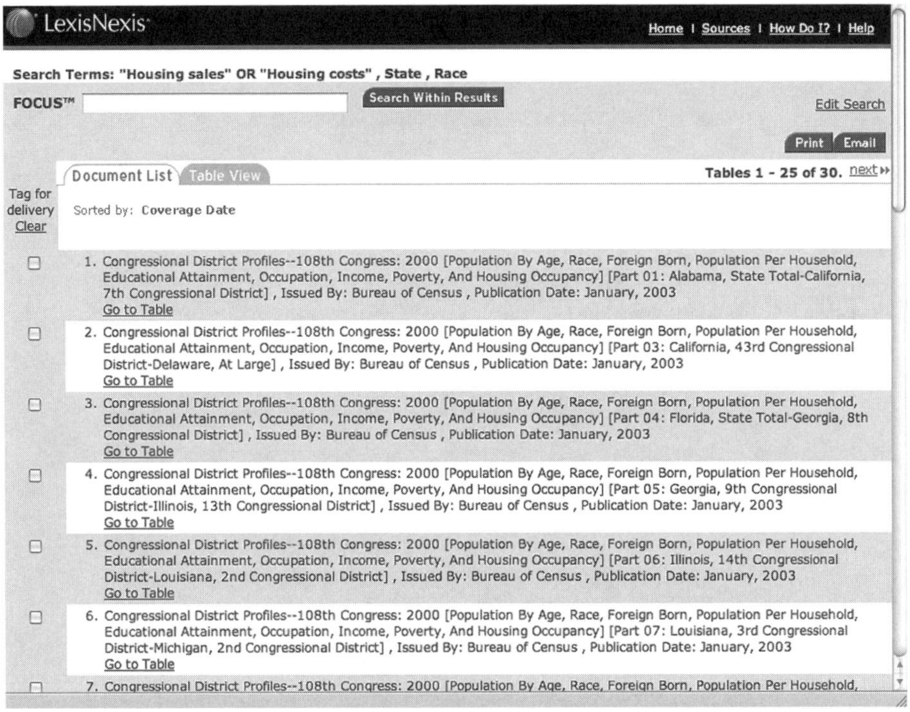

Fig. 8.8. Results showing a multipart report. Copyright 2008 LexisNexis, a division of Reed Elsevier Inc. All Rights Reserved.

as a keyword search, and adding various Geographic limits (e.g., Cities, County, or Metro Area) produces some results, but not as recent or as broadly applicable as we'd like (detailed information about every county in Idaho, while impressive, doesn't help me much for any other location). Let's extend the scope of what we're searching by changing to the Search Abstracts section. Hold this "search thought" while we introduce Search Abstracts.

The Search Abstracts Interface

The Search Abstracts interface (Figure 8.9) looks a lot like the Search Tables interface, with additional text entry search boxes (connected by Boolean operators), because we are now searching content with, in the words of Golderman and Connolly (2005), "meticulously detailed abstracting." The source limits for searching are also more clearly identified as the three major statistical publications published by LexisNexis (i.e., ASI, SRI, and IIS).

Getting to Full Text for Abstracts

If you're at a library that doesn't have a subscription to the microfilmed documents referred to by these indexes, getting to the source materials could be frustrating. However, sometimes the records contain links to online full text, or the documents indexed might be available in hard copy in your library: anything with "book" in the title would be worth looking for in your OPAC.

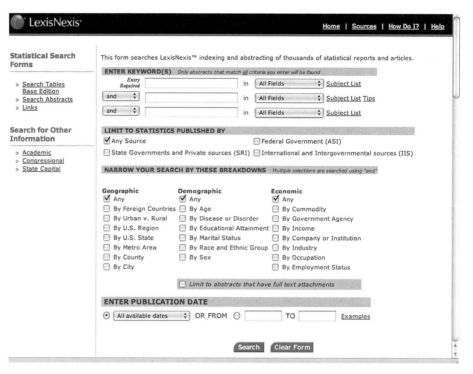

Fig. 8.9. "Search Abstracts" interface. Copyright 2008 LexisNexis, a division of Reed Elsevier Inc. All Rights Reserved.

Re-running Search Example 3

Here in Search Abstracts, a search on "Commuting" AND work by City produces many more results (174, as shown in Figure 8.10), and there are quite a few by Metro Area as well. The first item in Figure 8.10 is the *Statistical Abstract of the U.S., 2008: The National Data Book. Motor Vehicles*, published in October 2007. That even looks quite recent, for data! (This refers back to the point about the time it takes to assemble and publish data. Getting 2007 numbers in 2008 is remarkable turnaround; more common is about a 2-year lag time, which still represents—for academic purposes, at least—acceptably recent data.)

When we look at the full record for that first item, however, we find that the "Commuting to work" section is from 2005. That does seem old. Should we give up and accept that as the best data available? No, we're librarians; we like to search, and once a question sucks us in, it can be hard not to keep trying. Let's wrap up our tour of *Statistical* with an overview of output options, and then see what it's like to go directly to some of the sources for governmentally produced "numbers." We'll see if we can pursue our commuting time question there.

Working with Results: "Tag" and Output

Tag for Delivery

As you can see in Figure 8.10, the results lists in *Statistical* have the familiar checkboxes, for selecting those entries that you wish to output. This marking function is called "Tag for Delivery" in the LexisNexis databases.

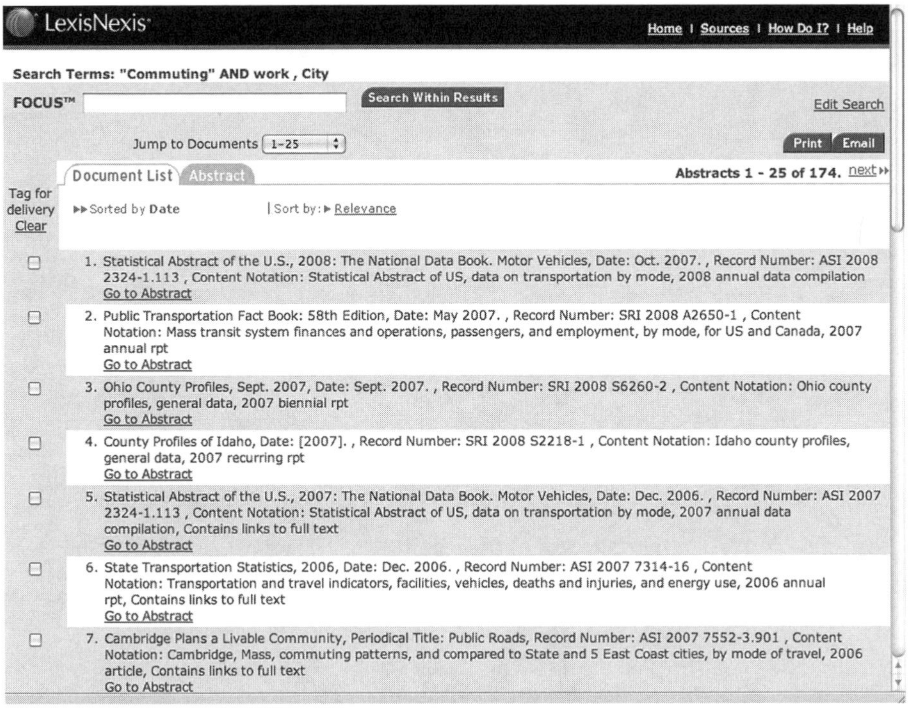

Fig. 8.10. Results: Search Abstracts commuting search. Copyright 2008 LexisNexis, a division of Reed Elsevier Inc. All Rights Reserved.

Print and E-mail

Having "tagged" your records, you can now choose the Print (which also includes a Save option) or Email function tabs; however, prepare yourself for a slight frustration. If you select multiple records and choose Print, only the citations (and, if you specify Expanded List, some indexing terms) will be printed, not the tables. To get hard copy output of the tables, you'll need to print the full records one at a time. The Email function has a similar limitation: the GIF images of the tables are not included in the e-mail output (even if it's only one record). The image would have to be saved on the desktop and then attached to a regular e-mail message. The Email function allows you to put in the "To" address, naturally, but does not allow you to provide the "From" address (e.g., from you) or a Subject line. It does allow you to include a note in the body of the e-mail. If you wish to send records from *Statistical* to someone else, it can be useful to send the information to yourself first, and then forward it to the other person, putting in your own Subject line. Coming from your e-mail rather than the vendor's, with your Subject line, helps to keep the message from getting caught by a spam filter.

Going from LexisNexis *Statistical* to Web Sites

The LexisNexis *Statistical* "Annotated links" page (Figure 8.11) gives us an easy way to connect to the government Web sites that you'll want to use most often. Our first stop is the Bureau of Census (http://www.census.gov), home of American FactFinder.

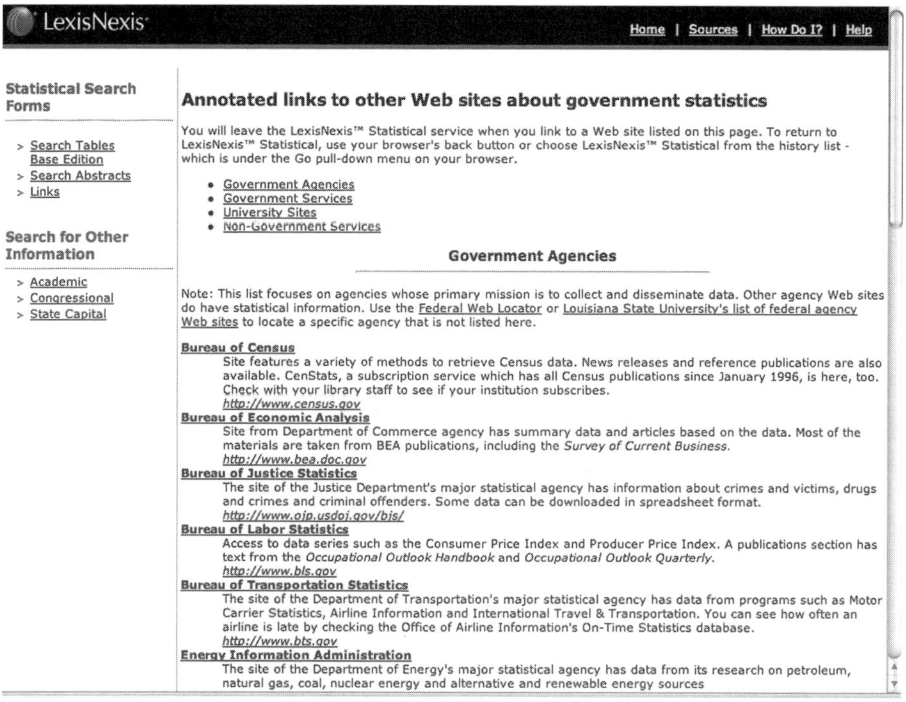

Fig. 8.11. Annotated links page. Copyright 2008 LexisNexis, a division of Reed Elsevier Inc. All Rights Reserved.

American Factfinder

Background and Coverage

At the Census Bureau Web site, one of the "variety of methods to retrieve Census data" referred to in the LexisNexis *Statistical* annotation is a wonderful database called *American FactFinder*. This is a good tool that keeps getting better: it was one of Péter Jacsó's "Picks" (i.e., a positive review) in 2000, and it has only gotten easier to use and understand since then. The folks at the Census Bureau deserve a lot of credit for continuing to work at understanding their users better, and making the incredible, complex wealth of information they collect more accessible to the public.

The data accessible through American FactFinder includes the latest Census information, but also information gathered in studies done more frequently, such as the annual American Community Survey, and the Economic Census, which is taken every 5 years. The "Getting Detailed Data" section of American FactFinder includes data from the latest two decennial censuses (i.e., 1990 and 2000), more years of the American Community Survey, the Puerto Rico Community Survey, annual Population Estimate reports, the 5-year Economic Census reports, and additional annual economic surveys such as the Annual Survey of Manufactures and County Business Patterns.

Notes and Search Examples

The U.S. Census Bureau homepage has many options but is laid out clearly enough to be navigable (Figure 8.12). It's very hard not to comment

Fig. 8.12. The U.S. Census Bureau home page, as of June 2008.

on all of the other interesting things available here, but I'm going to try to restrain myself. (Don't hesitate to explore on your own, however, especially some of the links associated with "People & Households" or "Special Topics.")

The link to American FactFinder is located in the list on the left side of the page. The American FactFinder homepage, as of June 2008, is shown in Figure 8.13.

Search Example 1: Getting a Community "Fact Sheet"

You'd like to know how well you "fit in," (statistically, at least) in your community.

It is interesting to examine statistics that have been gathered about the community you live in, and see how you fit, in terms of age, marital status, income, etc., in the place that you call home. The American FactFinder Fact Sheets provide a good profile of every community in the United States. On the American FactFinder page, get a Fact Sheet for the place where you live. If the Fact Sheet text entry box is on the homepage, as in Figure 8.13, simply type in your zip code. (If for some reason it has moved, look for a link to the "Fact Sheet" page, which will have this functionality on it.)

If you want to look up a place for which you don't have a zip code, type in the city or town name, with a state abbreviation to make it clear which one you mean (e.g., Richmond, VA, or Richmond, MI, or MN, or MO). If the name

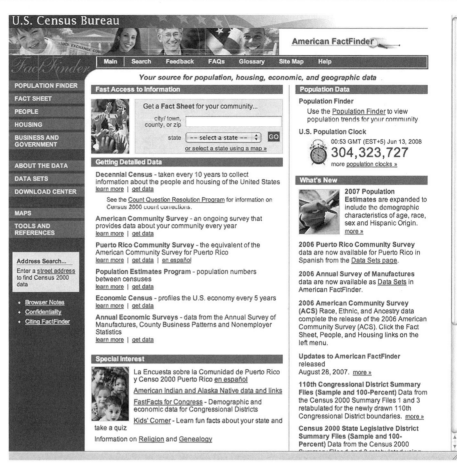

Fig. 8.13. The American FactFinder home page, as of June 2008.

still matches more than one geography, you'll have the option of choosing the place you want from a list.

Fact Sheet Contents

And look at what you get! Figures 8.14a and 8.14b show the Fact Sheet for Austin, TX, with data from the 2006 American Community Survey. In this version, as you move your mouse over the rows in the table, the highlight moves with you, helping you to see clearly which figures go with which heading. For example, highlighted in Figure 8.14*B* is the age group 65 years and over. The total number of people in this age group in Austin as of 2006 was 48,640, or 6.8 percent of the Austin population. This was about one half of the percentage in the U.S. population as a whole, where this age group represented 12.4 percent of the total population. So Austin is a "young" city demographically. This view is showing the most recent data available, but note there is also a "2000" tab. There you will find the data from the 2000 Census.

Using the Fact Sheet retrieved by your zip code, what can you find out about your community? Spend some time looking through this information, and experiment with the various links: on the tab for the 2000 Census data,

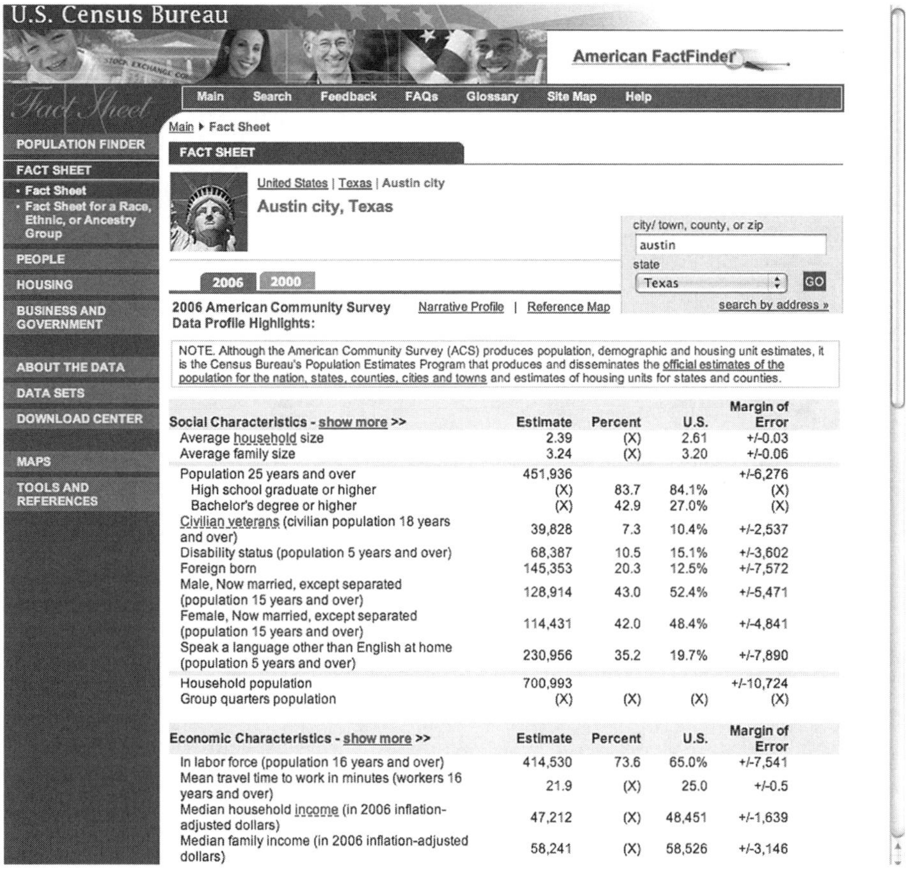
U.S. Census Bureau

American FactFinder

Fact Sheet

Main | Search | Feedback | FAQs | Glossary | Site Map | Help

POPULATION FINDER
FACT SHEET
• Fact Sheet
• Fact Sheet for a Race, Ethnic, or Ancestry Group
PEOPLE
HOUSING
BUSINESS AND GOVERNMENT
ABOUT THE DATA
DATA SETS
DOWNLOAD CENTER
MAPS
TOOLS AND REFERENCES

Main ▸ Fact Sheet

FACT SHEET

United States | Texas | Austin city

Austin city, Texas

city/ town, county, or zip: austin
state: Texas GO
search by address »

2006 | 2000

2006 American Community Survey Data Profile Highlights: Narrative Profile | Reference Map

NOTE. Although the American Community Survey (ACS) produces population, demographic and housing unit estimates, it is the Census Bureau's Population Estimates Program that produces and disseminates the official estimates of the population for the nation, states, counties, cities and towns and estimates of housing units for states and counties.

Social Characteristics - show more >>	Estimate	Percent	U.S.	Margin of Error
Average household size	2.39	(X)	2.61	+/-0.03
Average family size	3.24	(X)	3.20	+/-0.06
Population 25 years and over	451,936			+/-6,276
High school graduate or higher	(X)	83.7	84.1%	(X)
Bachelor's degree or higher	(X)	42.9	27.0%	(X)
Civilian veterans (civilian population 18 years and over)	39,828	7.3	10.4%	+/-2,537
Disability status (population 5 years and over)	68,387	10.5	15.1%	+/-3,602
Foreign born	145,353	20.3	12.5%	+/-7,572
Male, Now married, except separated (population 15 years and over)	128,914	43.0	52.4%	+/-5,471
Female, Now married, except separated (population 15 years and over)	114,431	42.0	48.4%	+/-4,841
Speak a language other than English at home (population 5 years and over)	230,956	35.2	19.7%	+/-7,890
Household population	700,993			+/-10,724
Group quarters population	(X)	(X)	(X)	(X)

Economic Characteristics - show more >>	Estimate	Percent	U.S.	Margin of Error
In labor force (population 16 years and over)	414,530	73.6	65.0%	+/-7,541
Mean travel time to work in minutes (workers 16 years and over)	21.9	(X)	25.0	+/-0.5
Median household income (in 2006 inflation-adjusted dollars)	47,212	(X)	48,451	+/-1,639
Median family income (in 2006 inflation-adjusted dollars)	58,241	(X)	58,526	+/-3,146

Fig. 8.14a. American FactFinder Fact Sheet for Austin, TX, upper half, data from the 2006 American Community Survey, page layout as of June 2008.

the "map" links take you to detailed, color-coded and interactive maps, and the "brief" links associated with many of the data items are PDFs of nicely produced, short ("brief") Census publications on the topic. On either tab, if you have more than one, the "Show More" links associated with the major categories will take you to more detail on that topic for your geographic area. Note: for the Map and Show More links, be sure to use the browser Back button to go back.

Commuting Time to Work Question: A Clue

Note that these Fact Sheets include a data category that relates to Search Example 3 from the LexisNexis section, about commuting time in U.S. cities. There must be a survey that asks this question, so there must be data available on this topic. Can you find the "mean travel time to work" for the place where you live? (Hint: this is an "Economic Characteristic.")

Advanced Search Example

The Fact Sheets are wonderful for easily finding a great deal of information about one location at a time. But what if you wanted one item of

dollars) Per capita income (in 2006 inflation-adjusted dollars)	28,250	(X)	25,267	+/-839
Families below poverty level	(X)	12.7	9.8%	(X)
Individuals below poverty level	(X)	17.7	13.3%	(X)

Housing Characteristics - show more >>	Estimate	Percent	U.S.	Margin of Error
Total housing units	324,528			+/-3,066
Occupied housing units	293,856	90.5	88.4%	+/-4,894
Owner-occupied housing units	138,851	47.3	67.3%	+/-4,447
Renter-occupied housing units	155,005	52.7	32.7%	+/-4,422
Vacant housing units	30,672	9.5	11.6%	+/-3,746
Owner-occupied homes	138,851			+/ 4,447
Median value (dollars)	173,000	(X)	185,200	+/-3,363
Median of selected monthly owner costs				
With a mortgage (dollars)	1,535	(X)	1,402	+/-37
Not mortgaged (dollars)	517	(X)	399	+/-19

ACS Demographic Estimates - show more >>	Estimate	Percent	U.S.	Margin of Error
Total population	717,100			+/-10,707
Male	373,902	52.1	49.2%	+/-6,497
Female	343,198	47.9	50.8%	+/-5,692
Median age (years)	31.2	(X)	36.4	+/-0.3
Under 5 years	60,064	8.4	6.8%	+/-2,365
18 years and over	548,548	76.5	75.4%	+/-7,283
65 years and over	48,640	6.8	12.4%	+/-1,768
One race	701,454	97.8	98.0%	+/-11,248
White	423,757	59.1	73.9%	+/-11,605
Black or African American	61,091	8.5	12.4%	+/-4,280
American Indian and Alaska Native	2,508	0.3	0.8%	+/-856
Asian	39,483	5.5	4.4%	+/-3,562
Native Hawaiian and Other Pacific Islander	57	0.0	0.1%	+/-100
Some other race	174,558	24.3	6.3%	+/-8,892
Two or more races	15,646	2.2	2.0%	+/-3,201
Hispanic or Latino (of any race)	257,774	35.9	14.8%	+/-5,536

Source: U.S. Census Bureau, 2006 American Community Survey

Explanation of Symbols:
'****' - The median falls in the lowest interval or upper interval of an open-ended distribution. A statistical test is not appropriate.
'******' - The estimate is controlled. A statistical test for sampling variability is not appropriate.
'N' - Data for this geographic area cannot be displayed because the number of sample cases is too small.
'(X)' - The value is not applicable or not available.

Fig. 8.14b. American FactFinder Fact Sheet for Austin, TX, lower half, data from the 2006 American Community Survey, page layout as of June 2008.

information for many places? As you recall, the original question in the LexisNexis *Statistical* Search Example 3 was about commuting, or travel time to work in *various* U.S. cities. The answer can be found here (finally), but requires working more directly with the original data sets. Luckily, the FactFinder creators have even made working with the original data sets manageable for nonspecialists. Go online, and see if you can walk through getting this data set with me. Since this is a free Web site, I know you can go see it for yourself, so I'm going to try explaining the process in words only. Use your eyes, see if you can follow along, and even adapt if necessary if something has changed.

1. On the American FactFinder homepage, find the Data Sets link. (In Figure 8.13, it appears both as a button on the left, and as the "get data" links in the middle section under the heading Getting Detailed Data.)

2. Hover your mouse over the Data Sets link, and choose "American Community Survey" (ACS) from the menu that appears. (In the first edition of this book, this exercise was done with Census data, but the ACS is more recent and somewhat easier to use.)

3. For the ACS, we're told that we can "Select from the following" and are given a list of (categories of) tables. There are now two possible routes to the answer to our question. We know we are looking for something that provides a geographic comparison among

places, and so we could choose the "Geographic Comparison Tables." There's also always the "brute force" approach of looking at everything available, provided by the "List all tables" link.

4. Let's try Geographic Comparison Tables. Click that, and the next screen should come up with the "geographic type" set to Nation. This is what you want: material from across the nation. (The other value for this drop-down menu, State, only allows you look at one State at a time.) The other variable to select on this page is the "table format." The nearest thing to "cities" in Census parlance is "metropolitan statistical areas," so we want the value called "United States—Metropolitan and Micropolitan Statistical Area, and for Puerto Rico." Select that and click Next.

5. On the next screen, we're almost there: simply scroll down through the list of tables to find "Mean Travel Time to Work" (table GCT0801), select that and click Show Result.

And there you are: a detailed set of data for travel time to work in every major metropolitan area of the United States (the uppermost part of the screen is shown in Figure 8.15). Look around on this page, and see what else you can do: for example, can you view the data as a "Thematic Map"? What most users immediately want is to be able to download the data, to load it into Excel to sort or otherwise manipulate it. In Figure 8.15, the "Print/Download" function is in the bar just above the name of the table.

See, you can do numbers! And isn't it interesting?

From "People" to "Workers"

The Bureau of Census keeps track of the state of "people" in the United States: that is, how many people there are, how old they are, what sex they are, what race they belong to, where they live, and so forth. The Census Bureau notes whether people are employed or not, their income, and whether they are below the poverty level. For more detail about "working America," however, we need to go to the Bureau of Labor Statistics.

Bureau of Labor Statistics

The Bureau of Labor Statistics, or BLS (http://www.bls.gov) tracks and provides exactly what the name says: everything about labor—working— in the United States. And it does mean *everything*, although since the first edition of this book, a "blizzard" of links on the BLS home page has been skillfully re-organized to try to make it less overwhelming and easier to use. As of this writing, a selection of news stories now occupies the center, and blocks of links are arranged in the side panels and across the bottom, as pictured in Figures 8.16*A* and 8.16*B*. I do love the BLS (how can you not love a government agency that uses a little green dinosaur icon to indicate "historical" data?), and am delighted to see their attempts to rationalize and simplify. It's true, now you have to roll your mouse over the link headings to get an idea of what is "underneath," but that change is well worth it, in my mind, to reduce the initial shock one used to get on seeing this page. Invest some time in studying what is included in the various links to get a sense of "what's where." It provides a vivid picture of working life in the U.S., and you will almost always find something new and useful, too.

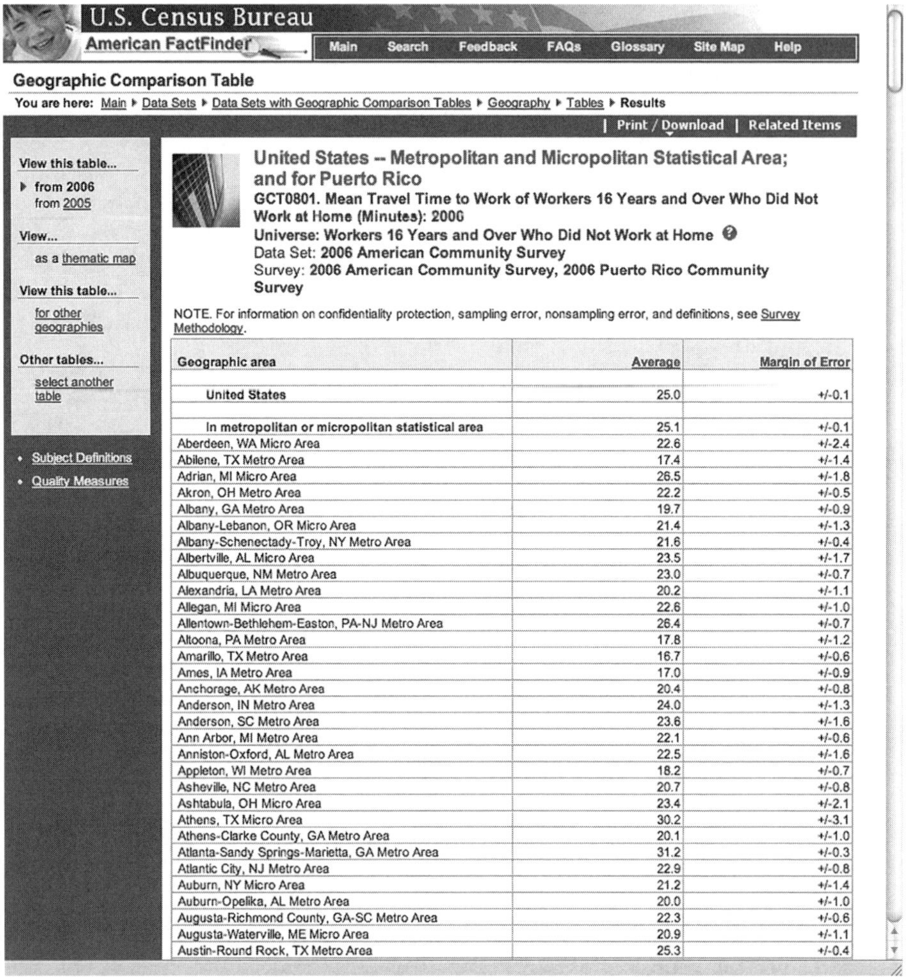

U.S. Census Bureau

American FactFinder

Main | Search | Feedback | FAQs | Glossary | Site Map | Help

Geographic Comparison Table

You are here: Main ▸ Data Sets ▸ Data Sets with Geographic Comparison Tables ▸ Geography ▸ Tables ▸ Results

| Print / Download | Related Items

View this table...
▸ from 2006
from 2005

View...
as a thematic map

View this table...
for other geographies

Other tables...
select another table

• Subject Definitions
• Quality Measures

United States -- Metropolitan and Micropolitan Statistical Area; and for Puerto Rico

GCT0801. Mean Travel Time to Work of Workers 16 Years and Over Who Did Not Work at Home (Minutes): 2006

Universe: Workers 16 Years and Over Who Did Not Work at Home

Data Set: 2006 American Community Survey

Survey: 2006 American Community Survey, 2006 Puerto Rico Community Survey

NOTE. For information on confidentiality protection, sampling error, nonsampling error, and definitions, see Survey Methodology.

Geographic area	Average	Margin of Error
United States	25.0	+/-0.1
In metropolitan or micropolitan statistical area	25.1	+/-0.1
Aberdeen, WA Micro Area	22.6	+/-2.4
Abilene, TX Metro Area	17.4	+/-1.4
Adrian, MI Micro Area	26.5	+/-1.8
Akron, OH Metro Area	22.2	+/-0.5
Albany, GA Metro Area	19.7	+/-0.9
Albany-Lebanon, OR Micro Area	21.4	+/-1.3
Albany-Schenectady-Troy, NY Metro Area	21.6	+/-0.4
Albertville, AL Micro Area	23.5	+/-1.7
Albuquerque, NM Metro Area	23.0	+/-0.7
Alexandria, LA Metro Area	20.2	+/-1.1
Allegan, MI Micro Area	22.6	+/-1.0
Allentown-Bethlehem-Easton, PA-NJ Metro Area	26.4	+/-0.7
Altoona, PA Metro Area	17.8	+/-1.2
Amarillo, TX Metro Area	16.7	+/-0.6
Ames, IA Metro Area	17.0	+/-0.9
Anchorage, AK Metro Area	20.4	+/-0.8
Anderson, IN Metro Area	24.0	+/-1.3
Anderson, SC Metro Area	23.6	+/-1.6
Ann Arbor, MI Metro Area	22.1	+/-0.6
Anniston-Oxford, AL Metro Area	22.5	+/-1.6
Appleton, WI Metro Area	18.2	+/-0.7
Asheville, NC Metro Area	20.7	+/-0.8
Ashtabula, OH Micro Area	23.4	+/-2.1
Athens, TX Micro Area	30.2	+/-3.1
Athens-Clarke County, GA Metro Area	20.1	+/-1.0
Atlanta-Sandy Springs-Marietta, GA Metro Area	31.2	+/-0.3
Atlantic City, NJ Metro Area	22.9	+/-0.8
Auburn, NY Micro Area	21.2	+/-1.4
Auburn-Opelika, AL Metro Area	20.0	+/-1.0
Augusta-Richmond County, GA-SC Metro Area	22.3	+/-0.6
Augusta-Waterville, ME Micro Area	20.9	+/-1.1
Austin-Round Rock, TX Metro Area	25.3	+/-0.4

Fig. 8.15. Results: top of the page showing travel time to work in major U.S. cities, data from the 2006 American Community Survey, page layout as of June 2008.

For our first example, we will focus on one section, about pay.

Pay & Benefits at the Bureau of Labor Statistics

Search Example 1: Part 1

Suppose the person closest to you announced that as soon as you get done with your MLS, he wants to go back to school and pursue *his* lifelong dream of becoming a registered nurse. This causes you to wonder about job prospects, and especially salaries for nurses.

On the BLS homepage, find the "Pay & Benefits" link under Subject Areas, which should include the "Wages by Area and Occupation" link. The next thing to decide is for what geographic area you want wage information: national, regional, state, or metropolitan area. When you're doing research for a particular person, it makes the most sense to look at data for a particular "metropolitan area," since you'll be living and working in some specific

Fig. 8.16a. Bureau of Labor Statistics home page, upper half, as of June 2008.

Fig. 8.16b. Bureau of Labor Statistics home page, lower half, as of June 2008.

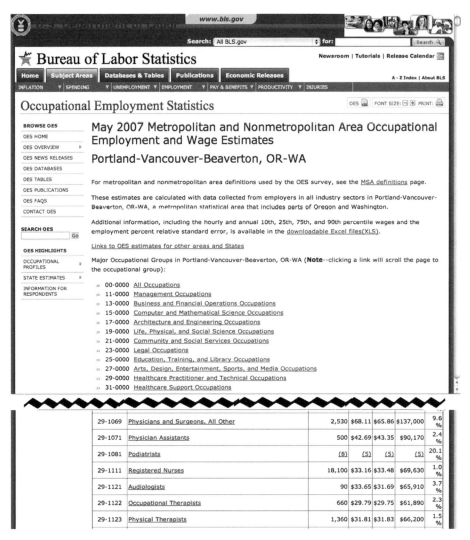

Fig. 8.17. BLS page for Occupational Employment and Wage Estimates for Portland-Vancouver-Beaverton, OR, selected portions, as of June 2008.

place. (The other categories are more appropriate for more theoretical, comparative research purposes.) So let's try the option that lists "For 375 metropolitan statistical areas (MSAs), 34 metropolitan divisions, and over 170 nonmetropolitan areas," because it seems to offer more than the "major metropolitan areas" option (which only offers "80 metropolitan areas").

Clicking this link takes us to a straightforward page where you simply have to scroll to the state you want and choose a city name. For instance, the "Employment and Wage Estimates" Web page for the metroplex of Portland-Vancouver-Beaverton, Oregon, is shown in Figure 8.17.

Oh no! more numerical codes and broad category headings to choose from—or is that really true? Note how tiny the scroll bar is in this screen-shot, indicating that this is a very long Web page. Here is a beautiful thing: you *don't* have to figure out that Registered Nurses fall under the heading "29–0000 Healthcare Practitioner and Technical Occupations." All you need

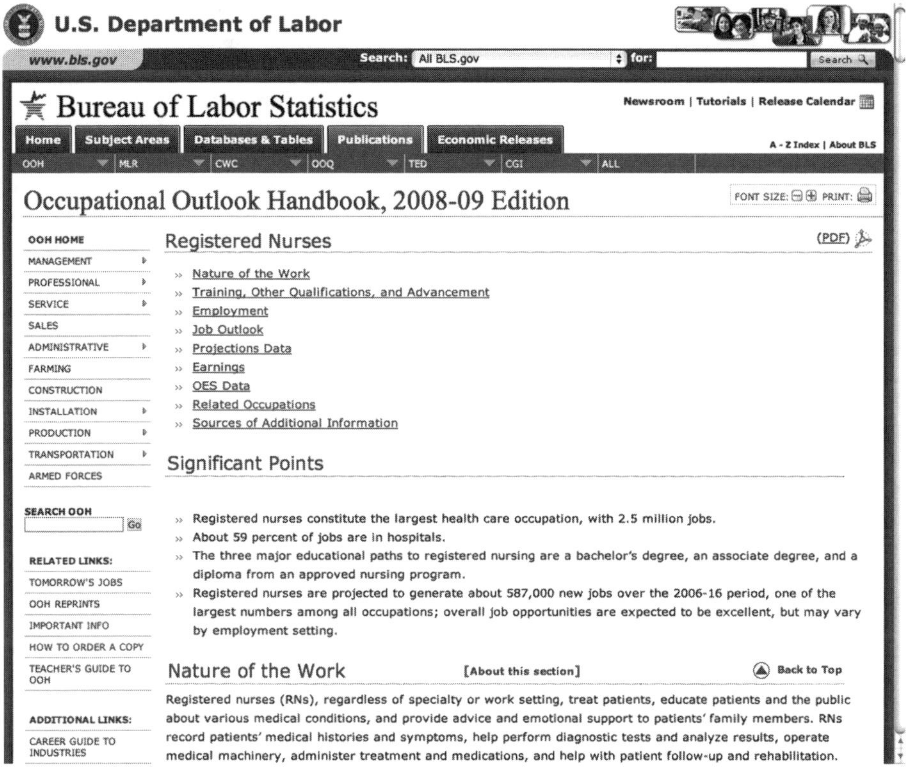

Fig. 8.18. Beginning of *Occupational Outlook Handbook* entry for Registered Nurses, as of June 2008.

to do is search the page for the word "nurses," using the Web browser's Find function. (Find is listed under the Edit menu, or can be invoked on a PC with "Control-f", on a Mac with the Apple (or splat) key-f).

Occupation Information at the Bureau of Labor Statistics

Search Example 1: Part 2

Continuing with the search example started earlier, your second concern was about the job outlook for nurses.

On the BLS homepage, you could use the Employment → Employment Projections link under Subject Areas, but if you scroll down, you'll see that the source we want, the *Occupational Outlook Handbook* (OOH), is listed right there, under Featured Publications. There are various ways to use the *Handbook*, depending on your interest (e.g., if you have a specific position in mind, as in this case, or you only want to browse a job category to get ideas). The Search OOH search box is usually the quickest way to find information on a specific line of work. If you are looking for a very specific job title, or the sorts of trendy titles that crop up in the tech industry ("chief creative officer"), you might not find an entry in the *Handbook*. But for a great many occupational titles, it brings together an extremely useful package of information: Nature of the Work; Working Conditions; Employment; Training, Other Qualifications, and Advancement; Job Outlook; Earnings; Related Occupations; and Sources of Additional Information.

Searching "Registered Nurses" rapidly brings us to the entry pictured in Figure 8.18, and the encouraging news that "Registered nurses are projected to generate about 587,000 new jobs over the 2006-16 period, one of the largest numbers among all occupations; overall job opportunities are expected to be excellent, but may vary by employment setting." This could be a good career move!

The only bad news is that this information is provided at the "nationwide" level only. Finding information on "job outlook" by state or city is, regrettably, beyond the entry-level scope of this text, and you are encouraged to go talk to your friendly local business librarian.

Quick Recap

LexisNexis *Statistical* is one of the few databases that act as an indexing and abstracting service for "numerical" information. The database content is drawn from three hard-copy A & I services: *American Statistics Index* (ASI), *Statistical Reference Index* (SRI), and the *Index to International Statistics* (IIS). LexisNexis offers three subscription options: the Base Edition, Research Edition, and Abstracts modules. The Base and Research Editions represent a basic and extended set of records from ASI, SRI, and IIS. These editions provide a GIF image of the associated data table with each record (the numerical equivalent of "full text"). The Abstracts modules act as an electronic version of the entire contents of the ASI, SRI, and IIS indexes, and can be used to point to the source document microfiche collections associated with these indexes. LexisNexis *Statistical* includes numerical information in all subject areas, although it is strongest in the type of information collected by U.S. government offices and agencies. Publication dates in the Base and Research Editions are generally from 1995 on, but current publications often contain many years of historical data. A general search strategy for *Statistical* is to start with fairly broad terms (either from the Subject List or as keywords), and then experiment with the many limits offered. The database also offers a list of Links to carefully selected government Web sites.

American FactFinder is an easy-to-use interface to find information from the latest Census, and other surveys done more frequently, collected by the Census Bureau. You can search by zip code, or by city/town, county, and/or state, to retrieve a Fact Sheet on a particular place. Fact Sheets offer data arranged under headings such as General (gender, age, and race), Social (education, disability status, married, etc.), Economic (employed, travel time to work, income, etc.), and Housing (ownership, value, etc.) Characteristics. Advanced queries, such as retrieving the same information about many places, can be carried out by means of the "Data Sets" interface.

The *Bureau of Labor Statistics* tracks and provides information about employment and occupations in the United States, as well as limited international information. As of June 2008, the BLS home page was organized into panels of information: Subject Areas, News, Latest Numbers, Featured Publications, Quick Links, etc. We looked at only two of the hundreds of resources at the BLS: wage information by occupation, based on geographic location (e.g., salaries for librarians in Boston versus Omaha), and the *Occupational Outlook Handbook* (OOH). The OOH pulls together a range of useful information for each job described: Nature of the Work, Working Conditions, Employment; Training, Other Qualifications, and Advancement; Job

Outlook, Earnings, Related Occupations, and Sources of Additional Information.

Numbers and the Reference Interview

Numeric Reference is somewhat of a specialty, involving a lexicon all its own. Information from surveys gets turned into data sets, which are then defined in terms of four distinct characteristics. I have listed here four specific things to try to find out during a reference interview with any patron requesting "data."

- The *population*, often referred to as the "universe" in data-speak: Whom is the patron interested in? All of the people who live in rural areas of the United States? Nurses? Railway workers in the nineteenth century?

- *Date*: Most current available? One particular date (usually a year) in the past? Or a "time series:" a set of values over a particular period? (e.g., the GNP for the United States from 1948 to now).

- *Frequency* (for a time series): Annually? Quarterly? Monthly?

- *Place, or geographic region*: The whole United States? Alabama? Spain?

It would be nice to provide you with a succinct, complementary list of actions to take based on the answers to these questions, but that probably requires a book unto itself. Suffice it to say that these definitely *are* the four questions to ask, and that eliciting information about these four things is useful in several ways, both practically and psychologically:

- The answers to these questions should help to determine if the patron really does want a data set, or just some statistics.

- If the request is vague, obviously the questions should help to clarify it, and asking them collects useful information (while also buying some time in which to rack your brains).

- Going through the process also provides a structured approach to fall back on (e.g., go back and ask the *right* questions), if you thought you understood the question and could get an answer pretty quickly, but your first resource isn't working out.

- Finally, answers to these questions are intended to help *you* to decide where to go looking for the information, but they will be equally helpful if you need to refer the patron to someone else in the library. Capturing the answers is a useful thing to do that makes the patron feel that a "help process" has been started, and forwarding the information will make the next librarian's task much easier, as well as saving time for both the librarian and the patron.

Exercises and Points to Consider

1. In the opening to this chapter, some broad categories of the following types of "numbers" were mentioned. If you are using this

book in a class, have a class discussion and see how many specific types of the following sorts of numbers or statistics you can come up with:

"People" type

"Business" type

"Financial" type

2. Fact-checker exercise. Working from an everyday newspaper article that mentions some statistics, see if you can verify the information, either by going to the source listed (if it is), or by searching on your own. The *Wall Street Journal* is an excellent source of this type of article and is good about mentioning the sources for its figures.

3. The BLS also tracks prices and costs. Importing and exporting goods is a "Business Cost." At the BLS homepage, see if you can find some data about the price changes (often referred to as *price indexes*) for imported oil (*petroleum* in the language of government). Hint: this is one of the "Most Requested" sets of statistics.

Suggested Readings

Anything that Stephen Woods has written for *DttP: Documents to the People*. His articles on various number-finding questions and resources appear regularly, and are useful, timely, and completely accessible. Different database vendors index his article titles differently: ProQuest calls them all "By the Numbers," the name of his column, whereas H.W. Wilson uses the more informative "headnote" titles, such as "Survey of International Criminal Justice Statistics" (2007), "Women Worker Series and the Bureau of Labor Statistics: Where Have All the Women Gone?" (2005), and "Comparing Apples and Oranges: Statistics over Time" (2004). Search by his name and the journal name to be sure of getting everything.

Vinyard, Marc. 2006. All the Right Numbers: Strategies for Locating Industry Sales. *Searcher* 14 (September): 54–59. More an introduction to industry research in general, Vinyard's article provides very useful descriptions of commonly available commercial resources (e.g., Datamonitor and Standard & Poor's *Industry Surveys*), as well as government resources and trade association Web sites. Very accessible and readable.

Ojala, Marydee. 2004. Statistically Speaking. *Online* (Weston, Conn.) 28 (March/April): 42–44. A more in-depth look at "where numbers come from," similar to the opening discussion in this chapter. Full of good advice and strategies from a master in the field.

Berinstein, Paula. 2003. *Business Statistics on the Web: Find Them Fast—At Little or No Cost*. Medford, NJ: CyberAge Books. Chapter 2, "Statistics Basics," and Chapter 3, "Who Generates and Publishes Statistics?" provide additional excellent background information for this topic. If you are in a position where you get "number" questions frequently, I recommend having a copy of this book close by to use as a reference.

Notes

1. Note that non-profits and trade organizations usually do not provide data for free; *non-profit* does not mean "no fee" (and trade organizations need to recoup their costs, too).

2. What one might call the "ha ha, you must be kidding!" price category.

3. Obviously, Google does a good job of finding Web sites for organizations, but *Associations Unlimited*, the database equivalent of that reference staple, the *Encyclopedia of Associations*, is handy for identifying associations—especially the international ones, whose Web site might not be in English.

4. Look for links with the word "Investor" in them: Investor Relations, Investor Center, etc.

5. A pretty close approximation to a comprehensive list of currently available data and statistics resources can be seen at the library Web site of a well-endowed university such as Princeton. The Subject List of databases for Economics & Finance at Princeton (further subdivided by "Economic Data" and "Financial Data") is impressive.

6. USA.gov is "the U.S. Government's Official Web Portal" and is actually fairly usable. FedWorld.gov (http://www.fedworld.gov) is both a portal and a search tool; Google U.S. government search (http://www.google.com/ig/usgov), and Search-Gov.com (http://www.searchgov.com) are good "government" search engines.

7. Why there isn't a "Part 02" for this report is a mystery. Five points to the first alert reader to figure it out.

9
Focus on People

This entire book so far has been concerned with the mechanics of databases: what they are, how to use them, and how they differ by discipline. But at any time it's important to pause and reflect on the ultimate reason *why* we're interested in learning this: to assist other people in their research process. Understanding the people who may benefit from using these databases and how they feel about doing research (there are a lot of emotions involved, it turns out) can inform how you interact with them. This chapter provides an examination of the general theoretical underpinnings of what your users are going through: the whole process of *information seeking*. Indeed, information seeking is all around us, "always embedded in the larger tasks of work, learning, and play" (Nel, 2001). Whether you're motivated by the question of locating the nearest coffee shop or a desire to find information on a rare form of cancer, although you might not have thought of it this way, those who study information-seeking behavior see you as engaged in a process to purposefully change your state of knowledge (Nel, 2001). If you are a librarian trying to facilitate information seeking, it's important to have the process in the back of your mind as you engage in a reference interview. Understanding the information-seeking process also helps to inform your whole strategy of questioning in the reference interview (e.g., the use of "open" and "closed" questions) and helps to ensure greater satisfaction on both sides: librarian and patron.

This chapter is based on selected articles and other sources from the library literature that I have found helpful for conveying the major points I wished to make. These articles range from scholarly and erudite to down-home and practical: often the informal, one- or two-page pieces offer some of the best down-to-earth advice. This is, however, by no means a comprehensive review of the literature. The information seeking literature is vast and continually being added to: as of June 2008, there were 578 records that had been assigned the pure Thesaurus subject heading "Information

Needs" ("used for: information-seeking behavior") in *Library Literature & Information Science*, dating from 1982 to May 2008. The phrase "information needs" was used on its own or as part of other subject headings in a total of 2,312 records! Entire journals are devoted to the study of information needs and seeking. *Information Research*, an "open access, international, scholarly journal" made its debut on the Web in 1995 and has been actively publishing ever since (IR homepage, 2008). *Information Research* probably now offers the largest freely available body of research papers on this topic in the world. Interest in information seeking has a remarkably long history, as demonstrated by a study of the reference interview dating from the nineteenth century (Green, 1876). Countless other studies have followed, continually analyzing how people go about fulfilling information needs and how librarians can better assist in the process.

Part 1: Information-seeking Behavior

The information seeking literature can generally be characterized as belonging to one of two groups: the theoretical, which discusses the topic in abstract terms and seeks to define it in terms of structured models, and the applied, which discusses it in terms of real-world observations and interactions. This section provides an introduction to some of the theory and the applied studies on people's information-seeking behaviors.

Some Theoretical Background on Information Seeking

Robert S. Taylor's 1968 article is a classic in the area of theoretical information seeking studies. In it, he presents a model that identifies four levels of questions:

- Q1 the visceral need
- Q2 the conscious need
- Q3 the formalized need
- Q4 the compromised need

According to Taylor, information seeking can range from an unconscious not-even-expressible information need, to a very fuzzy but vaguely discussible need, to a point at which the person can clearly voice the question, and finally—the compromised need is the question "*as presented to an information system*" (emphasis mine). An example of "the question as presented to an information system" is what a person types into the Google search box. (The source quoted lists library or librarian as the first kind of possible "information system," but as we know and is amply demonstrated in the literature, after friends or colleagues, the Web is by far the first choice of information seekers today.)

In his 2001 article, Johannes Nel surveys the subsequent theoretical literature and the models of information seeking, with an emphasis on the emotional states that accompany the various stages of the search process. He describes the classic model of the "information search process" by Carol Kuhlthau (1991) in detail; it has many stages and affiliated emotions, as indicated in Table 9.1.

Table 9.1. Information Search Process Stages in Kuhlthau's Model

Stage	Task	Emotions
Initiation stage	Recognize a need for information (result of awareness of lack of knowledge).	Uncertainty, apprehension
Selection stage	Identify and select general topic or approach.	Optimism (upon achieving task)
Exploration stage	Need to locate information about topic, become informed, integrate new information with previously held constructs, reconcile sources providing inconsistent or incompatible information	Confusion, uncertainty, discouragement, frustration, sense of personal inadequacy
Formulation stage	Focus, personalize topic by identifying and selecting ideas from all the information retrieved.	Increased confidence, sense of clarity
Collection stage	Gather information related to the restated, focused topic; clearer sense of direction allows for more efficient, relevant interactions with information systems.	Confidence increases, interest in project increases, uncertainty subsides.
Presentation stage	Prepare presentation of findings	Relief, satisfaction (or disappointment if search has not gone well)

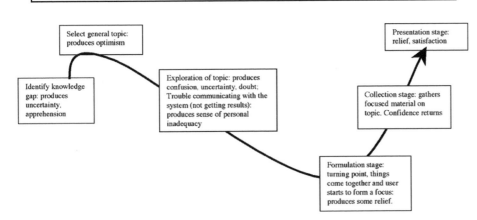

Fig. 9.1. The research roller coaster.

Taken overall, this process amounts to quite an emotional roller coaster for the poor information seeker. Looking over the stages, we could envision it as in Figure 9.1.

A study by Ethelene Whitmire (2003) demonstrates that when it comes to undergraduates faced with writing research papers, Kuhlthau's model fits exactly. This model also fits with my own experience with academic information seekers; although the process doesn't necessarily progress steadily from one stage to another. They frequently go through several iterations of the "select, explore, formulate, collect" stages. Kulhthau's model has also been applied to adolescent information seeking by Ross J. Todd (2003). His figure of the model also pulls in the associated cognitive processes (thoughts: from vague to focused to increased interest), and physical actions (exploring to documenting).

Dr. Jannica Heinström, who has worked closely with Professors Todd and Kuhlthau, has published several articles on her research in this area. Her work brings the ideas in Kuhlthau's model (i.e., stages, tasks, and emotions in information seeking) to a next step (i.e., testing the influence of disciplinary area, study habits, and personality on information seeking in students in higher education), within the current, online-dominant information world. She has looked at patterns in information seeking both in master's level students and in middle and high school students. She has identified three characteristic information-seeking patterns relating to the students' preferences for exploration or specificity, which she has named *fast surfing*, *broad scanning*, and *deep diving*. She found these various styles to be "grounded in personality traits" and could be "linked to the students' study approaches." In only one area, the social sciences, did discipline appear to have an influence on information seeking style (Heinström, 2006). Table 9.2 attempts to capture the results of her studies on master's level students in a shorthand format.

(Note the "good critical evaluation skills" of the broad scanners. In related research, the importance of critical thinking skills in determining a user's level of library anxiety—and, ultimately, information-seeking success—has been studied and is usefully discussed in Kwon et al. 2007.) In looking over this table, don't you find it easy to recognize fellow students or patrons of any kind that you have worked with? Theory, in all these cases, seems to accord well with reality, and the "reality" of information-seeking behavior is a favorite topic of library literature.

Applied Research on Information-seeking Behavior

There is a vast quantity of literature on information-seeking behaviors in academic settings. These studies have a long history, and include both specific and broader groups, such as:

- High school students (Chung and Neuman, 2007)
- Undergraduates in general (Foster and Gibbons, 2007; Novotny, 2004; Whitmire, 2003; Prince, 2003; Valentine, 1993)
- Veterinary students (Pelzer, Wiese, and Leysen, 1998)
- Business students (Makani and WooShue, 2006; Abels, Griner, and Turqman, 2004)
- Graduate students: international versus American (Liao et al., 2007), and in the humanities (Barrett, 2005)
- Sociology faculty (Shen, 2007), other social sciences faculty (Mayfield and Thomas, 2005), academic scientists (Hemminger et al., 2007), chemistry faculty (Flaxbart, 2001)

Table 9.2. Information Seeking by *Fast Searchers, Broad Scanners,* and *Deep Divers*

	Fast Surfers	Broad Scanners	Deep Divers
Amount of effort	Minimal	Active, but highly spontaneous, serendipitous	Considerable; strong search engagement
Information acquisition pattern	Hasty, unstructured	Unstructured exploration	Focused and structured, systematic: preference for precision over recall
Preferred types of content	Easily accessible and digestible: overviews, restatements of views already held	Inspiring, challenging, presenting new ideas	High scientific quality; specific
Discipline (area of study)	No influence	Significant connection found between social sciences students and this approach.	No influence
Study approach	Surface; low motivation	No influence	Focused, structured; desire for thorough understanding: deep or strategic approaches to studying. High motivation.
Personality traits	Low conscientiousness: "easily distracted, impatient, easygoing." Low openness to experience and high sensitivity result in "avoidance of challenging information content."	Extroversion, but low agreeableness, openness to experience: "outgoing, curious, and competitive." Good critical evaluation skills.	No "significant influence of personality;" but a positive connection between openness and conscientiousness to deep diving.

Based on Heinström, 2006.

- "Academics" in general (Borgman et al., 2005; Jankowska, 2004; Marcum and George, 2003; Massey-Burzio, 1998; Reneker, 1993; Ellis, 1993).

Medical librarians have published a great many articles on information seeking in health care, frequently focusing on the professional side: patient care teams (Reddy and Spence, 2008), speech-language pathologists (Nail-Chiwetalu and Ratner, 2007), health sciences faculty (Owen and Fang, 2003) and health sciences faculty in Ghana (Sulemani and Katsekpor, 2007), primary care practitioners (Andrews, 2005; Preddie, 2005), school of public health faculty (Wallis, 2006), on-duty critical care nurses (McKnight, 2006), nurses in Nigeria (Ajayi, 2005), and clinical research coordinators (Wessel et al., 2006). On the patient side, they have studied middle-aged women (Yoo and Robbins, 2008), women with uterine fibroids (Ankem, 2007), vulnerable populations (Dervin, 2005), and consumers looking for help in making screening test decisions (Burkell and Campbell, 2005).

School media specialists and public librarians have also actively contributed their observations and advice about the information-seeking behaviors that they observe in the clientele of their libraries (Perrault, 2007, Meyers et al., 2007, Leckie and Given, 2005; Eisenberg, 2005; Vesey, 2005; Minkel, 2004; Shenton, 2007; Shenton and Dixon 2004; Shenton and Dixon 2003; Todd, 2003; Loertscher and Woolls, 2002; Lorenzen, 2001).

Scanning the literature, we find other groups ranging from arts administrators (Zach, 2005, 2006) and other humanists: ethnomusicologists (Liew and Ng, 2006), composers of electroacoustic music (Hunter, 2006), and visual artists ("Information-Seeking Behavior," 2008), to scientists (Grefsheim and Rankin, 2007; Murphy, 2003) have been studied. Also of interest are lawyers (Booth, 2004; Makri et al., 2008), genealogists (Duff and Johnson, 2003), engineers ("Information Needs," 2007), and users of the European Parliamentary Documentation Centre (Marcella et al., 2007). It is a highly international topic as well, including small and medium-sized enterprises (SME) managers in Botswana (Jorosi, 2006), agricultural scientists in India ("Information Seeking Strategies," 2008); in Nigeria, oil palm scientists (Obasuyi, 2007) and fishermen (Njoku, 2004), and Jewish studies scholars in Israel (Bronstein and Baruchson-Arbib, 2008)—all have been the objects of scrutiny of their information-seeking behaviors. A study of physical science librarians shows that we even look at ourselves (Brown and Ortega, 2005).

Information Seeking in the Internet Era

The recent applied research on information seeking behavior in "wired" societies has consistent themes: people tend to turn first to the Internet or to friends or colleagues, when they have an information need. Much as they love the Internet, they still do like interacting with humans. Given the choice between someone they know: a friend, a teacher, or a colleague, and a librarian (whom they do not know), they'll start with the former. As Stephen Abram notes about Millennial students: "Need help? Ask the MySpace community" (Abram, 2007). With social networking sites, users now have the best of all worlds: doing their information seeking with "friends" and doing it conveniently, online. Another finding has to do with time: in the studies, users consistently complain about lack of time. Information seekers try to save time whenever possible, which leads to opting for "convenience over quality." In a study of gender differences in information seeking, the researchers found that men deal with this time problem by having a stronger preference for fast retrieval tools and are slightly more likely to go to the Internet as their first resource, but that women "perceived lack of time more intensely" (Steinerová and Šušol, 2007).

Although a major obstacle to doing research that is repeatedly mentioned is "knowing where to start," at the same time, elementary school children, teenagers, and undergraduates consider themselves skilled and quite capable of doing their own research. Users are also more and more aware of the enormous amount of information available, and in conjunction with the "lack of time" problem, complain about information overload (Young and

Von Seggern, 2001). Fast surfers have a "particular vulnerability to feelings of information overload" (Heinström, 2006).

Participants in Young and Von Seggern's (2001) study described a "dream information machine" as something intuitive (a mind reader), a thing they can interact with in natural language. Their dream information machine is also a single source: comprehensive, complete, portable, and accessible 24 hours a day, 7 days a week (24/7). Note that librarians are some of these things, but we are not portable or available 24/7. We tend to point you to several sources rather than one that has everything, but we are sometimes rather good at mind reading. Given this description, however, it's impossible not to pause and consider why people love the Internet.

Why People Love the Internet

According to the literature, at the beginning stages of the research process the information seeker is anxious and nervous (unless they are teenagers or undergraduates, born into the Web world and quite confident of their abilities to find things). One of the big problems is getting started: an information seeker gets very discouraged and might even quit if he or she doesn't get results. They prefer one source, they want it fast, and they want it everywhere, all the time. On the Internet:

- You do it on your own; among other things, your thoughts don't have to be as clearly formulated as they would be to express your question to someone you don't know well.

Embarrassment is therefore avoided, and:

- Starting is easier because you simply type something in and almost always get results.
- Anxiety is immediately reduced, because you got *something* (you probably have gotten much more than just something—you may have gotten thousands of hits—but it is better, quite literally, than nothing).
- You think that you must know what you're doing. Confidence is increased: you got something(s), so you don't need help.
- It appears to be "one source" because you can get something on practically any topic from one search engine.
- It's fast, it's available 24/7, and it's almost ubiquitous, especially now that you can get to it on your PDA or cell phone.

What's not to like? There are, however, many negative emotions connected with searching on the Internet.

Downsides of Internet Searching

Some of the negative emotions and aspects of doing one's own searching on the Internet include:

- Doubt, uncertainty
- Confusion
- Frustration

- Time pressure

- "Infoglut"—being overwhelmed with results (Young and Seggern, 2001)

- Never knowing when you're finished or if you've "found it all"

You have undoubtedly encountered many of these negative emotions yourself when searching the Internet. (Even Google is only as good as the search you give it.) Having to sift through long lists of results, visiting various pages, evaluating, clicking deeper within a site to try to figure out why it was included in the results, then backtracking and trying not to get lost can definitely elicit all of these emotions. From the literature and my own experiences with users, the user mindset appears to be something like this:

Web searching can be very frustrating, but at least you suffer in private. You don't have to confess or try to explain your topic to a stranger: a librarian (especially if it isn't totally clear to *you* yet). Or perhaps you've been working on this idea for while and think that you're quite on top of it: how could someone (a librarian) totally unfamiliar with it be any help? You'd have to explain so much, and that would take too much time. Besides, you got results, so you obviously know how to search, and you're sure the information you want is out there. You want it, and it sounds reasonable to you that such information should exist, therefore it must be there, because you can find anything on the Internet, right? Somewhere. It must just be a matter of trying again, and trying again, frustrating as it is.

Effect of the "Internet Mindset" on Information Seeking

The most recent literature about information-seeking behaviors scarcely questions that users go straight to the Internet; that is a given. Now what is studied is how the "Internet mindset" impacts their information seeking, or search, habits. The patterns that seem to be emerging are the use of very simplistic searches involving only one or two keywords, and many iterations: search and scan (the results), search and scan again, and again. Rather than trying to evaluate or analyze why a search didn't work, users immediately change a word and try again, rapidly abandoning searches that don't appear to work (Novotny, 2004). Users rarely if ever take advantage of advanced search features, and Boolean logic doesn't even enter the picture: presented with an advanced search interface, they still simply enter keywords (Minkel, 2004; Novotny, 2004). Users don't know how to refine large result sets, instead they scan quickly for one or two likely looking titles. Overall, current search habits seem to be characterized by a trial-and-error approach (Minkel, 2004), and a general lack of any kind of critical, analytical skills (Todd, 2003). The title of Eric Novotny's 2004 article captures it exactly: "I don't think I click." Although Heinström's (2006) study was not about the specific actions of the research participants, the type of searching described here sounds very much like what fast surfers and broad scanners would do, although she notes that the broad scanners are better at critiquing their results.

Is all this a death knell for the powerful, sophisticated interfaces developed for subscription databases? My hope is no: that features such as Boolean operators and field searching will continue to be available, to be used by those who know how (by Heinström's third group, the deep divers). At the same time, one can already see that the way keyword searches are handled "behind the scenes" in these databases is getting better and better, so that simple keyword searches in a sophisticated database produce useful results. We have also seen in previous chapters that many of the databases have started adding myriad features aimed at helping users to refine their results on the results page, if they don't choose to use the capabilities in the search interface. Is there any hope of teaching students and others to use more effective search methods: synonyms, Boolean logic, limits? In my opinion, trying to do this on the large scale, that is, teaching whole classes to be expert searchers, is probably not realistic. As "teaching moments" arise, one on one, introducing just one or two of these concepts with the appropriate hooks: "this will make your searching much more efficient—it'll be much easier to get the information you need, and you'll get a better grade on your paper"—that, in my experience, is possible. Woo them gently; the carrot is much more effective than the stick. The occasion for most of these "teaching moments" is in the reference interview, our next topic.

Quick Recap

The information-seeking process has been described in the theoretical literature with various models. Taylor's model uses levels of questions; Kuhlthau's model describes it as a series of stages and tasks, each with a good deal of emotion attached. Heinström, a colleague of Kuhlthau, studies information seekers in the Internet era, and characterizes them as fast surfers, broad scanners, or deep divers. Applied studies of academic users support these models and show two major trends: a person seeking information tends to consult the Internet or friends and colleagues, before turning to the library. Searching the Internet has many very appealing aspects for information seekers, as well as frustrations. The predominance of Internet usage has affected how the "Net generation" searches for information; their habits generally are characterized by speed, reliance on keyword searches rather than anything more sophisticated, and trial and error. The deep diver searchers are an exception.

Part 2: The Reference Interview

We hardly even need the authority of "the literature" to tell us about how people look for information, however, because the evidence from all of our lives probably bears witness to the reality every day:

People go straight to the Internet.

Or they ask other people.

Where do libraries and librarians fit in, then? It appears, for better or worse, that for most people librarians have become the resource of last resort. (Although women are more likely than men to seek out help from librarians, at least in Slovakia [Steinerová and Šušol, 2007]). Indeed, in a survey of MBA students (Abels, Griner, and Turqman, 2004), the answer with the highest response rate to the question: "Means of Contacting the Librarians" is "Would not consult a librarian." (Ouch.) The exception is a person you have worked with and helped before: once someone has experienced a "good search" that produces useful material in 5 to 10 minutes, he or she is likely to consider returning to you rather than continue to engage in marathon, fruitless sessions on the Internet. Even if the answer with the librarian is a Web search, it may well be more efficiently done and produce the needed results faster. Being a resource of last resort means we are not, perhaps, asked as many questions (chronically overworked reference librarians can throw things at me now), but the ones that we are asked are more difficult. Most of the time this makes the job more interesting. (The rest of the time—well, every job has its frustrations. It's better if you don't bash your head on the desk when people can see you, however.) Being a resource of last resort and having to work with more difficult questions means, however, that the topic of this section of the chapter, the reference interview, has only grown and not lessened in importance.

To sort out these more difficult questions and elicit useful information from people who are convinced that they are already good searchers who have done everything possible, you need all your best communication and people skills. Indeed, the oft-quoted dilemma, as phrased by Robert Taylor in 1968, still applies:

> Without doubt, the negotiation of reference questions is one of the most complex acts of human communication. During this process, one person tries to describe for another person not something he knows, but rather something he does NOT know.

What Is the Real Question?

One of the most challenging things about the reference interview is simply that people do not ask for what they really want. This is a recurring theme in the literature: "inquirers seldom ask at first for what they want" (Taylor, 1968), and "librarians have long recognized the tendency of library users to pose their initial questions in incomplete, often unclear, and sometimes apparently covert terms" (Dewdney and Michell, 1997). Mary Ellen Bates (1998) expressed the issue succinctly as "finding the question behind the question." Catherine Ross (2003) is strongly in favor of a reference interview in "almost every" transaction, because even a very brief exchange helps people to "clarify in their own minds what their question really is." In some musings about his work on a reference desk, Sean Scott (2004) has a humorous example of the type of question that makes any reference librarian's blood run cold: "Do you have anything on that gal who died?" ("That gal" turned out to be Anne Frank.)

Why is this asking of a question so difficult? Why don't people simply ask what they really want to know? It turns out there's a lot more to *asking* a question (let alone answering one) than meets the eye. For example:

- The question might be used as a way to make contact, to see if you're "available." Indeed, it has been suggested (Dewdney and Michell, 1996) that the initial question actually be treated as "four unspoken questions":
  - Am I in the right place?
  - Are you available to help me?
  - Are you listening and willing to help me?
  - Have you understood my topic (in general)?

- People all have worldviews and their own ideas (mental models) of how things work, even if they have no actual experience on which to base those ideas. Because of this, they ask a question that they think you can answer. They couch their need in terms of something they think that you can provide. This is what Taylor meant by his fourth type of question, the "compromised need." The person deliberately recasts the question "in anticipation of what the files can deliver" (Taylor, 1968), or in the form they think "is the sort of thing one should ask" (Fister, 2002).

- As illustrated by the extended quotation from Taylor at the beginning of this section, people don't ask an exact question because they might not themselves know very well what they want or of any better way to phrase what they want. If you were a 6-year-old trying to ask your school librarian for something to read that would explain why your parents always seemed to be taking your older brother to the doctor, how well do you think you could express it? You may discover that many people become about 6 years old on approaching a reference desk.

- Communication barriers can interfere in asking questions: barriers because of age, language, jargon, or mishearing or misinterpreting what was heard.

- There are many questions that can sound quite reasonable but just aren't. When you start to examine them more closely, they turn out to be impossibly broad.

- The exact information need might not be expressed because of embarrassment at having to ask, or because of the nature of the question.

- Even stronger than embarrassment, having to ask a question may bring up feelings of fear: fear from not knowing what to expect when they ask (what if it's a really stupid question and you become angry or say something belittling?) You can well imagine that a person in that situation would be very careful about the question they asked, and that it might be a long way from what they really want to know (Fister, 2002).

"Not the Real Question": Some Examples

Here are some examples, drawn from real life and from the literature, of questions that were asked based on the motivations described earlier, or questions that are open to several interpretations.

The totally misdirected question: "Could you read my paper and tell me if my arguments are right and if I've made any mistakes?" In reality, what the person wanted were some better, more scholarly sources.

The question that they think you're more likely to be able to answer: "Where are the issues of *Mergers & Acquisitions [M&A]*?" The real question: the student's professor had suggested a particular article in *M&A*, and the student was going to browse until he found it.

Here is a wonderful example of six possible situations that could be lurking behind the very simple question, "Where are the cookbooks?" (Peterson, 1997):

1. Polly wants to browse a wide range of cookbooks to get different recipe ideas.

2. Edna is looking for a specific recipe on authentic Italian *alfredo* sauce.

3. Mary is considering modifying her diet for health reasons and could really use some books on health and nutrition.

4. Jenny is conducting a cooking seminar and needs information on how to structure her classes.

5. Joe wants to be a chef, but he really needs books on job-hunting strategies.

6. Marty is looking for *The Anarchist's Cookbook*, which not a cookbook at all and is located in a completely different section.

The question that sounds reasonable and isn't: "I need a list of the top fifty undergraduate programs in Math, Computer Science, and Engineering worldwide." There are directories of such programs (in the United States), and one frequently sees lists in *Business Week* and similar publications of the "Top 50" or "Top 100" this or that, and so this seems like a reasonable request. (But it's not; don't try it!)

The failure of communication question (mishearing the original information): the undergraduate who asked for *Oranges and Peaches*, by Charles somebody, who gets more and more upset as the librarian can't find it, until he finally happens to say "but my professor said it was the Bible of evolution!!" and the librarian realized that what he meant was *Origin of Species*, by Charles Darwin (Dewdney and Michell, 1996).

Question Negotiation in the Reference Interview

It is possible to discover the real question, however. A combination of good communication skills, emotional intelligence, practice, and experience are the keys. The major component of good communication skills for the reference interview is known as *question negotiation*.

Question negotiation, although not a simple thing, does sound simple: you try to elicit information by asking questions. The questions have a particular style, known as open and closed. *Open questions* invite your interlocutor to tell you more, to expand on the topic in a freeform way (like the famous interview question: "tell me about yourself"), whereas *closed questions* are used to request a specific piece of information and usually require only a yes or no, or a one- to two-word response.

Open and Closed Questions

Here are some examples of open questions that are good to use in the reference interview (they tend to begin with words such as how, where, what, why, and the useful phrase, "can you tell me . . . "):

• Can you tell me something more about (the class assignment, the topic, etc.)?

• How much material were you hoping to find?

• What would you like to find out (about the topic)?

• How are you intending to use the information?

• What have you tried already?

- What else have you found, or do you already have any papers on this topic that we could look at?
- Where did you find (example, if presented)?

Similar to these, but with some interesting variations, is a lovely set of questions suggested by Mary Ellen Bates (1998), a notable authority on searching:

- What do you mean by ____?
- What do you already know about ____?
- What do you expect me to find?
- Are there any sources you have already checked or that you would recommend?
- If you were writing an article about this subject, what would the headline be?
- If I can't find exactly ____, what would be second-best?
- How will you be using the information?
- So, in other words, what you'd like me to find is ____, right?

Some examples of closed questions:

- Are you looking for a specific item or a list of materials on a topic?
- Do you want a comprehensive search or a few good items?
- Did you try (the catalog, the Web, or a particular database)?
- When do you need this by?
- Do you need scholarly (research, journal) articles or are popular (*Time*, *Newsweek*) articles okay?
- Are you looking for recent information or are you doing historical research?
- Have you used (particular resource) before?

Both open and closed questions are important and useful in question negotiation; don't fall into the trap of equating open with good and closed with bad. Open questions are a good way to get things going, to start developing a big picture, and to get the user talking and thus providing subject words. Closed questions are useful for focusing the topic, making sure the interaction proceeds efficiently, and helping to rule out courses of action. Strive to avoid a question negotiation session that uses only closed questions; rather, try to employ a mix of both. If you encounter a situation for which closed questions seem to be all that is required, don't feel guilty, however. It can happen, especially around basic questions, or in an instant messaging environment. What you want to avoid is getting into the habit of asking only closed questions from laziness or disinterest.

In coming up with questions, keep in mind the ultimate goals for the reference interview:

- Understand the problem and its literature—the topic.
- Find out what the person has already done (if anything).

- Develop search vocabulary and alternatives (synonyms).
- Determine limits (date, etc.) and levels (research or popular literature?).
- Discuss retrieval goals (How much/How many? How soon?).
- Develop an overall strategy to help you to select appropriate resources (database, Web, etc.)

Overall, the question negotiation process in the reference interview should help you to understand the problem context, that is, *who* and *why*. Who is your questioner: a 5-year-old, your mom, an undergraduate, or a sales manager in your company? Your choice of words, your questions, your suggestions, and the amount of time spent—every part of your interaction should be adjusted based on whom you are talking to. For example, most of the open questions suggested here aren't very appropriate for an elementary school student. The second primary part of the context is *why* are they asking—what is motivating the search? Is it just exploratory, a personal interest? Is it specific, a class assignment or preparation for an upcoming interview? Again, this affects the whole nature and direction of the search.

Interpersonal Communication Skills in the Reference Interview

Having lists of questions to ask will take you only so far, however. A successful reference interaction also requires a healthy amount of good interpersonal communication skills, such as:

- Active listening: verbally or nonverbally indicating interest, attentiveness (saying "uh huh," nodding), and empathy (facial expressions that mirror the other person's feelings, "ouch"), even humor (this seems to come up particularly in an instant messaging type of exchange [Fagan and Desai, 2002/2003]).
- Paraphrasing: "So you'd like (xyz); is that right?"
- Giving positive nonverbal cues: projecting an approachable attitude, using welcoming body language: smiling, eye contact, and an "interested face." The emotional underpinnings of the whole situation cannot be emphasized too much, and thus the need for "emotional intelligence" in conducting the exchange (Eidson, 2000). People generally pick up on tones of voice and negative body attitudes quickly and unerringly (Ross, 2003) and will be more satisfied with a helpful and friendly, even if incorrect or incomplete, answer than one that is correct but cold (Radford, 1999; Fagan and Desai, 2003).

As Tyckoson (2003) says: "It is the interaction, the process of communication, which is often more important than the content or a specific answer."

A school librarian's list of important communication skills emphasizes the following points, which are definitely applicable to any situation (Riedling, 2000):

- Positive, respectful responses
- Encouraging words
- Avoiding premature answers

The last point deserves extra attention, because it is a trap that is so easy to fall into. Even if students have been asking for the same thing for a week, it's important to treat each instance as if it were new. You never know—the fifteenth time it might actually be something a bit different.

In discussing communication skills and pitfalls, a public librarian is emphatic about not using library jargon, and points out terms that people frequently either mistake or use in a different sense from the "library" sense (Cramer, 1998):

- Bibliography for biography
- Reference book for nonfiction work
- Equating "fiction" with "not true," and thus pejorative
- "Check out" for "look at"

This point also bears some further elaboration. We need to remember that we use a very specialized professional vocabulary that is unfamiliar to most people outside our profession. For many people, "entering a library is like going into a foreign country, where a foreign language is spoken" (Ross, 2003). We should ask questions and provide an atmosphere that allows them to "describe their information need in their own terms" and in their own language (Ross, 2003).

Concluding the Reference Interview

One of the most important criteria of a "successful" reference interview is how it is concluded. It is crucial to leave the user with the feeling that the door is open to further interactions, by saying "if you don't find it, come back" or "if this doesn't work, come back, we'll try again." If you have the opportunity of seeing the person a bit later, asking a follow-up question (such as "Did you find it?" "How did that work out?") is also very powerful in terms of the user's sense of satisfaction, even if the question wasn't answered! Willingness and interest seem to count for as much, or even more, than accuracy in a reference interview situation. What you want to avoid is *negative closure*: simply sending someone off to another part of the building to "browse," not conducting any sort of question negotiation to determine the real need, not offering any sort of follow-up option, or any of several other negative verbal or body language tactics (Ross and Dewdney, 1998).

Know When to Stop

Finally, while you may now have the impression that every reference interview is going to be a huge affair, that you'll need to ask all kinds of questions, and should follow up on each one if possible—relax. They definitely won't all be like that. Some will be quite simple and brief, and even so, satisfying to both you and the patron. It's not only important to know about all these skills but also to employ them wisely. Use your emotional antennae and your ability to read the other person's body language, and don't go overboard if they are obviously in a hurry or not very interested. Give them what they seem to need and let it go. Something that is every bit as true today as when it was written in 1982 is Somerville's advice: "Part of the skill in conducting an effective interview is to know when to stop."

Beyond the Face-to-Face Reference Interview

There are many "modes" in which the reference interview can take place nowadays: the in-person reference desk still exists, and of course there is the telephone, but now reference interviews are also carried out by e-mail (an asynchronous exchange), and virtual reference, also called *reference chat*, which uses instant-messaging software (a synchronous exchange). Each move away from the face-to-face situation presents both hurdles but also, surprisingly, some advantages.

Reference Interviews on the Telephone

On the telephone, you have no visual cues, but the auditory ones are still there: you can tell a lot about people's ages and situations by their voices, and because it's usually easier to talk than to type, you can ask for and receive more information. On the negative side, you might find that conversing with a nonnative-English speaker over the phone seems much harder than in person; perhaps we unconsciously rely much more on visual cues, facial expressions, and the like when it is difficult to understand what we are hearing. It can also be more cumbersome to explain a process (e.g., navigating through various computer screens and interacting with an interface) over the telephone, but it's not terrible if the other person is sitting in front of their computer. On the plus side, you don't have to control your facial expression as rigorously as you do in person (some questions really do make you wince)! Also, there seems to be something about our "telephone" expectations: people are usually quite accepting of an offer to be called back if you aren't finding what they need immediately. This gives you time to think and explore without the pressure of being watched, or knowing that they are on hold.

Electronic Reference Interviews: E-mail and Chat

With e-mail and reference chat, even the auditory cues are gone, and all you have is words on a screen, which does present quite a challenge for nuanced communication. If you have no body language or gestures, and no voice intonation or accents, what do you do? In both e-mail and reference chat, you can use emoticons[1] and descriptions of gestures, and language that is more like how you would speak than write (Ronan, 2003). E-mail gives you plenty of time to think and compose a thoughtful, structured answer. You can attach files with screen snaps to help explain something if needed. You can check your "script," and always remember to have positive closure by adding "let me know how this goes" or "ask again if this doesn't work out; we'll think of something else." In e-mail, the requestor may very well follow up with you, and depending on the e-mail system, all of your exchanges might stay listed in the message, so you can quickly review what you've said and done so far. The typed environment can actually be a plus for people having to communicate in a foreign language, because accents are not in the way, and the people on both sides of the conversation have time to study the words to figure out what is being said. This typed environment is also such a part of our lives now that it is more nuanced than you would think: frustration and humor come through fairly obviously, and appropriate responses can be given. "[T]one and mood words, capital letters, and repeated punctuation reveal a lot about the writer's state of mind" (Fagan and Desai, 2003).

Reference chat often implies to the chat operator that there is a greater immediacy to the question than if the patron had e-mailed, but that is not necessarily so. Either by asking up front "do you need this right away?" (Ronan, 2003), or by frequently communicating to the user that you are working on the question, the person at the other end may turn out to be fairly patient (Kern, 2003; Fagan and Desai, 2003). After all, it's likely that if the person is of "student age," they are doing several other things at the same time and not just waiting for you (Carter, 2002/2003; Oblinger and Oblinger, 2005). The RUSA Guidelines for Behavioral Performance of Reference were amended in 2004 to address the additional electronic forms of reference encounters (ALA, 2004). Ronan does an excellent job of showing how to meet the RUSA Guidelines in a "chat" environment. She describes how to use the same time-honored techniques: open and closed questions, encouragement, interest, and follow up, but modify them for the medium. For example, try to keep both your questions and responses brief and relatively informal (Ronan, 2003). In a large study of chat reference transactions at a public library system, Kwon and Gregory found a definite correlation between following the RUSA Guidelines and patron satisfaction. The five behaviors most likely to result in user satisfaction were receptive and cordial listening, searching information sources with or for the patrons, providing information sources, asking patrons whether the question had been answered completely, and asking patrons to return when they need further assistance (Kwon and Gregory, 2007). You'll probably end up using mostly closed questions: that's all right; it's appropriate here. Throwing out a big open-ended question can be a useful way to stall for time while you are thinking or looking and can provide additional useful information as well (Carter, 2003).

Both e-mail and reference chat also offer some significant intangibles: gone is the embarrassment at having to approach a desk, where other people can see and possibly hear the interaction. Also gone is the reluctance to interrupt someone busily at work at something else. (If you're the chat operator, that's all you're doing, right? They can't see that you're multitasking as well.) Although there are no visual cues to use in positive ways, those same visual cues aren't there to influence either party in negative ways either: the librarian can't see that you have twenty-nine body piercings, and you can't see that the librarian looks like the neighbor that always yelled at you for playing ball in the back yard—someone who can't possibly understand you. That anonymity can be very freeing.

Can a True Reference Interview Happen Online?

Librarians have questioned whether a decent reference interview can occur at all in the online situation, but more and more voices have come out in support of it, saying that it can (Tyckoson, 2003; Fagan and Desai, 2003). As the Oblingers (2005) point out, "Personal does not always mean 'in person' to the Net Gen. Online conversations may be as meaningful as one that is face-to-face." My own experience bears this out as well. You are simply meeting the users where they are, instead of making them come into your physical space: it's convenient, it eliminates some of the worst impediments to asking questions (fear and embarrassment), it can definitely work, and the key remains communication.[2] Communication in the different media is different, but skills exist that can make it equally effective. Verbal, nonverbal, and textual: all offer ways to communicate effectively and positively. And "[s]uccessful communication...regardless of the medium over which that communication takes place—implies success in the reference process" (Tyckoson, 2003).

Why Is the Reference Interview So Important?

Obviously we can't all be subject specialists in everything, but we need to gain our patrons' confidence enough that they will work with us. Being attentive, asking questions, and taking an interest can help with this. You *are* a specialist in the search field. The person you are working with is, at the moment, the "specialist" in their field (i.e., what they want), while you are a layperson. You can still "achieve an intelligent and collegial interest" in their work, and this is "the level the search specialist should try to achieve" (Harter, 1986, 149). This situation calls for good communication skills and rapport, because you're depending a great deal on the person you're working with to supply the terminology describing their search need. You need to get as much out of your patron as you can. You then work with him or her to think of synonyms, and using that knowledge, try to match the terminology against an appropriate database's thesaurus, or simply try the terms given to you as keywords in a multidisciplinary database (or the Web), and proceed to pearl grow. The initial set of terms describing the topic usually needs to come from the patron, however.

The reference interview is how you are going to connect people to the information they need. Through an exchange of questions, you help them to clarify what their question really is, which ultimately saves their time, because you haven't, through misunderstanding or lack of probing, pointed them at something that is not useful (Kern, 2003). Tyckoson (2003) sums it up by saying: "The reference interview is the most important skill that a reference librarian can learn. Tools and sources will always change, but the process will always begin with the reference interview."

To me, it's really all about one simple thing:

You want them to come back.

A positive reference interaction, in person, on the phone, or online (accurate or not), helps that to happen.

Quick Recap

For several reasons, the questions that people ask in a reference situation frequently do not represent their real information need. The reference interview is meant to identify the "real question" and suggest terminology that can be used in a search. A good reference interview includes question negotiation, involving a good mix of open and closed questions, and good interpersonal skills: a positive, encouraging attitude, welcoming body language, and awareness of specialized vocabulary. How the interview is concluded and knowing when to stop are also important. Reference interviews over the phone, by e-mail, or by chat each have their advantages and disadvantages, but techniques can be employed to make non–face-to-face encounters equally successful. A good reference interview leaves the patron with positive feelings and more likely to return to the library with future questions.

Exercises and Points to Consider

1. School media specialists: what would be a good list of questions to use with your "clientele"?

2. Communication barriers were mentioned in a general way in this chapter, and a few examples were given (e.g., language, age differences). Can you elaborate on these? How many other communication barriers can you think of?

3. What would welcoming body language look like? How about unwelcoming?

4. How would you feel if you asked a question at a reference desk, and the librarian responded by turning immediately to his or her computer and typing?

5. Have you had many interactions with reference desks where you were the patron? Which ones do you remember? What do you remember about them?

6. Say that you were at the reference desk, and a woman approached and said she was looking for information about sign languages used with children who are *not* deaf. What are some questions you might try asking her? What are some other things you might do?[3]

Suggested Readings

The information-seeking literature can quickly become overwhelming. Rather than the myriad articles cited in this chapter, you might find it more manageable to look at just two books on the topic:

Case, Donald O. 2007. *Looking for Information: A survey of research on information seeking, needs, and behavior.* 2nd ed. Amsterdam: Academic Press.

Fisher, Karen E., Erdelez, Sandra, and Lynne (E. F.) McKechnie, eds. 2005. *Theories of Information Behavior.* Medford, NJ: Information Today, Inc.

Notes

1. Emoticons: Also known as *smileys,* emoticons are facial expressions created from punctuation, e.g., :-) :-(:-p or "abbreviated" forms, without "noses" :) :(.

2. In a review of nine discontinued chat reference services, the reasons for discontinuing were identified as low volume, funding, staffing and technical problems; not the ability to conduct reference transactions online (e.g., librarians' communication skills). See Radford, Marie L. and M. Kathleen Kern. 2006. A Multiple-case Study Investigation of the Discontinuation of Nine Chat Reference Services. *Library & Information Science Research* 28 (4): 521–547.

3. Skilled questioning, or even more likely, a session with appropriate databases employing good pearl-growing tactics, are needed to recast this question as "methods of nonverbal communication used with autistic children." Unless you're an expert in this field (in which case presumably you don't need help finding such information), this is not the language you are likely to use in everyday speech. But to get the best results most efficiently, it helps tremendously to have the question reformulated into this language.

10
Choosing the Right Resource for the Question

By this point in this book, or in your course if the book is being used as your textbook, you may be feeling somewhat overwhelmed: there are so many databases, and there's the whole Internet. How are you supposed to know what to use when? Specifically, you might wonder:

1. Should you always try to use a database first?

2. Is it "wrong" to use the Web?

3. Are there guidelines for when you should use a database and when you should use the Web?

4. Where do you start?

First and foremost: don't panic. Everybody feels this way at some point in his or her library school career, and frequently during the training on their first (and second, and third...) job as well. While there are no hard and fast rules for "what to use when" (like so many things, with time and experience you'll develop a style that is effective for you), there is an answer to the first two specific questions. Question 1: Should you always try a database first? Not at all, you should start with whatever seems most appropriate for the question and where you feel most comfortable starting, given the resources you have available. In answer to Question 2: It is never "wrong" to use the Web, as long as you also use database resources if the question suggests they might be helpful (and you have databases available to you).

The rest of this chapter is meant to help answer Questions 3 and 4. We'll address them in reverse order so as to begin at the beginning, and because the question, "Where do I start?" has a simple and direct answer.

It's the same answer that applies to anything in reference service: start with a good reference interview.

Start with the Reference Interview

The reference interview, whether it is in depth or only a two- or three-line dialogue, is the key to everything that happens next. That is how you find out what the patron wants, which should then suggest to you what resource(s) would meet the need. The reference interview should reveal factors such as:

- What is the subject area?
- What is the person looking for? For example, a specific factoid, a few good articles, an overview, or some statistics?
- Does he or she want current or historical information?
- How much material is needed: a great deal, or again, a "few good articles"?
- Does the person require "research" level material (also known as scholarly or peer-reviewed), or popular material?

These points are discussed in the reference interview section of Chapter 9. Your reference interview also should provide some keywords or phrases with which to start your search. You now have a body of information to work with (context, guidelines, intent, and subject), and can make an initial decision as to whether it sounds like a database question or a Web question. Note that I said "initial decision"—you can always change your mind and take a new approach as you work on the request; you don't have to get it right the first time.[1]

Now let's tackle the harder issue—guidelines for using databases or using Web search engines. What should you be looking for in the information that you gather during the reference interview to help address that issue?

Questions for Databases

When trying to decide when to use databases and when to use a Web search engine, remember that people are using the Web to answer many questions on their own, and by the time they approach a librarian, it's likely that more sophisticated techniques are called for. That said, in this section you'll find the hallmarks of questions that indicate *to me* that a database might be the answer, and questions for which a Web search might be a better approach. Never get the impression that any of this is carved in stone. As you gain experience, you will undoubtedly come to identify further or different indicators based on the clientele you are serving that will whisper to you: "database" or "Web." You will find yourself making good choices most of the time, instinctively.

Why and When to Try a Database

Why choose a database over a Web search engine? The reasons are basic: authority and credibility. Databases can contain material with errors, but in general, there is a presumption that the material has been vetted somewhere in the process, and part of what you are paying the database vendor for is taking some responsibility for the quality of the material. Nancy Bloggs, writing Web pages in her bedroom, doesn't necessarily assume any responsibility at all. You can be more confident providing patrons with information from a commercial database than the free Web in many cases. Even with information such as a formula from a *CRC Handbook* or a dictionary definition, which can be readily available on the Web, if this material is being provided to *someone else*, it is better if it can be printed out from a database and handed over. No one is left wondering, "Who wrote this? Can I trust it to be right?" in situations in which the patron really wants to be sure of getting credible information. The Web is a useful tool for starting searches, but it is not generally the provider of choice for content to hand over formally to the patron as a final product.

Inevitably in the following descriptions you will find that Web searching is mentioned as well. It really is impossible to draw hard and fast lines between the two types of resources, because so often they do complement each other well, but I have tried to keep the discussions focused as much as possible on databases.

Requests Involving Articles

If your reference interview has shown that *articles* are involved in any way, it is usually a strong indicator to try a database. Articles represent content that has been formally published, usually in hard copy, and then distributed and made available for a fee. The publishers of the magazines, journals, and newspapers the articles appeared in are (usually) not giving them away free on the Internet. Yes, it's true that on the Web you can find papers that authors have posted on their Web sites or archived in their organization's "institutional repository."[2] If you're after a known item, the Web might work, but it's not as organized, efficient, and comprehensive as a good commercial database. There is just no comparison (yet...although Google Scholar is getting there).

For example, in an academic situation involving a student writing a paper, in almost every case your best choice is an article or encyclopedia database. The ability to search by subjects, to use various limits, and to know that the material you'll retrieve has all made an appearance in the commercial press all firmly call for such a database. The full text or links to full text in so many commercial databases is another obvious reason to go to a database.

Another way articles can be involved is as citations. In any setting, if someone were trying to track down a citation or flesh out an incomplete citation, you should try appropriate databases first. (If it seems to be a history article, try a history database.) If you don't find what you need there, however, turn to the Web (see notes in the Questions for the Web section, below). If the patron wants to see who has *cited* an article recently, this is clearly a database question (and which database is fairly clear as well), although again, Google Scholar has links for "Cited by <number>." But how and where is Google getting that information? How do you know whether it's definitive? If the *Web of Science* is available to you, my advice is to try that first, every time.

Of course, articles come from journals. Although patrons seldom ask, "where is the *Journal of XYZ* indexed?" this often becomes an implied question for the librarian in the course of answering the question they did ask. Usually the most efficient course of action is to check the *UlrichsWeb* database to see where the journal is indexed. (Of course, you can also simply go to a likely database and use its "publication browse" feature, to see if the requested journal is listed.)

Requests for an "Overview Article"

Patrons often want an article that provides an *overview* of some topic. There are a couple of problems with such a request. One is, you hear the word *article*, and you do think database, which is right. The problem is, it is not that easy to find general, overview-type articles in the periodical literature, unless the author is writing a "review of the literature" or a "tutorial" on the topic,[3] or the topic falls within a discipline that publishes special-purpose "survey" journals, such as *Computer Surveys*. In general, articles tend to focus on a particular, finite topic rather than providing a broad introduction. A better source for an introductory or overview treatment of a topic is often an encyclopedia entry (or a chapter in a prominent textbook for that field). There are thousands of specific-topic encyclopedias available, and more and more of them are being offered in online versions. Such a commercial encyclopedia database could indeed provide an authoritative, trustworthy overview.[4]

Book Questions

With the advent of mega online book vendors such as Amazon.com, Barnes & Noble (at http://www.books.com), or Powells.com (which covers the gamut of new, used, and out of print), and the availability of WorldCat on the web at WorldCat.org, the line between whether to use a subscription database or a Web resource for "book" questions has grown much more indistinct. Obviously if the patron wants to know if your library owns a particular book, you'll go to your library's OPAC. After that, it may depend on what resources you have available. If you have access to WorldCat via FirstSearch (and enjoy all the options that interface offers), and *Books in Print*, you might try those databases first for book-related questions (e. g., verifying or completing book citations, finding books on a topic, identifying a particular title that might be old or unusual). Because the subscription databases are not trying to *sell* the books, there is less screen "noise" to ignore, and thus they can be more efficient. You cannot beat the comprehensiveness of WorldCat, which helps to avoid the possibility of having to look at several online book and out-of-print vendor Web sites. And if it's quicker and easier to type "worldcat.org" into your browser than to click through a couple of library web pages to find the link to the subscription version, by all means use the Web version. On the other hand, if the patron is a student who wants a textbook (and is surprised that you don't have all the textbooks on Reserve), head off to Amazon.com immediately, to show him the deals on used copies.

Business Questions

Just by the nature of the beast, if it's a business question, it is usually safe to assume that the answer is worth money and thus is less likely to be freely available on the Internet. Business questions frequently involve articles, which we have already discussed as a database indicator. Another typical business query is the request for lists of companies in a certain line of business or in a specific geographical area. Although there are free telephone directories and other similar resources on the Web, the best directories for companies are commercial databases, such as the *Million Dollar Database*, or *Business and Company Resource Center*. Business documents such as market research reports or analyst's reports almost without exception come from subscription or other fee-based resources. A major exception to this general rule of "using databases for business questions" is in the case of certain business numbers, which we encountered in Chapter 8. Stock quotes and the financial reports (e.g., Annual Reports) of current public companies can usually be found on the Web. Another exception has to do with research in the murky realm of "competitive intelligence," in which almost anything goes: almost any information could be valuable. Thus, information from blogs, wikis, newspaper websites (often providing content not available in their printed versions), etc., is becoming an important—although often frustrating—part of business research (Ojala, 2008).

Law Questions

In this highly specialized area of reference, official legal databases are definitely your first choice. Although it is possible to find the text of some states' statutes (e.g., Texas Statutes) or laws (often referred to as "code," as in U.S. Code or N.Y. Code) online, it probably is easier to find the information needed using a commercial legal database. Especially in this topic area, the authority of a commercial, subject specific database is very important. (And the assistance of a skilled law librarian is even more important.)

Medical Questions

Things become somewhat fuzzier when it comes to helping patrons with medical questions. Because, as with law, we are again working in a very serious and specialized topical area, you should start with databases if possible, to take advantage of their authority and credibility. If you are working with medical professionals or medical students, obviously you'll use MEDLINE or PubMed. There is also a database called CINAHL specifically aimed at nursing professionals. For the lay public, there is a very nice Gale database called *Health Reference Center*. However, there is also an immense amount of medical information available on the Web that people are more than happy to tap into on their own, usually without recognizing the risks involved: the need to be very aware of the credibility of the source, the date of the information, etc. We'll revisit this issue in the Questions for the Web section.

Quick Recap

Questions for which you will want to try to use databases are those hallmarked by an underlying need for authority and credibility. Requests that mention a need for articles, either for research purposes such as writing a paper or tracking down a specific citation, are usually best answered by appropriate databases. Requests expressed as a need for an "overview article" are often better served by material from an encyclopedia entry. Questions about books are sometimes answered equally well by subscription databases and free Web sites, such as Amazon.com or WorldCat.org. Business-related questions usually involve material that has been expensive to collect, and such questions are usually better addressed with commercial databases. Preference should also be given to commercial databases for law and medical questions, due to the specialized and serious nature of the topic areas. The particular need in those situations for authority and credibility demands that only professionally produced and professionally acknowledged resources be used.

Choosing a Database

If you're faced with a question that seems like a database question, you could be in one of three situations: having many databases at your disposal (the assumption so far in this book), a few databases, or none at all. In this section we'll look at the issue of making a choice in each of those three scenarios.

Scenario 1: An Embarrassment of Riches

If you're at an institution that subscribes to literally hundreds of databases, the natural question is: how do you decide which one to use? Determining which database to start with involves many of the factors you use to *evaluate* a database (a topic addressed again in Chapter 11):

- What subjects does the database cover? (If the topic is well defined, definitely in one subject area, a subject-specific database such as *Art Index* or *EconLit* could be the right resource. If the topic seems fuzzy, or interdisciplinary, a multi-subject database such as ProQuest's *Research Library* or EBSCO's *Academic Search* or *MasterFILE* may be a better answer.)

- What types of material are included? Magazines? Scholarly journals? Books or book chapters? "Working Papers"? Other materials? Or do you need a numeric or directory database?

- What *level* of material? (Is it "popular" level or research level?)

- What is the date coverage of the database? Does it cover the right time period? If you are trying to find or verify a really recent article, you'll want to check how frequently material is added to the database you're thinking of using, and how up to date it is.

- If the database does not provide full text, are the sources mostly available in your library (or in another database)?

- How "searchable" is the database: Does it offer controlled vocabulary to focus your search, or does it offer keyword searching of all fields, if you need to find a needle in the haystack? Which fields are searchable? If you only have one piece of information, but that field isn't searchable in the database you've picked out, you have a problem. If you're looking for a particular *kind* of article, like a book review, you want a database that lets you limit or search by article type. Is it possible to limit by scholarly or peer-reviewed articles, if that's what you need?

You also don't have to pick just one database. You could identify two or three candidates and test your most specific search term in each one to see which shows the most hits. Especially if you're venturing into a new subject area, try your most specific term in the database that you've chosen, and see how many hits there are. If the database has a subject list or thesaurus, look up your term to see if it is listed, and how many records are associated with it.

This list of factors to consider probably sounds like it would take far too much time, while the patron is sitting there expecting immediate action. As you gain experience, however, you will find that you can do this analysis of "database or the Web?" quite quickly, however. If you're at a major university or large public library that subscribes to a large number of databases, it's very likely that library staff have already created Web pages that organize the databases into groups by subject, and often by whether or not they are full-text. Start by looking at databases by subject, or at guides developed by librarians that might suggest the best databases for different subject areas. Quickly scan the descriptions of the databases' *coverage, currency,* and *material* types. Go into the database(s) that seem most appropriate and test them for subject coverage, availability of appropriate fields and limits as mentioned in the bulleted list above. This all comes across as "action on the question" to the patron, and results will probably follow pretty quickly.

Of course, you have the free Web as well. Even when you have hundreds of subscription databases at your fingertips, it's a perfectly acceptable strategy to run a quick Web search, just to see if the term is "out there," and what context it is used in, especially for an unfamiliar topic area (think of this as a "reality check"). As mentioned before, the two can complement each other well.

Scenario 2: A Few Good Databases

This scenario could apply to a school library with a handful of databases available, or to a corporate, law, or other special library as well. In each case, the limited number of databases was chosen for its appropriateness to your clientele and your mission, so in a way, you could consider this an advantage: some preselection has taken place, and these should already be the "most likely" databases for the questions that you expect to encounter. Given this, you can still look at your databases in light of the factors discussed above. Which one(s) might be most appropriate, given their *coverage, currency, searchability,* and *ability* to identify research? You can jump into one or more and test your search terms. Frankly, in many ways you have the advantage over those libraries that have hundreds of databases, because you can be thoroughly familiar with each of your resources, and have a much better idea which one is likely to be most useful for any given question, without any testing or analysis at all. And, of course, you have the free Web as well.

Scenario 3: No Subscription Databases at All

It would certainly be sad and frustrating, after learning about all these nifty fee-based resources, to find yourself in a situation in which you don't have any subscription databases available. No point in grousing and hand wringing, however: let's assume that at least you have an Internet connection. Two U.S. government agencies provide free versions of their database content on the Web: PubMed from the National Library of Medicine, and ERIC from the Department of Education. You also have the riches of OCLC's WorldCat now at your fingertips, at WorldCat.org. Google Scholar provides a way to search for peer-reviewed articles from scholarly journals; the effectiveness of this search engine varies according to the subject area of your search (definitely try it for an engineering literature search[5], for example), and the time period. You should be able to trust the authority of Web sites from the government (.gov), such as MedlinePlus.gov, or sites run by reputable organizations (.org), like the American Cancer Society (http://www.cancer.org).

Actually, you may find there are some (subscription) databases provided at no cost to you through your local public library system. This is something to have explored ahead of time, so you'll have some idea of what is there, and what you need to do to gain access (e.g., a current library card with a barcode number).

Each of these scenarios has included the Web, the last one relying solely on it. This seems the natural time to consider what questions are best answered by the Web.

Questions for the Web

One is tempted to say "what *isn't* a question for the Web?" because it seems that no matter what keywords you search for, they'll have appeared in some Web page, somewhere. There are certainly topics, however, that are much more likely, or only, answerable by a Web search.

Personal Uses of the Web

We use the Web endlessly for personal research: finding books at Amazon.com, getting weather reports, checking crossing delay times for the bridges to Canada, making travel plans, checking movie times, buying an answering machine (or buying anything), or trying to find an answer to a software question. It's quick, it's easy, and it's not the sort of information you'll find in databases. (For a review from *Consumer Reports* about something that we're thinking of buying, however, we wind up back at a database, because that's an article.) Because it's only for our personal information, we take the responsibility for deciding how authoritative the information is and whether that's important.

Professional Uses of the Web

Popular Culture, Local Information, and People

At the reference desk, questions about popular culture ("Who is the highest paid player in the NFL?"), or with daily life or local information ("Where are all the HSBC bank branches in (city X)?", "Can I get a list of all the choral societies in (city Y)?"), or one of my favorites: identifying the source of a song, poem, or quotation from a small fragment, are definitely Web search material. For anything to do with films, a part of popular culture, the Internet Movie Database (IMDb) is my resource of choice. The Web is also amazing (a little frighteningly so) for finding people. It doesn't always work, but we all know some pretty incredible stories about locating people by searching for them on the Web.

Citation Disambiguation

The Web is useful for tracking down citations. If you're not finding a citation in a database (even after leaving out part of what the patron has told you), don't hesitate to drop parts of the citation into Google (or your favorite search engine) to try to figure out where the problem lies. In doing a Web search, you are looking for the citation to appear on someone else's Web page (where one hopes that it's correct and complete), or at least to gain some sense of context that would indicate, for example, that you have chosen to look in a database in the wrong subject area. Maybe you can even find the author's Web page and see how he or she referred to the work in question. Try anything you can think of to provide a clue.

Rare or Obscure Topics

You can also start with a Web search when the patron indicates that what she is looking for is quite obscure, and you want the biggest haystack possible in which to look for that needle (think of the desperate parents in the movie *Lorenzo's Oil*). Of course, the patron has probably already searched on the Web, but perhaps you can do it better. Do a quick Web search if the topic is obscure *to you*, just to try for a quick sense of context and possibly some additional useful keywords.

Medical Questions from Laypeople

If you are working on a medical question with a patron who is not a member of the health services professions, it is hard not to use the Web in your research. As mentioned in the previous section about Medical Questions, the patron very likely has been searching the Web on his own, and one can't deny there is a great deal of medical information available there. What is imperative is that you impress on the patron that much of it is incorrect, misleading, and outright dangerous, unless it comes from a reputable source. Depending on the resources available in your library and the skill level of the patron, your approach might be to encourage a change not in *source* but in *methodology*. Rather than simply doing Web searches, you can try to get the patron to *browse* reputable sites, such as MedlinePlus.gov, or WebMD.com, and the sites of, again, reputable organizations. Use Web searches to find those associations and organizations, but then urge the patron to go into those sites and browse or search within the site. If at all possible, however, databases such as *Health Reference Center* or the *Virtual Reference Library*, both from Gale, would be preferable.

Standard Facts and Statistics

For someone looking for a specific, standard fact (e.g., in what year did the Berlin Wall fall?), the authority of an encyclopedia database is attractive, but you may well just try a Web search, because it might be quicker and just as useful. (It's a standard date, after all; if the page comes from a credible source, it might be right. You might even trust Wikipedia in this case.) Of course, if the patron then wanted historical background for the falling of the Wall, you should get back to the encyclopedia or article databases very quickly. The area of quotations and definitions can be equally murky: in a situation in which it doesn't matter that much, you can probably just do a Web search. At the reference desk, if you have a resource such as *Oxford Online*, it would be more authoritative and professional to use that.

As we found in Chapter 8, government agencies provide quite a wealth of statistical and numerical information on the Web. There aren't as many databases available in this area, so I often find myself using the Web as an equal partner when a question requires statistics or numbers to answer it. (But again, if I have access to an appropriate database, it almost always provides a much more *efficient* way of getting the information and usually is more authoritative as well.)

Quick Recap

Although you can certainly find academic material on the Web (papers, lectures, reports, etc.), organized, academic research is not yet its strongest point. (There are exceptions, of course, such as the arXiv site for high-energy physicists.) The overarching themes in this Questions for the Web section have rather been issues of daily life, popular culture, people, and connecting with the "informal college," that is, tapping into the "web" of other people's knowledge (e.g., for software questions, obscure topics, or "fragment" questions: lyrics, quotations, etc.). The Web is useful for providing clues, context, or a reality check. It is amazing—what *did* we do before?

Exercises and Points to Consider

1. What do *you* use the Web for? Try keeping a journal for a week in which you record every time you use the Web to answer a question, either at work or in your personal life. Can you detect any common themes in your Web use?

2. "Search madness" activity: if you are using this book as part of a class, have the group come up with a list of questions that they have encountered in a library, in their studies, or in their daily life. Then add in questions from earlier chapters in this book, or from search assignments. For questions that required databases before, try them as Web searches. For the questions submitted by the class, decide which seem suitable for the Web, and which are for databases. Spend a session just searching and comparing results.

Suggested Reading

Tenopir, Carol. "Sorting Through Online Systems." *Library Journal* (May 1, 2002): 32, 34.

This is the shortest, sanest set of tips and advice for keeping the plethora of databases "straight" in your head. Even though some of the names have changed since 2002, the advice still applies. A must read.

Notes

1. For the record, this is a "sea change" from the early days of searching on systems like Dialog, where you paid by the minute and often by each record displayed. Then you really did do your homework thoroughly before "going online," and it was generally expected that you would get it right the first time. The advent of databases on CD-ROM and now on the Web has totally changed this aspect of searching (for the better).

2. Google for "institutional repository" +DSpace or +Eprints for more information on this topic.

3. This varies a great deal by discipline: tutorial articles (which can also appear under a title of "Review" or "Survey") are common in the Engineering and Computer Science literature. There is a standard format for articles in medical journals that includes a literature review, and the more scholarly library science articles have this as well. A literature review might not be the same as an overview, however, and certainly in subject areas such as business, a real "overview" is fairly rare.

4. Unfortunately, I often find it hard to convince my patrons—who are generally undergraduates or graduate students—that an encyclopedia entry is a valid resource or way to start. I'm trying to point them to a specialized encyclopedia, but they seem to relegate anything with *encyclopedia* in the title to "little-kid" status.

5. In a study published in May 2008 comparing coverage of the engineering literature in *Compendex* and Google Scholar, the researchers found an almost 90 percent matching rate in Google Scholar for materials published after 1990. See Meiera, John J. and Thomas W. Conkling. 2008. Google Scholar's Coverage of the Engineering Literature: An Empirical Study. *Journal of Academic Librarianship* 34 (May): 196–201.

11
Evaluating Databases

This chapter provides a detailed list of issues to consider when evaluating a database: information to gather, factors to assess, and suggestions for benchmarking. It concludes with advice about how to use this information effectively in putting together a database purchase request. The previous chapter, on choosing the best resource for the question, also draws on this material; don't be surprised if you find yourself going back and forth between these two chapters.

In real life, occasions requiring an in-depth formal evaluation of a database are not going to arise that frequently. Institutions don't change their database subscriptions that often: getting anything new usually means giving up an existing service, and changing between relatively equivalent products tends to be held in check by the overall community's resistance to change. (Users generally prefer a status quo they are familiar with, rather than frequent changes. A replacement has to demonstrate obvious and significant improvements in ease of use or content to be accepted.) At the same time, you want to remain up to date on new databases in your subject area, and therefore familiarizing yourself with new and changing products may become a fairly steady undercurrent to your job (depending on the volatility of products in your subject area). Another motivation for doing a thorough study of a database is to write a review of it. Although reviewing is an excellent way to start getting published, it isn't something you do every day. Finally, you obviously want to master a database completely before teaching others about it, even though (as you'll find in the last chapter), you want to be judicious in how much of what you learn you choose to pass on to your audience.

Thus the position of this chapter in the book: almost at the end of the sequence rather than at the beginning. It's important, and I hope useful, but it is not information that you'll need to work through in its entirety very frequently. Note that I said, "in its entirety"—the information here is intended to be a fairly comprehensive list, for the special situations listed above. Some of these are major considerations, some are minor, and some you might not be able to find any information on, but it's still interesting to be aware of all the potential factors. You certainly will find that you use selected elements from this list regularly in your daily reference activities, as mentioned in the previous chapter. Factors of "database evaluation" such as topical coverage, date range, availability of full text, and usability of the interface, you'll find yourself assessing almost automatically and even memorizing for the databases you use frequently. For those situations requiring an in-depth examination, such as a database trial or writing a review for publication, the following two sections offer a list of categories and associated factors to consider in evaluating and testing databases.

Basic Facts and Figures

Initial Factual Information to Gather

Database Vendor(s)

As with anything else, the same databases are often available from different vendors, and it can pay to shop around. Vendors get the data in a raw format and then format and load it according to how they structure their database, what fields they want to use, whether those fields are searchable, etc. The search capabilities (and obviously the user interface) vary depending on the vendor, and you can have a really different experience searching the same database offered by different vendors. If you are seriously looking at a new database and more than one vendor provides it, be sure to try them all. It's a big investment, and you owe it to your organization, and especially to your users, to get the version that will best meet *their* needs.

Existing Reviews

Has anyone already written a review of this database? A thorough database review is a large task, requiring hours of research and testing. Although you may still need to check the latest facts and figures (number of sources, etc.) if the review is a few years old, and you will always want to do your own testing, someone else's review is a useful place to start. The *Charleston Advisor* is an excellent source of reviews. If you are using a database such as *Library Literature & Information Science* to locate reviews, look for document type "review," and author names such as Mary Ellen Bates, Péter Jacsó, Mary Dee Ojala, Barbara Quint, and Carol Tenopir. If the database is offered by more than one vendor, look for comparative reviews or individual reviews for the different versions.

Coverage

There are many aspects to "coverage," including:

Subject Coverage. This is also referred to as "scope." What is the subject emphasis of the database—what topical areas does it cover, or is it multidisciplinary? For the subject, what is the *level* of the material covered; that is, who is the intended audience? K–12 students? College students? Graduate students? Faculty? Specialists? The lay public?

Material Coverage. What types of material and formats are included? If only periodicals, what types? Popular or scholarly? Trade journals or newspapers? Is there one type that is emphasized; that is, are there many more popular or trade journals, with only a few scholarly titles? For articles containing tables or graphics, are these included? If yes, how are they reproduced? (A formatted table reproduced in plain text can be almost impossible to interpret.) If other kinds of documents are covered, what are they? (Possibilities include books, book chapters, theses, conference proceedings, government documents, speeches, audio transcripts such as NPR interviews, and photos or visual materials such as would be found in an image archive.) Are any primary source materials included? What formats are offered for full text: HTML, PDF, or both?

Source Coverage. How many sources are indexed[1]? More important, if both popular and scholarly sources are included, approximately how many of each are there? What is the *selection policy*: are the source publications indexed cover-to-cover, or only selectively? Is this policy universal for all titles in the database, or does it vary by title? How much information is provided: citations only, citations with abstracts, or citations and full text? This is also referred to as the breadth and depth of coverage: more source titles would indicate greater *breadth*, and cover-to-cover indexing would provide greater *depth* of coverage.

Date Coverage. Does the database provide current, or retrospective coverage (e.g., how far back in time does indexing for most of the titles go)? Does the database use a "moving wall" date coverage system, wherein titles are covered up to a set number of years in the past (e.g., JSTOR titles usually are covered from the first issue up to issues from 3 to 5 years ago. Each year one more new year is added, but current issues are not available.).

Geographic Coverage. Does the database index just U.S. publications, or is the source list international? If international, are the materials in their original language? How many and which languages are represented? Are article titles and abstracts (if available) offered in translation?

Availability of Sources

A major consideration for any database is how accessible the material that it indexes will be to your users. How many, or what percentage, of the sources are available in full text? If the records are mainly or all citations, does the database support linking technologies such as SFX? (Is your institution running such technology, and do you have other databases that might offer the content that is indexed in the database you are evaluating?) If the database is offered by multiple vendors, which ones support linking? Whether or not you can use a linking technology with a database that provides only citations, and how many of the sources indexed are physically available at your library should be key elements in a decision to purchase. Interlibrary loan is always an option, but people usually prefer to be able to put their hands on what they want locally.

Currency

How often is material added? How soon after a journal is published do records for its content appear in the database? (This can be a hard question to answer, but it's worth asking.) Are there embargoes on certain titles (e.g., the publisher has decided not to make the most current issues available)? How many titles are embargoed and for how long? (Are they embargoed for weeks, months, a year or more?) If there are embargoed titles that are of significant interest to your library, do you have subscriptions to the print versions, or a separate online access arrangement, so that users have access to the current issues? Here again, if the database is offered by more than one vendor, check the updating and embargo schedules for each one. Both of these factors can vary considerably by vendor.

So far this discussion has focused mainly on periodical databases, but what about a directory database? A list of associations might remain fairly stable, but matters in the corporate world are fairly dynamic: companies change their names, get bought, sold, and merged into other companies. For both associations and corporations, names of officers, their titles, phone numbers, etc., are likely to change. You should try to find out how often such a directory type of database is updated (and where do they get the information from)? For example, if you live in a place where the area code has changed, and records in a business or association database don't reflect that change after a year, this is a red flag that there might be problems with the vendor's updating system.

Size

Mainstream commercial databases can probably all be described as huge in terms of number of individual records; that is, the number of records is so large as to be meaningless. (For more on the question of database size, see Péter Jacsó's useful article, "How big is a database versus how is a database big" (2007).) What is likely to be more important is to find out how fast is the database growing? If the database is already very large, is it divided up into multiple sections? Are the sections by date (e.g., current, backfile), or by subject or material group? A database broken into sections can be annoying to use if you frequently have to rerun searches in each section. Last, a fairly uncommon concern: if the database is one that you load locally on your own server, how much space does it require?

Errors

Are you surprised to see this heading? Remember, databases are ultimately human creations, and therefore errors are definitely a possibility. Unfortunately, errors or error rates in a database are hard to determine empirically. You simply need to keep your eye out for them as you work with the database and decide for yourself if you're seeing too many.

Generally, there are three kinds of errors: factual, typos, and indexing errors. Factual errors are non-typo mistakes in numerical or other data (e.g., a date, an address, a phone number, or a name). Typos are things like transposition of letters or numbers, or inadvertent dropping or doubling of words. Usually fairly benign, typos become a big problem when you can't pull up an article because there's a typo in the title or author, etc., or if there is a typo in a "stable URL" link, so that the link does not function. Indexing errors are errors of judgment in assigning terms or categorizing records. This type of error is almost impossible to find deliberately; it is mentioned here only so that someday when you're looking at a record and thinking: "Why in the world did they assign *that* term?"—it could be an error. Some errors are acceptable, but when they start interfering with searching, or mean that the resource is simply providing wrong information, obviously you are moving into the unacceptable realm.

Unfortunately, it is very difficult to test for errors. In doing test searches, you can watch for typos to appear, or you can try keyword searching for words that are frequently mistyped (e.g., *serach* for *search*). In a directory database, you could randomly sample a few records and try to check the names and phone numbers against another source. Otherwise, the best thing to do is to tap the experience of all the other users out there: look for articles, even if not review articles, which mention the database. Do they say anything about errors? You could also post a question to an appropriate newsgroup or blog, and see what anecdotal evidence other users have to offer.

Database Aids

Database aids include both online and physical resources that provide help in using the database, teaching others to use it, and promoting it. You'll want to find out: Does the database have an online Help function? Is it easy to find, easy to understand, and easy to use? Is the help context sensitive, that is, different depending on which screen you are on, or always the same? Note that context sensitive is not necessarily always better than static: the system's interpretation of your "context" may leave you scratching your head and wanting to start at the beginning instead. Is there an online tutorial, and is it useful? Is there a printed manual? (Usually not, but it never hurts to ask.) Are there "quick start" or similar brief "how to" cards or leaflets that the vendor can provide? Will the vendor send you promotional materials to help market the new database? Does the vendor offer any "train-the-trainer" services, either in person or by Web-cast seminars (Webinars)?

Cost and Vendor Support

Vendors regularly experiment with new pricing models, and this can often be a more intricate question than you might think. In academic situations, the database cost is frequently based on FTE, or how many *full-time equivalent* students there are on campus. Such a charge model usually then means there is no limit to the number of people who can use the database at the same time. At the other end of the spectrum from this model, some databases charge by number of simultaneous users, or *seats*, that you opt for, meaning that only a limited number of people can use the database at the same time. Another model is to charge by the search, or to sell *blocks* or sets of searches. When the number of searches in the block is used up, access is suspended until you purchase more. A database with deep date coverage may be divided into sections, and it might be worth checking to see if you can purchase only the most recent section (if that would meet your needs). Price negotiation can be full of wheeling and dealing: discounts might be available based on the number of years that you sign on for or by the number of databases purchased from same vendor. No matter how you look at it, however, database subscriptions are expensive. Many libraries now participate in library consortia, which act together to negotiate pricing with vendors. Because there are so many possible factors, database prices are seldom (if ever) posted on vendor Web sites or listed anywhere. The best way to determine the cost for a particular database is to start with the Collection Development or Acquisitions Librarian in your library. If you are not currently in a library, call the vendor directly and speak with a sales representative.

It's also useful to explore the kind of support that the vendor offers, in particular for usage statistics. Are usage statistics available? How detailed are they? How do you access them, or can a report be automatically sent to you on a regular basis? Do the statistics adhere to the standards suggested by Project Counter? (See http://www.projectcounter.org.) Standardized statistics allow you to really know what you are looking at, what has been counted, and what it means. If you decide to invest the money, it's very important to have some idea of how much the database is getting used.

Other vendor support issues to explore are the nature and availability of technical and search support (by phone? e-mail? Web form? Is it 24/7 and 365?), and, as mentioned previously, train-the-trainer services. During your database trial period, besides working with the database itself, be sure to test the technical and search support services, not once, but a few times. Is it easy to reach a knowledgeable person? Were your questions answered accurately and in a timely fashion?

Finally, check to see if the database has any special platform (i.e., PC, Mac, Unix, or Linux) or Web browser requirements. If any of these would mean upgrades or new equipment in order to offer the database, it puts another cost consideration into your evaluation and planning.

Testing and Benchmarking

As mentioned earlier, prior to initiating a subscription request, you will want to get a database trial (or multiple trials if the database is offered by more than one vendor). This is a key component in your evaluation. I have never encountered a vendor who wouldn't offer some kind of trial access to their products. Do not abuse their good nature in this regard: don't ask for a trial if you aren't serious about the database for some reason (either for purchase or for review-writing purposes), or if you don't have the time to evaluate it properly. While you have the trial, make good use of it: if necessary, deliberately schedule several time slots on your calendar over the course of the trial to devote to working with the database. As they say, pound on it! You really need to know what you're talking about if you are going to recommend it for purchase. The following section describes aspects of the database to look for, assess, and compare (benchmark) during your database trial (your test period).

Testing

Record and File Structure

This topic takes us all the way back to the material in Chapter 1. Factors to assess include the following: What fields are available? Are the fields appropriate and useful given the subject matter of the database? Sometimes when vendors simply apply their standard interface to a new database, the result is less than optimal. Of the fields you see in a full record display, how many are also searchable? (Some fields may be "display only.") Another way to think of this is: how many ways can you look up same record? That is, how many "access points" do the records have? More fields aren't always better but can be helpful. Do the searchable fields each have their own index list, and can you browse that list? Think of the FirstSearch databases and their many indexes, which even distinguish single-word from phrase indexes. More indexes are great but not always better. The questions to have at the front of your mind at all times during an evaluation are "Does this make sense for this database? Is it helpful? Does it help get me to better results more efficiently?"

Linking is an aspect of record and file structure that you can divine simply by observation. In a record display, are there fields that are linked (e.g., Author or Subject), which allow you to pull up all other records with that author or subject immediately? Are there other linked fields in the record, and to what do they link?

Indexing and Cataloging Practices: Searchability

Don't be put off by the heading of this section: it is not a suggestion for you to try to find out the interior policies and work practices that the vendor uses. Rather, there are many things that you can observe during testing, or find out from the documentation, that reveal something about how the vendor has set up the indexes, and how much human intervention (cataloging) has been applied to the records. These things can be dubbed *searchability*, and you will find many of them familiar from earlier chapters:

- Are there stop words?
- Can you adjust the date range of your search?
- What are the limits that you have available? Are they useful?
- Controlled vocabulary:
  - Does the database use a set of a controlled vocabulary (e.g., subject terms)?
  - Is it a subject list, a straight alphabetical list of terms, as in EBSCO's *MasterFILE Select* or ProQuest's *Research Library*?
  - Or is it a thesaurus: a hierarchical system, with "broader," "narrower," and "related" headings, that shows relationships between terms, as you find in *Library Literature* or ERIC?
  - If it is a thesaurus, who created it—the original database *producer* (such as the American Psychological Association), or the database *vendor*? (Remember that these are often two very different organizations.)
  - With any kind of list of subject terms, can you browse the list?
  - Is there any kind of "mapping" functionality to help you to get to the right subject terms?
  - If subject terms are assigned to each record, how many are assigned? (2 to 3? 5? 10 or more?)
  - Are the subject terms broad or very specific? (What is the "specificity" of the indexing language?)
  - Consistency of indexing: has the subject list grown or changed over the years? If so, and if there are "discarded" headings, how is that handled? How do you know if a term has been discontinued?
  - Has some form of mass search and replace been performed, or do you need to search on both the old and the new term? (These are good nitty-gritty questions to ask the vendor's search help desk.)

- With any browsable indexes, do they offer a "paste to search" function, so you don't have to retype the entry in the search interface? (This saves time and the risk of typing errors.)
- Abstracts:
  - Do the records offer abstracts?
  - Are they simply replications of the first paragraph of the article, or are they actually evaluative or summarizing? (The former are more likely to have been machine generated, whereas the latter are most likely to have been written by a person.)
  - Are the abstracts generally long and detailed or short?
- Title enhancements:
  - If titles in this subject discipline's literature are frequently cute or clever rather than straightforward, is a supplemental title added, to clarify what the article is really about (and to give you a better chance of retrieving it with a keyword search)?
  - If the database offers materials in different languages, are the article titles offered in translation?
- Full text: If full text is available, is it searchable?[2] Are there better tools for searching full text available (e.g., proximity operators)?
- Does the database offer a "find more like this" function? If yes, does it pull up appropriate, useful material?
- Overall, does the database employ features and conventions that are similar to other databases?

An additional point that bridges both "searchability" and the next category, user interface, is the idea of search history. This is a user interface functionality that does not have to do with indexing or cataloging practices, but that certainly contributes to a database's searchability. Does the database keep track of your search history? Can you reuse previous searches; combine them with other previous searches or with new terms?

User Interface: Usability

This is an area that is open to both objective and subjective evaluation, and can be particularly important in the case of the same database offered by multiple vendors. As you work with the database, besides assessing the content and search function, keep track of your experiences and reactions to the interface—the *way* that you access that content and those search functions. In the broadest sense you should ask, "Does it work? How well?" When you are comparing vendors, searching the same information through a different interface can feel like a totally different experience. Some specific things to be look for are:

- Are different skill levels accommodated: novice, expert?
- Is the interface easily understood?
- Does the interface make it clear how to use it, both by layout and by the terminology used? For example, are field names clear and understandable to the user?

- If icons are used, are they meaningful?

- Is the interface so bare and simple that it's "naked," or is it cluttered, busy, or mysterious?

- Are there *too many* options (or too many ways to do the same thing)?

- How is color contrast used? Is color used to demarcate functional areas of the screen, or is everything uniform in color?

- Is the interface visually appealing? For instance, is the color scheme easy on the eyes? Are the fonts too small, too big, too hard to read, etc.? Are the colors or fonts adjustable, either on a user-by-user basis or globally for your account, by a local system administrator (or both)?

- Does it provide good navigation links? Is it well designed?

- How much control do the navigation links exert: for example, if you use the Back button rather than a "Modify search" link, does it wipe out your search? (This is very annoying.)

- Can you initiate a search by just pressing Enter, or is it necessary to always click a "Search" button?

- How many clicks does it take to get to your "goal" (i.e., abstract, full-text, etc.), and back?

- How easy is it to adjust or modify your search? Do you have to go back to a main search screen, or is a search interface, or other kinds of refining options, available on the results screen?

- How easy is it to find help? What terminology is used for help?

- Are functions such as save, e-mail, and download easy to see and understand?

- If the database has a "time out" function, that is, you get disconnected after a certain period of inactivity, does it provide a warning before disconnecting you? Can the time-out period be adjusted?

- If the subscription is based on a limited number of users, what sort of message is displayed if all the "seats" are in use when you try to sign on?

- Is the database browser or platform dependent, that is, will it work only with a specific Web browser, on a specific type of computer (usually Windows rather than Mac, Unix, or Linux)?

- If the database is browser dependent, what sort of warning does it provide if you attempt to use it with an unsupported browser?

- If you encounter non-functioning tools (i.e., buttons/features that don't work), is it because you are on an unsupported platform? This is another good excuse to call the vendor's tech support line.

Treatment of Research

How research is treated is an important factor for any institution that works with students who are writing papers. Terms frequently used for research articles are *peer reviewed*, or *scholarly*. Databases such as EBSCO's *MasterFILE Select*, ProQuest's *Research Library*, or Wilson's *OmniFile*, which offer both popular and scholarly articles, provide a limit function for "Peer Reviewed."[3] Provision of such a limit or similar functionality only makes sense when a database includes a wide range of materials, however. Databases that consist almost entirely of scholarly materials, such as the *Science Citation Index* or *EconLit*, do not need this type of filtering functionality. Questions to ask in evaluating a multidisciplinary database are:

- Does the database provide "research" level material?
- How can scholarly materials be identified? By a limit in the search interface?
- Is there a way to distinguish scholarly materials in search results, even if you haven't used a limit (e.g., by an icon in the record, or by a separate tab in the results display that filters for scholarly articles)?
- Is there anything in the product literature to indicate how many journals, or what percentage of the sources, are scholarly?
- One other point to check: scholarly articles almost always have a bibliography of sources at the end. If the database provides full text in HTML rather than PDF format, check to be sure that such bibliographies are included.

Sorting/Display/Output Capabilities

Sorting:

- What is the default sort order for displaying results? Can you change it?
- Where is the sort function offered: in the search interface, in the results display, or in both?
- What are the sort options?
- Is there a limit on the number of results that can be sorted? Some databases offer a "sort" option only on results sets of, for example, 500 or less.
- What fields can you sort by?
- If the database allows you to select certain records and create a list of just the selected or marked records, can those be sorted?

Displaying:

- How many results are displayed per page? Can you change the number?
- Are the search parameters (e.g., words searched, limits used) reiterated on the results list screen?
- What is the default record display: full or brief? Can you change it?
- Are search terms highlighted in the results display? If they are, is it possible to turn such highlighting off? (Many repetitions of

highlighted terms can sometimes turn out to be more annoying than helpful.)

- Are format options indicated for each record, for example, icons indicating HTML or PDF availability?

Output:

- What formats are offered for output, especially of full text? Plain text, HTML, or PDF?

- Can you e-mail records? What are the e-mail options offered: for example, sending the information formatted as plain text, HTML, or as a PDF attachment? How much can you customize the e-mail: can you enter your e-mail as the return address, put in your own Subject line, or add a note? Can you choose to include the search history with the e-mailed results?

- When printing records, do you get to choose what is printed (which fields)? Note especially in databases that provide full text: can you select a group of records, and then print the full records in one continuous stream? Or are you forced to print full text records one by one?

- If you have reason to believe that many of the people who would use this database use software programs such as RefWorks or EndNote to keep track of their citations, does the database offer an export function for bibliographic management software programs?

Benchmarking

The first three types of benchmark activities listed here are, obviously, most important when you are trying to choose between two databases, especially if you already subscribe to one and are contemplating whether to change to the other. The next point addresses the fact that in academia, there is always a set of schools with which your school compares itself, and such comparisons are important to administrators. The final point below is perhaps not a realistic goal but is a significant concept.

Source List Comparisons

In choosing between rival databases, a good first step is to compare their lists of sources; that is, which journals (or other document types) does each one offer? How much overlap is there? How many unique titles are there? Among the unique titles, which list has more titles that are of interest to *your* institution? Among the titles that are the same in both databases, is the coverage the same: that is, how do the dates of coverage and the availability of full text (if any), compare? If you can obtain the source lists in Excel format and merge them into one spreadsheet, it can greatly facilitate this comparison process. This comparison is also almost entirely quantitative and objective, and therefore it carries more weight in a request for purchase. And you might not have to do this comparison "by hand" with your own spreadsheets: check the recent library literature, and ask colleagues in Collection Development, Acquisitions, or Cataloging to see if any comparison products are available to you.

Search Result Comparisons

Just as it sounds, you should run the same searches in the databases that you are comparing, and see how the number and nature of the "hits" compares. The number refers to how many results, and the "nature" refers to the quality of the results: if one database yields ten more hits on a search, but of those extra ten, eight are from popular magazines or are only brief articles, are you really getting any significant advantage? Absolutely equal searches are somewhat difficult to achieve, because each database could use differing subject terms, the default fields that are searched might be different, etc., but this is still a very useful exercise to do. Experiment with keyword searches, phrase searches, and field searches. If there are subject terms that are the same in both databases, those are ideal for benchmark searches. Simply spending some time with the two subject lists side by side on the screen can be useful too: try to get a sense of the level of detail of subject terms used and the nature of the language. Even in the realm of "controlled vocabulary," there are some that are more formal, and others that sound more like natural language. Users are more likely to benefit by accident when the subject terms are less formal (e.g., because the terms they type in happen to match the subject vocabulary).

Be sure to keep a record of everything you do while you're "benchmark searching": exactly what the search was, the number of results, and comments on the results. Don't count on your memory: by the next day the similarities and differences will be a blur. Keeping a good log helps this activity stay in the quantitative, objective realm, rather than the gut instinct, subjective realm.

Finally, be sure to test searching at different times of day, to compare response times. Based on the vendor's location, figure out what represents "peak hours" and test during that time. Significantly slower response times or access refusals are not a good sign.

Technical Support Comparisons

If you are comparing two databases, come up with some questions for the technical support staff at both vendors. Compare the time required to get answers, how accurate the answers are, and the general effectiveness of the staff.

Peer Institution Holdings

As mentioned previously, administrators at colleges and universities are very aware of, and sensitive to, comparisons with other schools that are recognized as "peers." It has nothing to do with the intrinsic worth of the database at hand, but if you can show that a significant number of your school's peer institutions already subscribe to this database, it may be helpful in persuading your administration to fund the purchase.

Ideal Assessment of Coverage

The ideal assessment of coverage is represented by this question: how much (what is the percentage) of the total literature in the discipline is covered by this database? This is an ideal, because, frankly, I can't imagine how one would go about determining it with any kind of precision, but it is an interesting and thought-provoking point to raise. (If the database is subject specific, one strategy might be to see if there is a matching subject category in *Ulrich's*, and then compare numbers of titles. This is still bound to be somewhat crude, however.) It could be a good question for the database vendor.

Making a Request for Purchase

As mentioned as the beginning of this chapter, one of the reasons that you would choose to go through this much work is if you were considering a new database subscription. Now that you've done the work, what can you do to try to make the new subscription a reality? You've done your homework well, but keep in mind that administrators, like the rest of us, have limited time and attention spans. They don't want to read ten pages of detail, they just want to see a succinct argument that shows why database XYZ is necessary, how it will benefit library users, and, quite likely, how you propose to fund the purchase. Most organizations have a process in place for making such requests, but the following list of points probably meshes with, or can be used to enhance, the existing process.

Elements to Include in the Request

What Does This Database Bring to the Institution?

Show what material this database offers that is not available from any other existing service (this could include topic areas, material types, specific publication titles, date ranges, etc.). Use numbers rather than text as much as you can. Relate the database directly to the goals of your organization, for example, to specific classes, areas of expansion (new programs), and so forth. If you need to highlight textual elements such as publication titles, provide at most four key titles, and list any additional titles you think are important in an appendix. Once you have demonstrated why this database is unique, it is also important to address the following consideration.

How This Database Complements the Existing Collection

Although of course the database needs to bring something new to your organization (otherwise, why would you be interested in it?), it's also important to demonstrate how the material in this database could complement and extend the existing library collections. For example, if your library has a subscription to the ASI, SRI, and IIS fiche collections, you can make a strong argument for subscribing to the extended version of LexisNexis *Statistical*, because this provides an electronic index to the fiche collection. If your library doesn't have the fiche, however, it doesn't make much sense to get this version of the database: you'll only lead users to materials that you can't provide locally. Similarly, if you are trying to make a case for a new religion database, but your school doesn't offer any kind of religion degree, you certainly can say it brings something new to your resources, but what exactly would be the point? There would be little complementary material in the collection, and, unless there were popular religion courses offered in another department, it would be difficult to identify a strong user base.

If you are proposing to change from an existing database to a rival product, obviously you'll do many comparisons, as mentioned in the first two types of benchmarking. You'll want to emphasize differences in the new version of database that are important to your stated audience for the database. The following section discusses this key point, the potential database users.

Who Will Use the Database

Who will be interested in the material in this database? How many potential users will it have? If at all possible, try to get some of those potential users involved during the database trial period. Have them "test drive" the database, or at least take a look at the source list. Comments from users (e.g., "it helped me with a paper," "I needed this for my thesis research," "it seemed easy to use"), or even better, purchase requests from users (i.e., "the library should definitely have this resource"), can be very persuasive. If you found a database review that included a strong comment relating to the audience for the database, which matches your potential audience, include it here.

Marketing the Database

If you get the database, how will you let people know that the new resource is available? As always, strive for brevity, but try to outline all the avenues you propose to use to market the database. For example, try a mass e-mail to department faculty and students (possibly more than once), that includes links to appropriate Web pages, posters, flyers, brown-bag (or better, free pizza) information or training sessions, etc. People have a lot vying for their attention, and as vociferously as your users may have said they wanted this new database, you will still need to put out quite a bit of effort to get them to integrate the new tool into their work habits.

In addition, it's a good idea to include how you plan to evaluate database usage after a year. How well did your marketing work? Usage statistics are one obvious measure, but some kind of quick, informal survey (e.g., by e-mail or a Web page) of your target communities shows a bit more initiative on your part. Besides, such a survey has the added benefit of providing additional marketing as well as assessing!

How the Purchase Will Be Funded

Funding is usually the make-or-break factor: what is the cost, and where will the money come from? With the cost, indicate whether it includes any discounts, which pricing model was used (e.g., if you opted for only two simultaneous users rather than five), etc. If you have competing price quotes from multiple vendors, indicate that you've chosen the most economical one (or if you haven't, why). Where the money comes from might be from canceling something else (another database, or several serial titles), or, if your accounting system permits, a permanent transfer of funds from a monographic to a serial budget. If you feel that your case is strong enough, there is always the option of simply requesting additional funds to be added to your budget line to pay for the new subscription.

Addenda

If the database has been favorably reviewed, include citation(s) to the review(s) in an appendix. Particularly useful or pertinent quotes might be included in appropriate sections of the main document. If in the course of your review and testing you have discovered features that you feel are particularly compelling, mention those now. Indicate that you can provide detailed title comparisons, or search logs, if requested.

Your overall goal is to present a succinct, clear, and quantitative as well as qualitative case. Your first attempt might not be successful, but you will have shown that you can perform a rational and cogent analysis. Your funding agents are more likely to trust you and try to do their best for you when you try again. So take a refusal like a good sport, and just keep gathering data for the next attempt.

Exercises and Points to Consider

1. This list of things to consider in evaluating a database is fairly comprehensive (perhaps daunting?), but no list can ever be absolutely complete. You've been working with databases a lot by now: What other points or issues have *you* encountered that you'd add to this list? What points do you think aren't as important or that you wouldn't need to bother with?

2. A major project: choose a database that is new to you, either from the resources available at your institution, or by requesting a trial from a vendor. Do a thorough evaluation of it, from the point of view of either writing a review of the database for publication, or writing up a purchase request for your management. (If you aren't currently employed in a library or other type of information center, make one up.) Then either:

    Write the review.

    or

    Write up the purchase request.

    If you choose the review option, write the review as if you were going to submit it for publication. Include the name of the publication to which you would submit the review, and follow its guidelines in terms of formatting, length, etc. (See "Instructions for authors" on the publication's Web site.) After your professor has seen it, she might well encourage you to follow through with the submission; this is a realistic goal.

    If you choose the purchase request option, include a separate description of your (real or fictional) library or information center, to set the scene. Be sure to describe your user community, and your institution's overall budget situation. Make it as realistic as possible. If you are currently working in a library or information center, choose a database you'd actually like to obtain: you may be able to put your work here to good use on the job.

    In either case, do not feel compelled to work through every single point mentioned in this chapter: choose the ones that make sense and are feasible for your chosen project.

Suggested Readings

Powers, Audrey. 2006. Evaluating Databases for Acquisitions and Collection
    Development. In: *Handbook of Electronic and Digital Acquisitions*. Haworth

Press. Powers's chapter is pp. 41–60, and it covers much of the same ground as this chapter, but with some interesting differences, including a case study. It can be very helpful to read similar material presented in a different voice. Other chapters in this *Handbook* are useful as well; for example, chapter 4 discusses the special issues around aggregator databases.

Sabin-Kildiss, Luisa, Cool, Colleen, and Hong Xie. 2001. Assessing the Functionality of Web-Based Versions of Traditional Search Engines. *Online* 25(2): 18–26. Although we take it for granted now that databases are Web based, and the names of some of the products mentioned here have changed, the fundamentals of this article are still sound and useful.

Notes

1. The number of sources is usually easily found in the vendor's promotional literature for the database, because—dearly as we love them—vendors do love to play the "numbers game": that is, "we have more sources than vendor Y." Now, what really matters is what those sources *consist* of: are they all quality publications, or are the numbers being padded with the sort of titles you find in your dentist's office? Still, the number of sources is worth getting, if only because it provides another quantifiable piece of information for your purchase request.

2. This is not as silly a question as it sounds. For example, the *Investext Plus* database consists of nothing but full-text PDF documents, but you cannot search the full-text content. Only the material in the "citation" portion of the records is searchable, and the records are very brief.

3. Tip: if a database includes both popular and scholarly materials, but doesn't provide any functionality for distinguishing between them but does use subject headings, then some subject terms that might help sift out research articles are "methodology," "sampling," "populations," "results," "variables," or "hypotheses."

12
Teaching Other People about Databases

If the thought of getting up in front of other people and speaking makes your blood run cold, and you were hoping that by becoming a librarian you could avoid having to do that kind of activity[1] . . . *my* hope is that after reading through this chapter and getting some experience, you will change your mind, and come to understand that teaching and presenting are a vital part of librarianship. Let us consider the importance and ramifications of presenting for a moment, and then we'll get into some more specific nuts and bolts.

The library profession needs spokespeople and champions. The focus of this book has been, of course, databases, but what good are a group of wonderful databases if you can't convey to others that they exist and how to use them? How long do you think funding for these expensive resources will last if you can't defend them? In the larger scheme of things, it's never too early to get used to the idea of justifying your existence: public, school, and state-employed librarians need to be able to talk to their communities and to local and state legislatures. Academic librarians make points for their libraries in the eyes of the budget controllers by successfully engaging in the academic game: by giving presentations at conferences, and by holding offices in state and national professional organizations. Our profession might not be in crisis, but we certainly are challenged by the Internet as almost no other profession is. The Internet is "free," and libraries are expensive: we are cost centers, not profit centers. It's difficult to quantify the value we give back. If you've chosen to become a librarian, or are already in the profession, presumably you've made that choice because you enjoy and believe in libraries as an institution and librarianship as a vocation. Isn't it worth it to learn to get up in front of people and talk for a short time to ensure that your chosen path has a future? *Any* kind of speaking you do—whether it's an Information Literacy session for a freshman writing class, an evening program for adults at a public library, a talk at a conference, three minutes of impassioned defense before a state legislature, or even a brief discussion in an elevator—makes a difference. It makes a difference both for libraries in general and for your own career, to be able to tell others effectively what we do, why our (expensive) tools are useful, and the benefits they bestow.

Teaching means getting up in front of people and talking. Humans like to communicate (look at the popularity and omnipresence of cell phones), and teaching is just another form of communicating. It would be wonderful if "how to teach" were part of your library school curriculum (Meulemans and Brown, 2001), but maybe it wasn't, or maybe library school is a distant memory. Still, even if public speaking ranks right up there with getting a root canal in your list of favorite things to do, be assured that it can be done. It gets easier, and you might even enjoy it someday.[2] Honest. Maybe you enjoy teaching and presenting already; if so, good for you! If not, the following principles should help to make the experience manageable, if not totally enjoyable.

Teaching Principles

The second half of this chapter discusses the opportunities to teach people about databases that librarians commonly encounter. Of the four types of teaching or public speaking opportunities considered, I count myself as quite lucky to have experienced them all (with the exception of the public or school library versions of the second point). These experiences have informed my thoughts about what works and what doesn't, and what's important and what isn't, in the process of conveying skills or knowledge from one person to another, or from one person to a group. The process of writing up my thoughts for this chapter included double checking my instincts against some representative examples from the teaching literature (see the Suggested Readings at the end of the chapter), including essays by two professors who have been recipients of the undergraduate teaching award at my university. It was gratifying to find my instincts born out by this review. A particular acknowledgment goes to Celia Applegate, Professor of History at the University of Rochester, whose list of "Rules" both inspired and frequently informed the following list of Principles.

These are guidelines that can be applied to any type of teaching, not just of databases, although there are underlying assumptions (e.g., in the emphasis on use of technology) that what is being taught is technical or online in nature. You'll find the list ranges from the more philosophical "Teach to Your Audience" to the very directive and practical "wait for someone to answer when you ask a question." You will be able to use these principles as a kind of checklist and support system as you strive for all the hallmarks of an effective teacher. Repeated studies have shown that "concern for students, knowledge of the subject matter, stimulation of interest, availability, encouragement of discussion, ability to explain clearly, enthusiasm, and preparation" are the qualities that students cite most often in describing effective teachers (Feldman, 1976). Those are your goals, and these suggestions will help you achieve them.

Principle 1: Teach to Your Audience

Be very clear who your audience is, and keep them firmly in mind as you prepare the session. Make your teaching objectives, material, and handouts—everything about what you're doing—appropriate to the needs and interests of *that* audience. It's quite easy to decide what you want to tell people, but it takes a good deal more effort to determine how to deliver your message in a way they will really *hear* and perhaps remember. Ten-year-olds, undergraduates, lawyers, or the PTA are all very different groups of people, and your approach needs to be different in each case.

Sidebar 12.1: Teaching the "Millennial" Audience

Millennials, *Net gens*, or *Generation Next* are the various terms used to refer to people born between 1981–1982 and 2002 (also frequently spelled *Millenials*).

Characteristics of Millennials	Effective Teaching Strategies for Millennials
• Don't like being passive recipients of information	• More self-directed
	• Very little lecture
• Like trial and error (no fear of failure)	• Relaxed and informal
• Like to learn from each other	• Lots of student engagement and activity (for example, they like competition)
• Don't like formal instruction	
• Like to be engaged and entertained	

From Carter and Simmons, 2007.

Principle 2: Avoid Lecturing

Avoid pure lecture at every opportunity. As Professor Applegate (1999) puts it: "Never miss an opportunity to keep your mouth shut." You probably thought that if you were asked to teach or present, that you should fill every moment, but silence truly can be golden. Do not be afraid of silence (Applegate, 1999). People need time to process what you're saying, which means that you need to stop speaking from time to time. Give people time to "think about what they have been told" at regular intervals (Felder and Silverman, 1988). Something as simple as pausing to write a point on the board, and not talking while you do it, can provide a moment of needed silence. We're lucky in our subject matter, too, in that when you're teaching about databases, you have all kinds of ways you can stop lecturing and give your audience time to *use* what they've heard as well as think about it. For example:

- In a hands-on situation, have people start doing their own searching. Try to make the searching, not your lecture, fill the majority of the class time. Talk about one idea, then have them try it, then go on to another idea, and have them try it. Alternate between talking and activity.

- In a demonstration (not hands-on) situation, you might present them with a search statement, and then have them work alone or with the person next to them, to come up with as many synonyms as they can for each of the concepts in the search.

- Use the projector to display, or hand out a paragraph describing a search request, either in the form of discursive text, or a dialogue between a patron and a librarian. Have the class—individually, in groups, or as a whole—figure out one or more search strategies to try. Then have members of the audience come up and type in the chosen searches.

- If you are going over a computer function of some kind (e.g., looking materials up in the online catalog), ask the class if anyone has done it before. (*Wait* for an answer.) Then have one or two volunteers come up and demonstrate how they do it.

- Use questions such as "what are all the uses you can think of for (XYZ)?" to start discussions. To get even the quiet people involved, hand out brightly colored Post-it^{TM} notes to everyone, and have them *write* their ideas, one per note. Stick them up on a wall or a white board, in categories, and start a discussion from there.

In general, look at the list of concepts you wish to get across, and come up with alternatives to straight lecturing. Students in the "Net gen" or "Millennial" generation (1982–2002) seem to be especially adverse to lecture, and even the students' subject faculty have noticed that they learn from discussing issues with each other (Viele, 2006). Small groups, discussion, writing on the board, Post-its, other hands at the "instructor" keyboard, any kind of physical activity or acting out (you can do some fun things with people acting out Boolean logic)—all of these are lecture alternatives. People learn best when they are developing and putting concepts into practice themselves, so aim for that if possible. You don't have to come up with all these teaching ideas on your own. Brainstorm with a colleague; it will be fun for both of you.

Principle 3: *Wait* for Answers

When you ask questions (which is definitely a good thing to do), first, ask with a purpose: ask a question for which you really want an answer, and second, *wait* for someone to answer. Give your audience a chance to marshal their thoughts and come up with a response. Resist with every fiber of your being the desire to answer your own question. The moment you do, the audience will decide your questioning is all a sham, and they won't bother to make any further effort. You will have no chance of getting them to answer any subsequent questions.

Waiting for someone to answer is definitely one of the hardest things to do in a teaching situation. That silence seems to stretch out forever, but try to remember two things. One, the time seems much longer to you than it does to your audience. Two, the silence will eventually start to bother the people in your audience as well, and they will realize that you really mean it; you *do* want to hear from them. Sooner or later someone will crack and say something. If you really can't stand it, pick someone in the group and push the matter by asking, "what do you think?" in a friendly way.

Of course, the kinds of questions that you ask make a difference, too. Questions that ask people to relate things to their own lives or experience are generally more comfortable, and can usually get *someone* to pipe up. Once they do, if you're looking to foster more group discussion, don't immediately respond yourself—look around for someone else who looks on the verge of speaking and give that person an encouraging look, or just ask, "what do you think?" Try not to be the arbiter, the touchstone for every response from the group. It is not necessary to "respond to every response" (Applegate, 1999).

Principle 4: Less Is More

Don't overwhelm your audience by trying to do too much. Guided by Principle 1, choose only a limited number of concepts or instructions that you feel will be the most useful information for *that audience*. Take two or perhaps three things you think would be most helpful for *that audience* to remember or learn, and build your presentation around those items. One of the biggest pitfalls for new professors—and this extends to anyone new to teaching—is that they tend to over-prepare lectures and try to present too much material too rapidly. Successful teachers, however, present material "paced in a relaxed style so as to provide opportunities for student comprehension and involvement" (Boice, 1992).

This may well sound like an advocation that you set your sights pretty low, and you may feel that it's a disservice to show only a few features of a wonderful database that is loaded with functionality. The problem is, you can't possibly cover as much material in interactive, non-lecture classes; they aren't very efficient in that sense. If you are adhering to Principle 2, sincerely trying to avoid pure lecture (which is the most ineffectual form of instruction anyway), and instead trying to foster discussion and engagement and "active learning," you can't go over every bell and whistle. It will be frustrating at times: "They should know this! They should know that too! And this other thing!" Consider this, however: if you show them two or three things that get their interest, enough so that they go back on their own, don't you think they might discover some of the other "things they should know" on their own? It's likely that they can. Motivated, interested people are pretty smart that way.

Overall, the outcomes of a nonlecture style of teaching can be much more useful and rewarding to your students. If you cover only two or three things in an interesting way that shows, "here's how this will benefit you," the participants are much more likely to remember at least some of the content. And, if you manage *not* to alienate your audience, and *not* make the session one they can't wait to get out of, they are much more likely to seek you out again for help later, in what is probably the more useful one-on-one situation at the Reference Desk.

Principle 5: Transparency in Teaching

Don't be inscrutable (Applegate, 1999): lay out clearly the goals and objectives for the class, the assignment, or the exercise—whatever you are doing. Always keeping in mind Principle 1, relate the goals and objectives to your audience. Do your best to make them feel that it's worth their while to be there. Keep things simple, straightforward, and honest—you are not a god(dess) or keeper of keys to special mysteries, you just happen to have some useful knowledge you'd like to share that will, you believe, make your audiences' lives better in some way. Honesty is important because of the next principle.

Principle 6: You Have the Right to Be Wrong

It is acceptable to be wrong occasionally, or not to know the answer to every question. Acting inscrutable is often allied with trying to be infallible, and both are terrible ideas. Of course you will have done your best to master your material (Principle 8 below), but it is still inevitable that someone will ask you a question to which you don't know the answer, or that some alert person will point out something you've gotten wrong, pure and simple. Laugh at yourself, thank the person (sincerely) for noticing, make a note to fix it for next time, and get over it. No one is perfect, and most audiences will relate to you more easily if they think that you're human rather than a remote and infallible being. Consider this wonderful quotation:

> Arnold Schoenberg wrote in the introduction to his 1911 text on musical harmony that "...the teacher must have the courage to be wrong." The teacher's task, he continued, "is not to prove infallible, knowing everything and never going wrong, but rather inexhaustible, ever seeking and perhaps sometimes finding." The more we can involve the students with us in this task, "ever seeking and...sometimes finding," the better...(Applegate, 1999).

Ever seeking and perhaps sometimes finding—what a perfect expression for librarianship. So don't get upset if you make a mistake; you are in excellent company.

Principle 7: Teaching with Technology

If working with technology of any kind, there are two things to keep in mind: (1) slow down, and (2) anticipate technology failure.

When you are working with "technology," that is, either a projected computer screen or a hands-on computer classroom, you need to build more time into presentation plans. Especially in a hands-on situation, in which people are looking back and forth from your (projected) screen to their own (and maybe back to yours yet again), *slow down*. It's essential to take more time: you know where you're going, but your audience doesn't. It is all uncharted territory for them. You must give the people who are trying to follow you time to process. Even if they are not trying to replicate what you are doing on their own computers and are just watching the screen, take your speed down a few notches. Don't scroll rapidly up and down, and practice mousing from point A to point B without a lot of whizzing around on the screen. These may sound like small details, but again, your audience is madly trying to follow you (and might also be trying to take notes); this is new territory for them, and their minds will be doing a lot more processing than yours. Excessive scrolling and mousing in that situation is distracting, if not downright annoying, so work on keeping it to a minimum.

The other thing about technology: be ready for things to go wrong. Plan for how you will handle it if the projector bulb goes, or you can't get on the Net, or the computer crashes. For example, if you're leading a hands-on session and the projector malfunctions, simply designate one or two of the people in the class as your "hands," and have them follow your directions while the other students gather around those computers. Invite all the students to help as backseat drivers. They'll probably all have more fun and get more out of it than if things had gone according to plan! If you're presenting in a non–hands-on situation and your projector fails, start a discussion instead. Ask the group something about what you have just been trying to cover. As noted earlier, questions that relate the material to their own experience ("what do you folks usually do when you need to find XYZ?") are good for getting the ball rolling.

If you're presenting somewhere other than your home location and intend to show something live on the Internet, take a PowerPoint file (with screen snaps of what you intended to show live) along as backup. It's a fair amount of extra work (depending on the length of your presentation), and you might not need it, but oh, if you do need it, you will be intensely thankful that you took the time. So take the time. It also gives you a way to rehearse (if you take a laptop with you) on the plane or in the hotel room the night before.

If you're in your home situation and something goes wrong: first, call tech support (if you have it); second, restart the computer; third, start some kind of discussion.[3] With students, ask them about their assignment (or whatever has brought them to you today), what they've done so far with it, their familiarity with the library and its systems. In a non-academic situation, ask them what brought them to the session, what they hope to get out of it, etc.

Above all, in a technology failure situation, do not betray your anxiety. Don't wring your hands and whimper helplessly. Groaning is permitted, as long as you also laugh. Maintain your aplomb. This is much easier to do if you've rehearsed in your mind what you'll do if the technology lets you down. Because it will: not every time, but at least sometimes. Dave Barry says that your household plumbing makes plans in the middle of the night for how it will go wrong and disrupt your big party. These devices—computers, projectors, servers, etc.—undoubtedly do the same thing. And speaking of rehearsal....

Principle 8: Practice

There is an old gag that asks, "How do you get to Carnegie Hall?" Answer: "Practice, practice, practice." Practice is essential. If you are not used to presenting, or are uncomfortable with it, I cannot emphasize enough the importance of rehearsal. Practice is crucial for several reasons. First and foremost, the time you are alloted will always be limited, and a live run-through is the only way to find out how long the session you have planned actually lasts (and usually you will find you have more material than you think). Practicing also helps you to become more comfortable, and can help identify "bugs" in your presentation, saving embarrassment later. Let's look at the "limited time" issue in more detail.

No matter what sort of group teaching or presentation situation it is (Information Literacy, staff development, etc.) you will always be working within a specified time limit. Until you have run through what you plan to say—actually spoken the words *out loud*—you won't know how long your presentation really takes. Unless you have a lot of experience, you cannot mentally run through a talk at a slow enough pace to mimic a verbalized version reliably. Especially when a presentation or sample class is part of a job interview, practice it to be sure it fits within the time allotted. If you practice and find that your presentation is too long, the only option is reducing the amount of information that you attempt to convey. When in doubt, cut it out. Talking faster is *not* an option, nor is running over. Both things will irritate your audience. If you simply keep talking and have to be cut off before you're finished, you will look unprepared. Practice by yourself (but aloud!), even if it means talking to the wall and feeling like an idiot. If possible, the best option is to round up some classmates, friends, or family, and give your talk to them. Especially if you are trying to simulate a class situation, with questions and back and forth, practicing with friends is extremely helpful in determining your timing and pacing. They can also help identify any non sequiturs or outright errors in your talk. In a job interview situation, if you teach only one thing but do it well, appear relaxed, interact with your audience, and stay within your time limit, your prospective employers will feel as if you've taught them much more, and generally have far more positive feelings about you than if you try to cram in every last nuance, are forced to rush, and lecture the entire time. Unless you are really unusually gifted in this area, your audience will almost always be able to tell whether or not you have practiced.

At the same time, being well rehearsed doesn't mean rattling off your "script" like—well, like a memorized script. Rather, it means full mastery of your material, so that you are talking about your topic naturally and easily, you are able to field questions or take small side trips (or encounter technical difficulties) without getting flustered or derailed from your main intent, and your enthusiasm and enjoyment of your topic come through. If you are suffering, your audience will suffer as well. Take some lessons from Hollywood: rehearse, know your lines, and deliver them with sincerity and enthusiasm. Act like you're enjoying it, even if you aren't. Your audience will enjoy it a great deal more (and you might too). Remember to smile occasionally: write yourself a note if necessary, and breathe. You can't panic when you're breathing deeply and slowly. So practice, then breathe, smile, open your mouth, and share the wonderful information you have with your audience. You'll be great!

Database Teaching Opportunities

Let's take a look at the kinds of opportunities for teaching or presenting information about databases that you are likely to encounter as a librarian. In order of frequency of occurrence (from most to least), these can be summarized as:

- One on one, with a patron over a question at the reference desk.

- One-off, one-time sessions, often known as Information Literacy classes (or sometimes *bibliographic instruction* [BI]) in college and university settings. Presenting such a class is a common part of an academic job interview. In a school library, these are usually referred to simply as classes and tend to be quite brief: 15 to 20 minutes. The public library equivalent might be an evening or noontime continuing education session.

- A database introduction or review, such as one would present at a staff meeting or staff development session.

- A sustained, semester-long class.

These are all quite different sorts of encounters, yet you'll find that many of the principles given here apply to them all. What follows are some thoughts about applying the principles in each case to make your database instruction more effective.

Teaching at the Reference Desk

This is probably the type of "teaching encounter[4]" that people generally find most comfortable: it's intimate, one on one; you only have to deal with one person and can focus entirely on him or her. It's also reactive, rather than proactive: the person has *chosen* to approach you, and you can focus on the "topic of the moment," and then the encounter is over. True, you can't prepare (Principle 8), exactly, but that can be a plus: you won't be over-prepared. You have your life knowledge, your library science education, and your professional experience, and you simply apply these in various ways to meet each person's individual information needs.

Introducing a patron to a database at the reference desk provides an opportunity for a "teaching moment," but if you take advantage of that, keep it to a moment. Don't overwhelm (Principle 4, less is more). Pick one or two things to try to "teach" the patron, such as: "this is how you get to the list of databases on (subject X)" and "see this drop-down? If you change it to Subject, the articles you get should be right on target." *Suggest* the power of the database, but don't try to impart all your knowledge. (As Carol Kuhlthau (1988) says in more formal terms, the reference encounter represents the ideal in terms of teaching, because it offers "intervention that matches the user's actual level of information need.") Go through the process with the patron, asking questions about the topic, etc., and explaining in a general way what you're doing, but without necessarily going into all the details. In other words, try to be "transparent" (Principle 5) without being overwhelming or lecturing (Principle 2). For example: "let's try this database— it's got psychology articles" rather than "well, first you should go to the list of psychology databases, and then read the descriptions to decide which one to use. . . ." Attempt to engage the patron gently, as well as being quiet from time to time. A good time to be quiet is when you're looking at a list of results together, so that the patron can study the screen and process. It's much better to hold back a bit and have the patron ask "how did you do that?" than to overwhelm him or her with information. Let's face it, not everyone is that interested, or *needs* to do this kind of research again (Principle 1, Teach to Your Audience). Dropping a limited number of "teaching seeds" is more likely to result in further questioning and ultimate "skill flowering" than ten minutes of unmitigated, and probably unappreciated, lecture.

Teaching an Information Literacy Session

The classroom situation a librarian is most likely to encounter is really quite the hardest: the one-off, limited time (usually only around an hour) class, whose purpose might range from the typical Information Literacy, or "library," session for freshman English students, to how to search the Internet in an evening class for adults at the public library. Now you as an instructor are facing a roomful of people who may or may not wish to be there, and with whom you will probably only have one class session. You are supposed to have some idea of what makes them tick, make contact with them, communicate, and impart two or three chunks of useful knowledge about a fairly sophisticated topic (i.e., database or Web searching) in the limited time allotted. Certainly it is a challenge, but by keeping the principles in mind, you can meet that challenge.

Even in this situation, you can still teach to your audience: you will have advance notice that the session is coming, which gives you time to find out something about who your audience is going to be. In any kind of school situation, the instructor should be willing to tell you the reason that he or she has requested an instruction session in the library, and something about the class (e.g., personalities, skill levels, etc.). In a community education situation, talk to other librarians who have taught such classes before: who tends to show up? What are they usually most interested in? How are their skills? If you feel you need more information, do some reading: there has been plenty of research done on teaching adults (and every other age group). Here's your chance to go to ERIC and get "a few good articles."

We'll assume that, based on your research, some demonstration or hands-on training with a database will be part of your session, or possibly two databases, or a database and the library's online catalog—but that is probably pushing the limits of Principle 4 (less is more). It depends on the point that you are trying to make with each resource. For example, for a first freshman introduction to the library, you might decide that a multidisciplinary database that offers mostly full-text is the resource most attuned with their needs and interests, and therefore you will show them the pertinent features of that database. For an upper-level course, you might opt to demonstrate a subject-specific, abstracts-only database (or one of the *Web of Science* Citation Indexes), along with the library OPAC, with an explanation of how the two can be used in concert. Here is where you can use "self-exploration" to great advantage: you could divide the class into small groups and have each one explore and report back on a different resource, allowing the class as a whole to cover a lot more ground. (A scenario based on this idea is described below.) One thing you can almost be sure of, no matter who is in your class, is that they won't know about databases, but they will know about Google (or whatever search engine is hot at the moment). Use this to your advantage: you know one thing that represents familiar ground to them, so work it in: compare and contrast the search engine with the properties of databases to introduce what databases are. (What is frustrating is that having to explain that there are such things as databases always uses up one of the few, precious two to three learning objectives!)

Examples of Class Scenarios

Here is a step-by-step scenario that might be used in an introductory session for students (my experience is with undergraduates, but this might well work with high school students or graduate students as well). You will need to have prepared the handouts with the assignment for each group, and if possible, a Web page specifically for the class, with links to the database(s) that you want them to use. If your school uses a course management system and you have rights to add material there, that's ideal.

- Explain that the students' instructor has told you about their assignment, and you want to familiarize them with some resources that will help with the research for that assignment: make it go faster, be more efficient, and provide better quality information, so that they can write better papers. They are going to do most of the work, however, and need to do a good job, because they will be teaching the rest of the class. (Transparency, and some motivation.)

- If your school uses a course management system such as Blackboard (and you have rights to add material there), ask if any of them have used course pages on [whatever your institution calls the course system]. Don't forget to wait for an answer. If anyone has, ask if they knew that there was a course page for this course there.

- If you are simply using a Web page you have created that is not part of a course management system, show the students how to get there.

- Divide the class into small groups of three or four, and give each group a handout with its assignment. (Avoid lecturing; encourage "active learning.") For the assignments, give each group a search topic appropriate to the class, and have them search it in a subscription database. Ask them two to three "how do you...?" types of questions about the resource. (Less is more.) Then ask them to do the same things in a Web search engine. For example:

  - For a freshman composition class, two handout examples:

    (1) In *Project MUSE*, search for "fairy tales and strong women."

    Questions: How many results do you get? Are these articles scholarly or popular? How can you tell? Working from one result, how might you find "more like this"? (The purpose of the "more-like-this" question is to get them to notice and use subject headings.)

    Try the same search and answer the same questions using Google.

    (2) In *MLA*, search for criticism or interpretation of Grimm's Fairy Tales.

    Questions: Are there any special fields in the database that might help you do this search? What are the different kinds of publications included in *MLA*? How would you get from these records to the full text?

    Try the same search and answer the same questions using Google Scholar.

  - For an upper level Computer Science course:

    In the *ACM Digital Library*, search on "wearable computers."

    Questions: How many results do you get? How recent are they? Can you sort the results in different ways? How might you use one result to "find more like this"?

    Try the same search and answer the same questions using NCSTRL (www.ncstrl.org).

    (For other groups, substitute *Inspec* and Google Scholar or Scirus.)

  - For any class:

    In [your library's OPAC], try a keyword search on [appropriate topic].

    Questions: [two to three things you'd really like them to "get" about your online catalog].

    Try the same search and questions using Google Books. Which do you like better? What are the advantages and disadvantages of each?

- Even if you have enough computers for everyone, in your groups of three to four, have only one to two people manning the keyboards. Tell the others they are in charge of taking notes, because they will be presenting their group's results. (Active learning, engagement.)

- When the groups are finished, have each group come to the front and present their results. Only jump in and point things out or add material if they really seem to have missed something; you may be very surprised at how little you need to add. (Avoid lecturing.) Ask the rest of the group if they have any questions (wait for answers). Use your "talk time" to ask questions about their perceptions of similarities or differences among the various subscription resources.

Overall, you should find that this kind of hands-off, active learning approach will definitely be "teaching to your audience." You have done your "practicing" in coming up with the assignment handouts (obviously, you need to test drive them all and make sure they support whatever points you are trying to make, which counts as "practice"). Here are two additional variations on this theme, this time concerning a common teaching objective:

One of the most difficult things to convey to undergraduates seems to be how to identify and obtain scholarly articles, especially when the full text has to be tracked down from physical copies of journals in the library. You might decide that all you want to make sure the students come away with is (1) the idea that special purpose databases exist, and (2) databases provide an efficient means to identify articles on a topic. If you are at an institution that subscribes to many databases that offer full text, or that has implemented a link resolver system such as SFX, you might limit your goals to just those two basic ideas, and tell the students to ask at the reference desk when they need help accessing the physical journals. Then structure the session along the lines just described above, but focusing on databases that do not provide full text. Have every group address the question: how do you get from a citation to the full text?

Alternatively, you could start with the idea that (1) special purpose databases provide an efficient means of identifying articles. Then you might demonstrate a sample search (without trying to explain Boolean concepts, or the importance of synonyms or other searching concepts), whose results include a "perfect" article not available in full text online. Ask the students what they would do at this point. (Remember to *wait* for somebody to say something—anything!) Then go for your point (2): how to get from a citation to a physical bound journal on a shelf. If it's possible to have the class all look up the journal, get its call number, and head out into the stacks in search of, all the better. Give hints, but don't lead. Let them work together; perhaps divide the class into two or more teams and turn it into a competition (at this point, it would be even better to supply each group with a different citation on a slip of paper, so that they are heading in different directions). If all that isn't possible, bring the appropriate volume into class with you, and give it to one of the students to find the actual article within the bound volume. Encourage him to get help from a friend if he wants, and discuss something else while they work on that. Basically, don't try to do too much, and if possible, try to make what you *do* do interactive, collegial, and physical. If you should be lucky enough to have someone ask a question (and don't forget, of course, to solicit questions), great, explain, but otherwise remember the thought in Principle 2: never miss an opportunity to keep your mouth shut. Resist the urge to "data dump" to your audience. (For even more nifty ideas for "active learning" exercises to use with undergraduates, be sure to consult Burkhardt et al., 2003, listed in the References for this chapter.)

My examples are heavily oriented to undergraduates, since that is the group with which I am most familiar, but you should be able to turn the basic ideas, the principles outlined earlier, to your advantage for whatever group you are teaching. For example, a class of adults from the community will, of course, have quite different learning objectives: rather than finding articles to support research papers, they may want to learn how to find reputable health information on the Web, or how to assess the validity or quality of any Web resource. You might decide that your goals are to introduce the idea of Advanced Search, and how to use it to limit a Web search to .gov or .edu sites. If you are introducing article databases, it's probably for different purposes, for example, current events, genealogy, business, or investment research. No matter what the subject matter, the principles still apply: try to determine what information will be most pertinent to *that* audience; don't just lecture; definitely ask questions (an adult group might actually answer, and it can be easier to get an interesting discussion going); don't try to do too much; and finally, be extra careful to take it slow in a hands-on session. An adult group is also probably more likely to point out a mistake, or ask you a new question, and that's great: you'll learn something, and they'll secretly enjoy the idea that they stumped the teacher. It's a win-win situation.

In general, although the brief, "one-off" session[5] can be challenging, it is challenging in a good way. (For an even greater-but-good challenge, consider doing such a session in 15 minutes. Arant-Kaspar and Benefiel (2008) demonstrate a real mastery of "knowing their audience" and "less is more" in their description of their successful outreach program of brief instructional visits to classrooms.) True, you don't have the opportunity to establish much rapport with the group, to see their growth or progress, or to repair any blunders in this week's class next week. On the other hand, you are forced to be really rigorous in developing your one class (draw up your list of learning objectives, and then cross most of them out), so that what your attendees receive is a carefully honed, very targeted product. The quality is just as high, if not higher, than many of their regular classes, and the session is likely to be more interactive and memorable as well. If nothing else, the class will come away knowing that (1) you exist; (2) something other than Google exists; and (3) you were trying to show them something that would enhance some aspect of their life. Just as we discussed in the Reference Interview chapter, if you can leave them with a positive impression, it's more likely that individual students will later seek you out at the Reference Desk, or by e-mail, chat, etc.

Teaching a Class in a Job Interview

Presenting a class as part of a job interview has been mentioned a few times already, but let me add some specific notes about it here. First, the time will probably be shorter (20–30 minutes) than in any real class. This will tend to force you into more of a lecture style of presentation, which your audience is expecting, but try to surprise them: try to work in at least one of the interactive, nonlecture approaches suggested under Principle 2. Second, something that may sound obvious: do your homework. The library where you will be interviewing most likely has a Web site. If the library is part of an institution of higher education or a corporation, the organization probably has a Web site. Study these, and use them to inform your presentation: make the class you create look as if you already work there. Base your presentation on a database available at that library, and make your audience a group at that institution (a particular class, with a real class number and professor's name, or a real group within the company or organization). For a public library, study the schedule of classes already on offer, and try to come up with a session that would augment or complement an existing class. If you decide that you want to demonstrate a database that is available only at your target library, and not wherever you currently are, call up the vendor and ask for a trial so that you can learn it, and use the library's link when you are on site. (Create a PowerPoint as backup just in case.) Create one or more appropriate handouts to go with your presentation, and again, don't be shy about copying the library or organization's logo off their Web site to "brand" your handouts. In as many ways as possible, act like you're already on board. With this kind of preparation, perhaps you soon will be!

A Staff Presentation

Teaching your colleagues about a database is quite different from all of the other situations described here. For one thing, knowing your audience shouldn't be an issue: even if you are a new hire right out of library school, you should have a pretty good sense of what librarians are interested in and want to know. Because they are your peers and colleagues (which can make the whole thing both more and less comfortable), it should be much easier to plan and deliver your message. Note, however, that if your group includes members from throughout the library and not just reference librarians, it changes the playing field a good deal. Staff from departments outside of Reference, including computer support, may have little or no idea that databases exist or how they are used, and teaching in this situation is much more akin to teaching a group of adults from the community. But teaching a group of reference librarians about a database turns many of the formerly stated principles upside down

- Principle 2—Avoid Lecturing. You might be able to get away with more lecture here than in any other situation. It will still be appreciated if you try to break things up, however, and give your audience time to absorb what you're saying from time to time. I think you'll find, however, that a lecture naturally devolves into a more participatory session, for the reason noted in the next point.

- Principle 3—Wait for Answers. You probably won't have to wait for answers or need to work at fostering discussion; your colleagues likely will be very forthcoming with comments and questions. This is a group that is truly interested in what you are talking about and eager to explore it with you. (They are glad that you've done the work to master this database, so that they can ask *you* questions.)

- Principle 4—Less is More. You can set higher goals for the amount of information you plan to impart: again, this audience is *interested* and does want the details. They are already knowledgeable, and will be more interested in salient differences from what they know, rather than the basics. You can start at a much higher level of discussion. However, take some guidance from Principle 4 and don't overwhelm them. A rule of thumb might be to master as much of the database as you can, plan to present 50 to 60 percent of that (all of which is "beyond the basics"), and let questions bring out whatever else people want to know.

The other principles do not change much. Principle 5, Transparency, still applies. These librarians are likely to have chosen to attend your session, and so they are willing participants, but it's still a good idea to outline clearly the goals and objectives of your talk; that is, give them good reasons to stay and listen. You will very likely get a good workout of Principle 6 (you have the right to be wrong). You are talking to a very knowledgeable audience, who will undoubtedly catch something or know something that you don't. Don't worry about it! It's a benefit, not a contest. The two technology points of Principle 7 (go slower, and be ready for it to fail), both apply as in any other situation. Just because they are librarians doesn't mean they can look from their screen to your projected screen (or from your projected screen to their notes) any faster than anyone else. In fact, it may take them longer, because they are studying all the details more closely. So give everyone plenty of time. If the technology fails, you probably will have a whole roomful of people ready to jump in and help, so it's not all up to you. Still, you will want to show that you can stay calm, and have a plan in mind for what to do if the technology lets you down. Of course, Principle 8 applies to every situation: *practice* your database demonstration, in as realistic a situation as possible (e.g., out loud, in front of people if possible), before heading off to your staff development meeting.

If an Information Literacy session presents the most challenging *format* for teaching, a session for your colleagues undoubtedly presents the most challenging *audience* for your teaching. But again, let it be a good challenge. Learn the database, and practice, but don't kill yourself preparing. You'll never remember it all anyway, and you'll just make yourself nervous. If one of your "students" knows something that you don't, let him or her teach you. If someone asks a question that you don't know the answer to, and neither does anyone else in the room, make it an opportunity to explore and find out together. It's really much more interesting that way.

The Full Semester Class

Here at last we have a chance to aspire to what is truly important in teaching, that is, "connection, communication, and the stimulation of critical thinking" (Brown, 1999). Instead of one session, you'll see this class over and over, get to know your students, and get beyond a few nuts and bolts "how to's" of only one database to broader, philosophical and technical considerations of databases and information seeking. Sadly, these opportunities are quite rare for librarians, so I will not spend much time on this topic. I would like to say enough to indicate that this is a *feasible* project, however. Should you ever get offered the chance to develop and provide such a class, think seriously about taking it on.

A full semester class, obviously, requires considerable planning, and there are entire books devoted to teaching and curriculum planning (the Suggested Readings include two titles, and a search of WorldCat or Amazon.com reveals many, many more). However, it is not an insurmountable effort. Consider these six steps that are recommended in planning a course (Davidson and Ambrose, 1994):

- Assess the backgrounds and interests of your students.
- Choose the course objectives (note that these are often set by the department, and you simply need to determine how to achieve them).
- Develop the learning experiences within the course.
- Plan feedback and evaluation of student learning.
- Prepare a syllabus for the course.

You are already familiar with the concept in the first point: know your audience. With a full semester to work with, you can now choose overall course objectives, as well as objectives for each session. In both cases, however, you still need to be careful not to overwhelm your students. In each individual class meeting, you shouldn't try to deliver too much, and the sum total of all the sessions ultimately determines the amount of material that you can get through in a semester. You may find it useful to approach a semester-long course as an organizational activity: to work from large, overarching ideas, to the components of those ideas, and finally to the steps needed to teach those components. As you work out the steps, you can plan the best learning experiences to support them. As you determine the components, you can then plan ways to assess mastery of them. When all of that is done, you will have enough material to write up a syllabus.

A discouraging aspect of a whole semester's course for many people is that it seems like you have to come up with *so much material*. But, at least in the area of databases and research techniques, the large ideas—the overall objectives—can be broken down into many component parts. If you start analyzing, breaking down the knowledge or skills that you take for granted into a series of intellectually manageable chunks, you'll be surprised at the amount of material this represents. (Students like clearly defined "chunks" of information.) As you present the course, those component ideas build on each other, heading toward the overall course objectives. Along the way you are presenting learning experiences to convey those ideas, assessing to see if the ideas have been conveyed, and giving feedback. It's an organic, iterative, growing process. Go for it.

Exercises and Points to Consider

1. Think back over all your schooling. Which teachers do you remember most vividly (both good and bad)? See if you can come up with a list of reasons why those instructors either worked (or didn't) for you. Use this information to form your own list of "Teaching Principles."

2. A major effort: decide what type of library you would be most likely to apply for a job in, then develop a 20-minute mock teaching session that could be used in your interview. This could be an academic, school, public, corporate, law, or medical library.

   In real life, outreach is an increasingly important aspect in the services of all of these types of libraries (their very survival could depend on proving their value to the overall organization), so even if such a session is not listed as part of your interview schedule, be proactive: offer a session as an added extra to your interview.

Suggested Readings

Applegate, Celia. "Teaching: Taming the Terror." Chapter 2 in *How I Teach: Essays on Teaching by Winners of the Robert and Pamela Goergen Award for Distinguished Achievement and Artistry in Undergraduate Teaching*. Rochester, NY: University of Rochester, 1999. Available at http://hdl.handle.net/1802/2864.

Brown, Theodore. "Connection, Communication, and Critical Thinking." Chapter 1
in *How I Teach: Essays on Teaching by Winners of the Robert and Pamela
Goergen Award for Distinguished Achievement and Artistry in Undergraduate
Teaching*. Rochester, NY: University of Rochester, 1999. Available at
http://hdl.handle.net/1802/2862.

Lippincott, Joan K. "Net Generation Students and Libraries." In *Educating the Net
Generation*. Diana G. Oblinger and James L. Oblinger (Eds.). EDUCAUSE,
2005. Available at http://www.educause.edu/educatingthenetgen/. An excellent
source for learning more about and achieving a better understanding of this
particular audience.

McKeachie, Wilbert J. *Teaching Tips: Strategies, Research, and Theory for College
and University Teachers*. 9th ed. Lexington, MA: D.C. Heath and Company,
1994. A totally practical, down-to-earth guidebook, covering every aspect of
teaching. Although oriented toward the creation and delivery of a
semester-long class, Chapters 4 and 5, on Organizing Effective Discussions,
and Lecturing; Chapter 13, on Peer Learning, Collaborative Learning,
Cooperative Learning; and Chapter 19, Teaching in the Age of Electronic
Information, are all universally applicable.

Reis, Richard M. "Insights on Teaching and Learning." Chapter 11 in *Tomorrow's
Professor: Preparing for Academic Careers in Science and Engineering*.
Piscataway, NJ: IEEE Press, 1997. In the world of databases and technology,
we are operating closer to (computer) science and engineering than to the
humanities, which is why I deliberately chose this particular guidebook. Most
of the guidance provided could apply to any teaching situation, however, not
just science or engineering.

Veldof, Jerilyn. 2006. *Creating the One-Shot Library Workshop: A Step-by-Step
Guide*. Chicago, IL: American Library Association. If you didn't have the good
fortune to have taken a course in instructional design, here is the ideal
alternative. Veldof's guide is meant to address the need for a library session
that is "one shot," but frequently requested, and can be taught by different
people. This book will help you design a session that can be consistently
taught by different people and consistently received by any group of students,
but the instructional design principles are useful for improving any kind of
class development.

Notes

1. My opening statement to this chapter is based on years of informal observation
and interactions with librarians from many different libraries; an excellent study
by Kaetrena Davis now provides empirical evidence for it as well. In her survey,
she found that people don't go into librarianship specifically with teaching in mind,
most of the time: "more than two-thirds of the respondents (64%) chose librarianship
with a desire to help people, followed by a love of reading and literacy (52%)" (Davis,
2007).

2. The magic time for jettisoning pre-class nervousness and anxiety seems to be between 51 and 60 years of age according to Davis's study (2007).

3. Tech support people may hate me for presenting these actions in this order, but
if you restart the computer and that *doesn't* solve the problem, you've lost a lot of
precious time before initiating contact with tech support, who will inevitably take
some time to respond.

4. Frankly, it had never occurred to me to question that what happens at the Reference Desk is teaching, but if you have any doubts, there is a quantity of literature

available to support the idea: see the References list for Eckel, 2007; Elmborg, 2002; Gremmels and Lehmann, 2007, which all have strong "review of the literature" sections.

5. Actually, you might find you get invited back to give a library session every time the professor teaches the class, so definitely keep your notes and whatever materials (e.g., PowerPoint) you used.

References

Preface

Lampert, Lynn D. and Katherine S. Dabbour. 2007. Librarian Perspectives on Teaching Metasearch and Federated Search Technologies. *Internet Reference Services Quarterly* 12 (3/4): 253–278.

Tennant, Roy. 2003. *Endeavoring to Do Our Best: Library Systems as if Users Matter*. Endeavor General Session. Welcome and Keynote Speech, Endeavor User Group Meeting, April 25, 2003. Available at http://escholarship.cdlib.org/rtennant/presentations/2003end/enduserRT.ppt (accessed March 28, 2005; reconfirmed June 25, 2008).

Chapter 1

Computer History Museum. 2004. *Timeline of Computer History—Networking*. Available at http://www.computerhistory.org/timeline/?category=net (accessed June 20, 2008).

Dialog (a Thomson Reuters business). 2005. *Company Background—Dialog History Movie Transcript*. Available at http://www.dialog.com/about/history/transcript.shtml (accessed June 20, 2008).

Encyclopædia Britannica. 2008. s.v. "digital computer." Available at Encyclopædia Britannica Online, http://search.eb.com/eb/article-1825 (accessed June 20, 2008).

Lexikon's History of Computing. 2002. *Master Chronology of Events*. Available at http://www.computermuseum.li/Testpage/01HISTORYCD-Chrono1.htm (accessed June 20, 2008).

Chapter 2

Walker, Geraldene and Joseph Janes. 1999. *Online Retrieval: A Dialogue of Theory and Practice*, 2nd ed. Englewood, CO: Libraries Unlimited, p. 63.

Chapter 4

American Psychological Association. 2005. *PsycNET Guide to 2005 PsycINFO Changes.* Available at: http://www.apa.org/databases/training/psycnet_guide.pdf (accessed June 3, 2008).

American Psychological Association. 2008. *PsycINFO Fact Sheet.* Available at: http://www.apa.org/psycinfo/products/psycinfo.html (accessed June 2, 2008).

Institute of Education Sciences, U.S. Department of Education. 2005. *ERIC News—New Content Added to the ERIC Database.* Available at http://www.eric.ed.gov/ERICWebPortal/resources/html/news/eric_news_25.html (accessed July 2, 2005; reconfirmed June 25, 2008).

OCLC Adds to, Enhances the Content on FirstSearch. 1998. *Information Today* 15 (October): 19, 75.

Tenopir, Carol. 2003. Databases for Information Professionals. *Library Journal* 128 (October): 32.

Tenopir, Carol. 2004. Eric's Extreme Makeover. *Library Journal* 129 (September): 36.

Viadero, Debra. 2004. ERIC Clearinghouses Close; New System in Works. *Education Week* 23 (January): 20–21.

Chapter 5

NCBI *PubMed.* 2008. *PubMed Help.* Available at http://www.ncbi.nlm.nih.gov/books/bv.fcgi?rid=helppubmed.chapter.pubmedhelp (accessed June 5, 2008).

Tenopir, Carol. 2001. The Power of Citation Searching. *Library Journal* 126 (November): 39–40.

Thomson Scientific. 2005. The Index with All the Answers. *2005 A Year of Celebration.* Available at http://scientific.thomson.com/promo/celebration/sci (accessed May 6, 2005; reconfirmed June 25, 2008).

Thomson Scientific Press Room. 2008. The Scientific Business of Thomson Reuters Launches Expanded Journal Coverage in Web of Science by Adding 700 Regional Journals. Available at http://scientific.thomsonreuters.com/press/2008/8455931/ (accessed June 12, 2008).

U.S. National Library of Medicine. 2007. *Medical Subject Heading (MeSH) Fact Sheet.* Available at http://www.nlm.nih.gov/pubs/factsheets/mesh.html (accessed June 5, 2008).

———. 2008. *MEDLINE Fact Sheet.* Available at http://www.nlm.nih.gov/pubs/factsheets/medline.html (accessed June 5, 2008).

———. 2008. *What's the Difference between MEDLINE and PubMed? Fact Sheet.* Available at http://www.nlm.nih.gov/pubs/factsheets/dif_med_pub.html (accessed June 5, 2008). Fact Sheet includes additional added materials and a list of other *PubMed* services.

Chapter 6

Flagg, G. 2006. New WorldCat Search Site Offers Public Access. *American Libraries* 37 (September): 12–13.

Hane, Paula J. 2006. OCLC to Open WorldCat Searching to the World. *NewsBreaks* Information Today, Inc. Available at: http://newsbreaks.infotoday.com/ nbreader.asp?ArticleID=16951 (accessed June 9, 2008).

Helfer, Doris Small. 2002. OCLC's March into the 21st Century. *Searcher: The Magazine for Database Professionals* 10 (February): 66–69.

Hogan, Tom. 1991. OCLC Looks to End-User Market with FirstSearch. *Information Today.* 8 (November): 1, 4.

Jordan, Jay. 2003. Cooperating during Difficult Times. *Journal of Academic Librarianship* 29 (6): 343–345.

Murphy, Bob. 2008. OCLC and Google to exchange data, link digitized books to WorldCat. OCLC News Release 19 May 2008. Available at: http://www. oclc.org/news/releases/200811.htm (accessed June 9, 2008).

OCLC. 2008. *WorldCat homepage, WorldCat facts and statistics.* Available at http://www.oclc.org/us/en/worldcat/default.htm (accessed June 6, 2008).

OCLC Launches Eserials Holdings, WorldCat.org. 2006. *Advanced Technology Libraries* 35 (August): 1, 8–9.

WorldCat.org Adds New Features, Functionality. 2007. *Advanced Technology Libraries* 36 (March): 2–3.

WorldCat.org Adds List-Building Features, User Profiles. 2007. *Advanced Technology Libraries* 36 (August): 4.

Chapter 7

MLA. 2004. *Descriptors and Indexing.* Modern Language Association. Available at http://www.mla.org/publications/bibliography/bib_descriptors (accessed August 2, 2005; reconfirmed June 10, 2008).

MLA. 2007. *Frequently Asked Questions.* Modern Language Association. Available at http://www.mla.org/publications/bibliography/bib_faq (accessed June 10, 2008).

ProQuest LLC. 2008. *Information Centre: About MLA International Bibliography. Chadwyck-Healey Literature Collections.* Available at http://collections. chadwyck.com/infoCentre/products/about_ilc.jsp?collection=mla (accessed June 10, 2008).

Speck, Vicky H. 2002. *America: History and Life on the Web. Product Information Sheet.* ABC-CLIO. Available at http://www.abc-clio.com/ visitortools/productSheet/preview.aspx?productid=109711 (accessed June 16, 2005).

Chapter 8

Bates, Mary Ellen. 1998. Statistical Universe. *Database* 21 (October/November): 96.

Gauthier, Jason G. 2002. *Measuring America: The Decennial Censuses From 1790–2000.* (U.S. Bureau of the Census/Dept of Commerce), Washington, DC: U.S. Government Printing Office. Appendix A, p. A-1. Quoted in Joe Beine, The Cost of the U.S. Census. Available at http://www.genealogybranches.com/ censuscosts.html (accessed June 21, 2005; reconfirmed June 25, 2008). Cost per person figures calculated and added by Mr. Beine.

Golderman, Gail and Bruce Connolly. 2005. Numbers Beyond Borders. *Netconnect* (Spring): 28–35.

Jacsó, Péter. 2000. Peter's Picks & Pans. *Econtent* 23 (August/September) (accessed online via WilsonWeb).

Kmetz, Tom. 2003. LexisNexis Statistical (Base Edition). *The Charleston Advisor* 4 (January): 34.

O'Leary, Mick. 2006. DataPlace to the Rescue. *Information Today* 23 (December): 47, 52.

Chapter 9

Abels, Eileen, Lily Griner, and Maggie Turqman. 2004. If You Build It Will They Come? *Information Outlook* 8 (October): 13–17.

Abram, Stephen. 2007. Millennials: Deal with Them! Part II. *School Library Media Activities Monthly* 24 (October): 55–58.

Ajayi, N. A. 2005. Information Seeking by Nurses in the Obafemi Awolowo University Teaching Hospital, Nigeria. *Information Development* 21 (June): 121–127.

ALA. 2004. *Guidelines for Behavioral Performance of Reference and Information Service Providers.* American Library Association. Available at http://www.ala. org/ala/rusa/protools/referenceguide/guidelinesbehavioral.cfm (accessed June 25, 2008).

Andrews, James E., Kevin A. Pearce, and Carol Ireson. 2005. Information-Seeking Behaviors of Practitioners in a Primary Care Practice-Based Research Network (PBRN). *Journal of the Medical Library Association* 93 (April): 206–212.

Ankem, Kalyani. 2007. Information-Seeking Behavior of Women in their Path to an Innovative Alternate Treatment for Symptomatic Uterine Fibroids. *Journal of the Medical Library Association* 95 (April): 164–172.

Barrett, Andy. 2005. The Information-Seeking Habits of Graduate Student Researchers in the Humanities. *Journal of Academic Librarianship* 31 (July): 324–331.

Bates, Mary Ellen. 1998. Finding the Question behind the Question. *Information Outlook* 2 (July): 19–21.

Booth, Sally. 2004. Getting It Off the 'Net: Use of the World Wide Web in a Firm of Solicitors. *Legal Information Management* 4 (Summer): 97–104.

Borgman, Christine L., Laura J. Smart, and Kelli A. Millwood. 2005. Comparing Faculty Information Seeking in Teaching and Research: Implications for the Design of Digital Libraries. *Journal of the American Society for Information Science and Technology* 56 (April): 636–657.

Bronstein, Jenny and Shifra Baruchson-Arbib. 2008. The Application of Cost-Benefit and Least Effort Theories in Studies of Information Seeking Behavior of Humanities Scholars: The Case of Jewish Studies Scholars in Israel. *Journal of Information Science* 34 (2): 131–144.

Brown, Cecelia M. and Lina Ortega. 2005. Information-Seeking Behavior of Physical Science Librarians: Does Research Inform Practice? *College & Research Libraries* 66 (May): 231–247.

Burkell, Jacquelyn and D. Grant Campbell. 2005. 'What does this Mean?' How Web-Based Consumer Health Information Fails to Support Information Seeking in the Pursuit of Informed Consent for Screening Test Decisions. *Journal of the Medical Library Association* 93 (July): 363–373.

Carter, David S. 2002/2003. Hurry Up and Wait: Observations and Tips about the Practice of Chat Reference. *The Reference Librarian* 79/80: 113–120.

Cramer, Dina C. 1998. How to Speak Patron. *Public Libraries* 37 (November/December): 349.

Chung, Jin Soo and Delia Neuman. 2007. High School Students' Information Seeking and Use for Class Projects. *Journal of the American Society for Information Science and Technology* 58 (August): 1503–1517.

Dervin, Brenda. 2005. Libraries Reaching Out with Health Information to Vulnerable Populations: Guidance from Research on Information Seeking and use. *Journal of the Medical Library Association* 93 (October): S74–S80.

Dewdney, Patricia and Gillian Michell. 1996. Oranges and Peaches: Understanding Communication Accidents in the Reference Interview. *RQ* 35 (Summer): 520–535.

Dewdney, Patricia and Gillian Michell. 1997. Asking Why Questions in the Reference Interview: A Theoretical Justification. *Library Quarterly* 67 (1): 50–71. Quoted in Marshall Eidson, 2000.

Duff, Wendy M. and Catherine A. Johnson. 2003. Where Is the List with All the Names? Information-Seeking Behavior of Genealogists. *The American Archivist* 66 (Spring/Summer): 79–95.

Eidson, Marshall. 2000. Using Emotional Intelligence in the Reference Interview. *Colorado Libraries* 26 (Summer): 8–10.

Eisenberg, Michael B. 2005. Stage 2—Information Seeking Strategies (Big6 Special Section). *Library Media Connection* 23 (March): 34–37.

Ellis, David. 1993. Modeling the Information-Seeking Patterns of Academic Researchers: A Grounded Theory Approach. *The Library Quarterly* 63 (October): 469–486.

Fagan, Jody Condit and Christina M. Desai. 2002/2003. Communication Strategies for Instant Messaging and Chat Reference Services. *The Reference Librarian* 79/80: 121–155.

Fister, Barbara. 2002. Fear of Reference. Chronicle of Higher Education 48 (14 June): B20.

Flaxbart, David. 2001. Conversations with Chemists: Information-Seeking Behavior of Chemistry Faculty in the Electronic Age. *Science & Technology Libraries* 21 (3/4): 5–26.

Foster, Nancy Fried and Susan Gibbons. 2007. *Studying Students: the Undergraduate Research Project at the University of Rochester.* Chicago: Association of College and Research Libraries.

Green, Samuel Swett. 1876. Personal Relations between Librarians and Readers. *Library Journal* (October): 74–81. Quoted in David Tyckoson, 2003.

Grefsheim, Suzanne F. and Jocelyn A. Rankin. 2007. Information Needs and Information Seeking in a Biomedical Research Setting: A Study of Scientists and Science Administrators. *Journal of the Medical Library Association* 95 (October): 426–434.

Harter, Stephen P. 1986. *Online Information Retrieval: Concepts, Principles, and Techniques.* Orlando, FL: Academic Press.

Heinström, Jannica. 2006. Broad Exploration or Precise Specificity: Two Basic Information-seeking Patterns among Students. *Journal of the American Society for Information Science and Technology* 57 (11), 1440–1450. See also other works, available at: http://cissl.scils.rutgers.edu/staff/docs/CV_Heinstrom_012007.pdf (accessed June 14, 2008).

Hemminger, Bradley M., Lu Dihui, K. T. L. Vaughan, and Stephanie J. Adams. 2007. Information Seeking Behavior of Academic Scientists. *Journal of the American Society for Information Science and Technology* 58 (December): 2205–2225.

Hunter, Ben. 2006. A New Breed of Musicians: The Information-Seeking Needs and Behaviors of Composers of Electroacoustic Music. *Music Reference Services Quarterly* 10 (1): 1–15.

Information Seeking Strategies of Agricultural Scientists Working in the ICAR Institutions in India. 2008. *DESIDOC Journal of Library & Information Technology* 28 (May): 37–45.

The Information-Seeking Behavior of Visual Artists: A Literature Review. 2008. *Journal of Documentation* 64 (3): 343–362.

Information Needs and Information-Seeking Behaviour of Engineers: A Systemic Review. 2007. *Mousaion* 25 (2): 72–94.

IR Homepage. 2008. *Information Research: An International Electronic Journal.* Available at: http://informationr.net/ir/. (accessed June 14, 2008).

Jankowska, Maria Anna. 2004. Identifying University Professors' Information Needs in the Challenging Environment of Information and Communication Technologies. *Journal of Academic Librarianship* 30 (January): 51–66.

Jorosi, Boemo Nlayidzi. 2006. The Information Needs and Information Seeking Behaviours of SME Managers in Botswana. *Libri* 56 (June): 97–107.

Kern, Kathleen. 2003. Communication, Patron Satisfaction, and the Reference Interview. *Reference & User Services Quarterly* 43 (Fall): 47–49.

Kuhlthau, Carol C. 1991. Inside the Search Process: Information-Seeking from the User's Perspective. *Journal of the American Society for Information Science* 42 (5): 361–371. Quoted in Johannes G. Nel, 2001.

Kwon, Nahyun and Vicki L. Gregory. 2007. The Effects of Librarians' Behavioral Performance on User Satisfaction in Chat Reference Services. *Reference & User Services Quarterly* 47 (2): 137–148.

Kwon, Nahyun, Onwuegbuzie, Anthony J., and Linda Alexander. 2007. Critical Thinking Disposition and Library Anxiety: Affective Domains on the Space of Information Seeking and Use in Academic Libraries. *College & Research Libraries* 68 (May): 268–278.

Leckie, Gloria J. and Lisa M. Given. 2005. Understanding Information-Seeking: The Public Library Context. In *Advances in Librarianship* 29, edited by Danuta Nitecki and Eileen Abels. New York: Academic Press.

Liao, Yan, Mary, Finn and Jun Lu. 2007. Information-Seeking Behavior of International Graduate Students vs. American Graduate Students: A User Study at Virginia Tech 2005. *College & Research Libraries* 68 (January): 5–25.

Liew, Chern Li and Siong Ngor Ng. 2006. Beyond the Notes: A Qualitative Study of the Information-Seeking Behavior of Ethnomusicologists. *Journal of Academic Librarianship* 32 (January): 60–68.

Loertscher, David V. and Blanche Woolls. 2002. Teenage Users of Libraries: A Brief Overview of the Research. *Knowledge Quest* 30 (May/June): 31–36.

Lorenzen, Michael. 2001. The Land of Confusion? High School Students and Their Use of the World Wide Web for Research. *Research Strategies* 18 (2): 151–163.

Makani, Joyline and Kelli WooShue. 2006. Information Seeking Behaviours of Business Students and the Development of Academic Digital Libraries. *Evidence Based Library and Information Practice* 1 (4): 30–45.

Makri, Stephann, Ann Blandford and Anna L. Cox. 2008. Investigating the Information-Seeking Behaviour of Academic Lawyers: From Ellis's Model to Design. *Information Processing & Management* 44 (March): 613–634.

Marcella, Rita, Graeme Baxter, Sylvie Davies and Dick Toornstra. 2007. The Information Needs and Information-Seeking Behaviour of the Users of the European Parliamentary Documentation Centre: A Customer Knowledge Study. *Journal of Documentation* 63 (6): 920–934.

Marcum, Deanna B. and Gerald George. 2003. Who Uses What? Report On a National Survey of Information Users in College and Universities. *D-Lib Magazine* 9 (October). Available at http://www.dlib.org/dlib/october03/george/10george.html (accessed April 17, 2005).

Massey-Burzio, Virginia. 1998. From the Other Side of the Reference Desk: A Focus Group Study. *Journal of Academic Librarianship* 24 (May): 208–215.

Mayfield, Tracey and Joy Thomas. 2005. A Tale of Two Departments: A Comparison of Faculty Information-Seeking Practices. *Behavioral & Social Sciences Librarian* 23 (2): 47–65.

McKnight, Michelynn. 2006. The Information Seeking of On-Duty Critical Care Nurses: Evidence from Participant Observation and In-Context Interviews. *Journal of the Medical Library Association* 94 (April): 145–151.

Meyers, Eric M., Lisa P. Nathan, and Matthew L. Saxton. 2007. Barriers to Information Seeking in School Libraries: Conflicts in Perceptions and Practice. *Information Research* 11 (January). Available at http://InformationR.net/ir/12-2/paper295.html (accessed June 16, 2008).

Minkel, Walter. 2004. They Can't Always Find What They Want. *School Library Journal* 50 (August): 29.

Murphy, Janet. 2003. Information-Seeking Habits of Environmental Scientists: A Study of Interdisciplinary Scientists at the Environmental Protection Agency in Research Triangle Park, North Carolina. *Issues in Science & Technology Librarianship* 38 (Summer). Available at http://www.istl.org/03-summer/refereed.html (accessed June 11, 2005).

Nail-Chiwetalu, Barbara and Nan Bernstein Ratner. 2007. An Assessment of the Information-Seeking Abilities and Needs of Practicing Speech-Language Pathologists. *Journal of the Medical Library Association* 95 (April): 182–188.

Nel, Johannes G. 2001. The Information-Seeking Process: Is There a Sixth Sense? *Mousaion* 19 (2): 23–32.

Njoku, Ifeanyichukwu Faith. 2004. The Information Needs and Information-Seeking Behaviour of Fishermen in Lagos State, Nigeria. *International Information & Library Review* 36 (December): 297–307.

Novotny, Eric. 2004. I Don't Think I Click: A Protocol Analysis Study of Use of a Library Online Catalog in the Internet Age. *College & Research Libraries* 65 (November): 525–537.

Obasuyi, Luke. 2007. Factors Influencing Information-Seeking Strategies and Sources used by Oil Palm Scientists in Nigeria. *African Journal of Library, Archives & Information Science* 17 (October): 79–87.

Oblinger, Diana G. and James L. Oblinger, Eds. 2005. Is it Age or IT: First Steps toward Understanding the Net Generation. In: *Educating the Net Generation.* EDUCAUSE. Available at http://www.educause.edu/ir/library/pdf/pub7101b.pdf (accessed June 12, 2005).

Owen, David J. and Min-Lin E. Fang. 2003. Information-Seeking Behavior in Complementary and Alternative Medicine (CAM): An Online Survey of Faculty at a Health Sciences Campus. *Journal of the Medical Library Association* 91 (July): 311–321.

Pelzer, Nancy L., William H. Weise, and Joan M. Leysen. 1998. Library Use and Information-Seeking Behavior of Veterinary Medical Students Revisited in the Electronic Environment. *Bulletin of the Medical Library Association* 86 (July): 346–355.

Perrault, Anne Marie. 2007. An Exploratory Study of Biology Teachers' Online Information Seeking Practices. *School Library Media Research SLMR* 10. Chicago, IL.: American Association of School Librarians.

Peterson, Lisa C. 1997. Effective Question Negotiation in the Reference Interview. *Current Studies in Librarianship* 21 (Spring/Fall): 22–34.

Preddie, Martha Ingrid. 2007. Time, Cost, Information Seeking Skills and Format of Resources Present Barriers to Information Seeking by Primary Care Practitioners in a Research Environment. *Evidence Based Library and Information Practice* 2 (3): 105–107.

Prince, Monique. 2003. *Changes in the Information Use Patterns of College Freshmen.* MSLS thesis, University of North Carolina at Chapel Hill.

Radford, Marie L. 1999. *The Reference Encounter: Interpersonal Communication in the Academic Library.* Chicago: Association of College and Research Libraries. Quoted in Catherine Sheldrick Ross, 2003.

Radford, Marie L. and M. Kathleen Kern. 2006. A Multiple-case Study Investigation of the Discontinuation of Nine Chat Reference Services. *Library & Information Science Research* 28 (4): 521–547.

Reddy, Madhu C. and Patricia Ruma Spence. 2008. Collaborative Information Seeking: A Field Study of a Multidisciplinary Patient Care Team. *Information Processing & Management* 44 (January): 242–255.

Reneker, Maxine H. 1993. A Qualitative Study of Information Seeking Among Members of an Academic Community: Methodological Issues and Problems. *The Library Quarterly* 63 (October): 487–507.

Riedling, Ann Marlow. 2000. Great Ideas for Improving Reference Interviews. *Book Report* 19 (November/December): 28–29.

Ronan, Jana. 2003. The Reference Interview Online. *Reference & User Services Quarterly* 43 (Fall): 43–47.

Ross, Catherine Sheldrick. 2003. The Reference Interview: Why It Needs to Be Used in Every (Well, Almost Every) Reference Transaction. *Reference & User Services Quarterly* 43 (Fall): 38–42.

Ross, Catherine Sheldrick and Patricia Dewdney. 1998. Negative Closure: Strategies and Counter-Strategies in the Reference Transaction. *Reference & User Services Quarterly* 38 (2): 151–163.

Scott, Sean Cunnison. 2004. Process, Practice, and Psychic Stress at the Reference Desk. *OLA Quarterly* 10 (Fall): 19–23.

Shen Yi. 2007. Information Seeking in Academic Research: A Study of the Sociology Faculty at the University of Wisconsin-Madison. *Information Technology and Libraries* 26 (March): 4–13.

Shenton, Andrew K. 2007. The Information-Seeking Behaviour of Teenagers in an English High School. *The School Librarian* 55 (Autumn): 125–127.

Shenton, Andrew K. and Pat Dixon. 2003. Youngsters' Use of Other People As An Information-Seeking Method. *Journal of Librarianship and Information Science* 35 (December): 219–233.

Shenton, Andrew K. and Pat Dixon. 2004. The Nature of Information Needs and Strategies for their Investigation in Youngsters. *Library & Information Science Research* 26: 296–310.

Somerville, Arleen N. 1982. The Pre-Search Reference Interview—A Step by Step Guide. *Database* 5 (February): 32–38.

Steinerová, Jela and Jaroslav Šušol. 2007. Users' Information Behaviour—a Gender Perspective. *Information Research* 12 (April). Available at: http://informationr.net/ir/12-3/paper320.html (accessed June 14, 2008).

Sulemani, Solomon Bayugo and Seth Agbeko Katsekpor. 2007. Information Seeking Behavior of Health Sciences Faculty at the College of Health Sciences, University of Ghana. *Information Development* 23 (February): 63–70.

Taylor, Robert S. 1968. Question-Negotiation and Information Seeking in Libraries. *College & Research Libraries* 29 (3): 178–194.

Todd, Ross J. 2003. Adolescents of the Information Age: Patterns of Information-Seeking and Use, and Implications for Information Professionals. *School Libraries Worldwide* 9 (2): 27–46.

Tyckoson, David. 2003. Reference at Its Core: The Reference Interview. *Reference & User Services Quarterly* 43 (Fall): 49–51.

Valentine, Barbara. 1993. Undergraduate Research Behavior: Using Focus Groups to Generate Theory. *Journal of Academic Librarianship* 19 (November): 300–304.

Vesey, Ken. 2005. Eliminate Wobbly Research with the Information Resource Tripod. *Teacher Librarian* 32 (February): 35–37.

Wallis, Lisa C. 2006. Information-Seeking Behavior of Faculty in One School of Public Health. *Journal of the Medical Library Association* 94 (October): 442—446.

Wessel, Charles B., Nancy H. Tannery, and Barbara A. Epstein. 2006. Information-Seeking Behavior and Use of Information Resources by Clinical Research Coordinators. *Journal of the Medical Library Association* 94 (January): 48–54.

Whitmire, Ethelene. 2003. Epistemological Beliefs and the Information-Seeking Behavior of Undergraduates. *Library & Information Science Research* 25: 127–142.

Yoo, Eun-Young and Louise S. Robbins. 2008. Understanding Middle-Aged Women's Health Information Seeking on the Web: A Theoretical Approach. *Journal of the American Society for Information Science and Technology* 59 (February): 577–590.

Young, Nancy J. and Marilyn Von Seggern. 2001. General Information-Seeking in Changing Times: A Focus Group Study. *Reference & User Services Quarterly* 41 (Winter): 159–169.

Zach, Lisl. 2005. When Is Enough Enough? Modeling the Information-Seeking and Stopping Behavior of Senior Arts Administrators. *Journal of the American Society for Information Science and Technology* 56 (January): 23–35.

Zach, Lisl. 2006. Using a Multiple-Case Studies Design to Investigate the Information-Seeking Behavior of Arts Administrators. *Library Trends* 55 (Summer): 4–21.

Chapter 10

Ojala, Marydee. 2008. Business Research 2.0. *Online* 32 (March/April): 45–47.

Chapter 11

Jacsó, Péter. 2007. How Big Is a Database Versus How Is a Database Big. *Online Information Review* 31 (August): 533–536.

Chapter 12

Applegate, Celia. 1999. Teaching: Taming the Terror. In: *How I Teach: Essays on Teaching by Winners of the Robert and Pamela Goergen Award for Distinguished Achievement and Artistry in Undergraduate Teaching.* Rochester, NY: University of Rochester, pp. 23–36. Available at http://hdl.handle.net/1802/2864 (accessed June 23, 2008).

Arant-Kaspar, Wendi and Candace Benefiel. 2008. Drive-by BI: Tailored In-class Mini-instruction Sessions for Graduate and Upper-level Undergraduate Courses. *Reference Services Review* 36 (1): 39–47.

Boice, R. 1992. *The New Faculty Member: Supporting and Fostering Professional Development.* San Francisco, CA: Jossey-Bass. Quoted in Richard M. Reis, *Tomorrow's Professor: Preparing for Academic Careers in Science and Engineering.* New York: IEEE Press, 1997, p. 276.

Brown, Theodore M. 1999. Connection, Communication, and Critical Thinking. In: *How I Teach: Essays on Teaching by Winners of the Robert and Pamela Goergen Award for Distinguished Achievement and Artistry in Undergraduate Teaching.* Rochester, NY: University of Rochester, pp. 9–20. Available at http://hdl.handle.net/1802/2862 (accessed June 23, 2008).

Burkhardt, Joanna M., Mary C. MacDonald, and Andrée J. Rathemacher. 2003. *Teaching Information Literacy: 35 Practical, Standards-based Exercises for College Students.* Chicago, IL: American Library Association.

Carter, Toni and Beverly Simmons. 2007. Reaching Your Millenials: A Fresh Look at Freshman Orientation. *Tennessee Libraries* 57 (1): 1–4. Available at http://www.tnla.org/displaycommon.cfm?an=1&subarticlenbr=124&printpage=true (accessed June 21, 2008).

Davidson, C. I. and S. A. Ambrose. 1994. *The New Professor's Handbook: A Guide to Teaching and Research in Engineering and Science.* Bolton, MA: Anker Publishing. Quoted in Richard M. Reis, *Tomorrow's Professor: Preparing for Academic Careers in Science and Engineering.* New York: IEEE Press, 1997, p. 277.

Davis, Kaetrena D. 2007. The Academic Librarian As Instructor: A Study of Teacher Anxiety. *College & Undergraduate Libraries* 14 (2): 77–101. Available at http://hdl.handle.net/2197/272 (accessed June 21, 2008). Excellent review of the literature, interesting and useful study.

Eckel, Edward J. 2007. Fostering Self-Regulated Learning at the Reference Desk. *Reference & User Services Quarterly* 47 (Fall): 16–20.

Elmborg, James K. 2002. Teaching at the Desk: Toward a Reference Pedagogy. *portal: Libraries and the Academy* 2 (July): 455–464.

Felder, R. M. and L. K. Silverman. 1988. Learning and Teaching Styles in Engineering Education. *Journal of Engineering Education* 77 (2). Quoted in

Richard M. Reis, *Tomorrow's Professor: Preparing for Academic Careers in Science and Engineering*. New York: IEEE Press, 1997, p. 265.

Feldman, K. 1976. The Superior College Teacher from the Students' View. *Research in Higher Education* 5 (3): 243–288. Quoted in Richard M. Reis, *Tomorrow's Professor: Preparing for Academic Careers in Science and Engineering*. New York: IEEE Press, 1997, p. 261.

Gremmels, Gillian S. and Karen Shostrom Lehmann. (2007). Assessment of Student Learning from Reference Service. *College & Research Libraries* 68 (November): 488–501. Results of a study that provided quantifiable proof of reference as an instructional activity; article includes their survey instruments as appendices.

Kuhlthau, Carol C. 1988. Developing a Model of the Library Search Process: Cognitive and Affective Aspect. *RQ* 28 (Winter): 232–242. Quoted in Edward J. Eckel, Fostering Self-Regulated Learning at the Reference Desk. *Reference & User Services Quarterly* 47 (Fall 2007): 16–20.

Meulemans, Yvonne Nalani and Jennifer Brown. 2001. Educating Instruction Librarians: A Model for Library and Information Science Education. *Research Strategies* 18 (4): 253–264.

Viele, Patricia T. 2006. Physics 213: An Example of Faculty/Librarian Collaboration. *Issues in Science and Technology Librarianship* 47 (Summer). Available at http://www.istl.org/06-summer/article2.html (accessed June 21, 2008).

Index

ABC-CLIO, 148
Abstracting & Indexing (A & I) services, 1–3, 123; *See also* America: History and Life, ERIC, MEDLINE, PsycInfo, Web of Science
Academic job interviews, teaching as part of, 265–66
Active learning, class examples, 262–64
Adapting to change, importance in searching, 49, 121 n.4; exercise illustrating, 84 Q.2
Alternative spellings, 11, 45
America: History and Life, 147–57, *149–57*; exercises using, 171
American FactFinder, 190–95, *191–94*
American Statistics Index (ASI), component of LexisNexis *Statistical*, 178, 179, 181, 187
AND, Boolean operator, 20–21, *20*; *See also Notes and Search Examples for specific databases in the text*
Annual Bibliography of English Language and Literature (ABELL), 158–59
Answers, waiting for when teaching: principle, 256–57; examples, 262, 264, 266
Arts & Humanities Citation Index, component of *Web of Science*, 102–3
Audience, teaching to a specific: principle, 255; examples, 261, 262, 264, 265, 266
Author as subject searches, in *MLA International Bibliography*, 161, *162*; exercise using, 171 Q.10
Authority control, 25, 38 n.6
Auto-Explode, in OVID interface, 74, 90, *75, 91*

Bates, Mary Ellen, author of database reviews, 238; useful reference interview questions from, 217
Book reviews: finding in *America: History and Life*, 149–50, *149–50*; not included in *MLA*, 158
Books, reference questions involving, 228
Boole, George, 20, 37 n.1
Boolean logic and operators, 19–24, 37 n.2, *20, 22, 24*; pitfalls, 34, *34–35*; used in exercises, 35; *See also* OR, Boolean operator; *specific database Notes and Search Examples in the text*
Brief History of Time, A, used in search example, 113–15, *113–15*
Broad scanning, information seeking pattern, 208, 212
Bureau of Labor Statistics (BLS) website, 195–200, *197–99*; exercise using, 202 Q.3
Business and Company Resource Center, 229
Business reference questions, 228–29
Businesses, collection of data about, 175, 176

Census Bureau website, 189–95, *191–94*
Chadwyck-Healey databases, 158–59
Charleston Advisor, source of database reviews, 238
Chat (instant message systems): conducting reference interviews via, 220–21, 223 n.2; used in search example, 59–60, *59*
CINAHL, nursing database, 229
Citation indexes, history and use, 102–4

Citation management programs, outputting to. *See Output sections for specific databases in the text*

Citation preview feature, in EBSCO databases, 32, 151, *33*

Citations: importance of, in academia, 87–88, 104; verifying, 227, 232–33

Cited reference searching: in *America: History and Life*, 152–54, *153–55*; in *Web of Science*, 103–4, 108–15, *110–15*

Closed questions, 216–17

Communication skills: in the reference interview, 214, 216, 218–19; online, 221–22

Content Discovery Keys, in *Library Literature*, 57–58, *58*

Controlled vocabulary: description and advantages, 24–26; factor in database evaluation, 243; in ERIC (descriptors, thesaurus, subjects), 14, 64–66, *14–15, 64–66, 69*; in LexisNexis *Statistical*, 180, 181, 182, 184, *182–84*; in *Library Literature & Information Science*, 53–57, 59–60, *54, 56, 59*; in *MasterFILE Select*, 12–13, 29–32, *12, 31, 33*; in MEDLINE (MeSH), 89–90, 96, *91–92*; in *MLA International Bibliography*, 161, 163, 164–65, 169, *165*; in *PsycINFO*, 74–75, 81, *75–76, 83*; lack of in *Web of Science*, 105

Cross-dressing in Shakespeare's works, used in search example, 159–160, *160–61*

Customization features: in *Web of Science*, 105; in WorldCat.org, 137–38

Data and statistics: defined, 174; resources for, 175–77, 203 n.5, 203 n.6

Database evaluation, 237–48, 252 n.1–2

Database vendors. *See EBSCO, H.W. Wilson, LexisNexis, OCLC, Ovid, ProQuest, Thomson*

Databases: bibliographic, compared to article, 123, 127; choosing which to use, 230–31; contrasting with Google, in teaching, 262, 263; free versions, 231–32; history, 3–4; medical, for laypeople, 92; pricing, 241; purchase requests, 249–51; research articles in multidisciplinary, 245–46, 252 n.3; structure and design of, example, 4–11, 15, *6, 8*; subject, introduced, 51–52; use of in reference, versus the Web, 226–29

Deaf students, teacher training, used in search example, 64–69, *67, 69*

Deep diving, information seeking pattern, 208, 213

Descriptors. *See* Controlled vocabulary

Dialog, online search system, 3, 234 n.1

Double Helix, used in search example, 110–12, *111*

Double posting, 10

Dow Jones databases, *Factiva*, 41, 42, 44

Dystopian literature, used in search example, 165–66, *166*

E-mail, conducting reference interviews via, 220–21

E-mailing database results: desirable features in, 116, 157, 168, *117, 168*; *See also Output sections for specific databases in the text*

EBSCO databases: *America: History and Life*, 147–57, *149–57*; citation preview feature, 32, 151, *33*; *MasterFILE Select*, 12–13, 29–34, *12, 30–35*; search functionality, 41, 42, 45, *44*

Education Resources Information Center. *See* ERIC database

Emoticons, 220, 223 n.1

Employment, information from Bureau of Labor Statistics, 196, 198–200, *198–99*

Engerman, Stanley L., used in search example, 149–50, *149–50*

ERIC database, 13–15, 61–71, *13–16, 63–70*; exercises using, 84

Facebook, integration with WorldCat.org, 138

Fact Sheets, in American FactFinder, 191–93, *193–94*

Factiva database, 41, 42, 44

Fallibility of instructors is acceptable: principle, 258; examples, 265, 267

False drops: defined, 27; in search examples, 32, 39–40, 129

Fast surfing, information seeking pattern, 208, 211, 212

Field indexes, 6–15, *12–15*; in *America: History and Life*, 149; in ERIC, 63, 66, *64, 66*; in *Library Literature*, 58–59, *59*; in WorldCat, 132, *132*

Fields, in databases, 4–6, 15, *6, 16*; factor in database evaluation, 242–43; searching, introduced, 26; *See also Notes and Search Examples for specific databases in the text*

Financial information, collection of data about, 175, 177

Find in a Library, WorldCat.org feature, 137

Find in page function, in web browsers, 198?

FirstSearch databases: ERIC, 13–15, 61–71, *13–16, 63–70*; exercises using, 84, 143–44; WorldCat, 124–36, *126, 128–36*

Flexibility, importance in searching, 49, 121 n.4; exercise illustrating, 84 Q.2

Focus, in OVID interface, 74–75, 81, 90, *75, 91*

Gale databases: *Health Reference Center, Virtual Reference Library*, 229, 233
Garfield, Dr. Eugene, 102
Goals and objectives (transparency), in teaching: principle, 257; examples, 261, 262, 266
Google: Books, integration with WorldCat.org, 138; contrast with databases, in teaching, 262, 263; example of recall and precision, 28; Scholar, 231, 235 n.5
Government websites: Bureau of Labor Statistics (BLS), 195–200, *197*; MedlinePlus.gov, 233; sources for numerical information, 175, 176, 203 n.6; U.S. Census Bureau, 190–95, *191*
Grey literature, in ERIC, 62, 68

H.W. Wilson Company databases, *Library Literature & Information Science*, 52–61, *53–54, 56, 58–59, 61*; exercises using, 83–84
Hawking, Stephen: used in search example, 108, 113–15, *113–15*; used in exercise, 120 Q.7
Health Reference Center, medical database for laypeople, 92, 229, 233
Heart attacks in adult women, used in search example, 89–91, 97–98, *91–92, 97–98*
Heinström, Jannica, information seeking patterns model, 208, 212, *209*
Help files: consulting for database functionality, 42, 44–45; factor in database evaluation, 241

ICPSR (Inter-university Consortium for Political and Social Research), 175
Index to International Statistics (IIS), component of LexisNexis *Statistical*, 178, 179, 181, 187
Indexes of articles: history, 2–4, *2*
Indexes of database fields, 6–15, *12–15*; in *America: History and Life*, 149; in ERIC, 63, 66, *64, 66*; in *Library Literature*, 58–59, *59*; in WorldCat, 132, *132*
Information literacy classes, teaching principles and scenarios, 261–65
Information Research, 206
Information seeking behavior, 205–13, *207*
Institute for Scientific Information (ISI), 102
Internet, impact on information seeking behavior, 210–13
Internet Movie Database (IMDb), resource for film information, 232
Inverted file, 6

Jacsó, Péter, author of database reviews, 238
Journals, identifying and locating using WorldCat, 131–35, *132–35*
JSTOR, integration with other databases, 148, 158

Kulhthau, Carol, information search process model, 206–8, *207*

Law reference questions, 229
Lecturing, avoiding in teaching: principle, 255–56; examples, 261, 263, 264, 265, 266
Less is more, in teaching: principle, 257; examples, 261, 262, 263, 265, 266
LexisNexis databases: search functionality, 42, 45, *44, Statistical*, 177–89, *181–90*
Library Literature & Information Science, 52–61, *53–54, 56, 58–59, 61*; exercises using, 83–84; source for database reviews, 238
Library school curriculum, used in search example, 55–57, *56*
Limits: defined, 46; in *America: History and Life*, 149, 151, 152, *149, 151, 153*; in ERIC, 63–64, 70, *63, 70*; in LexisNexis *Statistical*, 181–82, 185–86, *183*; in *Library Literature*, 52–53, 57–58; in MEDLINE, 89, 91, *90, 93*; in *MLA International Bibliography*, 159, 164, *160, 164*; in PsycINFO, 74, 79; in PubMed, 95; in *Web of Science*, 105, 107, *108*; in WorldCat, 126–29, 133, *126, 129*
Link resolver systems (SFX), 101, 148, 158, 239, 264
Literature Online (LION), 158–59

Map to Subject Heading function, in OVID databases, 74–75, 77, 87, 90–91, *75–76, 91, 92*
MasterFILE Select database, 12–13, 29–34, *12, 30–35*; exercises using, 35–36
Medical reference questions, 229, 233
MEDLINE® database, 88–93, *90–94*
MedlinePlus.gov, medical website for laypeople, 92, 233
Mental Toolkit, 48–49
MeSH (Medical Subject Headings), MEDLINE thesaurus, 89–90, 96, *91–92*
Millennials, teaching, 255, 262–63
Million Dollar Database, 229
MLA International Bibliography, 158–70, *160–68, 170*; exercises using, 171–72
Modern Language Association of America, 158

Monetary information, collection of data about, 175, 177

Negative closure, avoiding in the reference interview, 219
NOT (used for AND NOT), Boolean operator, 22–23, 37 n.2, *22*
Numerical information, 174–77; reference interview questions to ask, 201

Occupational information, finding at the Bureau of Labor Statistics, 196–200, *198–99*
Occupational Outlook Handbook, used in search example, 47, 199–200, *199*
OCLC (Online Computer Library Center), 123–25; libraries, finding symbols for, 133, *133*; WorldCat.org, 136–43, *137–42*
OCLC FirstSearch databases: ERIC, 14–15, 61–71, *16, 63–70*; search functionality, 13–15, 42, *13–15, 44*; WorldCat, 124–36, 143–44, *126, 128–36*
Ojala, Mary Dee, author of database reviews, 238
One-on-one instruction, at the reference desk, 261, 269 n.4
OPACs (Online Public Access Catalogs), 123–24, 143
Open questions, 216–17
OR, Boolean operator, 21–22, *22*; effect on PubMed search results, 97–100; used in search example, 77, 165, 184, 185, 186, *185–86*
Order of operation, of Boolean operators, 23–24, 34, 37 n.3, *24, 34–35*
Organized crime, used in search example, 151, *152*
OVID databases: MEDLINE, 88–93, *90–93*; PsycINFO, 71–81, 84–85, *73, 75, 76, 77–80, 82–83*; useful interface features, 72–73, 77, 79

Patrons, interactions with librarians, 213–16
Pearl growing: defined, 46, 50 n.5; used in search example, 32–33, 47, 68–69
Peer pressure and self esteem, used in search example, 74–81, *75–80*
People: collection of data about, 175, 176; statistics about, from American FactFinder, 190–93, 195, *192–94*
Phrase searching, 42–43
Popular culture questions, 232
Practice, importance in teaching: principle, 259–60; examples, 261, 264, 267
Precision: and Recall, 27–28, 36–37; enhancing in searches, 26, 40, 42–43, 46; in PubMed, 100

Presentations, importance in librarianship, 253–54
Pricing models for databases, 241
Printing. *See Output sections for specific databases in the text*
ProQuest databases: *ABI Inform*, used in example, 47; Chadwyck-Healey imprint, 158–59; search functionality, 40–41, 42, 15, 50 n.2, *44*
Proximity searching, operators and examples, 39–43; *See also Notes and Search Examples for specific databases in the text*
PsycINFO database, 71–81, *73, 75–80, 82–83*; exercises using, 84–85
PubMed, 93–101, *94–100*; exercises using, 119–20
Purcell, Henry, used in search example, 140, *139*
Purchase requests for databases, 249–51

Questions, and the reference interview, 214–18
Quint, Barbara, author of database reviews, 238

Recall: and Precision, 27–28, 36–37; enhancing in searching, 43–45; in PubMed, 100
Record structure, examples of detailed, 15, 160, 163, *16, 162–64*
Records, in databases, 4–6, *6, 8, 16*
Reference Desk Rule No. 1, 50 n.3, 115
Reference interviews, 213–22; for data or statistics requests, 201
Related records: in *America: History and Life*, 154, *155*; in PubMed, 88, 96; in *Web of Science*, 88, 104, *109*
Results screens, revising searches in: in *America: History and Life*, 151–52, *152–53*; in *Library Literature*, 57–58, *58*; in *Web of Science*, 107, *108*; in WorldCat.org, 139–40, *140*
Reviews of databases, sources, 238
RSS feeds: in *Library Literature*, 57; in WorldCat.org, 137
RUSA Guidelines for Behavioral Performance of Reference, 221

Salary information, finding at the Bureau of Labor Statistics, 196, 198, *198*
Saving. *See Output sections for specific databases in the text*
Scholarly (peer-reviewed) limits: factor in database evaluation, 245–46, 252 n.3; in *Library Literature*, 52–53, 57–58; in *MLA International Bibliography*, 164, *164*
Science Citation Index, 102–3, 105
Search result comparisons, benchmarking tool for databases, 248

Search revision, in results screens: in *America: History and Life*, 151–52, *152–53*; in *Library Literature*, 57–58, *58*; in *Web of Science*, 107, *108*; in WorldCat.org, 139–40, *140*

Searchability, factor in database evaluation, 243–44

Searcher's Toolkit: 19–26, 39–47; mental "tools," 48–49; *See also Notes and Search Examples for specific databases in the text*

SFX linking technology, 101, 148, 158, 239, 264

Social networking: features, in WorldCat.org, 137–38; sites, effect on information seeking, 210

Social Science Citation Index, 102–3

Source list comparisons, benchmarking tool for databases, 247

Spellings, alternative, 11, 45

Statistical Reference Index (SRI), component of LexisNexis *Statistical*, 178, 179, 181, 187

Statistics and data: defined, 174; resources for, 175–77, 203 n.5, 203 n.6

Statistics websites: American FactFinder, 190–95, *191–94*; Bureau of Labor Statistics (BLS), 195–200, *197–99*; links from LexisNexis *Statistical*, 189, *190*

Stock quotes, sources for, 176

Stop words, 8, 10, 27

Subheadings, in MEDLINE, 90–91, *92*; in PubMed, 98, *98*

Subject databases, compared to Web searching, 51–52

Subject headings. *See* Controlled vocabulary

Summit, Roger, founder of Dialog, 3–4

Taylor, Robert S.: information seeking model, 206; on the reference interview, 214

Teachers: fallibility in permissible, 258, 265, 267; qualities of effective, 254

Teaching: as part of academic job interviews, 265–66; opportunities, 260–68; principles, 254–60

Technology, advice for use in teaching: principle, 258–59; examples, 265, 267

Tenopir, Carol: author of database reviews, 238; suggested readings by, 50, 234

Thesaurus: defined, 25, 38 n.4; factor in database evaluation, 243; in ERIC, 65–66, *65*; in *Library Literature*, 53–57, 59–60, *54, 56, 59*; in MEDLINE (MeSH), 89–90, 96, *91–92*; in *PsycINFO*, 81, *83*

Thomson Corporation databases, *Web of Science*, 103–119, *106–11, 113–19*

Trade organizations, as sources for numerical information, 176, 203 n.3

Transparency in teaching: principle, 257; examples, 261, 262, 266

Trials, factor in database evaluation, 242

Truncation, 43–45, *44*; used in search example, 66, 132, 185, *132*

U.S. Census Bureau, American FactFinder website, 190–95, *193–94*

U.S. Department of Labor, Bureau of Labor Statistics website, 195–200, *197–99*; exercise using, 202 Q.3

Usability, factor in database evaluation, 244–45

Usage statistics, factor in database evaluation, 242

Venn Diagrams, 20, *20, 22, 24*

Victorian mysteries, used in search example, 141–42, *141–42*

Virtual Reference Library, medical database for laypeople, 233

Watson, James, used in search example, 110–112, *111*

Web of Science databases, 103–119, *106–11, 113–19*; exercises using, 120 Q.6–8; search functionality, 42, 45, *44*

Web search engines: compared to subject databases, 51–52; use of in reference, versus databases, 232–34

WebMD.com, medical website for laypeople, 233

Wildcards, 44–45, *44*; used in search example, 144 Q.8

WorldCat, 124–36, *126, 128–36*; exercises using, 143–44

WorldCat.org, free version of WorldCat, 136–43, 231, *137–42*; exercises using, 144

About the Author

SUZANNE S. BELL is the Economics/Data Librarian in the Rush Rhees Library Reference Department at the University of Rochester, and an adjunct faculty member with the Department of Library & Information Studies, SUNY Buffalo.